GW01401347

DATA JUSTICE AND THE
RIGHT TO THE CITY

Studies in Global Justice and Human Rights
Series Editor: Thom Brooks

This series publishes ground-breaking work on key topics in the area of global justice and human rights including democracy, gender, poverty, the environment, and just war. Books in the series are of broad interest to theorists working in politics, international relations, philosophy, and related disciplines.

www.euppublishing.com/series/sgjhr

DATA JUSTICE AND
THE RIGHT TO THE CITY

Edited by Morgan Currie, Jeremy Knox
and Callum McGregor

EDINBURGH
University Press

Edinburgh University Press is one of the leading university presses in the UK. We publish academic books and journals in our selected subject areas across the humanities and social sciences, combining cutting-edge scholarship with high editorial and production values to produce academic works of lasting importance. For more information visit our website: edinburghuniversitypress.com

We are committed to making research available to a wide audience and are pleased to be publishing Platinum Open Access ebook editions of titles in this series.

© Editorial matter and organisation Morgan Currie, Jeremy Knox and Callum McGregor, 2022, 2024
© The chapters their several authors, 2022, 2024

Edinburgh University Press Ltd
The Tun – Holyrood Road
12(2f) Jackson's Entry
Edinburgh EH8 8PJ

First published in hardback by Edinburgh University Press 2022

Typeset in 11/13 Palatino LT Std by
Cheshire Typesetting Ltd, Cuddington, Cheshire, and
printed and bound by CPI Group (UK) Ltd,
Croydon, CR0 4YY

A CIP record for this book is available from the British Library

ISBN 9781474492959 (hardback)
ISBN 9781474492966 (paperback)
ISBN 9781474492973 (webready PDF)
ISBN 9781474492980 (epub)

The right of Morgan Currie, Jeremy Knox and Callum McGregor to be identified as the editors of this work has been asserted in accordance with the Copyright, Designs and Patents Act 1988, and the Copyright and Related Rights Regulations 2003 (SI No. 2498).

CONTENTS

FIGURES AND TABLES

FIGURES

TABLES

NOTES ON EDITORS AND CONTRIBUTORS

AlgorithmWatch is a non-profit research and advocacy organisation committed to evaluating and shedding light on algorithmic decision-making processes that have a social relevance, meaning they are used either to predict or prescribe human action or to make decisions automatically. AlgorithmWatch was founded by Lorena Jaume-Palasí, Lorenz Matzat, Matthias Spielkamp and Katharina Anna Zweig. The organisation (gGmbH) is run by Lorenz Matzat and executive director Matthias Spielkamp.

Jessica Brand is a research assistant at the Data Justice Lab and has worked on a number of projects since joining in 2017. These include investigating the impact of automated child welfare services, exploring the possibilities and limits of platform regulation, documenting data harms for the Lab's data harm record as well as researching the inter-section between data justice and the Wellbeing of Future Generations (Wales) Act. She is currently working on projects relating to the Lab's ongoing research on the theme of civic participation in data-driven decision making. Before joining the Lab she was an intern at Privacy International and is a former student of Cardiff University's MA Digital Media and Society.

Benedetta Catanzariti is a PhD candidate in Science, Technology and Innovation Studies at the University of Edinburgh. She is currently looking at the social and political dimensions shaping the design and development of AI systems, as well as the data practices that underlie machine learning models. Her research sits at the intersection of science and technology studies and feminist studies and explores the material practices, histories and epistemologies of computer vision technology.

Morgan Currie is Senior Lecturer in Data and Society in Science, Technology and Innovation Studies at the University of Edinburgh. Her research and teaching interests focus on open and administrative data, algorithms in the welfare state, activists' data practices, cultural mapping and critical GIS. She is principal investigator of The Culture & Communities Mapping Project and the Automating Universal Credit research project and co-leads the Digital Social Science Research Cluster at Centre for Data, Culture & Society. She earned a PhD in information studies from the University of California, Los Angeles.

Huw C. Davies is a Lecturer in Digital Education (Data and Society) at the University of Edinburgh and a Research Associate at the Oxford Internet Institute, and is affiliated to the Edinburgh Futures Institute. His research and teaching locates digital education with the wider sociologies of education and digital technology. He specialises in operationalising social theory with quantitive and qualitative digital and ethnographic methods. Huw has published articles about digital literacy, knowledge graphs, AI in education, and the tension between structure and agency in digitised societies.

Jessica Feldman is a researcher and an artist. She is an Assistant Professor/Enseignante-Chercheuse at the American University of Paris in the Department of Communication, Media and Culture, and the Director of the University's Civic Media Lab. Her research focuses on the intersection of new information and communication technologies and social justice, mainly by connecting ethnographic fieldwork with social movements and design collaborations with engineers. Her current book project articulates core design priorities that emerge in alternative computing tools developed by grassroots social movements focused on values of democracy, solidarity and inclusive participation. Her artwork addresses similar issues by experimenting with emerging technologies and practices of listening. Her research has been published in English and French in international journals and edited volumes and her artwork has been shown internationally in venues such as galleries, museums, concert halls, public parks and city streets.

Cailean Gallagher is a union organiser and historian based in Edinburgh. As an officer of the Scottish Trades Union Congress and coordinator of the Workers' Observatory, Cailean supports workers to organise in un-unionised and precarious work. He is also involved in a range of workers' education projects including the Sma Shot School and Falkland Summer School. Cailean recently completed a PhD at the University of St Andrews on the political and economic thought of Jacobite rebels and is researching the history of Scottish gig work and working time. He is co-author of *Roch Winds: A Treacherous Guide to the State of Scotland*.

Karen Gregory is a Senior Lecturer in Sociology at the University of Edinburgh, where she directs the MSc in Digital Sociology. Her research explores the nature of work in the platform economy and her writing has been published in *Work, Employment and Society*, *American Behavioural Scientist*, and *Information, Communication & Society*, among other journals. She is the co-editor of *Digital Sociologies* (Policy Press, 2016) and an Associate Editor at the *Journal of Cultural Economy*.

Fieke Jansen is a PostDoc at Cardiff University's School of Journalism, Media and Culture and the Data Justice Lab. She is interested in repoliticising data and technology by understanding its historical, social, cultural and political context in Europe. Her PhD research focusesd on the impact of the turn to data-driven policing by European police forces. Prior to starting her PhD, Fieke worked as a practitioner on the intersection of human rights, Internet and artificial intelligence. She can be reached at jansenf@cardiff.ac.uk.

Jeremy Knox is co-director of the Centre for Research in Digital Education at the University of Edinburgh, where he leads a research theme on the 'Data Society'. His research interests include the relationships between education, data-driven technologies and wider society. Jeremy's published work includes critical perspectives on artificial intelligence (AI), learning analytics, data and algorithms, as well as Open Educational Resources (OER) and Massive Open Online Courses (MOOCs). He is associate editor of *Postdigital Science and Education*, and co-convenes the Society for Research in Higher Education (SRHE) Digital University network.

Vili Lehdonvirta is Professor of Economic Sociology and Digital Social Research at the Oxford Internet Institute, University of Oxford. He has published extensively on the online gig economy and digital market-place platforms, including on their implications to workers, businesses and policy makers. His new book on the power of platform companies and how to govern them is forthcoming from MIT Press in 2022.

Callum McGregor is a Lecturer in Education at the Institute for Education, Community and Society, University of Edinburgh. He teaches on the MSc 'Social Justice and Community Action' and the MA 'Learning in Communities' courses. Callum is also an affiliate of the Edinburgh Futures Institute (EFI). Callum's research interests are interdisciplinary and address the relationship between democratic citizenship, education and the politics of policy. Within this broad context, he has published recently on topics as broad as education for climate justice, learning for democracy in the context of populism and radical digital citizenship.

Philippa Metcalfe is a PhD candidate at the ERC-funded DATAJUSTICE project, based at the Data Justice Lab at Cardiff University, UK. She has conducted empirical research in Greece and the UK exploring how datafied border and asylum regimes in Europe are both implemented and experienced, and examining the ways in which they further entrench historical bordering practices. Philippa has previously carried out research on migration and European asylum policy, conducting fieldwork in Greece with migrant solidarity groups. She completed a BA in Social Anthropology at the University of Sussex (2013) and an MSc in Social and Public Policy at Cardiff University (2017). Her work has been published in *First Monday* and *Geopolitics* peer review online journals.

Britt Paris is an Associate Professor of Library and Information Science at Rutgers University and an affiliate at the Data & Society Research Institute. She is a critical informatics scholar using methods from discourse analysis and qualitative social science to study how groups build, use and understand information systems according to their values, and how these systems influence evidentiary standards and political action. Her work focuses on developing a broader understanding of the social, political, economic and historical forces that have shaped our current technological environment to allow us to envision new systems that might better support the future we want.

Irene Pasquetto is a scholar in the field of information and communication science. She holds a position as Assistant Professor at the University of Michigan School of Information where she teaches Ethics of Information Technologies and Digital Curation. Her most recent research work focuses on science mis- and disinformation, open science practices, and public understanding and use/misuse of science products and infrastructures. From 2018 to 2020 she was a postdoctoral fellow at the Shorenstein Center on Media, Politics, and Public Policy, at the Harvard Kennedy School. At the Kennedy School, Irene co-founded and chief-edited the *Harvard Kennedy School Misinformation Review*. Irene earned a PhD in Information Studies from the University of California, Los Angeles (UCLA), where she also worked as a research assistant at the UCLA Center for Knowledge Infrastructures (CKI) and the UCLA Institute for Society and Genetics.

Jennifer Pierre, PhD, is a user experience and human–computer interaction researcher with expertise in social media, games, critical data studies and social informatics. She received her doctorate from the Department of Information Studies at UCLA, where she focused her dissertation on how youth use social media for social support. She holds an MLIS from the same department. Jennifer is currently working as a User Experience Researcher at YouTube. Her work can be found in the CHI, HICSS and CSCW proceedings, *Big Data & Society* and *InterActions*, and has been recognised by ACM SIGCHI, the Ford Foundation and the Bouchet Honor Society. In addition to her research and industry work, Jennifer has worked as an instructional designer with the UCLA Library WI+RE team, and has fuelled her passion for inclusion in STEM, higher education and tech as a member and leader of several diversity, equity and inclusion initiatives.

Joanna Redden is an Assistant Professor at the Faculty of Information and Media Studies, Western University and Co-Director of the Data Justice Lab. Joanna researches the social justice implications of government uses of AI and automated decision-making systems. This work has involved mapping and analysing changing government data systems across Western democratic countries, investigating data harms and the work being done to redress these harms as well as work to advance greater civic participation in these areas. Her work has been published in popular sites like *Scientific American* and leading journals like *Big Data & Society*. She is author of *The Mediation of Poverty* and co-editor of *Compromised Data: From Social Media to Big Data.*

Ina Sander is a postgraduate researcher and research assistant at the Data Justice Lab, Cardiff University, Wales, and a research fellow at the Helmut-Schmidt-University, Hamburg, Germany. Her research is located in the field of critical data studies and examines how data systems transform our societies and how citizens can be critically educated about this datafication. Her main research interest lies in conceptualising 'critical data literacy' and examining ways to implement this literacy, for example through online educational resources. She is also the co-founder and co-coordinator of the Critical Big Data and Algorithmic Literacy Network, and a former research fellow at the Centre for Advanced Internet Studies, Bochum, Germany.

Pip Thornton is a Chancellor's Fellow in GeoSciences at the University of Edinburgh. Her theory and practice explore the politics of existence in online spaces, critiquing and making visible structures of power within the digital economy with creative methods. She gained her PhD in Geopolitics and Cybersecurity from Royal Holloway, University of London in 2019. Her thesis, 'Language in the Age of Algorithmic Reproduction: A Critique of Linguistic Capitalism', put forward a theoretical, political and creative critique of Google's search and advertising platforms, and included an artistic intervention into Google's monetisation of language called {poem}.py. Shown at the Edinburgh Fringe, her 2019 piece *Newspeak* was shortlisted for the 2020 Lumen Prize for Art and Technology and was awarded an honourable mention in the Surveillance Studies Network Biennial Art Competition (2020). Pip's work has featured in *WIRED UK, New Scientist* and at the Open Data Institute in London.

Harry Warne is a postgraduate researcher at Aberystwyth University, Wales. Whilst a researcher with the Data Justice Lab, Cardiff University, Wales, he researched topics including uses of data systems within the public sector, police uses of live facial recognition, and the potential of democratic innovations for opening up government decision-making processes relating to data systems. His research into cancelled data systems for this volume focused on examples from New Zealand (Aotearoa) and Australia. His current research sits at the intersection of sub-state and democratic innovations theory with a particular interest in contemporary indigenous political formations.

Ben Williamson is a Chancellor's Fellow in the Centre for Research in Digital Education at the University of Edinburgh, focusing on digital technology and data in education policy and governance. He is an editor of the journal *Learning, Media and Technology*, and the author of *Big Data in Education: The Digital Future of Learning, Policy and Practice*.

Alex J. Wood is an economic sociologist at the University of Bristol and lectures on the Future of Work. He is also a Research Associate at the Oxford Internet Institute. His most recent research investigates worker voice, organisation and collective action in the gig economy and how digital technology shapes workplace regimes. His publications include the book *Despotism on Demand* (Cornell University Press, 2020) and articles for leading academic journals such as *Sociology, Work, Employment and Society, Human Relations* and *Socio-Economic Review*. He is PI of the British Academy funded 'Gig Rights Project', which uses an innovative quantitative methodology to explore labour rights and collective politics in the UK gig economy.

Nicolas Zehner is an ESRC-funded PhD candidate in sociology at the University of Edinburgh and a visiting research fellow in the Science, Technology & Society Program at the Harvard Kennedy School. In his research, he aims to shed light on the practice of city-making by investigating the ways in which urban planning agents imagine futures and the sociotechnical conditions that help establish the credibility of their expectations. His dissertation focuses on the role of scientific expertise in the drive for 'smart urbanism' and examines higher education institutions as central sites for the evolution and expansion of urban-regional sociotechnical imaginaries.

FOREWORD

The datafication of urban life is part of reconfiguring not only how we might access resources and services, but, perhaps more fundamentally, how we come to understand our cities, how we relate to them, and what matters in them. The use of data for capital, control, capture and contestation plays out in our city landscapes in ways that demand an engagement with justice not as a stable and universalist concept, but rather one that needs to be grounded in the complex practices and lived experiences of datafication. Bound up in discourses of the 'smart' city, urban living has rapidly become a hub for experimentation and technological innovation. With the global crisis of the COVID-19 pandemic, the relevance of the changing configuration of space and data has only become more pressing. Connecting data justice with the 'right to the city' framework is therefore a fruitful way to identify synergies, entangle demands and advance our understanding of societal shifts in more concrete terms.

Finding ways to advance and apply ideas of data justice is crucial as the rapid acceleration of data-intensive technologies across social life is often met with rather timid responses. Whilst there is widespread recognition that datafication brings with it significant transformations to our cities, we are often left with narrow parameters for how to address such transformations in a way that centres our rights, well-being and human flourishing. Often we are forced into thinking about broadening data collection, improving algorithms, or governing automation better as a way to ensure that the 'smartening' of our cities is done 'responsibly'. Connecting data justice to a right to the city framework allows us to nurture more radical imaginations for what we want our cities to be, how they should be organised, and what the place of technology should be in them.

The right to the city tradition also clearly marks out a central role for the people living *in* our cities to be the voices *of* our cities; that is, it is a city's residents who should be at the forefront of transformations, technological or otherwise. In this sense, it aligns with data justice debates that have sought to change the current make-up of the decision-making table towards impacted communities having a much bigger stake in both the framing of the problems and the nature of solutions that pertain to datafication. Moreover, the call for the right to the city alerts us to the collective dimension of any such endeavour, recognising that data is always relational, as must any data governance and data justice framework be.

In navigating the multitudes of urban life, we can begin to pinpoint how processes of datafication are being entrenched and how they impact on different dynamics in the city, whether it is how we are educated, work, access welfare, move or are policed. The task for data justice scholars when engaging with such dynamics must be to attend to the underlying power structures against which injustices come to be understood. The question is what function datafication – as a discourse and practice – serves in different contexts, the social, economic and political organisation that enables it, and who benefits. Making claims to a city, or seeking demands for rights to a city, is as much a call for making our cities more just as it is an intervention into how justice is constructed and defined.

In this sense, mobilisation for social justice in the datafied city has to tackle the actual conditions that lead to experiences of injustice as they exist on the ground rather than necessarily pouring efforts into appealing to ideal formations of data and technology. Similarly, the aim of social justice cannot simply be the creation of just institutions that enact justice 'from above'; justice must reside within and through social relations as they currently exist. The right to the city in the context of contending with the way urban life is being reconfigured through and within visions of a datafied future speaks to a form of mobilisation that therefore requires *political* engagement from the outset. What is at stake is more than legal remedies, technical fixes or procedural safeguards; a call for data justice and the right to the city has to also ensure *political capability* – a configuration of civic life that can enable and nurture solidarity as grounds for struggle.

The collection of chapters put together in this book by Morgan Currie, Jeremy Knox and Callum McGregor does much to deepen our understanding of what this 'new politics' of data justice and the right to the city looks like. By joining together two frameworks that have previously existed primarily in silos, the book advances a radical demand for a different vision for data and space than what is being offered by the prolific 'smart' city prophets. Instead, the book forces us to revisit ongoing struggles over inequality, discrimination, privatisation, welfare, migration, education and work that have long shaped the cities we live in. As these struggles are increasingly bound up with the rollout of data-driven technologies, the question is the extent to which these developments change the conditions within which justice can be pursued and achieved. In bringing together such a rich and diverse set of contributions, this book does much to answer this critical question.

Lina Dencik
Cardiff University, UK

ACKNOWLEDGEMENTS

We thank the authors in this book, first and foremost, for their valuable contributions to the book's themes. Several of these authors took part in the 2019 Data Justice Week at the University of Edinburgh, and we appreciate that they continued to work with us throughout the production of this publication. We are very grateful to our major funder, the Edinburgh Futures Institute, who funded the 2019 event and made it possible for this work to be open access. Many thanks to Melissa Terras, who originally suggested we send a book proposal to the University of Edinburgh Press. Thanks to the folks we worked with at the Edinburgh University Press: Ersev Ersoy, Sarah Foyle, Gillian Leslie and Jenny Daly, and Thom Brooks, series editor for Studies in Global Justice and Human Rights. Thanks as well to the anonymous reviewers of our original proposal and final manuscript. And thanks to AlgorithmWatch, who make their important work available under public licences, allowing that content to be republished here.

ABBREVIATIONS

ADMS – automated decision-making systems
AI – artificial intelligence
ANPR – automatic number-plate recognition
APIs – application programming interfaces
BLM – Black Lives Matter
DDI – Data-Driven Innovation initiative
EFI – Edinburgh Futures Institute
EU – European Union
FACS – Facial Action Coding System
FOI – Freedom of Information
GDPR – General Data Protection Regulation
HCI – human–computer interaction
HEIs – higher education institutions
IABS – Immigration and Asylum Biometrics System
ISPs – Internet service providers
LAN – local area network
MOOCs – Massive Open Online Courses
MoUs – Memorandums of Understanding
NASS – National Asylum Support Service
Nesta – National Endowment for Science, Technology and Arts
NGOs – non-governmental organisations
NHS – National Health Service
NRPF – no recourse to public funds
OER – Open Educational Resources
OWS – Occupy Wall Street

POC – people of colour
RTTC – right to the city
STS – science and technology studies
TRADE – talent, research, adoption, data and entrepreneurship
UKVI – UK Visas and Immigration

INTRODUCTION: DATA JUSTICE AND THE RIGHT TO THE CITY

Morgan Currie, Jeremy Knox and Callum McGregor

This chapter argues that the concept of data justice can inform and enrich practices motivated by the Right to the City (RTTC). RTTC is, at heart, a radical concept of citizenship that calls for the collective design of urban life, of 'affordable housing, a decent school for the kids, accessible services, reliable public transport. The right to have your urban horizon as wide or as narrow as you want' (Merrifield 2017). The comparatively nascent concept of data justice seeks to understand how datafication of everyday life, predominantly but not solely in urban contexts, compounds existing social injustices and creates new ones. While the lens of data justice helps illustrate how and why an analysis of datafication is today integral to the RTTC, the RTTC cautions against the political co-option of data justice into technocratic and privatised 'data for good' initiatives.

Emerging work on data justice discourages the data fetishism tainting public, commercial and academic discourse on emerging data industries. By 'fetishism' we mean the habit of endowing objects and entities with an almost magical, or at least intrinsic, power to shape the world around us (Harvey 2003). Data fetishism is a form of post-politics par excellence that casts aside theory and ideology and reduces various social problems to systems engineering conundrums solvable with sufficient data and processing capacity (Han 2017; Eubanks 2018). Instead, data justice scholarship and activism in all its diversity understand datafication as a political phenomenon related to more established structural dynamics of social injustice, whether distributive (economic), recognitive (cultural) or representational (political) (Fraser 2005).

1

FRAMING SOCIAL JUSTICE

A social justice approach focuses on the agency of those groups disproportionately impacted by datafication and urbanisation. We find it useful to draw on Nancy Fraser to frame social justice as participatory parity – that is, 'social arrangements that permit all to participate as peers in social life' (2008: 405). Distributive, recognitive and representational injustices are different dimensions of social justice that can be understood in terms of their combined impact on participatory parity in concrete situations (Fraser 2005). Constraints on participation can be attributed to the unfair distribution of economic goods, or the institutionalised cultural marginalisation of group identities, or to rules or institutions that suppress political voice, or a combination of all these.

Following Fraser and Iris Marion Young, this framing means paying attention to the entanglement of economic injustice with the politics of difference. The cultural domination of certain social groups reinforces material economic inequality, just as structural economic inequality in turn reproduces social problems (ill health, high crime rates, violence, addiction etc.) in poor and often racialised communities through the perpetuation of conservative policy discourses. In Fraser's more recent work, representational injustice is concerned with the asymmetrical distribution of power to determine what defines political space itself. Fraser identifies representational injustice at work where 'the division of political space into separated bounded polities deprive[s] some of the chance to engage politically with peers on matters of common concern' (Fraser 2008: 286). In short, there can be no recognition or redistribution without representation.

Dencik, Jansen and Metcalfe (2018) foreground how the emerging political economy of datafication and the politics of difference are intertwined, as opaque proprietary algorithms classify and sort social groups on the basis of 'group commonalities that are fundamentally alien to individuals and groups themselves' (p. 4). Transnational data infrastructures act as black boxes with real material consequences for people (most notably refugees and asylum seekers) who have no agency to speak back to systems that govern their daily lives. Distributive, recognitive and representational injustices are manifested in a panoply of concrete data justice issues: the automation and digitisation of social welfare, the datafication of border regimes, racist police profiling, the surveillance of social justice activism and the exploitation and precaritisation of labour through automation and platform capitalism, to name but a few. All of these issues and dynamics cut across different axes of oppression, including race, class, gender and legal status, and can ultimately be understood by asking how the dynamics of datafication enhance or inhibit participatory parity, a concern at the heart of RTTC struggles.

Historically, struggles for the RTTC find solidarity in difference, underpinned by a radically inclusive vision of citizenship that isn't contingent on legal status. Collective struggles over housing, policing, urban pollution, green space, transport, education, energy and food sovereignty (to name but a few) have all historically found common cause under the RTTC. Ideologically, what sets the RTTC apart from a more liberal discourse of rights, including human rights, is that it challenges the individualistic and post-political nature of such discourse. The RTTC is fundamentally about the right to 'change and reinvent the city more after our hearts' desire' (Harvey 2012: 4). At its best, the RTTC raises questions over the use and production of urban space that bring together citizens with heterogeneous interests and positions in often unpredictable ways (Lefebvre 1992). Thus, the RTTC is fundamentally sensitive to the question of building political solidarity in the face of difference. The salience of the RTTC today is the promise, at a municipal scale, to construct an alternative narrative of the people that rejects the false choice between a neoliberal technocratic oligarchy (with some progressive concessions) and right-wing xenophobic and racist nationalist populism in particular (Mouffe 2018).

The growing density of urban space, the proliferation of data produced by the concentration of inhabitants, and the technical expertise that cities attract have stimulated ideas about efficient governance and the city as an engine of economic growth. Policy makers and industry players envision data-driven technologies animating regional development in the form of entrepreneurial start-ups, data-science expertise and venture capital investment. In the fetishistic fervour to datify our cities (and their attendant institutions such as schools and health and welfare services), a focus on data justice is a necessary pillar of any effective RTTC activism. The struggles of digital rights activists and community activists organising for the RTTC are intimately entangled (Dencik, Hintz and Cable 2016). The RTTC opposes the unmitigated privitisation of public space and the commodification of the commons. As the informational commons become invisibly commodified, entire areas of urban life (education, health, transport, policing, tourism, housing, energy etc.) are mediated through digital infrastructures and the data they amass and process. Francesca Bria terms data a 'meta utility':

> [W]hat does energy sovereignty mean once we transition onto the smart grid, and firms like Google offer to cut out bills by a third if only we surrender our energy data? Does the struggle for 'energy sovereignty' mean anything if it is not tied to the struggle for technological sovereignty? Probably not. (Bria 2020: 166)

When sutured together, data justice and the RTTC are radical demands that form the starting point of a new politics. The next important step is to design paths to civic participation, resistance and the invention of creative alternatives to otherwise inevitable futures of corporate power and rising inequality.

This introduction makes connections between an existing and substantive body of literature on the RTTC with more recent and explicit calls for justice where data-driven systems increasingly suffuse our social institutions. The first section provides an overview of the RTTC as an enduring conceptual lens looking at the civic, participatory and creative production of urban space. As much work in this area has already established, policies and pundits have normalised the imaginary of datafication most explicitly in urban contexts. The second section will elaborate on the ways that notions of data justice expand upon the intersection of critical data studies and social justice studies, bridging an interest in the social impact of 'Big Data', algorithms, artificial intelligence (AI) and other data-intensive technologies, with established concerns for fairness, rights and opportunity in society. We connect data justice literature to established debates in social justice theory, considering the extent to which the current paradigm of datafication troubles many of the assumptions that underpin prevailing understandings of fairness in contemporary society. Just as the subsequent contributions in this book do, we suggest frameworks and practices through which datafied cities and citizens might engage in more justice-oriented relationships.

A RETURN TO THE RIGHT TO THE CITY

The term 'right to the city' largely originated with Henri Lefebvre, Marxist philosopher and social scientist, writing in the period leading up to 1968 protests in Paris. For Lefebvre, the material spaces of the city are implicated in all social and political aspects of urban life. Because our daily environment constitutes social relations, it follows that the only way for urban citizens to exercise their rights fully is to have the capacity to design their environment and participate in struggles over its development. In Mark Purcell's (2002) reading, Lefebvre offers a radical approach to political inclusion: all inhabitants – not only legal citizens, but all who live in a city – should make these decisions about urban space through direct forms of participation. The RTTC is relevant to a broad spectrum of historical upheavals and gentrification processes driven by often racialised financial capitalism, including 'slum clearance, demolition and displacement of communities in Haussman's Paris in the 19th century, Robert Moses in 20th century New York and contemporary development in cities like Seoul, Delhi and Mumbai' (Minton 2017: 55). The most radical potential of the RTTC therefore lies in an intersectional approach, directly challenging racist, patriarchal, capitalist and ableist social relations that underpin the production of urban space.

Social movements were quick to adopt 'the right to the city' as a slogan in their efforts to resist gentrification and development backed by global capital (Brenner, Marcuse Mayer 2012) and in popular struggles against austerity, globalisation and the destruction of open spaces and land (Mayer 2009). In Brazil, the 'right to the city' gained legal meaning when it enshrined its 2001 City Statute, giving citizens more rights to shape development of public land (Fernandes 2007). The United Nations and the World Social Forum adopted the phrase as a theme during several global gatherings in the 2000s (Kuymulu 2013); in these cases, RTTC reflects global concerns that in cities, democracy and enfranchisement are on the decline, both through the outsourcing of public services and thanks to capitalism's unrelenting emphasis on the exchange value – rather than use value – of space.

RTTC took on new academic significance in the 2000s when critical urban theorists revived the phrase to analyse class struggle, antiracism and radical democracy in the face of globalisation and later the 2008 financial crisis and Occupy Wall Street. In David Harvey's (2008) critique, the phrase describes how cities have long been battlegrounds for capitalist surpluses that are reinvested in city planning and infrastructure, leading too often to commercialisation of common spaces, gentrification, assaults on unions, and environmental degradation through new forms of extraction. 'Since the urban process is a major channel of surplus use, establishing democratic management over its urban deployment constitutes the right to the city', argues Harvey – as opposed to privatisation that colonises public space for the rich. The right to the city mobilises certain rights – of social justice and having a high standard of living and dignity – over others, such as the right to property and to participate in the free market. For Harvey, the RTTC is always commons-based and collective, taken up by communities, not exercised by individuals. At all steps are questions of social justice and participatory parity: Who determines what a good city should be? How might we design a world of justly distributed public resources?

RTTC has supplied scholars with a rich framework to understand urban grassroots efforts. Kuymulu (2013) views the Gezi Park uprisings in Istanbul through this lens – the occupation of the park was a reaction to government plans to turn this green space into a shopping mall. A band of activists, occupying the park for three days, effectively stopped the construction and sparked nation-wide protest as citizens reacted to police brutality against the occupiers. Weinstein and Ren (2009) use the RTTC framework to compare formal housing rights protections and the work of housing rights activists across Shanghai and Mumbai. Shillington (2013) uses the concept to look at how inhabitants of Nicaragua's cities use household fruit trees to challenge food insecurity.

Debates also characterise this literature. Exactly what rights does the right to the city encompass (Attoh 2011)? Is the phrase used so often that it risks dilution (Plyushteva 2009)? Should rights even be the focus, over other ethically resonate terms, such as 'needs' (Mitchell 2003)? Does the phrase signal too much about the process, and not enough about the values that should drive the process (Purcell 2002)? These questions become less important when we understand the RTTC as a set of demands enacted through struggle, rather than an objective sociological category. As a discursive practice, the RTTC 'does not exist previously to its political articulation' (Mouffe 2018: 62).

Despite its contingency, we can identify four principles that characterise literature on RTTC: (1) resisting the privatisation of public space and services, which historically entails treating space in terms of its surplus value rather than civic use value due to government austerity and privatisation; (2) fighting for a more equitable distribution of the benefits of city life to all inhabitants; (3) introducing more democratic practices determining urban development and resource distribution; and (4) guiding these processes using a particular set of rights that emphasise social justice over property ownership.

RIGHT TO THE DATAFIED CITY

The question of technology and its influence on social relations has always been central to RTTC struggles, since urban technologies implicitly encourage and facilitate certain social relations while excluding others. Take Winner's (1980) famous example of how Robert Moses used urban planning as a racist tool to undermine desegregation efforts by constructing freeway bridges that blocked public transport from reaching all-white suburbs. As Winner (1980) observed in his landmark work, people often adjust to social relations resulting from 'technological' change that they would resist if resulting from overt politics. So the question of technology in the RTTC is not new.

Datafication introduces new sets of problems that recharacterise RTTC principles. Shaw and Graham (2017) reanimate a particularly important aspect of Lefebvre's work in this context: the 'right to information', which constitutes part of the broader conceptualisation of the 'right to the city' (Lefebvre 1996). Digital information collected by 'GPS devices, Uber, Wikipedia and TripAdvisor' create digital reproductions of cities' infrastructure that are 'often as important as their bricks and mortar' (Shaw and Graham 2017: 908). Shaw and Graham focus on the power implicit in this shift to urban data, tracing the ways in which powerful corporations such as Google 'reproduce and control urban space itself' (2017: 921). 'In this capacity, [tech companies] have now joined – and in some cases, perhaps even superseded – the ranks of urban planners, developers and landlords from Lefebvre's era in terms of their power over the city and its many problems' (Shaw and Graham 2017: 921). Datafication, in this sense, is increasingly indistinguishable from the privatisation of the city, where civic use value is subordinated to profit-seeking behaviour of a technology sector increasingly controlled by a small group of dominant corporations. Today, regional city deals view data-intensive industry as a panacea for competitive advantage and a site for surplus reinvestment and growth. State-based services rely more and more on private platforms. Thus, the RTTC is partly about challenging the 'accumulation by dispossession' of data generated by citizens and the Faustian pact we make daily when we exchange data for services, such that it might be controlled democratically and operationalised in more emancipatory directions.

Kitchin and colleagues further renew the 'right to the city' literature through the examination of the smart city, a much more overt datafication of urban space involving embedded technologies that administer city functions (Kitchin, Cardullo and Di Feliciantonio 2019: 1). Algorithmic and automated systems, while not overtly disciplinary, create forms of control that steer and nudge citizens (Kitchin et al. 2019: 4). This kind of social control entrenches forms of inequality by reconfiguring citizens as productive consumers, forming divisions between those who fuel the tech-infused urban economy and those that ultimately benefit from it. 'Citizens . . . can browse, consume, and act. If there is civic engagement, it is in the form of a participant, tester, or player who provides feedback or suggestions, rather than being a proposer, co-creator, decision-maker, or leader' (p. 6). Kitchin et al. (2019) draw on the 'right to the city' to propose alternative community- and justice-oriented visions of the city. As Morozov and Bria (2018) detail, many cities are grappling with the neoliberal model of the data-driven city, and are proposing community-driven datafication that provides more equitable distributions of the benefits of city life. The city of Barcelona is a key example: since 2015 it has attempted to adopt the practice of 'technological sovereignty' – designing technology to serve local residents 'and be owned as a commons, rather than applying a universal, market oriented proprietary technology' (Kitchin et al. 2019: 10). Gabrys (2019) offers another example of participatory, community-driven practices for urban development through citizen sensing of air pollution. Gabrys takes inspiration from Lefebvre to characterise 'the city as an ongoing collective project' driven by 'staving off and surviving dispossession, pollution and injustice that often accompany increasing urbanization' (Gabrys 2019: 250–1). Drawing on Lefebvre's underlying philosophical direction, Gabrys asserts that:

> the right to the city is more relational rather than teleological, since it is less focused on arriving at a finished urban form, and more attuned to the ways of life that are experienced and sustained,

as well as the political subjects that urban inhabitants become in these collective urban projects. (Gabrys 2019: 252)

As the following section will elaborate, data justice literature is also concerned with lived experience and the ongoing articulation of everyday injustices in ways that constitute more radically democratic practices. While this section has made connections between the concept of the 'right to the city' and the politicisation of data in urban contexts, the next defines the term 'data justice' and highlights several themes it shares with the RTTC literature.

DATA JUSTICE – POLITICS AND PERSONALISATION

As Dencik, Jansen and Metcalfe (2018) suggest, the central thrust of work in data justice is 'to situate data processes within historical and on-going struggles for justice claims'. This work should therefore be understood in a context of broader critical responses within the social sciences to the often evangelistic and celebratory discourses that tend to accompany technology development. Dencik et al. (2018) further clarify this reversal of the dominant narrative, suggesting 'datafication is not a revolution that is drastically changing the structural power and political economy of modern society, but an extension of conditions that have resulted in grievances and injustices towards historically marginalised and politically sculpted targets' (Dencik et al. 2018: 6). In this sense, both critical data studies that draw on RTTC and work in data justice call for a sea change in the hyperbole and sense of triumph surrounding technical progress, and a much more in-depth engagement with social justice concerns in the era of datafication.

Echoing RTTC, a central concern for data justice is the manifestation of power. A number of recent works in data justice have examined the ways in which the political economy of datafication has concentrated power within an elite few and amplified the marginalisation, misrecognition and liability of many (O'Neil 2018; Taylor 2017; Eubanks 2018; Noble 2018). Nancy Fraser's formulation of justice as participatory parity is powerful in this context. Automated welfare services, for instance, typically signal cuts in staff, involve contracts with private firms whose patented systems evade public scrutiny, and facilitate surveillance through algorithmic risk assessment, creating opaque systems with little public oversight. Work in data justice views these automated systems as 'a new form of governance that advances particular social, economic and political agendas, benefitting some and disadvantaging others' (Hintz, Dencik andWahl-Jorgensen 2019: 143). Another pertinent example is Crawford and Joler's study of a 'virtual assistant', which, rather than focusing on the technical features of the device or the functions defined by its designers, describes and visualises a 'map of human labor, data and planetary resources' (2018) that constitute the gadget. Crawford and Joler (2018) chart, amongst other relationships, the '[p]rivatization and exploitation' of rare earth elements used in the production of the virtual assistant, with the '[u]npaid immaterial labour' of users who train the system through their everyday use of voice commands.

While there has been a long-established critique of the consumerist model of public service governance (Clarke 2007), we now must pay attention to public services transformed by data-driven technologies. Examining the ways public services are being revisioned through relationships between public and private intermediaries, Williamson outlines a method of personalisation, which:

> involves the use of sophisticated software and algorithms that can be used to collect and analyse 'big data' on service users, consisting of personal information and individual behavioural data, in order to anticipate or even predict citizens' future lives, behaviours and requirements. (Williamson, 2014: 292)

Such services constitute a shift from generalised public services to highly customised and automated relationships between individual citizens and local authorities. Under the guise of this supposedly beneficial 'personalisation', such approaches tend to build in a form of isolation, where individuals lose shared experiences of public services, and therefore connections to each other. As Hintz et al. (2019) note, such data-driven personalisation works against notions of collective citizenship, further entrenching an ideology of individual responsibility and personal culpability. For Lake, this 'hyperindividualism' surfaces most intensely in urban governance, which is reduced to 'the management of atomistic behavior' (2017: 8). Further, such personalisation 'undermines the contribution of urban complexity as a resource for governance, erodes the potential for urban democracy, and eviscerates the possibility of collective resistance' (p. 8). In this sense, public services that are reconstituted as personalised data-driven transactions undermine the very notion of the 'public' as representing mutual experiences, united causes, or indeed the capacity for collective action.

A further concern of data justice is around public space and services, where such notions are becoming increasingly contested in city contexts. The data justice literature, as with RTTC, is concerned about how datafication enables the impoverishment of public space and city services. This is particularly evidenced in new investments in the digital platform sector that sets out to 'unlock the potential' of big datasets as a kind of raw material, but ends up drawing new lines of power between those that store and organise data, and those of us who have less understanding of or control over these information flows. An important, and under-explored, aspect of the existing RTTC literature to date, which the literature on data justice has richly contributed to, is the rise of surveillance systems that encroach on daily life and public space through predictive analytics and facial recognition software, which have been found to embed racial bias (though see Mitchell and Heynen 2009). At the same time that citizens are ceding control of their statistical representations through their online behaviour, automated data collection increasingly privatises and marketises activities in public space – as we witness with the rise of profitable data analytics industries that monetise data on students at public universities (Williamson 2017). Contemporary social justice movements from 15-M in Spain to Occupy to Black Lives Matter have recognised that reshaping public space is also an issue of reaching publics through technical platforms over which they have little control. Both data justice and the RTTC call for collective, democratic oversight of these platforms and to exercise this right by drawing on long-standing social justice principles. By combining the strengths of these two literatures, we can start examining how these trends are particularly amplified in urban contexts.

Another key dimension of data justice work that mirrors RTTC literature is to promote a return to community-driven goals and technological designs that promote shared experiences and action. Perceiving data-driven systems as inherently social quite literally opens up ways of identifying and comprehending the impact of technology in general, and issues of marginalisation and injustice in particular. A pertinent example here is the Algorithmic Justice League,[1] who, through unmasking the racial and gender biases built into various AI products (Buolamwini and Gebru 2018; Raji and Buolamwini 2019), engage in a range of high-profile advocacy and policy work in the US, for example testifying to the Committee on Oversight and Reform in the House of Representatives concerning the impact of facial recognition and bio-metric surveillance.

Finally, there is growing interest in not only critiquing the inher-ent biases and politics of data-driven systems, but also attempting to transform design practices themselves to engage in the 'dismantling or transforming [of] systems of oppression' (Costanza-Chock 2019). Contends Costanza-Chock:

> the design of AI, or machine learning, is still deeply inequitable. It's inequitable in terms of: who gets to build it; who the paid AI workers are; who the imagined users are; the goals of the systems; the sites in which we're building these things; the power rela-tions that these systems support and strengthen; the pedagogy that we're using to teach the people who are learning how to build these systems in computer science departments around the country and around the world. (Costanza-Chock 2019)

Green critiques the discipline of data science, calling it 'a form of politi-cal action' (2019: 7) and asking data scientists to view themselves as doing politics through their work, which can make such an impact in people's daily lives. Green's depiction is in stark contrast with the insular approach to computer science, where emphasis tends to be placed largely on cohesive design at the expense of considerations of their wider social impact. This notion of 'design justice'

> goes beyond fairness. It entails thinking about the matrix of domi-nation – about intersecting systems of oppression – and what it means to design sociotechnical systems that can transform or overturn these systems, rather than constantly reproducing them in technology, in design, and in machine learning. (Costanza-Chock 2019)

While encompassing a much broader approach to design than simply working with data-driven technologies, the Design Justice Network Principles[2] offer a tangible set of guidelines for avoiding the kind of biases and marginalisation identified in much of the data justice litera-ture. However, this concern for formalising justice from the outset of design exists in tension with calls to focus research on lived encounters with data and the everyday experiences of often unpredictable injustice.

In the final section of this chapter, we examine the contribution that the data justice literature has made to our understanding of social justice itself, and ask how this perspective intersects with the praxis-oriented development of RTTC.

JUSTICE IN TIMES OF DATAFICATION

As the previous section discussed, work in data justice is clearly grounded in wider sociological and political critiques of technology; it is oriented towards countering much of the mainstream advocacy and promotion of Big Data, AI and machine learning through centring issues of inequality, discrimination and injustice in public discourse around data-driven technologies. However, in doing so, notions of data justice also offer some productive and pertinent critical commentary on social justice theory itself, and on the general ways in which issues such as fairness, accountability and transparency are discussed in the contemporary context of increasing data governance. Key to this contribution of data justice research is the way in which it draws upon sociological understandings of data and social life, in order to trouble many of the assumptions that tend to underpin prevailing understandings of justice and fairness. Dencik et al. (2018) highlight two principal areas of social justice theory for which the paradigm of datafication provides a pertinent contemporary context: Fraser's concept of 'abnormal justice' (2008), which, rather than attempting to define the fair distribution of resources in society, focuses on the conditions in which the very notion of justice itself is framed; and the work of Amartya Sen (2009) and Iris Marion Young (2011), which foreground the lived experiences of injustice. Across these critical perspectives, Dencik et al. (2018) highlight the ways in which current and pervasive data practices hold particular resonance for understanding social justice differently. For example, the significance of Fraser's work has been to highlight conditions in which 'normal justice' – where 'those who argue about justice share a set of underlying assumptions', and 'contests assume a relatively regular, recognizable shape', and in which justice is constituted 'through a set of organising principles and manifesting a discernible grammar' (2008: 393–4) – fails to occur. Better understood as 'abnormal justice', such scenarios call into question fundamental assumptions about the ontology of justice, the scope of actors, and the very procedures through which it might be pursued (Fraser 2008). As Dencik et al. (2018) highlight, the omnipresent regimes of data collection and processing, and their fine-grained entanglements with everyday social life, present precisely such abnormalities, where data itself is questioned as a tangible commodity, the extent to which particular groups or populations are disadvantaged is contested, and the routes to claiming or practising justice are opaque.

Once again, work in data justice is a challenge to dominant discourses, this time those in the guise of fairness, privacy and the protection of individual rights, which have tended to characterise broader discussions of the social impact of data-driven technologies. Dencik et al. (2018) specifically question the relevance of more prevalent Rawlsian notions of distributive justice, where the principal focus is to achieve the equitable dissemination of resources in society. As Dencik et al. suggest, the underlying assumptions of distributive justice are 'not enough to question the implications of obscure, unaccountable and interwoven decision making created by datafication' (2018: 4–5), due not only to the abstruse modes through which data-driven systems might identify and categorise populations in ways that result in marginalisation or injustice, but also in relation to the extent to which such processes are traceable and amenable to processes of public scrutiny. In other words, where a notion of fairness underpins the understanding of justice, within which the primary concerns are located in concepts of privacy and the protection of personal rights, assumptions are made about the coherence, agency and permanence of the actors involved, as well as the space in which the very question of justice can be posed and understood. For Dencik et al., the path to understanding such abnormal justice contexts lies in drawing from the work of Sen (2009): to foreground 'social conditions and lived experiences' (Dencik et al. 2018: 4), rather than develop theoretical principles, or indeed assume the fair and unbiased conduct of civic institutions. As such, comprehending the (in)justice of datafied societies comes from examining the struggle between the ways people form their own identities and social groupings, and the pervasive sorting, ordering and categorisation undertaken by often concealed technologies (Terranova 2004), producing automated affinity groups (Gillespie 2014) to which citizens are unknowingly assigned, and with which they are appraised.

Heeks and Renken (2018) also work with social justice concepts to offer new theorisations of justice and human rights in light of datafication in global development contexts. The authors begin by pursuing three possible theories of data justice based on widespread social justice literature – what they call 'mainstream' theories. The first is *instrumental* data justice, which puts a focus on whether the outcome of the use of data is fair and just – here this can mean deploying data in a way that leads to discrimination of those with protected attributes, or to a violation of a subject's legal rights to privacy and data protection. Second, a *procedural* notion of justice examines the processes of data creation and handling; this valuation places a strong emphasis on whether individuals have consented to the use of their data, or whether stakeholders have any due process over the handling of the data. Third and final, *distributive* justice looks at who controls and accesses the data; this emphasis might ask whether data privacy protections are in place or whether an individual or groups can control their own data representations. Distributive justice would look not only at how fairly data is distributed, but also at whether the benefits of data control are distributed in equitable ways.

Heeks and Renken, however, critique and nuance these ideas by arguing they ignore the social structures that determine, in part, the relationships and data flows under scrutiny in the three mainstream theories. A structural perspective prompts different types of questions, such as '[w]hy is access to data maldistributed in the global South? Why is participation in data processes unequally distributed? Why do the benefits of data systems in developing countries include some and exclude others?' Heeks and Renken's structural critique shows the limitations of instrumental, procedural and distributive approaches; it focuses instead on the societal conditions shaping data infrastructures and systems – on how society enables the circumstances that shape the creation, exchange and ownership of data. Heeks and Renken draw on Iris Marion Young's network view of social structure and data assemblage analysis to ask how capitalism or governance regimes produce structural inequalities in developing countries, which in turn bear on the inequitable distribution of data and data rights. The authors also propose a capabilities approach, but one slightly amended from Amartya Sen's work. From this perspective, data justice for development is not only about fairly distributing data or giving equal access to its control – it would also include fairly distributing the means to achieve with it, along with creating contexts and institutions that enable people to make good use of data and put related protections and rights into place.

Data justice advocates' insistence that we ground social justice claims in structural, political-economic critiques and lived experiences is a clear intersection with the RTTC. RTTC literature, as described above, cannot disentangle theoretical analyses from actual political-economic struggles of urban life. The RTTC must arise from a contingent set of principles that are shaped through ongoing contention and the political articulation of rights in different contexts. In sum, we find that the RTTC is now being reframed and refreshed, yet again, through the rise of urban datafication, and new understandings of justice in light of datafied citizenship is just another illustration of this dialectic that animates both areas of scholarship.

REPOLITICISING DATA FOR THE RIGHT TO THE CITY

This chapter has brought together long-standing interests in 'the right to the city' with emerging calls for 'data justice'; it has highlighted the pressing need to (re)politicise data, particularly in urban contexts where neoliberal ideologies and tech-fuelled entrepreneurial capitalism are at their most acute, but also where citizens might have the greatest opportunities to mobilise tangible community-driven approaches. We suggest that (re)politicising data is both a critical response to the instrumentalist discourses of technological progress and a methodological practice for surfacing issues of injustice, authentic to the lived experiences of communities in the midst of datafication regimes. We have drawn on literature both from RTTC and data justice that argues for recognition of the politics of data (see Ruppert, Isin and Bigo 2017; Bigo, Isin and Ruppert 2019), and for the need to embrace an essential condition of contestation through which data-driven technologies are necessarily developed (Crawford 2016).

Embracing such tensions and contests is precisely where the work of RTTC and data justice intersect: to '(re)politicize data and demonstrate its relevance to social justice issues and advocates' (Dencik et al. 2018). Hintz et al. further suggest such political work as 'a strategy for connecting concerns with data to broader movements for social justice to develop an integrated approach capable of challenging the dominant datafication paradigm' (2019: 152). Political struggle becomes crucial amidst the fog of the common-sense techno-capitalist vision of the future city, where neoliberal forms of data-driven technology are portrayed as not only inevitable, but without rational or feasible alternatives. The contribution of this chapter is to show how these two theories together take on this challenge, purposefully discounting the certainty of data-driven innovation in the city, offering critical perspectives on the prevailing discourses of efficient, market-led urban futures, and opening up creative and community-centred alternatives.

THE ORIGINS AND STRUCTURE OF THE BOOK

The inspiration, and perceived need, for this book materialised from the editors' experience of organising a week of interdisciplinary events on the theme of data justice, 20–24 May 2019. This programme was funded and supported by the University of Edinburgh's interdisciplinary and civic-facing Edinburgh Futures Institute (EFI), which also generously agreed to support the open-access publication of this book. This book is a product of its environment in the sense that a number of authors not only write from, but also about Edinburgh and urban datafication in Scotland. To the extent that Edinburgh can be viewed as an emerging hub of urban datafication, we, as editors, are accountable to this partial perspective – both the insights that it generates as well as its inevitable blind spots. It is important to state that the University of Edinburgh itself is a powerful player shaping the production of its urban surroundings, through a largely economic narrative that aims to position the region as the 'data capital of Europe'. As academics based at this institution at the time of writing, we are committed to confronting and working through this ambivalent positionality in order to better understand possibilities for intervention. We are also keenly aware of the omissions of this collection and, as such, we view this as a partial and situated form of knowledge, accountable to the manifold mediations and local roots that birthed it.

However, neither is the book solely confined to this local context. The book's contributions have been thematically organised into four sections: the automation of welfare and social services; education; labour; and activism. In each of these sections, we find bold, urgent and diverse analyses of the manifold ways in which data injustices and global struggles over the right to the city intersect: take, for example, AlgorithmWatch's stories of automation in seven cities across the world; Jansen's study of predictive policing in Europe; and Paris et al.'s critical analysis of calls for data transparency in police officer-involved homicides in the US, following the 2014 police murder of Michael Brown in Ferguson, Missouri. What this book does not offer is a comprehensive overview of the ways in which global concerns about data justice and the right to the city intersect. However, what it does offer is a contribution to ongoing critical praxis in the face of urban datafication. In this spirit, we welcome you to this edited collection.

NOTES

1. Algorithmic Justice League: https://www.ajlunited.org/.
2. Design Justice Network Principles: https://designjustice.org/read-the-prin ciples.

REFERENCES

Attoh, K. A. (2011) What kind of right is the right to the city? *Progress in Human Geography*, 35(5), 669–85. doi: 10.1177/0309132510394706.

Bigo, D., Isin, E. and Ruppert, E. (2019) *Data Politics: Worlds, Subjects, Rights.* London: Routledge.

Brenner, N., Marcuse, P. and Mayer, M. (2012) Cities for people, not for profit, an introduction. In N. Brenner, P. Marcuse and M. Mayer (eds), *Cities for People, Not for Profit: Critical Urban Theory and the Right to the City.* London: Routledge, pp. 1–10.

Bria, F. (2020) A new deal for data. In J. McDonnell (ed.), *Economics for the Many.* London: Verso.

Buolamwini, J. and Gebru, T. (2018) Gender shades: intersectional accuracy disparities in commercial gender classification. In S. A. Friedler and C. Wilson (eds), *Proceedings of Machine Learning Research, vol. 81: Conference on Fairness, Accountability and Transparency*, 23–24 February 2018, New York, USA, pp. 1–15.

Clarke, J. (2007) 'It's not like shopping': Citizens, consumers and the reform of public services. In M. Bevir and F. Trentmann (eds), *Governance, Consumers and Citizens. Consumption and Public Life.* London: Palgrave Macmillan.

Costanza-Chock, S. (2019) *Designing AI with Justice.* Public Books. Available at https://www.publicbooks.org/designing-ai-with-justice/ (last accessed 3 January 2022).

Crawford, K. (2016) Can an algorithm be agonistic? Ten scenes from life in calculated publics. *Science, Technology, & Human Values*, 41(1), 77–92.

Crawford, K. and Joler, V. (2018) Anatomy of an AI system. Available at https://anatomyof.ai/ (last accessed 3 January 2022).

Dencik, L., Hintz, A. and Cable, J. (2016) Towards data justice? The ambiguity of anti-surveillance resistance in political activism. *Big Data & Society* (July–December), 1–12.

Dencik, L., Jansen, F. and Metcalfe, P. (2018) A conceptual framework for approaching social justice in an age of datafication. Working paper. Available at https://datajusticeproject.net/wp-content/uploads/sites/30/20 18/11/wp-conceptual-framework-datajustice.pdf (last accessed 3 January 2022).

Eubanks, V. (2018) *Automating Inequality: How High-Tech Tools Profile, Police, and Punish the Poor*. New York: St. Martin's Press.

Fernandes, E. (2007) Constructing the 'right to the city' in Brazil. *Social & Legal Studies*, 16(2), 201–19. doi: 10.1177/0964663907076529.

Fraser, N. (2005) *Reframing Justice*. Assen: Uitgeverij Van Gorcum.

Fraser, N. (2008) Abnormal justice. *Critical Inquiry*, 34(3), 393–422.

Gabrys, J. (2019) Data citizens: how to reinvent rights. In D. Bigo, E. Isin and E. Ruppert (eds), *Data Politics: Worlds, Subjects, Rights*. London: Routledge, pp. 248–66.

Gillespie, T. (2014) The relevance of algorithms. In T. Gillespie, P. J. Boczkowski and K. A. Foot (eds), *Media Technologies: Essays on Communication, Materiality, and Society*. Cambridge, MA: MIT Press, pp 167–94.

Green, B. (2019) Data science as political action: grounding data science in a politics of justice. *Computers and Society*, arXiv:1811.03435.

Han, B.-C. (2017) *Psycho-Politics: Neoliberalism and new Technologies of Power*. London: Verso.

Harvey, D. (2008) The right to the city. *New Left Review*, 53 (Sept/Oct).

Harvey, D. (2012) *Rebel Cities: From the Right to the City to the Urban Revolution*. London: Verso.

Heeks, R., and Renken, J. (2018). Data justice for development: What would it mean? *Information Development*, 34(1), 90–102. doi: 10.1177/ 0266666916678282.

Hintz, A., Dencik, L. and Wahl-Jorgensen, K. (2019) *Digital Citizenship in a Datafied Society*. Cambridge: Polity Press.

Kitchin, R., Cardullo, P. and Di Feliciantonio, C. (2019) Citizenship, justice, and the right to the smart city. In P. Cardullo, C. Di Feliciantonio,and R. Kitchin (eds), *The Right to the Smart City*. Bingley: Emerald.

Kuymulu, M. B. (2013) 'Right to the city' at a crossroads. *International Journal of Urban and Regional Research*, 37, 923–40. doi: 10.1111/1468-2427.12008.

Lake, R. W. (2017) Big Data, urban governance, and the ontological politics of hyperindividualism. *Big Data & Society*. doi: 10.1177/2053951716682 537.

Lefebvre, H. (1992) *The Production of Space*. Chichester: John Wiley.

Lefebvre, H. (1996) *Writings on Cities: Henri Lefebvre*. Selected, translated and introduced by E. Kofman and E. Lebas. Oxford: Blackwell.

Mayer, M. (2009) The 'right to the city' in the context of shifting mottos of urban social movements. *City*, 13, 362–74. doi: 10.1080/13604810902982755.

Merrifield, A. (2017) Fifty years on: the right to the city. In Verso Books (ed.), *The Right to the City: A Verso Report*. London: Verso.

Minton, A. (2017) Who is the city for? In *The Right to the City: A Verso Report*. London: Verso.

Mitchell, D. (2003) *The Right to the City: Social Justice and the Fight for Public Space*. New York: Guilford Press.

Mitchell, D. and Heynen, N. (2009) The geography of survival and the right to the city: speculations on surveillance, legal innovation, and the criminalization of intervention. *Urban Geography*, 30(6), 611–32. doi: 10.2747/0272-3638.30.6.611.

Morozov, E. and Bria, F. (2018) *Rethinking Smart Cities: Democratizing Urban Technology*. New York: Rosa Luxemburg Stiftung. Available at http://www.rosalux-nyc.org/rethinking-the-smart-city/ (last accessed 3 January 2022).

Mouffe, C. (2018) *For a Left Populism*. London: Verso.

Noble, S. U. (2018) *Algorithms of Oppression: How Search Engines Reinforce Racism*. New York: New York University Press.

O'Neil, C. (2018) *Weapons of Math Destruction: How Big Data Increases Inequality and Threatens Democracy*. London: Penguin.

Plyushteva, A. (2009) The struggle over public citizenship. *The Urban Reinventors Online Journal*, 3.09, 1–17.

Purcell, M. (2002) Excavating Lefebvre: the right to the city and its urban politics of the inhabitant. *GeoJournal*, 58, 99–108. https://doi.org/10.1023/B:GEJO.0000010829.62237.8f

Raji, I. D. and Buolamwini, J. (2019) Actionable auditing: investigating the impact of publicly naming biased performance results of commercial ai products. Association for the Advancement of Artificial Intelligence (www.aaai.org). Available at https://dam-prod.media.mit.edu/x/2019/01/24/AIES-19_paper_223.pdf (last accessed 3 January 2022).

Ruppert, E., Isin, E. and Bigo, D. (2017) Data politics. *Big Data & Society*. doi: 10.1177/2053951717717749.

Sen, A. (2009) *The Idea of Justice*. Cambridge, MA: Harvard University Press.

Shaw, J. and Graham, M. (2017) An informational right to the city? Code, content, control, and the urbanization of information. *Antipode*, 49(4), 907–27. https://doi.org/10.1111/anti.12312

Shillington, L. J. (2013) Right to food, right to the city: household urban agriculture, and socionatural metabolism in Managua, Nicaragua. *Geoforum*, 44, 103–11. doi: 10.1016/j.geoforum.2012.02.006.

Taylor, L. (2017) What is data justice? The case for connecting digital rights and freedoms globally. *Big Data & Society*, 4. doi: 10.1177/2053951717736335.

Terranova, T. (2004) *Network Culture: Politics for the Information Age*. London: Pluto Press.

Weinstein, L. and Ren, X. (2009) The changing right to the city: urban renewal and housing rights in globalizing Shanghai and Mumbai. *City & Community*, 8, 407–32. doi: 10.1111/j.1540-6040.2009.01300.x.

Williamson, B. (2014) Knowing public services: cross-sector intermediaries and algorithmic governance in public sector reform. *Public Policy and Administration*, 29(4), 292–312. doi: 10.1177/0952076714529139.

Winner, L. (1980) Do artifacts have politics? *Daedalus*, 109, 121–36.

Young, I. M. (2011) *Justice and the Politics of Difference*. Princeton, NJ: Princeton University Press.

Part I

Algorithmic Government

Dr Morgan Currie

Virginia Eubank's 2018 book, *Automating Inequality*, put sharply into focus a little-known issue at the time of its publication: how municipal and state governments around the US were quietly adopting algorithms to make life-or-death decisions around housing for the homeless, child protection and benefits for welfare recipients. Historically, decisions about government welfare provisioning such as these would be made by a human or a team of people, drawing on statistics, experience and other factors, including personal bias, intentional or not. In each of the three cases Eubanks examines, government staff saw algorithms as a welcome, efficient, neutral arbiter, offering a set of universal rules that could take prejudice out of their public assistance systems.

What Eubanks found, however, is a new form of control of America's poor, and a refrain of old societal biases perpetuated through these systems. Eubanks shows how the algorithm used to flag that a vulnerable child may need protection services draws on data that correlates with poverty – being poor, in essence, makes you more visible to the system. Eubanks's overall worry is that the people who access these services receive differential treatment by society; they are more likely to be controlled and penalised by these systems than those who can escape their logics by using private services. Just as alarming is the technocratic faith she found people put in algorithmic solutions to deeply structural problems, such as the algorithm that decides who gets the limited number of housing units available for Los Angeles County's growing homeless population, and the work this faith does to shift responsibility from political to technical solutions.

A year after Eubanks's book shed light on these issues, the *Guardian* began its series on Automating Poverty to investigate the global spread of automated and data-driven systems. In India, the *Guardian* reports,

1.2 billion citizens have been assigned a 12-digit identification number, linked to their biometric and demographic data, that people must use for public assistance. In some cases, reporters found that glitches – those times when the ID number doesn't compute in a local system – have meant people were denied food rations, leading to starvation and even death. In the UK, the Department for Work and Pensions uses automation to determine the benefits claimants can receive, which they access through an online process. Claimants have called the process hostile and confusing, putting undue burden on them to dispute incorrect verdicts about their claim. In 2019, Philip Alston, who was at the time United Nations Special Rapporteur on extreme poverty and human rights, decried that, around the world, digital social services increasingly punish and conduct undue surveillance on beneficiaries. In case after case, with the introduction of these algorithmic systems, certain services were eliminated, beneficiary pools reduced, and beneficiaries themselves suffered greater sanctions and more demanding conditions for accessing benefits. Alston warned of 'a complete reversal of the traditional notion that the state should be accountable to the individual' (2019: 3).

This section tackles these issues in depth and head on. The contributors are associated with two of the most impactful research centres focused on issues of algorithmic welfare and governance at the time of this book's publication: the Data Justice Lab, based in Cardiff University, and AlgorithmWatch, a German-based non-profit organisation. Contributors Fieke Jansen, Philippa Metcalfe, Joanna Redden, Jessica Brand, Ina Sander and Harry Warne are all affiliated with the Data Justice Lab, one of the major academic hubs supporting research on social justice, Big Data and algorithmic decision making at all levels of government service.

Jansen's chapter focuses on law enforcement and how predictive policing technologies in the European Union (EU) reshape the city through anticipatory governance and risk calculations, turning the entire cityscape into a tool for algorithmic governance. Jansen reports how, using automated licence plate readers, the police turn city streets into a datafied infrastructure that they use to determine who is risky. Police mandates also increasingly determine how public health authorities interact with risky individuals, showing the creep of law enforcement into other social service domains. In her chapter, Metcalfe examines how automated data sharing across government agencies shapes border politics and produces new spaces hostile towards refugees and migrant populations. Metcalfe's chapter draws on Lefebvre's right to the city concept to think beyond formal rights enacted through the state to include a right to difference, to *not* be classified and categorised by systems that try to deny illegalised migrants' access to basic services. The chapter by Redden, Brand, Sander and Warne looks at predictive analytics used by child welfare agencies. Drawing on four international case studies, the chapter asks how and why government agencies wound up cancelling plans to pursue predictive analytics that informed decisions about families and services. The chapter argues that we have much to learn about automated decision-making support systems by paying attention to the rationalities behind decisions *not* to pursue them. In each contribution, the author offers a strong theoretical and empirical basis to understand the rise of algorithmic and datafied governance, arguing that these trends require new conceptions both of citizenship and the right to the city.

The fourth contributor to this section is AlgorithmWatch, an organisation that combines research on algorithmic decision making with advocacy for transparent and ethically designed automated systems. AlgorithmWatch's campaign work includes their crowdsourced OpenSHUFA project, which enlisted citizens to share their credit scores to reverse engineer Germany's primary, and entirely opaque, credit scoring institution. AlgorithmWatch also put out a comprehensive 'Automating Society' report, a wide-ranging look at the automated decision-making systems growing around Europe, from welfare and law enforcement to education and health.

Here we have reprinted seven stories from AlgorithWatch's website about automation in cities around the world, from home evaluation algorithms in Amsterdam to facial recognition systems used by local European law enforcement and a COVID-19-related social scoring system in Suzhou, China. Two of the stories give a glimpse of algorithms that can be used for more just and ethical ends, as in the case of a French city that adopted an algorithm to fight the cronyism that plagues the allotment of coveted daycare slots, and in Tartu, Estonia's capital, where officials are combining subsidies for green retrofitting with automated systems that nudge residents to reduce energy consumption, helping to cut residents' heating bills in half. These stories point the way to the various futures of algorithmic governance we currently face – one of control, opacity and punitive measures that reinforce social and political stratification, versus one of greater fairness, transparency, public oversight and social and environmental care.

REFERENCES

Alston, P. (2019) Report of the special rapporteur on extreme poverty and human rights. Seventy-fourth session, Item 72(b) of the provisional agenda. 11 October. Available at https://srpovertyorg.files.wordpress.com/2019/10/a_74_48037_advanceuneditedversion-1.pdf (last accessed 3 January 2022).

Eubanks, V. (2018) *Automating Inequality: How High-Tech Tools Profile, Police, and Punish the Poor*. New York: St. Martin's Press.

Chapter 1

PREDICTIVE POLICING: TRANSFORMING THE CITY INTO A MEDIUM FOR CONTROL

Fieke Jansen

INTRODUCTION

Cities are increasingly becoming sites where data about people and objects are abstracted and made calculable to optimise a range of public services, from algorithmic welfare fraud detection and automatic crowd monitoring, to mobility and policing systems (Dencik et al. 2019). These forms of algorithmic governance, referring to the way in which algorithms reproduce social order (Katzenbach and Ulbricht 2019), have been made possible through rapid technological developments, the ever-expanding volumes of data that can be captured about people and objects in contemporary data infrastructures (boyd and Crawford 2011; Mayer-Schönberger and Cukier 2013: 30; Andrejevic 2020) and the belief in data to quantify, track and predict human behaviour objectively (Van Dijck 2014). Often advanced on the premise of effectiveness and efficiency, algorithmic governance has become controversial as it further institutionalises 'long-standing binaries of "deserving" and "undeserving" citizens that influence how they are valued and treated' (Redden 2018). In the context of the city, these controversies demand our attention in relation to the police as the enforcer of the state's monopoly of violence, where the turn towards algorithmic governance introduces key questions around harm, inequality, discrimination and exclusion. This becomes especially pertinent as the police are the front-running public authority when it comes to piloting algorithmic systems within the city.

In recent years, police have come to rely upon a range of data-driven technologies (Jansen 2018; Williams and Kind 2019). This chapter will focus on predictive policing, as it is one of the most prominently tested and debated forms of algorithmic governance. Predictive policing practices have been introduced with the promise that analysing historic and real-time data allows for the prediction of when and where a crime is most likely to occur or who is most likely to engage in or become a victim of criminal activity in the near future (van Brakel 2016; Brayne 2017; Ferguson 2017; Egbert and Leese 2021). The assumption embedded within these technologies is that it will allow police to deploy their limited resources more efficiently by engaging in pre-emptive interventions, where taking action before a crime has occurred is believed to lead to crime reduction. Since its introduction, predictive policing has evolved from predicting the locations of where crime is most likely to happen (Brayne 2017), to predicting which individuals have the highest likelihood of becoming a perpetrator or victim of crime (van Brakel 2018), to even predicting which objects (i.e. cars) are most likely to be used in criminal activity (Amnesty International 2018). This latest turn in predictive policing suggests that the police are not merely trying to pre-empt criminal activity by classifying which locations and individuals are considered 'risky', but increasingly seeing the city as a data infrastructure for its analysis. As such, this chapter argues that predictive policing offers a way to understand how the city has become an important stage for the struggle between algorithmic governance and people's life chances.

The implications of predictive policing have been explored from different scholarly perspectives, some foregrounding issues around bias (Lum and Isaac 2016; Buolamwini and Gebru 2018), while others question the assumed relationship between technology and the managerial logic of effectiveness and efficiency (Egbert and Leese 2021). Those approaching predictive policing as sociotechnical assemblages understand these forms of algorithmic governance as a symbiosis between human and machine or organisation and machine, arguing that while these systems might not lead to crime reduction, they are contributing to the digitisation of the police (Egbert 2019; Egbert and Leese 2021). Critical race scholars argue that these technologies are just another medium through which Black and Brown communities are criminalised and controlled, a racial justice lens that allows scholars to account for the historic and ongoing struggles over how society is organised and whom these technologies aim to exclude (Williams 2015). In this chapter, I unpack and build on these critiques and contextualise predictive policing within the structures and political ideologies that police in Europe inhabit. I'm particularly interested in engaging with the relationship between datafication and control and how the notion of risk has become central to questions of governance in contemporary society.

Approaching predictive policing as a manifestation of social structures that determine how crime is problematised and controlled allows this chapter to decenter technology (Peña Gangadharan and Niklas 2019) and understand it as a governance mechanism that is transforming the city. As such, analysing predictive policing as a social structure embedded in an institutional context offers an entry point into the historic and existing political ideologies that are driving these implementations and the interests it (pre)serves. This entry point allows for a deeper understanding of the structures and mechanisms that create conditions of domination and control in society (Young 2011). This chapter draws on research carried out as a part of a multi-year project, Data Justice, which aims to understand datafication in relation to social justice, and how datafication of police intersects with social justice concerns (Dencik, Hintz and Cable 2016; Taylor 2017). Drawing on Foucault's (1977; Gordon 1980) notion of governmentality and Beck's (1992) conceptualisation of risk society, I will advance the argument that risk has become a key technology of governance and is reshaping the state–citizen nexus, creating spatio-temporal structures within the city that appropriate existing public infrastructures to manage crime. Here, this chapter refers to both the city's material public infrastructures, such as green spaces and roads, and its social public infrastructure, such as social security and health services, social services and schools, which indicate the significance of algorithmic governance based on risk beyond policing (Dencik et al. 2019).

PREDICTIVE POLICING

Predictive policing is a policing strategy that can be placed in a broader pre-emptive policing approach that builds on well-established criminological theories (Ferguson 2019; van Brakel 2020; Egbert and Leese 2021). This strategy follows the logic that analysing known criminal behaviour from the past allows us to make statistical predictions about criminal behaviour in the near future, which in turn can inform police strategies and the allocation of resources (Brayne, Rosenblat and boyd 2015). While this logic is at the heart of predictive policing, not all predictive approaches are the same; as such, this chapter will first explore three distinct types of predictive policing systems – hotspot policing, predictive identification of individuals and predictive identification of objects – before engaging with its critiques and exploring the relationship between society and the concept of risk as a mechanism of governance.

Hotspot policing relies on the identification of patterns in the distribution of crime to predict the locations where crime is most likely to happen in the near future (Kaufmann, Egbert and Leese 2019). This type is mostly directed at predicting high impact crime, such as robbery, burglary and theft, and it can inform the extent to which police patrol certain areas. European police departments have tested a range of different systems, including the Crime Anticipation System in the Netherlands (Willems 2014; Drenth 2017), PredPol, Azevea and Palantir in the UK (Beckford 2018; Couchman 2019), and PreCob, PreMap, KLB-operativ, Scala and KrimPo in Germany (Knobloch 2018; Seidensticker, Bode and Stoffel 2018; Egbert and Leese 2021). The main distinction between these different tools is in ownership structures: some models have been developed in-house by police, while others are developed in cooperation with universities, and others have been bought off the shelf from commercial providers. A second differentiating characteristic is how the models are constructed. While most primarily rely on police data (the type, location and date and time of crime) to calculate the spatio-temporal distribution of crime, others also include variables such as weather, holidays, events and distance to highways (Ferguson 2017; Hardyns and Rummens 2018), arguing that certain seasonal factors and proximity to highways have historically contributed to an increase in criminal activity in certain areas.

Despite the wide range of tools tested across Europe in recent years, there have only been a few external evaluations of predictive policing; these have concluded that there is no evidence base that suggests a clear relationship between the use of predictive policing tools and the reduction of crime. Despite these observations and the fact that some trials have since been halted due to disappointing results, the interest in and overall deployment of these systems in Europe has not decreased (Monroy 2017; Egbert 2019; van Brakel 2020). Here it is important to distinguish between the actual impact of these tools on crime reduction and their ability to predict where crime will most likely take place in the near future (Harcourt 2007) and their perceived positive impact on the operations and practice of policing. Empirical research on the use of hotspot policing in Germany and Switzerland by Egbert and Leese (2021) offers some insight into both, as they found that these models 'need not necessarily be "true" but merely accurate enough to inform operational measures' (Egbert and Leese 2021: 3). The term 'operational measures' refers to adjusting the patrol frequency in neighbourhoods that are identified as being at risk. Analysing the actual practice of predictive policing shows that these tools are merely an additional information source that informs operational decisions, where the sum of intelligence should in theory allow the police to deter criminal activity. In addition, Egbert (2019) argued that the benefits of testing and deploying predictive systems go beyond their intended purpose, in that they both reinforce a belief in the ability of data to better analyse and represent criminal activity and normalise the practice of data collection and algorithmic governance.

Predictive identification of people, also known as risk scoring, aims at predicting who is most likely to become a potential offender or potential victim of a predefined crime priority. In most cases, police use these tools to identify, rank and intervene in the lives of individuals who are already known to the police (van Schendel 2019). These tools, which label and sort a person according to the likelihood they will engage in criminal activities or escalate in levels of violence, become a funnelling mechanism through which known suspects or perpetrators are shortlisted for a specific intervention. This category of risk modelling is more diffuse as it is applied to a range of crime priorities; for example, risk scoring in relation to high impact crime is used to identify individuals at different stages of their 'criminal career', from young adolescents showing concerning behaviour to known criminals who can be classified as prolific offenders (Abraham et al. 2011; Wientjes et al. 2017). Risk scoring in relation to 'gang activity' is used to identify individuals who have been seen with 'known gang members' or share data attributes with a profile of a gang member and so become suspect by association (Amnesty International 2018; Williams and Clarke 2018). Police also deploy these tools as a strategy to predict which known criminal offenders and terrorists are at risk of using increased force and violence in future criminal offences (Quinsey et al. 2006; Jansen 2018). There are even risk models being developed that calculate the likelihood that a sexual abuse or rape victim is at risk of being revictimised due to the conditions that shape their life chances, such as working at night or

living in a certain neighbourhood, or as a result of their interactions
with the police when first reporting the crime.

Each model of predictive identification has its own unique approach
and data inputs, ranging from analysing historic police data, as is the
case in Prokid, Top 600 and the 'persoonsgerichte aanpak' (person-
based approach) in the Netherlands (van Ham 2003; Wientjes et al.
2017), to collecting new data from targeted police observations, as
done by the RADAR-iTE of the BKA in Germany (Sonka et al. 2020).
Still, common to all approaches is that risk can be made calculable
through statistical models that analyse historic datasets to attribute one
or more group traits to a specific criminal offence (Harcourt 2007). A
second important shared characteristic is that these models are often
designed to make police data actionable for an integrated care and
control approach. Here, we see activities of surveillance, arrest and
conviction combined with interventions aimed at addressing the mul-
titude of problems that exist in the life of an individual labelled as risky
by a predictive policing tool, such as debt, unemployment, addiction,
psychosocial problems and mental disabilities (van der Put et al. 2013;
Ferguson 2017). This 'carrot and stick' approach, argued to be part of
the Integrated Offender Management programme in the UK, the Gang
Matrix in London and the Top 600 in Amsterdam (van der Put et al.
2013; Amnesty International 2018; Cram, 2020), is more invasive than
normal crime deterrence approaches. The individual being classified
as at risk is often subjected to increased surveillance and interference
by police and other state actors. Institutionally these care and control
approaches materialise in inter-agency collaboration between the
police, municipality, parole office, public health services, child protec-
tive agencies and others, who collectively try to address a specific crime
type (Amnesty International 2018; Jansen 2018). It is imperative to note
that while the coordination task of the inter-agency collaboration can
be located within another public authority, the statistical analysis is
based on police data that was subsequently shared with third parties;
as such, only those individuals known to police will be nominated for
the intervention.

A lesser known form of predictive policing is that of identifying
objects in city infrastructures which share characteristics attributed to
a specific crime priority (Meijer, Ruijer and Dekker 2020). This development is enabled by the rise of sensors and smart cameras in city
infrastructures which increasingly capture larger volumes of granular

data about people and objects in real time. In the context of predictive policing, smart cameras used for automatic number-plate recognition (ANPR) can now also be used to recognise objects, behaviour and faces (de Jonge 2017; Meijer et al. 2020). An Amnesty International (2020) report, 'We Sense Trouble', exposes this type of predictive policing tested by the police in the city of Roermond in the Netherlands. The aim of this programme is to pilot a risk-scoring algorithm on ANPR cameras to prevent 'Eastern European mobile banditry' in a specific area. Mobile banditry refers to the criminal offence of pickpocketing and shoplifting. The proposition made by the police is that they analyse camera footage to detect vehicles and movement patterns that are deemed risky, which will prompt a response before an incident occurs, allowing them to prevent crime through targeted patrolling and car stops (Meijer et al. 2020). Trained on historical data, the system constructs a risk score based on both the make and model of a car and movement patterns to predict the likelihood that the driver and passengers will engage in mobile banditry in a demarcated area, a shopping district in the city of Roermond. What characterises this type of predictive policing is that it is implemented on top of an existing surveillance infrastructure, in this case automated number-plate recognition, thus expanding the logic of risk to objects and further integrating risk scores within automated systems. Consequently, objects become proxies for the classification of specific communities – in this case, people with Eastern European nationalities and Roma ethnicity.

These developments show how policing is becoming more reliant on data collection and automated processes. Moreover, these specific use cases show how both the city's material public infrastructures, like roads, and its social public infrastructure, like welfare and public health organisations, are harnessed for police interventions. This situation normalises the notion that roads are data infrastructures for police to calculate who is risky, and police mandates become the lens through which public health and care authorities interact with risky individuals. As such, the city itself becomes a tool for algorithmic governance.

CRITIQUING THE TOOLS OF PRE-EMPTION

As noted above, predictive policing is a category that encompasses a range of spatio-temporal crime preventions, as police continue to test statistical models on a variety of crime priorities. Whilst these tools are often presented as isolated technological artefacts that facilitate the operational side of policing, academic analysis and critique are beginning to engage with the social structures, political drivers and organisational cultures that shape the conditions for these technologies to manifest. Engaging with predictive policing tools as a sociotechnical assemblage enables a better understanding and critique of the complex relationship between crime, police and society (Egbert and Leese 2021). Initial scholarly inquiries into hotspot policing advanced the notion that this practice shifts the nature of policing from reactive to pre-emptive: instead of investigating a crime once it has occurred or as it happens, policing becomes reliant upon statistical probability to intervene and take action before a criminal act can materialise. Pre-emption could mean patrolling certain areas in a city at a specific time, intercepting some objects for identification checks or even structurally interfering in some individuals' lives through a care and crime approach (Brayne 2017: 986; Hardyns and Rummens 2018; Amnesty International 2020; van Brakel 2020). Critics argue that this shift towards deterrence and control does not actually pre-empt where crime is most likely to happen, but instead identifies where arrests are most likely to happen, prioritising management over crime reduction (van Brakel 2016).

Recognising that pre-emptive crime intervention is at odds with the presumption of innocence until proven guilty, this chapter argues that the turn to predictive policing reflects how political and organisational contexts increasingly assume crime can be eliminated or managed through statistical predictions. Here, predictive policing builds on a technological deterministic imaginary, 'as if the solution to societal and political conflict were simply a matter of perfecting information systems' (Andrejevic 2020: 101). The turn to data-driven decision making in policing places a greater emphasis on understanding the 'what' over the 'why' of crime, as data analysis privileges correlation over causation (Andrejevic 2014), producing intelligence that something might come about but not why or how something comes into being. Kaufman, Egbert and Leese (2019) argue that 'patterns themselves do not invite reflections about how they came into being, but they feed into requirements and ideals of efficient policing. They nurture the goal to reduce crime by being faster and smarter than offenders – rather than understanding motives and motivations' (Kaufmann et al. 2019). As such, the implementation of predictive policing relates more to organisational aspiration, something the police can control, than the context which nurtures criminal behaviour, something the police cannot control. Building on Andrejevic (2020) and Kaufmann et al. (2019), this chapter argues that these predictive policing approaches depoliticise and reduce crime to something that can be measured, calculated and predicted. Such a move privileges intervention that aligns with organisational aspirations of efficient policing, and as a result prioritises deterrence over prevention and managing crime over engaging with the structural conditions that shape a person's life chances.

When approaching predictive policing from a racial justice lens it becomes evident that these systems further embed normative notions about which locations, individuals and objects are undeserving enough to become the object of increased state scrutiny and control. In adopting this lens, we see that not everyone, nor every location in a city, is being abstracted and classified according to risk; thus, these tools run the risk of perpetuating and reinforcing existing inequalities. Take, for example, the use of hotspot policing in the US. To understand the relationship between bias, police data and predictive policing algorithms, Lum and Isaac (2016) engaged in an experiment that compared drug crimes recorded by Oakland police department with survey data from the 2011 National Survey on Drug Use and Health, which offered the researchers an estimate of illicit drug use in the city from a non-criminal justice data source. This comparison clearly demonstrated that while drug use is distributed equally across the city, drug arrests recorded in police records are concentrated in 'two areas with largely non-white and low-income populations' (Lum and Isaac 2016). The authors then applied the Predpol predictive policing model on Oakland's drug arrest data and found that the tool reinforces existing bias in police data, directing patrols to those areas in town that have historically been over-policed, creating a negative feedback loop that would increase policing on Black and Brown communities. Looking at the predictive identification of individuals, as with the Gang Matrix in London, and objects, as in the sensing project in Roermond, it is clear that these models attribute one or more group traits to a specific criminal offence, such as a young Black man with gang activity, or an Eastern European man in a car with a German licence plate with mobile banditry (Amnesty International 2018, 2020). When race and ethnicity become group attributes associated with criminality, these associations inevitably further the criminalisation of communities of colour (Williams 2015; Williams and Clarke 2018). The targeting of these communities is then rationalised through

the use of these seemingly neutral predictive models, cloaking political choices and institutional racism in the assumptions that technology
is neutral, or that data doesn't lie (Van Dijck 2014). Such disparities
highlight the importance of understanding predictive policing not as a
merely technological object but as the manifestation and reproduction
of social structures that disproportionately impact those communities
considered 'the other' in an imagined 'white society'.

The above examples clearly demonstrate how predictive policing
can negatively shape the life chances of individuals and communities
of colour. Moreover, relying on statistical tools for crime prevention
allows police to engage in the management of crime by prioritising
punitive interventions over addressing structures that create inequality (Harcourt 2007). This strategy is what critical criminologists call the
'orthodox approach' to crime, a tactic that sees crime as a flaw of the
individual who commits it, rather than the result of unequal distribution of power, material resources and life chances in societies that
'breed, create, and sustain criminality' (DeKeseredy and Dragiewicz
2018). Here, I argue that these critiques do not fully account for how
the logic of predictive policing is transforming society, as pre-emptive
crime approaches do not limit themselves to police but encapsulate
part of the city's broader public infrastructure. Even when the predictive approach is said to combine control with care, changing the
living conditions of a risky individual, I argue that this should still
be considered punitive. The lists of individuals are constructed from
police data, which classifies individuals as being at risk of engaging in
criminal activities; as such, care is provided from a security perspective.
Accordingly, interventions become focused on preventing a person
from continuing in a life of crime, rather than addressing what the
more fundamental needs are of a person and their family. This perspective also places the orthodox approach to crime at the centre of police
action as well as affecting the mandate of care authorities. Arguably,
the police become the data infrastructure for pre-emptive intervention
in the city, and public health and care authorities engage with those
deemed risky from a risk and criminality perspective as constructed by
police data.

The predictive object identification programmes, such as those that
target mobile banditry in the Netherlands, show a continual pursuit by
police for new ways to capture data, moving prediction into the material infrastructures of the city. Not only do these programmes reveal an

incentive to increase the interoperability of databases both within the police and between different public authorities (Leese 2020), but they also build on top of, and expand, existing surveillance infrastructures by exploiting ANPR cameras for predictive policing and expanding the spatial areas in which these cameras can be activated. The disciplinary system of the police is now no longer subject-oriented but extends to the environments that people inhabit by pre-emptively intervening when 'risky' objects are flagged on city infrastructures. These different forms of predictive policing show how predictive systems have evolved from controlling incidents and individuals to managing environments, a phenomenon Andrejevic (2020) describes as 'environmentality'. Here, Andrejevic builds on Foucault's notion of 'biopolitics' to analyse these interventions, which are not directed at the subject but at controlling the context around them; in this way, the city becomes a medium for governance through the use of surveillance infrastructures (Andrejevic 2020: 104). In the context of predictive policing, police appropriate the material public infrastructures for the management of crime through which the city itself becomes a tool for exclusion.

RISK AS A POLITICAL RATIONALE

The emergence and evolution of predictive policing is part of a larger trend in which algorithmic governance shapes people's life chances. Amoore (2020) argues that algorithmic systems of governance are transforming who and what is made visible and calculable; they should be scrutinised as 'ethicopolitical' arrangements that generate new conditions of what someone can be in the world. Algorithmic systems should therefore be understood as 'regimes of recognition' that institutionalise classification to further the notion of 'deserving' and 'undeserving' citizens (Redden 2018). This type of power is evident in how predictive systems ascribe risk to some locations, individuals and objects but not others. Bourdieu (2018) refers to these forms of control as 'struggles over classification', since who and what is classified shapes people's social, cultural and economic position in society. Seeing predictive policing as political arrangements that are the continuation of historic struggles over classification allows this chapter to frame these algorithmic governance systems as manifestations of larger social structures (Jessop 2005) that create the conditions for control, which in turn reproduce social justice concerns. As such, this chapter takes lead from Peña Gangadharan and Niklas (2019), who argue that we need to decentre technology to give nuance to the discussion about the role and place of technology in the production of social inequalities.

Here, this chapter is particularly concerned with risk as the political rationale through which the relationship between the police and society is constructed. I draw on Foucault's 'governmentality framework' (Foucault 1977; Gordon 1980), in which he advances the idea that governance should be understood as the interplay between the 'governing of the self' and the 'governing of others', and that 'the modern sovereign state and the modern autonomous individual codetermine each other's emergence' (Lemke 2002: 51). Where technologies of governance aim to preserve state power, existing power structures and the interests of the political and economic elite work to systematise and regulate the power relationship between the state, market and citizen nexus. This effort refers both to reinforcing the more institutionalised modes of power and bolstering the rationale that underpins these modes of power. More specifically, Foucault points out that governmentality involves a dialectical relationship between 'political rationalities', the discourse that justifies governance, and 'technologies of government', the means through which this ideology is translated into action (Henman 2011). Thus, understanding the structures and conditions that shape people's lives requires studying both the technologies of government and the political ideologies that underpin them (Lemke 2002).

In the field of criminology, the concept of 'governmentality' is influential as it provides a framework to analyse how crime is problematised and controlled in neoliberal societies (Garland 1997). Here, I argue that engaging with the political rationale of risk will offer a new entry point into the relationship between crime, police and society. Beck (1992) first articulated the prominence of risk in contemporary politics through his work on the 'risk society', in which he argued that, since the Industrial Revolution, society has entered into a process of 'reflexive modernisation', as man-made risks, an unwanted side effect of modernity, create social uncertainties that force societies to change. 'As a result of this process, society in the "second modernity" is no longer concerned with the distribution of power and wealth, but instead with the way it handles risks' (Wimmer and Quandt 2007). By putting Beck's concept of the risk society in conversation with Foucault's notion of governmentality, this chapter situates risk as a rationale of governance that informs and justifies specific practices. Governmental risk approaches are what Beck calls 'procedures in order to secure or repair credibility, without fundamentally questioning the form of power or social control involved' (Beck 1992). Predictive policing becomes a technology of governance that classifies certain environments, subjects and objects as 'risky' and in need of monitoring, control and discipline – all justified by the assumption that identifying risks will allow society to mitigate the negative consequences of our neoliberal economy (Beck 1992; Fressoz 2007; Wimmer and Quandt 2007; McQuillan 2015).

Risk as governance can take two forms. The first fundamentally seeks to address the root causes of human-made risks that emerge from neoliberal economies, while the second focuses on managing the consequences of these risks. Predictive policing technologies fall firmly in the second category. These systems do not address the risk posed to society by the increasingly unequal distribution of power and material resources, expedited by information capitalism (Srnicek 2017; Cohen 2019). Instead, these technologies aim to control those who do not fit the norm of society, the 'undeserving' citizen, the 'criminal' – the physical manifestations of the invisible threats of neoliberalism (Fressoz 2007). Risk therefore becomes the centre of social conflict, materialising in modes of governance and the discourse driving the public's perception of danger. Here, risk becomes the driver of state intervention rather than exploring how social, economic and legal structures make contemporary criminality a consequence of modernity (Krahman 2011). Building on Foucault (Foucault 1977; Gordon 1980) and Beck (1992), it is imperative we understand predictive policing not as something radically different or new but as the continuation of the existing rationality of governance, which manifests itself in the conceptualisation of 'problems' in the city and algorithmic governance as a solution.

A diffuse range of city infrastructures are now directed as mechanisms for disciplining and controlling some individuals and communities, transforming the spatio-temporal horizons of the police to determine people's life chances. To grasp the relationship between predictive policing and the city, it is significant to understand risk not only as a paradigm to engage with the consequence of emerging from modernity but also as a market opportunity. Entire industries have emerged that profit from managing the risks they and others have created (Beck 1992; Krahman 2011). Seeing how predictive policing is placing risk and security at the centre of governance, using both the city's physical infrastructure and public health and care authorities as environments through which criminality is managed, I argue that risk is not merely creating market opportunities but is also creating governance opportunities. The political rationale of risk allows police to further their crime prevention logic beyond their organisational structures and mandate. The notion that an increasing number of public resources in cities are directed at crime reduction through algorithmic governance is significant for understanding not only who is made visible (Amoore 2020) but also who decides who is made visible to the algorithmic risk gaze (Fraser 2008).

CONCLUSION

At a time of increased reliance on algorithmic governance systems by public authorities in the city, the question of how technology mediates power relations in society has gained new significance. The police, as the public authority that is at the forefront of experimenting with algorithmic governance systems, offers an entry point into understanding how rights to the city are transforming, which political ideologies are being served, and at what costs. In the range of technologies currently being tested by police, predictive policing has become a prominent feature of how crime prevention is organised, expanding the spatio-temporal structures of pre-emption beyond police agencies themselves. While predictive policing might foreground new concerns relating to the changing nature of police, bias and the criminalisation of communities of colour, what is equally concerning is that pre-emptive intervention to manage crime has become a central component of city infrastructures.

The expanding reach of police through centralising crime prevention in a range of public services and public infrastructures has been in the making for some time. The desire to quantify risk and make certain parts of the population visible and calculable is a natural consequence of the belief in data's ability to quantify, track and predict human behaviour and the perceived power associated with those actors who know how to wield algorithmic power. Still, building on Beck's argument that, in contemporary societies, risk is at the centre of social conflict, this chapter argues that predictive policing further obfuscates and intensifies the allocation of public resources towards managing social risk rather than addressing the increasingly unequal distribution of power. Managing risk through quantification as such becomes a governance opportunity to further transform the city and its infrastructures into a medium for control. Predictive policing is a tool of governance that not only informs decision making, but also transforms how we understand society. This situation normalises the notion that roads are data infrastructures for police to calculate who is 'risky' and police mandates become the lens through which public health and care authorities interact with risky individuals.

ACKNOWLEDGEMENTS

Research for this article is part of a large multi-year project called 'Data Justice: Understanding Datafication in Relation to Social Justice' (DATAJUSTICE) funded by an ERC Starting Grant (no. 759903).

REFERENCES

Abraham, M., Buysse, W., Loef, L. and Dijk, B. van (2011) *Pilots ProKid Signaleringsinstrument 12- geëvalueerd*. Amsterdam.

Amnesty International (2018) Trapped in the Matrix: secrecy, stigma, and bias in the Met's Gangs Database. Amnesty International. Available at https://www.amnesty.org.uk/files/reports/Trapped%20in%20the%20Matrix%20Amnesty%20report.pdf (last accessed 3 January 2022).

Amnesty International (2020) We sense trouble: automated discrimination and mass surveillance in predictive policing in the Netherlands. Amnesty International.

Amoore, L. (2020) *Cloud Ethics: Algorithms and the Attributes of Ourselves and Others*. Durham, NC: Duke University Press.

Andrejevic, M. (2014) The Big Data divide. *International Journal of Communication*, 8(1), 1673–1689.

Andrejevic, M. (2020) *Automated Media*. New York: Routledge.

Beck, U. (1992) *Risk Society: Towards a New Modernity*. SAGE.

Beckford, M. (2018) Police computer 'predicts' who is likely to commit crime. *Mail Online*, 23 December. Available at https://www.dailymail.co.uk/news/article-6523997/Minority-Report-police-computer-predict-likely-commit-crimes.html (last accessed 3 January 2022).

Bourdieu, P. (2018) *Bourdieu: Classification Struggles*. Cambridge: Polity Press.

boyd, d. and Crawford, K. (2011) Six provocations for Big Data. (SSRN Scholarly Paper No. ID 1926431). doi: 10.2139/ssrn.1926431.

Brayne, S. (2017) Big Data surveillance: the case of policing. *American Sociological Review*, 82(5), 977–1008.

Brayne, S., Rosenblat, A. and boyd, d. (2015) Predictive policing. *Data & Civil Rights: A New Era of Policing and Justice*. Available at https://www.datacivil rights.org/pubs/2015-1027/Predictive_Policing.pdf (last accessed 3 January 2022).

Buolamwini, J. and Gebru, T. (2018) Gender shades: intersectional accuracy disparities in commercial gender classification. Conference on Fairness, Accountability and Transparency. *Proceedings of Machine Learning Research*, 81: 1–15. Available at https://proceedings.mlr.press/v81/buolamwini18a/bu olamwini18a.pdf (last accessed 3 January 2022).

Cohen, J. E. (2019) *Between Truth and Power*. Oxford: Oxford University Press.

Couchman, H. (2019) Policing by machine: predictive policing and the threats to our rights. Report. Liberty.

Cram, F. (2020) The 'carrot' and 'stick' of integrated offender manage-ment: implications for police culture. *Policing and Society*, 30, 378–95. doi: 10.1080/10439463.2018.1547719.

de Jonge, E. (2017) Projectplan Smart City Security Concept: Landelijk Project Operationele Proeftuinen Programma Sensing. Politie.

DeKeseredy, W. and Dragiewicz, M. (2018) Introduction: Critical criminol-ogy: past, present, and future. In W. DeKeseredy and M. Dragiewicz (eds), *Routledge Handbook of Critical Criminology*, 2nd edn. London: Routledge, pp. 1–12.

Dencik, L., Hintz, A. and Cable, J. (2016) Towards data justice? The ambiguity of anti-surveillance resistance in political activism. *Big Data & Society*, 3. doi: 10.1177/2053951716679678.

Dencik, L., Redden, J., Hintz, A. and Warne, H. (2019) The 'golden view': data-driven governance in the scoring society. *Internet Policy Review*, 8, 1–24. doi: 10.14763/2019.2.1413.

Drenth, A. (2017) Ervaringen van straatagenten met het Criminaliteits Anticipatie Systeem. *Het Tijdschrift voor de Politie*, 79(3/17), 6.

Egbert, S. (2019) Predictive policing and the platformization of police work. *Surveillance & Society*, 17(1/2), 83–8.

Egbert, S. and Leese, M. (2021) *Criminal Futures: Predictive Policing and Everyday Police Work*. London: Taylor & Francis.

Ferguson, A. G. (2017) *The Rise of Big Data Policing*. New York: New York University Press.

Ferguson, A. G. (2019) Predictive policing theory. In T.R. Lave and E. J. Miller (eds.), *The Cambridge Handbook of Policing in the United States*. Cambridge: Cambridge University Press, pp. 491–510. doi: 10.1017/9781108354721.025.

Foucault, M. (1977) *Discipline and Punish: The Birth of the Prison*. London: Allen Lane.

Fraser, N. (2008) Abnormal justice. *Critical Inquiry*, 34, 393–422. doi: 10.1086/589478.

Fressoz, J.-B. (2007) Beck back in the 19th century: towards a genealogy of risk society. *History and Technology*, 23, 333–50. doi: 10.1080/07341510701527419.

Garland, D. (1997) 'Governmentality' and the problem of crime: Foucault, criminology, sociology. *Theoretical Criminology*, 1, 173–214.

Gordon, C. (ed.) (1980) *Michel Foucault Power/Knowledge: Selected Interviews and Other Writings 1972–1977*. New York: Vintage.

Harcourt, B. E. (2007) *Against Prediction: Profiling, Policing, and Punishing in an Actuarial Age*. Chicago: University of Chicago Press.

Hardyns, W. and Rummens, A. (2018) Predictive policing as a new tool for law enforcement? Recent developments and challenges. *European Journal on Criminal Policy and Research*, 24, 201–18. doi: 10.1007/s10610-017-9361-2.

Henman, P. (2011) Conditional citizenship? Electronic networks and the new conditionality in public policy. *Policy & Internet*, 3, 1–18.

Jansen, F. (2018) *Data Driven Policing in the Context of Europe*. Data Justice Lab report. Available at https://datajusticeproject.net/wp-content/uploads/sites/30/2019/05/Report-Data-Driven-Policing-EU.pdf (last accessed 3 January 2022).

Jessop, B. (2005) Critical realism and the strategic-relational approach. *New Formations*, 56(1), 40–53.

Katzenbach, C. and Ulbricht, L. (2019) Algorithmic governance. *Internet Policy Review*, 8, 1–18. doi: 10.14763/2019.4.1424.

Kaufmann, M., Egbert, S. and Leese, M. (2019) Predictive policing and the politics of patterns. *The British Journal of Criminology*, 59, 674–92. doi: 10.1093/bjc/azy060.

Knobloch, T. (2018) *Vor Die Lage Kommen: Predictive Policing in Deutschland: Chancen und Gefahren datananalytischer Prognosetechnik und Empfehlung Fur den Einsatz in der Polizeiarbeit*. Stiftung Neue Verantwortung & Bertelsman Stiftung.

Krahman, E. (2011) Beck and beyond: selling security in the world risk society. *Review of International Studies*, 37, 349–72.

Leese, M. (2020) Fixing state vision: interoperability, biometrics, and identity management in the EU. *Geopolitics*, 1–21. doi: 10.1080/14650045.2020.1830764.

Lemke, T. (2002) Foucault, governmentality, and critique. *Rethinking Marxism*, 14, 49–64.

Lum, K. and Isaac, W. (2016) To predict and serve? *Significance*, 13(5): 14–19.© 2016 The Royal Statistical Society.

Mayer-Schönberger, V. and Cukier, K. (2013) *Big Data: A Revolution That Will Transform How We Live, Work and Think*. London: John Murray.

McQuillan, D. (2015) Algorithmic states of exception. *European Journal of Cultural Studies*, 18, 564–76. doi: 10.1177/1367549415577389.

Meijer, A., Ruijer, E. and Dekker, R. (2020) *Navigatiestrategie: Lessen uit drie casusstudies over de kennispositie van de Tweede Kamer op het gebied van digitalisering*. Universiteit Utrecht.

Monroy, M. (2017) Disappointing results for predictive policing. Available at https://digit.site36.net/2017/09/25/disappointing-results-for-predictive-policing/ (last accessed 3 January 2022).

Peña Gangadharan, S. and Niklas, J. (2019) Decentering technology in discourse on discrimination. *Information, Communication & Society*, 22, 882–99. doi: 10.1080/1369118X.2019.1593484.

Quinsey, V. L., Harris, G. T., Rice, M. E. and Cormier, C. A. (2006) *Violent Offenders: Appraising and Managing Risk*. London: American Psychological Association.

Redden, J. (2018) The harm that data do. *Scientific American*, 1 November. Available at https://www.scientificamerican.com/article/the-harm-that-data-do/ (last accessed 3 January 2022).

Seidensticker, K., Bode, F. and Stoffel, F. (2018) Predictive policing in Germany. Available at https://kops.uni-konstanz.de/bitstream/handle/123456789/43114/Seidensticker_2-14sbvox1ik0z06.pdf?sequence=5 (last accessed 3 January 2022).

Sonka, C., Meier, H., Rossegger, A., Endrass, J., Profes, V., Witt, R. and Sadowski, F. (2020) RADAR-iTE 2.0: Ein Instrument des polizeilichen Staatsschutzes. *Kriminalistik*, 74, 386–92.

Srnicek, N. (2017) *Platform Capitalism*. Chichester: John Wiley & Sons.

Taylor, L. (2017) What is data justice? The case for connecting digital rights and freedoms globally. *Big Data & Society*, 4, 205395171773633. doi: 10.1177/2053951717736335.

van Brakel, R. (2016) Pre-emptive Big Data surveillance and its (dis)empowering consequences: the case of predictive policing. *SSRN Journal*. doi: 10.2139/ssrn.2772469.

van Brakel, R. (2018) Taming by chance? A rhizomatic analysis of pre-emptive surveillance of children. PhD dissertation, Vrije Universiteit Brussel.

van Brakel, R. (2020) Rethinking predictive policing: towards a holistic framework of democratic algorithmic surveillance. In M. Schuilenburg and R. Peeters (eds), *The Algorithmic Society Technology, Power, and Knowledge*. London: Routledge.

van Brakel, R. (2020) Een reflectie over het huidig toezicht van het gebruik van surveilancetechnologie door de lokale politie in België. *Cahiers Politiestudies*, 55, 139–60.

van der Put, C., Assink, M., Bindels, A., Stams, G. J. and de Vries, S. (2013) Effectief vroegtijdig ingrijpenEen verkennend onderzoek naar effectief vroegtijdig ingrijpen ter voorkoming van ernstig delinquent gedrag. Ministerie van Veiligheid en Justitie.

Van Dijck, J. (2014) Datafication, dataism and dataveillance: Big Data between scientific paradigm and ideology. *Surveillance & Society*, 12(2), 197–208. doi: 10.24908/ss.v12i2.4776.

van Ham, T. (2003) 18. High impact crimes: profielen van plegers en kansen voor de aanpak. *Tijdschrift voor Criminologie*, 127–39.

van Schendel, S. (2019) Risk profiling by law enforcement agencies in the Big Data era: is there a need for transparency? In E. Kosta, J. Pierson, D. Slamanig, S. Fischer-Hübner and S. Krenn (eds), *Privacy and Identity Management. Fairness, Accountability, and Transparency in the Age of Big Data*: 13th IFIP WG 9.2, 9.6/11.7, 11.6/SIG 9.2.2 International Summer School, Vienna, Austria, 20–24 August 2018. Revised selected papers, IFIP Advances in Information and Communication Technology. Cham: Springer, pp. 275–89.

Wientjes, J., Delsing, M., Cillessen, A., Janssens, J. and Scholte, R. (2017) Identifying potential offenders on the basis of police records: development and validation of the ProKid risk assessment tool. *Journal of Criminological Research, Policy and Practice*, 3, 249–60. doi: 10.1108/JCRPP-01-2017-0008.

Willems, D. (2014) CAS: Crime anticipation system: predictive policing in Amsterdam. Available at https://event.cwi.nl/mtw2014/media/files/Willems,%20Dick%20-%20CAS%20Crime%20anticipation%20system%20_%20predicting%20policing%20in%20Amsterdam.pdf (last accessed 3 January 2022).

Williams, P. (2015) Criminalising the other: challenging the race–gang nexus. *Race & Class*, 56(3), 18–35.

Williams, P. and Clarke, B. (2018) The black criminal other as an object of social control. *Social Sciences*, 7, 234. doi: 10.3390/socsci7110234.

Williams, P. and Kind, E. (2019) *Data-Driven Policing: The Hardwiring of Discriminatory Policing Practices Across Europe*. European Network Against Racism. Available at https://www.enar-eu.org/IMG/pdf/data-driven-profiling-web-final.pdf (last accessed 3 January 2022).

Wimmer, J. and Quandt, T. (2007) Living in the risk society. *Journalism Studies*, 7, 336–47. doi: 10.1080/14616700600645461.

Young, I. M. (2011) *Justice and the Politics of Difference*. Princeton, NJ: Princeton University Press.

Chapter 2

'HOSTILE DATA', MIGRATION AND THE CITY: ENACTING AND RESISTING SPACES OF HOSTILITY IN THE UK

Philippa Metcalfe

INTRODUCTION

Introducing her flagship policy in 2012, Theresa May famously proclaimed, 'the aim is to create, here in Britain, a really hostile environment for illegal immigrants' (Hill 2017). And so, everything from housing to health care, bank accounts to education became a part of a push to identify, track and target migrants across the country. Accordingly, we saw the incorporation of wider logics of a datafied border cemented within and across British society, as efforts grew to identity, sort, criminalise and govern anyone subject to immigration controls (Metcalfe and Dencik 2019). As people across society became part of an augmented and dispersed border force, the key to enacting these policies became the sharing of information between government departments. Consequently, data became the lynchpin of hostile environment policies, creating systems of 'hostile data' capable of labelling someone as 'illegal' and 'deportable' (Corporate Watch 2018). These data systems determine overarching societal power structures, working to design and create space and social relations, and so data has become a means of enacting control within a city. In other words, hostile data makes salient existing practices of exclusion as a part of the British border regime, further entrenching logics of hostility and control in the lived reality of illegalised migrants. I use the term 'illegalised migrants' to refer to individuals deemed illegal by the state, including people refused asylum with no safe place to go home to, or people who have overstayed their visa. To some degree, 'illegalised migrants' also includes people seeking asylum, who are often labelled as 'illegal immigrants' despite there being a legal right to enter a country and

46

claim asylum. This illegalisation of people seeking asylum stems from the illegalisation of routes of entry as border regimes work to maintain a level of control over mobility through limiting legal means of travel.

Using Lefebvre's (1968) theories of the right to the city, this chapter will explore how hostile data systems, in relation to wider hostile environment immigration policies, work to reproduce dominant structures and power systems across society. Specifically, the chapter will explore how datafied controls entrench bordering logics into everyday space, shaping the interactions that people seeking asylum or illegalised migrants have with the state.

There has long been research on the implications of datafication and the impact on politics, economy, social relations and urbanity (Castells 1988; Mitchell 1995; cf. Kitchin, Cardullo and Di Feliciantonio 2019). In this chapter, I suggest that Lefebvre's theories of the right to the city and production of space serve as a useful format for placing struggles over space, inclusion and recognition of rights. Particularly, in relation to migration, questions become prevalent over the right to enter, remain and live safely in the city, without fear of deportation or detention (Trimikliniotis et al. 2015). The right to the city ultimately demands a fundamental change to systemic injustice wrought through segregation, domination and exclusion within urban life and across society. As such, the concept works to situate oppressive systems of power within a society hostile to migration, as well as to frame demands for justice, wherein without systemic change, injustice will continue. I argue that the hostile environment, and with it the complex and overarching databases and data-sharing agreements, must thus be looked on as an extension of long-standing and oppressive power structures within society and the borders of nation-states.

To begin, I introduce the theories of Lefebvre's right to the city to explore the production of spaces of hostility. I then move on to outline the key elements of hostile environment policies, interrogating their role in furthering exclusionary and harsh border politics and governance by disseminating controls across society. Within this, I will explore the use of data as enacting this hostility, wherein systems of data sharing become both key to implementing these policies, as well as making that implementation less visible. For example, compared with the '"go home" vans' that drew high levels of criticism from urban dwellers (Travis 2013), automated data sharing between the National Health Service (NHS) and the Home Office is much less visible. Finally, through using the right to the city theories as a framework for reimagining rights as not exclusive to citizens, but instead to those who inhabit the space of the city, legally or illegalised, I argue that the right to the city retains its usefulness in placing struggles over space, resisting oppression and retaining agency in the face of datafied systems that aim to control. Whereas current efforts focus on, for example, firewalls between the Home Office and other government departments (Hermansson et al. 2020), we see, through using Lefebvre's theories, that we must demand a more fundamental restructuring of society, along with national and global systems of power, to bring about data justice and systemic change.

THE RIGHT TO THE CITY AND STRUGGLES OVER SPACE

Although Lefebvre speaks of a right to the city (1968), it is about much more than that; it becomes about commanding the entire societal process, beyond the city itself, challenging the very consolidation of power by the state or elites (Attoh 2011; Harvey 2008). As Lefebvre says, the right to the city is 'a cry and a demand' (1968), a demand for a radical reorganisation of dominant and oppressive social, political and economic relations, a restructuring of capitalism and liberal democratic citizenship (Purcell 2002: 100). It is about moving decision making away from centralised state power and instead towards those who live in, and produce, urban space (Purcell 2002: 101; see also Mitchell 2003; de Lange 2019; Manfredi-Sánchez 2020). As such, we see that the right to the city is a 'right to change and reinvent the city more after our hearts' desire . . . a collective rather than individual right' (Harvey 2012: 4; see also Marcuse 2012). The right becomes about being a part of the creation of social worlds, being allowed to be included in decision-making processes shaping the lives of those who live in the city (de Lange 2019: 72). Moreover, the right to the city argues for seizing power and space away from the elites and from the state, and a radical democratising of urban life for those who build and sustain it (Isin 2000; Harvey 2012: xvi). This, Lefebvre claims, challenges traditional claims to rights through national citizenship and instead replaces them with the rights of 'citadins', that is, those who inhabit and shape urbanity (Lefebvre 1991; cf. Purcell 2002: 102).

As Lefebvre famously claimed, 'there is a politics of space because space is political' (Elden 2007). Space remains a contentious topic in relation to borders and migration, where it is often seen in relation to national territory, shaping interactions, exclusion and controls over individuals outside of state-defined parameters of 'citizen'. Moreover, questions of inclusion are complex as visibility and invisibility become interchangeable and desirable at different times as people make their way through border regimes until 'legality' is won from the state (Trimiklionitos et al. 2015: 28; see also Metcalfe 2022). This visibility/invisibility becomes interesting when confronted with the implementation of datafied governance, which works to reconfigure and perpetuate existing forms of control into less visible structures whilst simultaneously making illegalised migrants more visible to the state. How should a person claim the right to the city if there is a power in staying invisible to expansive datafied systems of governance that work to identify people for violent exclusion, such as deportation? This is an important point of contention, as spaces of exclusion move to invisible and often unknown and complex databases with less accountability yet harsher outcomes. As systems become datafied, should responses be focused on datafied protections to guard from data sharing without consent, or to stop data sharing between government departments completely? Here, campaigns often decry the need for firewalls between government departments (for example, Patients Not Passports et al. 2020) or expanded data ownership rights for migrants, who currently remain exempt from GDPR (General Data Protection Regulation) rules (for example, Bradley 2018). However, through applying Lefebvre's theories, I ask if efforts should instead be focused on a more fundamental reorganising of society and reclaiming of rights and power that datafied systems entrench but that historical forms of governance, from capitalism to colonialism, created. In other words, is it enough to offer small protections within a hostile society, or should we demand a reorganisation of society as a whole? This chapter is not looking to give an answer to this, or indeed offer proposals for how this would happen, but instead hopes to raise important questions about what we mean when we ask for data justice for all, and question whether this can happen without a larger shift in societal power.

Though often overlooked in the writing of Lefebvre, who focuses on the proletariat as the key antagonist over the right to the city, questions over space and inclusion are arguably equally as important for non-citizens; for illegalised and precarious migrants who resist the racist city as well as the capitalist city (Purcell 2002: 106). This resistance,

I argue, becomes more pertinent than ever as automated systems of data sharing and new interoperable databases work to enact overarching spaces of hostility. Importantly, the right to the city offers another form of inclusion beyond formally recognised citizenship, where the collective struggle of all those who live in, and produce, the city and the social worlds within it claim the right to shape the urbanism and society they want to live in (Harvey 2012). Moreover, the right to the city, as Trimikliniotis et al. (2015) argue, is a central marker for distinguishing between those who are given permission and included in the city, and those who are not, who must then fight for inclusion themselves (p. 101). These authors present Lefebvre's ideas on the 'right to enter', the 'right to inhabit', the right to 'adapt one's built, cultural and social environment according to one's habitus', and the 'right to transform the environment to belong, the right to move on to another city and country' (Lefebvre 1996; Trimikliniotis et al. 2015: 112–13). The authors note that, with regard to the first two points raised – the right to enter and the right to inhabit – it becomes key to remain invisible, indistinguishable and unnoticed due to hostile and exclusionary border and migration regimes that seek to deny both of these things; so, they argue, we must consider the 'right to remain informal but safe'. Through looking at the more nuanced rights to the city, we see that formal recognition and granting of immigration status will not dispel the wider levels of marginalisation and segregation that migrants face; from housing to jobs to education (Gilbert and Dikeç 2008: 256), there remains a power in creating more substantive forms of inclusion. Likewise, inscribing anti-discriminatory practices or firewalls within punitive immigration databases will not dispel this level of societal segregation. Important to this discussion is that this inclusion is becoming harder as datafied systems work to make visible illegalised migrants as a means of identifying people for exclusion as a part of hostile environment policies.

A HOSTILE ENVIRONMENT

So, how are these spaces of segregation constructed and enacted in the UK towards illegalised migrants? As Theresa May famously declared in 2012 when introducing new immigration and asylum policies in the UK, the aim was to 'create a really hostile environment for illegal migrants', through cutting off access to basic rights such as housing, health care and support in the hope it would force illegalised migrants to leave 'voluntarily'. This was implemented through the 2014 and 2016 Immigration Acts and relied upon establishing means of information and data sharing between government departments, schools, hospitals, housing and even banks (Price 2014; Corporate Watch 2018; Quille 2018; Goodfellow 2019).

Important to note is that hostile environment policies are not a new political mission. The 1996 Asylum and Immigration Act, which had focused on reducing the 'attractiveness' of welfare for asylum seekers and other illegalised migrants (El-Enany 2020: 161), arguably acted as a precursor for the politics shaping the hostile environment policies of today (Goodfellow 2019). Indeed, New Labour then took the helm of implementing restrictive asylum policy in the late 1990s (Webber 2012). This approach was outlined by the New Labour government in a 1998 White Paper called *Fairer, Faster and Firmer: A Modern Approach to Immigration and Asylum* (Home Office 1998), which engrained deeper than ever before the notion of 'bogus' asylum claims, shining light on undesirable 'economic migrants' (Corporate Watch 2018). This focus on fairer and faster is also reflected in the language used within data-driven systems, which often tout the 'efficiency' of datafied systems (Redden, Dencik and Warne 2020). In 1999, the Immigration and Asylum Act (United Kingdom 1999) provided legislation that enabled a comprehensive system for data sharing between the Home Office, police, crime databases and customs (Webber 2012: 149). Thus, we again see the formalisation of a specific mode of migration govern-ance based on information gathering and data sharing to enact restric-tive policies and surveillance. This act also created a National Asylum Support Service (NASS), moving welfare support for people seeking asylum away from mainstream welfare benefits and furthering levels of surveillance through tying together housing and financial support, which became used as a tool for geographical containment. Often NASS accommodation is in areas where housing stock is the cheapest, meaning there is also a physical exclusion from the urban spaces and from community. This practice of physical exclusion from the urban city reflects what Gilbert and Dikeç (2008: 255) deem 'discriminatory and segregated organization not only of urban space but of society', and speaks to the core theories of Lefebvre's right to the city, which fights against this removal from 'urban reality' through punitive and discrimi-natory practices (Lefebvre 1996).

Over the next ten years, there followed numerous restrictive and exclusionary immigration and asylum policies that expanded detention capacity and practices (Squire 2011), introduced biometric cards and databases (Amoore 2006), restricted welfare and appeals rights, and gave way to a strong anti-migrant rhetoric that allowed for the introduction of the hostile environment policies (Goodfellow 2019). Here, the logics of criminalisation are advanced both through datafied mechanisms for categorisation, as well as punitive immigration policies and techniques for social control (Aas and Bosworth 2013), resulting in a 'crimmigration control system' (Webber 2012; Quille 2018; Bowling and Westernra 2020; Hendry 2020).

More recent hostile environment policies, with a physical presence in the streets – including '"go home" vans' and early morning immigration raids – made obvious practices of exclusion towards illegalised migrants (Jones et al. 2017). Though public engagement was encouraged through an 'Immigration Enforcement Hotline',[1] encouraging another form of data collection through the reporting of people suspected of 'illegality' (Bowling and Westenra 2020: 169), these actions also drew attention for the callousness in their delivery, where these overtly visible efforts to discriminate and intimidate migrants were met with criticism across society. Demonstrating a form of enacting the right to the city, activists protested against the immigration raids and vans, and anti-raid solidarity networks worked together to reclaim the streets through showing up in large numbers when immigration raids took place (Corporate Watch 2019).

However, these practices became seemingly less visible as they moved towards data sharing and surveillance, which took place through intergovernmental Memorandums of Understanding (MoUs) and by creating new databases, infrastructures and data sharing agreements. This development is visible in the MoU between the NHS and Home Office (Department of Health and Social Care and Home Office 2017), which later evolved into the MESH database (NHS 2021), and worked to check the immigration status of any current or prospective patients. Important here is that not everyone was aware of these instances of data sharing taking place. The campaigns Docs Not Cops[2] and Patients not Passports,[3] for example, highlight that many medical practitioners, as well as people subject to migration controls, remained unsure of how processes of data sharing between the NHS and the Home Office take place, even if they suspected that this data sharing was likely happening. And so these data systems retain an inaccessible and unchallengeable position, often employed without our knowledge and without corresponding to lived experiences (Hintz, Dencik and Wahl-Jorgensen 2017: 734), thus creating a feeling of powerlessness by those affected (Andrejevic 2014: 1682; Taylor 2017). The disconnection for practitioners between actions and consequences as a result of confusion around how data systems function allows for a 'performance of indifference in the face of tragedy' (Leurs and Smets 2018: 5), as a lack of transparency obscures violent outcomes.

Despite this invisibility, hostile immigration policies enacted through data sharing still claim space within the city and work to exclude those deemed 'illegal'. These policies also work to remove the moral conflict inherent in witnessing overtly violent practices of exclusion due to practices becoming less perceptible through their automation (Bowling and Westenra 2020: 164). Notably, these developments see the incorporation of wider logics of a datafied border, which seek to identify, sort, criminalise and control migrants for political goals of reducing illegalised migration (Metcalfe and Dencik 2019). Thus, we see new means of making illegalised migrants visible to the state through often imperceptible mechanisms that further exclude them from the city and wider society. Below I will outline the key databases and data-sharing practices before moving on to examine how theories of the right to the city can be used to tease apart the struggles over space, inclusion and, importantly, resistance and reclaiming of power within a datafied system of control.

HOSTILE DATA

Hostile environment policies have become reliant upon data sharing and automated practices of checking eligibility to basic services such as health care or housing. Often this data sharing is done through MoUs, though ongoing efforts are being made to create shared platforms through application programming interfaces (APIs), which would allow for faster sharing and queries between departments to become standardised. Before moving to analyse these developments within the framework of Lefebvre's theories, it is necessary to outline some of the key instances of data sharing and how these represent hostile data in many aspects of welfare, health care, housing and policing (it is beyond the scope of this chapter to outline every single instance of data sharing, and so, for a detailed overview of this, please see Corporate Watch 2018).

Possibly the most widely noted instance of data sharing with the Home Office occurs in the NHS (Hiam, Steele and McKee 2018). Data sharing that began between the Home Office and NHS as early as 2016 became formalised in an MoU in 2017. However, this arrangement sparked huge controversy and was withdrawn in 2018 after a legal challenge questioning the secrecy of the MoU (Bowcott 2018). Nevertheless, unbeknownst to many, more recently the MESH database was created to facilitate ongoing data-sharing practices; it works to check for chargeability of patients in hospitals through examining a person's immigration status. The process works through an automated check of NHS numbers of patients, which are run through the MESH system, creating red, amber or green 'banners'.[4] This system of data sharing in health care has led to high levels of fear and mistrust amongst migrant communities, who reportedly avoid interactions with health care out of fear of detention and deportation or high charges (Patients not Passports et al. 2020). The harms of this distrust have been especially felt during the pandemic, where people have died of COVID-19 through fear of seeking medical help (ibid.), and where fear is leading to low uptake of vaccines for people with insecure immigration status (Walker 2021). This system of red, amber or green categorisation echoes theories scrutinising the filtration of travellers (Broeders and Hampshire 2013) and is evident in other instances, such as the recently abandoned 'racist algorithm' used by the Home Office (Foxglove 2020). This algorithmic system was only dropped after a legal challenge that argued that the black box algorithm used to sort visa applications through a traffic light system of ratings for travellers was inherently problematic and discriminatory (Warrel 2020). Here, some nationalities were flagged as 'suspicious' or 'risky', placing individuals from these countries under far higher levels of scrutiny and affecting their ability to cross borders.

Another database used to identify illegalised migrants and exclude them from social care is NRPF Connect,[5] which identifies people with no recourse to public funds (NRPF). Local councils can use this system to deny people access to social services, financial support and council accommodation; the system works through sharing information with the Home Office to determine a person's immigration status (Project 17, 2018). Again, this database will flag up those with NRPF as potentially 'illegal' and liable to be reported to the Home Office for detention and potential deportation. Additionally, as with MESH, NRPF Connect works to create mistrust and fear of local authorities, pushing people underground into unsafe and insecure living situations or homelessness, and leaving them vulnerable to exploitation.

We also see the use of data sharing to conflate the immigration and criminal databases IDENT1 and the Immigration and Asylum Biometrics System (IABS) through the introduction of the Biometric Services Gateway (Home Office 2017). This new data infrastructure works through capturing fingerprints and checking them against data on both IDENT1 and IABS simultaneously. The database is being implemented through mobile fingerprinting units used by twenty-two police forces across the country to stop and scan people without identification on the street (Home Office 2018). Civil society groups have raised concerns over the impact on marginalised and historically targeted communities, who often face racial discrimination at the hands of the police, as well as the impact on trust in the police for people without immigration status (Racial Justice Network and Yorkshire Resists 2021). Ultimately, many argue that this use of biometric data by the police for immigration purposes has a hugely detrimental impact upon heavily policed and racialised communities, once more creating unnecessary fear and shaping interactions across the city as people move to avoid the police. The Biometric Services Gateway is part of a larger Home Office biometrics programme, which seeks to provide a 'Biometric Matching Service delivering biometric search, identification and verification capabilities across multiple biometric modalities (initially fingerprints and face) and for multiple data sets (immigration, citizenship, law enforcement, etc)' (Privacy International 2019: 5). This program would work by creating a single online cloud system where multiple checks can be conducted simultaneously by police, UKVI (UK Visas and Immigration) and the Border Force, bringing together and furthering many existing aspects of hostile environment policies.

Datafied surveillance of asylum seekers also becomes easier through the use of ASPEN cards – limited debit cards topped up weekly by the Home Office – which enable the Home Office to monitor where and on what asylum support is spent (Tillyard 2019). Importantly, the separation between asylum support and mainstream welfare systems allows a much closer tracking and surveillance of spending, as people seeking asylum are made exceptional and segregated from wider welfare recipients. This exceptionality also imposes stringent controls on where and how the money is spent. As asylum support dictates that it is only to meet 'essential needs', the spending of money on, for example, petrol, can be prohibited. Likewise, as a person is not allowed to leave their NASS accommodation for extended periods of time, if someone spends their asylum support outside the area in which they have been officially housed, the Home Office is able to check and will threaten suspension of support. Thus, through this we see another example of hostile data within asylum support. Arguably, this level of surveillance not only works to isolate people seeking asylum or with NRPF from wider society, but also means ongoing geographical control is enacted through data surveillance.

Ultimately, increased datafication leads to greater regulation of borders and restricts freedom of movement (Ajana 2015: 13). Here, it is useful to draw on critical data studies, where questions are asked pertaining to power dynamics involved within data-driven processes that create and reproduce social and cultural divisions (Andrejevic, Hearn and Kennedy 2015: 385), limit privacy (Ohm 2010; Pasquale 2015), result in a lack traditional informed consent (Fairfield and Shtein 2014; Metcalf and Crawford 2016), further discrimination (boyd and Crawford, 2012) and effectively enact exclusion and hostility. Specifically, datafied or 'smart' borders, Vukov suggests, create a new intersection between biopolitical and algorithmic forms of governance (2016: 81; see also De Genova 2013). In other words, as Kitchin et al. (2019: 9) argue, 'smart technologies can be used to suppress dissent and reproduce a particular polity'. Specifically, we see that datafication facilitates hostile environment policies, where border logics shape not only the physical external border, but also the everyday lives of people subject to immigration controls.

From the perspective of the British state, datafication as described above advances the framing of illegalised migration as a social ill, a problem needing to be solved or fixed, and enables exclusion of illegalised migrants from basic services. Datafication also creates spaces of exclusion from wider society, as people targeted through these policies come to fear interactions with the state through concerns over data sharing. These issues become key when considering the need for some illegalised migrants to remain invisible from the state to avoid detention and deportation. Simultaneously, however, the state endeavours to make the very same individuals visible and traceable through expansive data infrastructures. Importantly, with the datafied systems listed above, to stay invisible means no interaction with any services, as interaction will mean data sharing, in turn facilitating tracing and surveillance, and potentially resulting in detention and deportation. Arguably, the hyperbolic language of 'illegal immigrants', 'bogus asylum seekers' or 'dangerous individuals' legitimises these exclusionary data infrastructures, dispelling moral concerns over surveillance and following the logics of categorisation as 'worthy' recipients of support, or as 'illegal' migrants needing to leave the country.

Within critical data studies, some argue that using data as a form of governance is nothing new, but a continuation of capitalist uses of technologies to control and subjugate certain members of society (Thatcher, O'Sullivan and Mahmoudi 2016: 1000). Thus, it should come as no surprise that processes that further stratify society and consolidate power should disproportionately affect the most vulnerable, marginalised and excluded (Taylor 2017: 3), in this case precarious illegalised migrants in the UK. Casting the net wider, we see how datafication of border regimes more widely has resulted in the perpetuation of violent border controls, making it harder to cross borders and claim asylum or settle in a new country (Pallister-Wilkins 2016). Ultimately, the goal of the datafied hostile environment is to make visible illegalised migrants in order to facilitate deportations or 'voluntary' return – in other words, to identify people to be violently excluded from society and national territorial space. When the logics behind border regimes are to reduce migration and deny freedom of movement to illegalised travellers, the datafied systems will further this work and make it more difficult to evade control. Moreover, whilst hostile environment policies see the containment of people seeking asylum in segregated accommodation, hostile data simultaneously means people are more visible to the state than ever before.

In response to this, I argue that there is strength in applying Lefebvre's right to the city theories as a means of conceptualising struggles over space within an urban environment and beyond, where participation in the everyday production of space acts to counter (in) visible attempts to exclude an individual. Accordingly, the rallying cry and demand of the right to the city is more pertinent than ever. Specifically, Lefebvre's notion of a 'citadin' becomes highly pertinent when considering illegalised migrants who are denied citizenship. Below, I will explore how these theories can be used to tease apart the specific effects of datafied logics and practices of governance, where the lack of transparency obfuscates the process, yet ultimately perpetuates long-standing practices of exclusion.

DATAFICATION AND THE CITY

At the time of Lefebvre's writing on the right to the city, we saw the encroachment of neoliberal logics entering the world stage and shaping urban life accordingly, where there was a mobilisation of 'technocratic knowledge and politico-institutional power in order to produce, manipulate, manage, and regulate' the ordering of societies, and relations within and across them (Brenner and Elden 2009: 32). Some may argue we are seeing a similar turn of events with the datafication of society, which once again capitalises on technocratic knowledge and power to control and govern societies; though, however much datafication may have changed the tools of governance, the grounding principles largely remain the same. And so, the right to the city remains a useful paradigm for understanding ongoing spaces of control, oppression and resistance. What becomes increasingly worrying is the invisible ways in which these structures of power, driven through capitalist and neoliberal global systems that demand the free movement of goods at the cost of freedom of movement of people, are furthered with data-driven tools for governance (Besteman 2020).

When we consider this in relation to ongoing hostility towards migrants, which have become entrenched in datafied systems that become harder to see and resist, the need for societal reorganisation is more evident than ever. Looking back at the data systems in place for the identification of illegalised migrants in the UK, and the outcomes of them, we see that this has impacts far beyond the technology itself. That someone may forego lifesaving treatment during a pandemic for fear of data sharing with the Home Office and deportation is a clear example of this. On top of this, when those implementing datafied systems, from nurses to social workers, are unsure of the mechanisms in place for data sharing due to their automation, or indeed the long-term impacts of data sharing, the systems of governance become obfuscated. This may mean that practitioners forced to use data infrastructures they do not understand may unintentionally become part of implementing exclusionary immigration policies that endanger the very people they are working to try and support. This in turn means governance becomes naturalised by technology and thus rendered more invisible. Consequently, we must focus efforts on dismantling the system as a whole, and not merely the technological tools that discourage and exclude those illegalised by the state from basic universal rights.

In reference to migration and the city, some argue that Lefebvre's theories have shaped 'cities of sanctuary' in the UK (Foerster 2019), where local councils work to offer hospitality, countering national narratives of hostility through limiting cooperation with restrictive state immigration policies (Squire and Bagelman 2012). Within this movement, we see attempts to create 'enacted citizenship' where the goal is not granting nationality but recognising everyone regardless of their legal status and including them in day-to-day city life (Manfredi-Sánchez 2020: 3; see also Bauder 2016). This recognition has echoes of movements such as the 'sans-papiers' struggle in France, where new ideas of citizenship were invoked through the inhabiting of the city (Gilbert and Dikeç 2008: 254). However, in reference to datafied cities, questions arise over the ability of local-level councils and government to challenge nationwide automated data systems. As such, we must ask how far is the reach of cities of sanctuary? For example, are local councils able to prevent police going onto the streets with mobile fingerprint scanners? Such questions bring focus back to who the power holder in the city is, and where efforts to challenge oppressive powers must be focused.

Research within critical data studies has also talked of the 'right to the datafied city' or the 'digital rights to the city' (Shaw and Graham 2017; de Lange 2019; see Kitchin et al. 2019: 15). Specifically, Kitchin et al. (2019) have written about the right to the city in reference to the development of smart cities, where smart cities continue to reproduce inequalities and special segregation though the ongoing advancement of capitalist, neoliberal, colonial and nationalistic interests (p. 5). Though the systems of hostile data described above may not add up to a smart city, patterns of data collection for an apparent societal goal finds resonance with the language of smart cities. These hostile systems become particularly pertinent in line with the disciplinary elements of datafied cities, where techniques of governance become internalised (de Lange 2019: 76). Importantly for this discussion, Kitchin et al. (2019) argue that we must continue to interrogate how space is created and citizenship is framed and changed in times of datafication, as social worlds move into algorithmic governance and the visibility of structures of dominance and exclusion become obfuscated and complex (p. 4). They ask: what kind of smart city do we want to enact, create and live in? Yet, it is not merely an issue of smart cities or data, but a more fundamental issue in relation to the structural organisation of society and social worlds. Ultimately, we must ask what kind of society we want to live in, datafied or not, and demand a reorganisation of society accordingly. As such, questions over the framing of citizenship and rights become central in relation to hostile border regimes, where the demand may be justifiably focused on the abolition of borders in their entirety (Mezzadra 2019).

In parallel to this, Trimiklionitos et al. (2015) talk of digital mobilities and the 'ontology of moving people' (p. 19) in reference to subaltern and precarious migrants as they make their journeys across external borders and grapple with the everyday internal borders they face when they arrive at their destination. Here, the authors talk of a 'mobile commons', consisting of shared knowledge and mutual support and care between migrants, shaped by their journeys and resulting socialities. The mobile commons is a result of 'migrant digitalities' and works to reclaim 'the commons' (p. 12). Within this, migrant digitalities both result in precaritisation and exclusion, which remain implicit to social structures and inequalities, but also demonstrate human and social agency through finding ways to reclaim, create and share knowledge (p. 10). Thus, the authors argue that the mobile commons become a 'revolutionising and transforming' power, shaping both the experiences of people on the move and wider societal developments, thus 'giving flesh and bone' to Lefebvre's theories (p. 9). Such an approach is key to realising that not all technological advancements are punitive, and that there remains autonomy in migration and agency of people on the move. As such, survival tactics, informed by the mobile commons, come to shape interactions with the state and the city, whilst also fighting for a larger overhaul of societal organisation.

The right to the city thus becomes a useful tool in formulating a call for this reorganisation as it speaks of challenging overarching systems that demand formal regularisation as dictated by the state. The language of Lefebvre's theories reframes 'us' and 'them', where the 'us' becomes co-inhabitants of the city, opposed to an 'us' based on sharing the same national identity (Purcell 2002: 105; see also Isin and Nielsen, 2008; Nyers, 2010). This repositioning brings into question the very notion of citizenship, speaking to key issues within migration studies, where Lefebvre introduces the notion of 'citadins', who are essentially urban dwellers, as a means of reframing who has the right to this creation and inhabitation of urban life (Lefebvre 1991; see Purcell 2003: 577). Whereas traditional forms of inclusion in urban life rest upon national citizenship, the right to the city empowers those who inhabit the city, legally or not. This, Purcell argues (2003: 581), becomes increasingly pertinent in times of the 'global city' (Sassen 1991), where, more than ever before, international migrants become concentrated in urban spaces. Moreover, it speaks to the substantive dynamics of urban life that recognises the urban and responding social relations as a means of producing space and politics (Gilbert and Dikeç 2008: 254–5). Consequently, we must interrogate what it means to reclaim space, where illegalised migrants hold power as citadins. This point is not to replace or refute the importance of gaining legal immigration status but challenges the right of the state to define interactions within social spaces.

An important point to ascertain is whether or not datafied forms of identification and categorisation shift or displace these issues sur-rounding space and segregation within and across society and the city, or whether data systems work to enact existing power structures in control of societal space. For this discussion, the British state's immi-gration policies, with the aim of reducing the number of migrants in the country through creating an inhospitable space, form the structures of power dominating the urban landscape and social worlds through-out the country. Though these policies are reliant on data systems for their implementation, just as Lefebvre highlights, there are more fun-damental aspects to consider when demanding a restructuring: that of challenging global border regimes and the limited view of national citizenship as a parameter for facilitating inclusion and rights.

CONCLUSION

Though it is data that enacts hostile environment policies, it is not the key behind the politics, and so we see that the logics of dispossession, of exclusion and identification, that rule border regimes are the real issue to be addressed. I have argued that a powerful framing for resist-ing these dominating and powerful logics is Lefebvre's theories of right to the city, and with it a radical reorganisation of existing social spaces and societal structures. Whilst new datafied immigration controls may make it harder for illegalised migrants to remain invisible, the cry and demand of Lefebvre's theories speak of the need for long-term structural change. Accordingly, Lefebvre's theories remain relevant in the face of the datafication of immigration techniques that aim to track, identify, monitor and deter, as they maintain the cry and demand to occupy, reclaim and reshape social and formal structures regardless of these controls. Specifically, within hostile data systems, which work to deny illegalised migrants' access to, amongst other things, health care and housing, control is garnered through making migrants visible and traceable to the state, or through pushing people into unsustainable and precarious situations.

Moreover, the right to the city foregrounds important issues concerning injustice within datafied societies, and particularly within datafied border regimes. Here, we can see a different approach to data justice to those given, for example, by Taylor (2017), who focuses on invisibility and disengagement with technology and anti-discrimination in existing mechanisms for governance. Importantly, the right to the city moves beyond demanding formal rights enacted through the state, recognising that this alone will not work to remove historical marginalisation, nor give those excluded in society a real stake in how things are organised on an everyday level. And so, change comes through working 'through and ultimately against marginalisation' (Gilbert and Dikeç 2008: 258). Accordingly, this demand offers a right to difference, where there is a right 'not to be classified forcibly into categories which have been determined by the necessarily homogenizing powers' (Lefebvre 1976: 3, cf. Gilbert and Dikeç 2008: 259). This language speaks directly to fundamental harms within datafication, which not only seeks to deny this right to difference but works to entrench practices of categorisation by the state.

ACKNOWLEDGEMENTS

Research for this article is part of a large multi-year project called 'Data Justice: Understanding Datafication in Relation to Social Justice' (DATAJUSTICE), funded by an ERC Starting Grant (no. 759903).

NOTES

1. https://www.gov.uk/report-immigration-crime.
2. http://www.docsnotcops.co.uk.
3. https://patientsnotpassports.co.uk/act/.
4. This information was learnt during interviews with NHS Overseas Visitors Managers, conducted in December 2020 as part of research for the project 'Data Justice: Understanding Datafication in Relation to Social Justice' (DATAJUSTICE), funded by an ERC Starting Grant (no. 759903).
5. https://www.nrpfnetwork.org.uk/nrpf-connect.

REFERENCES

Aas, K. F. and Bosworth, M. (2013) *The Borders of Punishment: Migration, Citizenship, and Social Exclusion*. Oxford: Oxford University Press.

Ajana, B. (2015) Augmented borders: Big Data and the ethics of immigration control. *Journal of Information, Communication and Ethics in Society*, 13(1), 58–78.

Amoore, L. (2006) Biometric borders: governing mobilities in the war on terror. *Political Geography*, 25(3), 336–51.

Andrejevic, M. (2014) The Big Data divide. *International Journal of Communication*, 8, 1673–89.

Andrejevic, M., Hearn, A. and Kennedy, H. (2015) Cultural studies of data mining: introduction. *European Journal of Cultural Studies*, 18(4–5), 379–94.

Attoh, K. (2011) What kind of right is the right to the city? *Progress in Human Geography*, 35(5), 669–85.

Bauder, H. (2016) Sanctuary cities: policies and practices in international perspective. *International Migration*, 55, 174–87.

Besteman, C. (2020) *Militarised Global Apartheid*. Durham, NC: Duke University Press.

Bowcott, O. (2018) Home Office scraps scheme that used NHS data to track migrants. *The Guardian*, 12 November. Available at https://www.theguardian.com/society/2018/nov/12/home-office-scraps-scheme-that-used-nhs-data-to-track-migrants (last accessed 4 January 2022).

Bowling, B. and Westenra, S. (2020) 'A really hostile environment': Adiaphorization, global policing and the crimmigration control system. *Theoretical Criminology*, 24(2), 163–83.

boyd, d. and Crawford, K. (2012) Critical questions for Big Data. *Information, Communication & Society*, 15(5), 662–79.

Bradley, G. M. (2018) *Care Don't Share*. Liberty. Available at https://www.libertyhumanrights.org.uk/issue/care-dont-share/ (last accessed 4 January 2022).

Brenner, N. and Elden, S. (2009) Introduction: *State, Space, World,* Lefebvre and the survival of capitalism. In N. Brenner and S. Elden (eds), H. Lefebvre, *State, Space, World; Selected Essays.* Translated from the French by G. Moore, N. Brenner and S. Elden. Minneapolis, MN: University of Minnesota Press.

Broeders, D. and Hampshire, J. (2013) Dreaming of seamless borders: ICTs and the pre-emptive governance of mobility in Europe. *Journal of Ethnic and Migration Studies,* 39(8), 1201–18.

Castells, M. (1988) *The Informational City: Information Technology, Economic Restructuring and the Urban-Regional Process.* Oxford: Blackwell.

Corporate Watch (2018) *The UK Border Regime, A Critical Guide.* Corporate Watch.

Corporate Watch (2019) Immigration raids: how direct action got UK's ICE squads on the run. Available at https://corporatewatch.org/immigration -raids-how-direct-action-got-uks-ice-squads-on-the-run/ (last accessed 4 January 2022).

De Genova, N. (2013) Spectacles of migrant 'illegality': the scene of exclusion, the obscene of inclusion. *Ethnic and Racial Studies,* 36(70), 1180–98.

de Lange, M. (2019) The right to the datafied city: interfacing the urban data commons. In P. Cardullo, C. Di Feliciantonio and R. Kitchin (eds), *The Right to the Smart City.* Bingley: Emerald, pp. 71–83.

Department of Health and Social Care and Home Office (2017) Memorandum of understanding between the Home Office, NHS Digital and the Department of Health. Available at https://www.gov.uk/government/pub lications/information-requests-from-the-home-office-to-nhs-digital (last accessed 4 January 2022).

Elden, S. (2007) There is a politics of space because space is political: Henri Lefebvre and the production of space. *Radical Philosophy Review,* 10(2), 101–16.

El-Enany, N. (2020) *(B)ordering Britain, Law, Race and Empire.* Manchester: Manchester University Press.

Fairfield, J. and Shtein, H. (2014) Big Data, big problems: emerging issues in the ethics of data science and journalism. *Journal of Mass Media Ethics,* 29(1), 38–51.

Foerster, A. (2019) Solidarity or sanctuary? A global strategy for migrant rights. *Humanity & Society,* 43(1), 19–42.

Foxglove (2020) Home Office says it will abandon its racist visa algorithm – after we sued them. Foxglove, 4 August. Available at https://www.foxglove .org.uk/news/home-office-says-it-will-abandon-its-racist-visa-algorithm -nbsp-after-we-sued-them (last accessed 4 January 2022).

Gilbert and Dikeç (2008) Right to the city, politics of citizenship. In K. Goonewardina, K. Stefan, R. Milgrom and C. Schmid (eds), *Space, Difference, Everyday Life.* London: Routledge, pp. 250–64.

Goodfellow, M. (2019) *Hostile Environment: How Immigrants Became Scapegoats.* London: Verso.

harvey, d. (2008) the right to the city. *New Left Review*, 53, 23–40.

Harvey, D. (2012) *Rebel Cities, From the Right to the City to Urban Revolution.* London: Verso.

Hendry, J. (2020) The hostile environment and crimmigration: blurring the lines between civil and criminal law. *Soundings: A Journal of Politics and Culture*, 76, 26–36.

Hermansson, L., Lundburg, A., Gruber, S., Jolly, A., Lind, J., Righard, E. and Scott, H. (2020) Firewalls: a necessary tool to enable social rights for undocumented migrants in social work. *International Social Work*, 1–15.

Hiam, L., Steele, S. and McKee, M. (2018) Creating a 'hostile environment for migrants': the British government's use of health service data to restrict immigration is a very bad idea. *Health Economics, Policy and Law*, 13(2), 107–17.

Hill, A. (2017) 'Hostile environment': the hardline Home Office policy tearing families apart. *The Guardian*, 28 November. Available at https://www.theguardian.com/uk-news/2017/nov/28/hostile-environment-the-hardline-home-office-policy-tearing-families-apart (last accessed 4 January 2022).

Hintz, A., Dencik, L. and Wahl-Jorgensen, K. (2017) Digital citizenship and surveillance society: introduction. *International Journal of Communication*, 11, 731–9.

Home Office (1998) *Fairer, Faster and Firmer: A Modern Approach to Immigration and Asylum.* The Stationery Office. Available at https://assets.publishing.service.gov.uk/government/uploads/system/uploads/attachment_data/file/264150/4018.pdf (last accessed 4 January 2022).

Home Office (2017) Home Office biometric programme – privacy impact assessment – Biometric Services Gateway. Available at https://assets.publishing.service.gov.uk/government/uploads/system/uploads/attachment_data/file/721100/Biometric_Services_Gateway_PIA__Final_.pdf (last accessed 4 January 2022).

Home Office (2018) Police trial new Home Office mobile fingerprint technology. Press Release. Available at https://www.gov.uk/government/news/police-trial-new-home-office-mobile-fingerprint-technology (last accessed 4 January 2022).

Isin, E. F. (2000) Introduction. In E. F. Isin (ed.), *Democracy, Citizenship and the Right to the City.* London: Routledge, pp. 24–41.

Isin, E. F. and Nielsen, G. (2008) *Acts of citizenship.* London: Zed Books.

Jones, H., Gunaratnam, Y., Bhattacharyya, G., Davies, W., Dhaliwal, S., Forket, K., Jackson, E. and Saltus, R. (2017) *Go Home? The Politics of Immigration Controversies.* Manchester: Manchester University Press.

Kitchin, R., Cardullo, P. and Di Feliciantonio, C. (2019) Citizenship, justice, and the right to the smart city. In P. Cardullo, C. Di Feliciantonio and R. Kitchin (eds), *The Right to the Smart City*. Bingley: Emerald, pp. 1–24.

Lefebvre, H. (1968) *Le Droit à la ville [The right to the city]*, 2nd edn. Paris: Anthropos.

Lefebvre, H. (1976) *The Survival of Capitalism: Reproduction of the Relations of Production*. Translated by F. Bryant. London: Allison & Bushy.

Lefebvre, H. (1991) *The Production of Space*. Translated by D. Nicholson-Smith. Oxford: Blackwell.

Lefebvre, H. (1996) *Writing on Cities*. Edited and translated by E. Kofman and E. Lebas. London: Blackwell.

Leurs, L. and Smets, K. (2018) Five questions for digital migration studies: learning from digital connectivity and forced migration in(to) Europe. *Social Media + Society* (January-March),1–16.

Manfredi-Sánchez, J. (2020) sanctuary cities: what global migration means for local governments. *Social Sciences*, 9(8), 146.

Marcuse, P. (2012) Whose right(s) to what city. In N. Brenner, P. Marcuse and M. Mayer (eds), *Cities for People Not for Profit: Critical Urban Theory and the Right to the City*. London: Routledge.

Metcalf, J. and Crawford, K. (2016) Where are human subjects in Big Data research? The emerging ethics divide. *Big Data & Society* (January–June), 1–14.

Metcalfe, P. (2022) Autonomy of migration and the radical imagination: exploring alternative imaginaries within a biometric border. *Geopolitics*, 27(1), 47–69, doi.org/10.1080/14650045.2021.191755.

Metcalfe, P. and Dencik, L. (2019) The politics of big borders: data (in) justice and the governance of refugees. *First Monday*, 24(4). doi: 10.5210/fm.v24i4.9934.

Mezzadra, S. (2019) Abolitionist vistas of the human: border struggles, migration and freedom of movement. *Citizenship Studies*, 24(4), 424–40.

Mitchell, D. (2003) *The Right to the City: Social Justice and the Fight for Public Space*. London: Routledge.

Mitchell, W. J. (1995) *City of Bits: Space, Place and the Infobahn*. Cambridge, MA: MIT Press.

NHS (2021) Message Exchange for Social Care and Health (MESH) Available at https://digital.nhs.uk/services/message-exchange-for-social-care-and -health-mesh (last accessed 4 January 2022).

Nyers, P. (2010) No one is illegal between city and nation. *Studies in Social Justice*, 4(2), 127–43.

Ohm, P. (2010) Broken promises of privacy: responding to the surprising failure of anonymization. *UCLA Law Review*, 57, 1701.

Pallister-Wilkins, P. (2016) How walls do work: security barriers as devices of interruption and data capture. *Security Dialogue*, 47(2), 151–64.

Pasquale, F. (2015) *The Black Box Society: The Secret Algorithms That Control Money and Information.* Boston, MA: Harvard University Press.

Patients Not Passports, Medact, Migrants Organise and New Economics Foundation (2020) *Migrants' Access to Healthcare During the Coronavirus Crisis.* Available at https://neweconomics.org/uploads/files/Patients-Not -Passports-Migrants-Access-to-Healthcare-During-the-Coronavirus-Cri sis-FINAL.pdf (last accessed 4 January 2022).

Price, J. (2014) The hostile environment. In B. Anderson and M. Keith (eds), *Migration: The COMPAS Anthology.* Oxford: COMPAS, pp. 193–4.

Privacy International (2019) *Home Office Biometrics (HOB) Programme Brief.* Open Space Home Office Biometrics Programme Briefing Paper. Available at https://privacyinternational.org/sites/default/files/2020-08/OP1071%20 -%2017072019%20Item%208.1%20LEDSHOB%20Open%20Space%20 -%20HOB%20Programme%20Briefing_0.pdf (last accessed 4 January 2022).

Project 17 (2018) *In the Night We Didn't Know Where We Were Going.* Available at https://www.project17.org.uk/media/67646/hotel-fund-report-pdf-final -copy.pdf (last accessed 4 January 2022).

Purcell, M. (2002) Excavating Lefebvre: the right to the city and its urban politics of the inhabitant., *GeoJournal,* 58(2–3), 99–108.

Purcell, M. (2003) Citizenship and the right to the global city: reimagining the capitalist world order. *International Journal of Urban and Regional Research,* 27(3), 564–90.

Quille, N. (2018) The Windrush generation in Britain's 'hostile environment': racializing the crimmigration narrative. Criminal Justice, Borders and Citizenship Research Paper No. 3274533. SSRN. Available at https://ssrn .com/abstract=3274533 (last accessed 4 January 2022).

Racial Justice Network (RJN) and Yorkshire Resists (2021) *Public's Perception on Biometric Services Gateway (mobile fingerprint app).* Available at https:// racialjusticenetwork277579038.files.wordpress.com/2021/01/report-public -perception-biometric-gateway.pdf (last accessed 4 January 2022).

Redden, J., Dencik, L. and Warne, H. (2020) Datafied child welfare services: unpacking politics, economics and power. *Policy Studies,* 41(5), 507–26.

Sassen, S. (1991) *The Global City.* Princeton, NJ: Princeton University Press.

Shaw, J. and Graham, M. (2017) *Our Digital Rights to the City.* London: Meatspace Press.

Squire, V. (2011) *The Contested Politics of Mobility: Borderzones and Irregularity.* London: Routledge.

Squire, V. and Bagelman, J. (2012) Taking not waiting: space, temporality and politics in the City of Sanctuary movement. In P. Nyers and K. Rygiel (eds), *Citizenship, Migrant Activism and the Politics of Movement.* London: Routledge, pp. 146–64.

Taylor, L. (2017) What is data justice? The case for connecting digital rights and freedoms, *Big Data & Society* (July–December), 1–14.

Thatcher, J., O'Sullivan, D. and Mahmoudi, D. (2016) Data colonialism through accumulation by dispossession: new metaphors for daily data. *Environment and Planning D: Society and Space*, 34(6), 990–1006.

Tillyard, G. (2019) Big Brother says 'no': surveillance and income management of asylum seekers through the UK ASPEN Card. *OpenDemocracy*. Available at https://www.opendemocracy.net/en/digitaliberties/big-brother-says-no-surveillance-and-income-management-of-asylum-seekers-through-the-uk-aspen-card/ (last accessed 4 January 2022).

Travis, A. (2013) 'Go home' vans resulted in 11 people leaving Britain, says report. *The Guardian*, 31 October. Available at https://www.theguardian.com/uk-news/2013/oct/31/go-home-vans-11-leave-britain (last accessed 4 January 2022).

Trimikliniotis, N., Parsanoglou, D. and Tsianos, V. (2015) *Mobile Commons, Migrant Digitalities and the Right to the City.* New York: Palgrave Macmillan Pivot.

United Kingdom: Immigration and Asylum Act (1999) *United Kingdom of Great Britain and Northern Ireland*. Available at https://www.refworld.org/docid/3bce94c44.html (last accessed 4 January 2022).

Vukov, T. (2016) Target practice: the algorithmics and biopolitics of race in emerging smart border practices and technologies. *Transfers*, 6(1), 80–97.

Walker, P. (2021) Hostile environment 'will cut Covid vaccine uptake among migrants. *The Guardian*, 8 February. Available at https://www.theguardian.com/society/2021/feb/08/undocumented-uk-migrants-to-be-offered-covid-vaccine-without-any-checks (last accessed 4 January 2022).

Warrel, H. (2020) Home Office drops 'biased' visa algorithm. *Financial Times*, 4 August. Available at https://www.ft.com/content/a02c6c42-95b1-419c-a798-0418011d2018 (last accessed 10 February 2022).

Webber, F. (2012) *Borderline Justice: The Fight for Refugee and Migrant Rights.* London: Pluto Press.

Chapter 3

DATAFIED CHILD WELFARE SERVICES AS SITES OF STRUGGLE

Joanna Redden, Jessica Brand, Ina Sander and Harry Warne

Predictive analytics is increasingly being used by child welfare agencies in many countries to influence decisions about resources, services, risk, and when and how to intervene in the lives of families. This chapter draws on international case study investigations of government agencies that have tried and *cancelled* their plans to pursue the use of predictive analytics to inform decisions about families and services. The chapter makes the case that we can learn a great deal by paying attention to the rationalities and decision-making practices that inform people's decisions not to pursue automated decision support systems. Through interviews and document analysis the chapter details the rights, efficacy and social justice concerns that have led government agencies to take a critical position towards the use of predictive analytics to inform decision making. The chapter concludes by arguing that there needs to be greater debate about whether or not these systems should be used in areas of social care. In order for such debate to occur there needs to be (1) more information provided about where and how these systems are being adopted; (2) greater effort by those wanting to implement these systems to justify their use in terms of efficacy, accuracy, fairness, bias and impact; and (3) democratic audits that involve stakeholders and affected communities to investigate impact and ensure a means for meaningful individual and collective intervention.

BRINGING ADMS TO CHILD WELFARE

Government agencies around the world are currently testing and implementing automated decision-making systems (ADMS), generally defined as technical systems designed to help or replace human decision making. These systems rely on large, linked datasets and are introduced with the aim of improving services and productivity and often involve the collection and sharing of data in real time; some make use of data analytics to predict the likelihood of particular outcomes (Gillingham 2019). Government agencies are using ADMS in the areas of fraud detection, benefit administration, policing and immigration, to inform decisions about sentencing, bail and immigration applications, among other assessments. In some cases, governments use these systems in attempts to target resources better, as government agencies struggle to meet public need in contexts of resource constraint and cuts to services.

In child welfare services, the subject of this chapter, ADMS are introduced to try and predict the likelihood that a child will suffer abuse and neglect. The agencies that adopt them argue that they have a responsibility to take advantage of all of the tools necessary to prevent harm to a child and help families before they are in crisis (Drake et al. 2020). Private companies who provide technological services to government and administrators claim that these systems provide a means to do more with less.

Previous research on the use of ADMS in the area of child welfare, however, raises concerns about the quality of the data held about children and families, relating in part to the limits of the data collection tools themselves and the challenges of trying to categorise and streamline information systems about people's incredibly complex lives. There are also ongoing apprehensions about how the data collected from families and children may infringe upon their rights, and how sharing data about families and children may even lead to harms, particularly if this involves sharing inaccurate or biased risk scores about people. Researchers have also worried that requiring frontline workers to input ever more data into databases limits opportunities to foster relationships and takes time away from these relationships (Anderson et al. 2006; Peckover, Hall and White 2008; Munroe 2010; White et al. 2010; Gillingham 2015). Others raise concerns about how ADMS are being used to socially sort in ways that disproportionately and negatively affect Black, indigenous and people of colour as well as those living in poverty (Lyon 2002; Gandy 2005; Benjamin 2019). Researchers note that in the models studied, some of the most highly weighted variables used to estimate risk were proxies for poverty (Keddell 2015; Gillingham 2016; Eubanks 2018). Another common problem that spans a range of uses of ADMS is a lack of transparency and access to the means to interrogate how the systems work (Pasquale 2015; O'Neil 2016).

At the Data Justice Lab we have been studying the social justice implications of government uses of data-driven systems since the Lab's founding in 2017. The research discussed in this chapter builds on our previous work of mapping and analysing government data-driven systems in the areas of fraud detection, justice and child welfare (Dencik et al. 2019; Redden, Dencik and Warne 2020), investigations into data harms caused by the uses of Big Data, and how people are working to redress and prevent such problems (Redden et al. 2020).

In our previous work on child welfare, we first conducted a review of research that focused on the social justice implications of predictive analytics in child welfare (Redden, 2020). This literature survey argues that previous research pointed to five significant concerns about the use of predictive analytics for risk assessment in child welfare: the lack of transparency surrounding these applications, which makes it difficult for them to be interrogated and challenged by users and those affected; that these systems can reinforce and exacerbate discrimination; that these systems are inaccurate and unreliable a lot of the time; that these inaccuracies can lead to stigmatisation of parents and the implications of this are not being considered; and that the data informing the systems is itself limited and problematic.

Research suggests that ADMS are often developed locally, at the municipal and city level. In response to this, we also conducted a political economic analysis of data linking and predictive analytics by UK local authorities for child welfare services, drawing on Kitchin and Lauriault's (2014) work on data assemblage as an analytical framework to argue for the need to situate and contextualise the forces leading to these systems (Redden et al. 2020). The key contextual forces we identified as driving the use of these systems include an austerity context fuelled by a neoliberal ideology that has led to major cuts, forcing local authorities to do more with less; the Troubled Families programme, introduced by the Conservative UK government in 2012, which compels local authorities to collect and combine more data about families in order to label them to access funds; a problematic legal justification for these data practices that does not fully address how rights to privacy are being compromised; a growing datafied marketplace, as companies enter into new kinds of arrangements with local authorities; differing levels of transparency, suggesting this is a contentious area requiring greater debate; a longer history that these systems are a part of, and that has involved instrumentalising and rationalising social work; and, finally, ongoing processes of negotiation, repurposing and resistance in the places where these systems are being implemented.

There have also been significant recent interventions into public debates about the use of predictive analytics in child welfare, which advance this previous research. Notably, the What Works for Children's Social Care Centre designed predictive analytics models for child welfare, then worked with four local authorities to develop risk assessment models for these systems. Their aim was to assess how well this kind of system worked. The Centre concluded:

> In summary, we do not find evidence that the models we created using machine learning techniques 'work' well in children's social care. In particular, the models built miss a large proportion of children at risk which – were the models to be used in practice – risks discouraging social workers from investigating valid concerns further, potentially putting children and young people at risk. (Clayton et al. 2020)

In response to their findings, the chief executive of the Centre, Michael Sanders, argued that now is the time for organisations to stop and think before implementing predictive analytics in the area of child welfare. Further, Sanders points out that it is the responsibility of government agencies and the companies promoting predictive analytics in this area both to be more transparent about their systems and to be required to prove they work (Sanders 2020).

Other stakeholders have taken issue with the ability of data systems to predict life outcomes at all. A global group of researchers recently came together to predict six life outcomes using machine learning methods (Salganik et al. 2020). In this case, 160 teams built predictive models to forecast six life outcomes based on data from the Fragile Families and Child Wellbeing Study, a rich dataset. The teams found that even the best predictions were not very accurate and that, overall, there are limits to our ability to use such methods to predict life outcomes.

Government agencies and civil societies across continents are also raising questions about the use of ADMS for social services. Our work at the Data Justice Lab falls in this area – we have been conducting a collaborative project with the Carnegie UK Trust to investigate the rationales informing government agencies who are making the decision to pause or cancel their use of ADMS.

STUDYING CANCELLED ADMS SYSTEMS

Our project, Automating Public Services: Learning from Cancelled Systems, involved a scoping exercise to identify paused or cancelled data systems in Australia, Canada, Europe, the United Kingdom and the United States (Redden et al. forthcoming). We argue that researching the factors and rationales leading to cancellation offers a way to get beyond the myths of technology to better understand its limits. That is, corporate and government materials often promote data-driven systems as a means to increase efficiency and to enhance organisational decision making by enabling greater insights – a phenomenon referred to by Evegny Morozov as 'technological solutionism' (Morozov 2014). This discourse has been criticised for not attending to the limits of data-driven systems, particularly to where and how these systems fail or work in ways not intended (Mosco 2014; Beer 2018). Further, it is difficult to find out where and how government ADMS are operating, let alone when and where decisions are made not to pursue these systems. Better understanding of the reasons people are choosing *not* to continue ADMS benefits those who are making their own decisions on whether and how to implement these systems.

Our research reinforces those arguing that how technologies are developed and implemented is not inevitable, and that technologies are sites of struggle (Eubanks 2011). There are competing values, politics and understandings of rights and justice informing these struggles, and paying attention to where these struggles occur helps us understand that our shared futures are undetermined. Important work remains to be done to determine the kinds of datafied futures we want – rendering these struggles and points of contention visible can show when there is need for wider public debate and consideration of ADMS.

To this end, Automating Public Services: Learning from Cancelled Systems identified sixty-one cancelled systems in the areas of justice (32), welfare and benefits fraud detection (12), child welfare (5), education (4), immigration (3), finance (2), border control (1), city planning (1) and health (1). Building on this scoping research, the second phase of the project involved twelve case study investigations of cancelled

Table 3.1 Child welfare systems studied by the Automating Public Services: Learning from Cancelled Systems project.

Denmark	Denmark decides not to pursue use of Gladsaxe model.
United States, Illinois	Illinois Department of Children and Family Services (DCFS) stops use of Rapid Safety Feedback (RSF).
New Zealand	Government decides not to use Predictive Risk Modelling (PRM) to identify children at risk of abuse and neglect.
United Kingdom, Hackney	Hackney Council decides not to pursue use of Early Help Profiling System (EHPS).

systems. This chapter draws on the results of the four case study investigations conducted of cancelled ADMS in the area of child welfare. Table 3.1 provides a list of the cancelled systems studied and which country they are located in.

For each case study, we collected legal documents, government reviews and audits, research reports and media reports. We planned to interview two to three people who had direct experience with the ADMS cancelled per case study, sending interview requests to government administrators, lawyers, politicians, civil society organisation representatives and community activists. In the case of the Denmark Gladsaxe model, we interviewed a municipal representative, but it proved very challenging to interview government representatives in the other three case studies in the US, UK and New Zealand; for these, we relied on quotes that officials had made to media outlets and drew on expert interviews for the New Zealand PRM model (two interviews), as well as previous interews with the developers of Hackney's EHPS model (two interviews).

Across our case studies we relied heavily on government documents. For the New Zealand PRM model we looked at an ethical review, a feasibility study and academic publications. In the case of the Denmark Gladsaxe model, we used a government review, a presentation by municipal officials about the Gladsaxe model as well as a list of potential indicators. To understand the Illinois RSF system, we analysed government and corporate promotional material about RSF, a review by the Office of the Inspector General and the Child Welfare Strategic Plan. Finally, for the UK Hackney EHPS, we drew on Freedom of Information (FOI) requests submitted by the Data Justice Lab and those published on the What Do They Know platform, as well as information provided across government websites.

The case studies reveal that the use of ADMS in the area of child welfare is being problematised by a range of actors, including those working within government as well as civil society, and within academia and the press. These concerns – raised around questions of privacy, rights, justice, transparency, accountability, fairness and impact – demonstrate that these systems are viewed as much more than benign government administrative technologies. Localised contexts figure heavily across our case studies, as local administrations pursued ADMS in two of our case studies: the Gladsaxe and Hackney authorities. Further, as we will show, critical media coverage presents both locally and nationally, as does community resistance.

FINDINGS: WHEN AND WHY ADMS ARE CANCELLED

The ADMS systems we reviewed were cancelled at different stages: both the Denmark Gladsaxe model and the New Zealand PRM model were cancelled at the stage of development; the UK's Hackney EHPS was cancelled after a two-year pilot and the US Illinois RSF system was cancelled after it was implemented. Across all cases, the decision to cancel the system involved a range of concerns including privacy and data protection, the potential for bias and discrimination and the effectiveness of the system and quality of the data.

The Gladsaxe model proposed for Denmark and the PRM considered in New Zealand were both developed to identify children in need of help for early intervention. But when information about the plans for these systems became publicly known, they were criticised by researchers and politicians for reasons similar to those raised about predictive policing systems in Los Angeles, as well as the fraud detection systems referenced in our other case studies. These criticisms centred on the potential for ADMS to further embed discrimination and lead to greater inequality, in addition to concerns about accuracy and bias. Unique to the case of New Zealand was that some details about the model were made public, enabling review and debate.

In contrast to these two systems, little is known about why the Illinois Department of Family Services stopped using the Rapid Safety Feedback programme, beyond a quote made publicly by the Director of the Department of Children and Family Services saying that the system was cancelled due concerns about unreliability and inaccuracy. Similarly, little is known about why Hackney decided not to proceed with the EHPS after its pilot; as with some of the other case studies, news reporting suggests it was cancelled due to issues with effectiveness, as there were concerns with accuracy and false positives and negatives. In the UK, a government spokesperson linked the Early Help Profiling System to concerns about limitations of the system's data.

Pre-emptive Cancellations

Both the Denmark Gladsaxe model and New Zealand PRM system were cancelled before their implementation, after civil society raised concerns about the further development and implementation of these models. These instances of critical public reception to the announcement of ADMS for child welfare suggests the need for more public debate about if and how ADMS should be used in this area.

In Denmark, the Gladsaxe model was a classification system developed by the Gladsaxe municipality in 2017 to trace 'children who were vulnerable due to social circumstances before they presented as in need' (AlgorithmWatch 2019). The model was never implemented. Before it could be tried, the Gladsaxe municipality as well as two other municipalities, Guldborgsund and Ikast-Brande, requested exemption from the national Personal Data Act, which restricted government bodies from linking personal data across professional systems and administrations in order to use the system. The government declined the exemption request because they wanted to change the legislation to allow *all* municipalities to use this model – a decision that soon led to critical media coverage along with public and academic concern. *Politiken*, for instance, published news stories that expressed concerns with this development around the tracking of families based on their data, the use of a points system to score families, and concerns about invasions of privacy and mass surveillance. Civil society critics, including the think tank Justitia, similarly raised concerns about the use of the model being a violation of the Personal Data Act (Anderson 2019). In December 2018, there was also an unrelated leak of about 20,000 people's personal data in the Gladsaxe municipality, which led to widespread public concerns about the municipality's ability to protect its citizen's personal data in the future (Kjaer 2018). In reaction, the government stopped plans to alter the legislation, a move that prevented

Gladsaxe from implementing their model. The governing Liberal Alliance's spokeswoman, Christina Egelund, stated that municipalities were not equipped to deal with 'the great responsibility that lies in taking care of the personal data of the citizens'.

In New Zealand, the government also shelved the PRM programme after similar critical responses to news that it would automate the risk assessment of children and families. In 2012, the New Zealand government had begun exploring a predictive risk modelling tool to identify children with the highest risk of neglect and abuse. As noted by Gillingham (2019), administrators wanted the system to combine multiple datasets to identify children in families with parents claiming public benefits who were most at risk of abuse and neglect, with the stated aim to provide supportive services to families. In an interview we conducted in 2020 with Neil Ballantyne, who has researched the events surrounding the plans to implement then shelve the model, he told us that a team at Auckland University developed the system; it relied on a statistical method to identify and risk score children under the age of two for the likelihood they would experience harm or neglect within a population. The system based these scores on family histories and circumstances; those with high risk-scores would be targeted for in-home interventions to prevent maltreatment (Vaithianathan et al. 2012; Vaithianathan et al. 2013; Wilson et al. 2015). The model was based on New Zealand's social investment approach to welfare services, which prioritised targeted practices instead of universal provision (Ballantyne 2020). As Ballantyne told us, when the government announced the system as part of a 2012 government White Paper on Vulnerable Children, it was the first time a government had publicised an attempt to use predictive risk modelling for child maltreatment.

The government trialled the system but never implemented it. In response to widespread public outcry, the government and researchers published details about the model to seek input, a move that enabled researchers to review the model and raise concerns. Heated debates ensued about the potential benefits and risks posed by the system (Dare, Vaithianathan and de Haan 2014; de Hann and Connolly 2014; Wilson et al. 2014; Gillingham 2015; Keddell 2015; Oak 2015). The criticisms focused on privacy concerns; also, people feared that the system presented too many false positives and that the data used was inaccurate. Public stakeholders raised questions about what rights and protections families would have, given the high number of inaccurate predictions (Gillingham 2015), and about how many families would be worse off because of unjustified suspicion and the negative potential impact of stigmatisation (Oak 2016). Further, the system threatened to individualise social problems instead of addressing their structural causes (Keddell 2015). But perhaps the largest concern was over the potential of the system to embed bias and lead to greater inequality. The system, in effect, threatened to punish the poor, as the highest weighted variables used were proxies for poverty, which could disproportionately affect low-income families – creating a feedback loop of increasing surveillance focused on the poor. Among the academics who made their criticisms public were Patrick Kelly, Philip Gillingham, Emily Keddell, Eileen Oak and Ian Hyslop; their complaints were joined by members of the the Social Workers Association and the Green Party, while Radio New Zealand and the *New Zealand Herald* gave the project critical media attention.

After the government acknowledged that the model raised significant ethical questions, it conducted a feasibility study and commissioned an ethical review conducted by the Head of Philosophy at Auckland University, Professor Tim Dare. The review ultimately concluded that the application of predictive risk modelling raised significant ethical concerns, but that many of these could be mitigated (Dare 2013). In the end, Minister of Social Development Anne Tolley cancelled the system in 2015, before an observational study was due to take place.

The decision to cancel the system ultimately appears to be a political decision. In our 2020 interview with Ballantyne, he argued,

> It is interesting to note that in spite of the ethical review commissioned by the MSD [Minister of Social Development] and the heated debates in academic journals and news media, in the end New Zealand's experiment with predictive risk modelling in child protection services was closed down as the result of an intervention by a government Minister, it was a political decision. It is not possible to be certain of the detailed rationale for that decision, but the reasons the Minister gave to the press (Kirk 2016), suggest that running an algorithm on all newborn children and intervening in cases not already known to social services – over half of which would be false positives – may have been a step too far for a neoliberal democracy.

This case is significant, because it is one of the few examples of a PRM model in child welfare being made public. The developers of this model would go on to assist with the implementation of the Alleghany Family Screening Tool in Alleghany County in the United States, where similar heated debates have emerged around the use of a similar model (Eubanks 2018).

Post-use Cancellations

In the other two case studies, the systems were cancelled after use. The Hackney Early Help Profiling System was cancelled after being piloted, while the Illinois Rapid Safety Feedback System was cancelled after being implemented. Both systems, in this regard, provide a learning opportunity about how ADMS systems work in practice and the internal dynamics surrounding their use, as well as the rationales behind decisions to forego them. However, we know the least about why these systems were cancelled, as we were unable to obtain interviews with government officials about the projects. Our situation demonstrates how challenging it can be to gain access to information about ADMS and raises important questions about the need for greater transparency by the agencies using these technologies.

In 2015 Hackney Council started using Xantura's Early Help Profiling System (EHPS) to risk-assess families. Initially the Hackney system was set up to help the council identify families that would qualify for the UK's Troubled Families programme. As with the other systems, the EHPS relied on combining multiple data sources, including school attendance and attainment, health records, family housing data and economic indicators, to flag those identified as needing extra support. Hackney Council also used the system to trial predictive analytics. The predictive system would send an alert and a report to case workers if the model detected that a risk threshold had been crossed, based on an automated scan of data. Every month the system provided social workers with a list of twenty families whose risk score indicated they needed help – it was then up to the social worker to determine if there should be an intervention. In previous interviews, developers stressed that the system was to support social workers' decision making, not replace it (Redden et al. 2020).

The council was attracted to the programme for the potential it had to save money by reducing screenings done by humans, along with better and more cost-saving early interventions and easier data sharing. London Councils, an umbrella body that oversees London's thirty-two councils, was a key driver leading to the piloting of this system, as it encouraged those councils to make greater use of ADMS. Another major influence was London Ventures, who, in partnership with the professional services firm EY, began providing grants for those who wanted to pilot ADMS.

Early reports suggested the system led to early interventions for more people, but we have not been able to identify what kind of impact the system had on service provision and people's lives, as impact was never studied. Indeed, the lack of effort to study the impact of ADMS on those who are affected by them, including social workers and service users, is a significant problem across all areas where ADMS are being implemented.

Ultimately, the council dropped the pilot scheme in 2019, four years after it started. That same year, the *Hackney Citizen* quoted a Hackney Council spokesperson saying,

> At the conclusion of the pilot we had not been able to realise the expected benefits and decided to not continue beyond the pilot stage. We found that the data available was more limited than had initially been envisaged and issues of variable data quality meant that the system wasn't able to provide sufficiently useful insights to justify further investment in the project. (Sheridan 2019)

Earlier investigative reporting by the *Guardian* (McIntyre and Pegg 2018) and a local politician also raised concerns about privacy and the fact that consent was not sought to use the data of citizens (Sheridan 2019).

Our fourth case study looked at how the Illinois Department of Family Services implemented the Rapid Safety Feedback (RSF) system in 2015, then stopped using it in 2017. The RSF system is a predictive analytics tool brought in amid concerns about an increase in the deaths of children. A non-profit organisation, Eckerd Connects, developed the system along with a for-profit partner, Mindshare Technology. Eckerd Connects (based in Florida and formerly Eckerd Kids) took responsibility for project management, case selection criteria and critical investigations of the project (DCFS 2015) but sub-contracted the development, implementation and ongoing maintenance of the predictive model to Mindshare. The project was reported to cost $366,000. The system analysed case tracking data and assigned a score from 1 to 100 to every abuse allegation through the agency's hotline (DCFS 2015; Jackson and Marx 2017).

There has been little published on why the system was cancelled, and we were again unable to obtain interviews with government officials in this case. A new director, Beverly Walker, who was brought in to lead the department, appears to be a key factor leading to the change; she is quoted in the *Chicago Tribune*, one of the media publications to write about the system's cancellation, saying that the contract was not renewed because 'predictive analytics [wasn't] predicting any of the bad cases' (Jackson and Marx 2017). In *The Imprint*, Kelly (2017) summarises that the decision for cancellation was connected to social workers' alarm at the inaccuracy of the system, possibly due to a lack of quality data, as it drew too many false positives and false negatives; it wrongly identified too many children as at risk in some cases, while failing to predict the deaths of children in two cases (Wood 2015). The *Chicago Tribune* reported that 'caseworkers were alarmed and overwhelmed by alerts as thousands of children were rated as needed urgent protection' (Jackson and Marx 2017). Illinois' Executive Inspector General raised concerns about how the contract for the system was awarded, and a 2017 audit summary notes that the DCFS wrongly processed the no bid contract as a grant instead of a sole source contract and without competitive bidding (OEIG 2017a, 2017b). The *Chicago Tribune* followed this development by criticising the no bid contract, leading to the resignation of the previous director (Kelly 2017; Jackson and Marx 2017).

CONCLUSION: MAKING SYSTEMS VISIBLE

Our investigations of cancelled ADMS for child welfare demonstrate the importance of learning about *why* government agencies are making these decisions. Whilst there is a great deal of corporate and government material promoting their use (Beer 2018; Edwards, Gillies and Gorin 2021), there is still little information publicly available about how these systems are used in practice and their limitations. Research on ADMS challenges this promotional material, raising concerns about the effectiveness of these systems for child welfare and to predict life outcomes at all (Clayton et al. 2020; Salganik et al. 2020). Our research demonstrates that a number of government agencies are landing on the more critical side of this discourse, as reflected in decisions to cancel ADMS across several government areas.

A range of public concerns raised by those operating outside of government agencies fuelled the decisions to cancel systems pre-emptively. These include worries that ADMS disproportionately target those receiving benefits, exacerbating discrimination and inequality, and concerns about the protection of personal data being linked and held by government agencies. In the case of the New Zealand PRM model, the government made details about the model itself public and open to scrutiny, a level of transparency that did not occur in any of our other case studies. With the two systems that were cancelled after implementation, news outlets quoted public officials saying they were cancelled out of concerns about their accuracy and effectiveness, including limited data quality.

In all cases, critical media coverage and concerns raised by civil society organisations and academic research played a role in making debates, as well as the systems in question, more visible. In three of our case studies, elected representatives made the final decision to cancel the ADMS. The ongoing struggles about whether ADMS should be used in public services are informed by competing values and political perspectives related to a number of areas: people's rights to privacy and dignity, justice as related to the right to due process, the role that labels and categories can play in stigmatisation and life chances, the need for enhancing democratic processes towards better transparency and accountability and for meaningful investigations into the impact of these kinds of systems. These struggles are an important indication of the need for more widespread debate going beyond questions of technological fixes, to ask deeper questions about politics, inequality and democratic process (Gangadharan and Jedrzej 2019; Hoffman 2020). Greater effort to politicise these debates is a necessary step to widespread and meaningful discussions about the kind of datafied societies we want to live in and the steps needed to get us there, together.

REFERENCES

AlgorithmWatch (2019) *Automating Society: Taking Stock of Automated Decision Making in the EU*. Available at https://algorithmwatch.org/en /wp-content/uploads/2019/02/Automating_Society_Report_2019.pdf (last accessed 5 January 2022).

Anderson, R., Brown, I., Clayton, R., Dowty, T., Korff, D. and Munr, E. (2006). *Children's Databases – Safety and Privacy: A Report for the Information Commissioner.* Foundation for Information Policy Research. Available at https://ora.ox.ac.uk/objects/uuid:5f8fccf1-e816-420b-a706-38074eeed6e3 /download_file?file_format=pdf&safe_filename=3878.pdf&type_of_work= Report (last accessed 5 January 2022).

Anderson, T. (2019) Gladsaxe talks about data monitoring: we want to make a 'black box'. Justitia. Available at https://www.version2.dk/artikel/gladsa xe-taler-ud-dataovervaagning-vi-vil-gerne-lave-black-box-1087552 (last accessed 5 January 2022).

Ballantyne, N. (2020) Interview. By Harry Warne. 3 July.

Beer, D. (2018) *The Data Gaze: Capitalism, Power and Perception.* London: SAGE.

Benjamin, R. (2019) *Race After Technology: Abolitionist Tools for the New Jim Code.* Cambridge: Polity Press.

Clayton, V., Sanders, M., Schoenwald, E., Surkis, L. and Gibbons, D. (2020) *Machine Learning in Children's Services Summary Report. What Works for Children's Social Care.* Available at https://whatworks-csc.org.uk/wp-con tent/uploads/WWCSC_machine_learning_in_childrens_services_does_it _work_Sep_2020_Accessible.pdf (last accessed 5 January 2022).

Dare, T. (2013) *Predictive Risk Modelling and Child Maltreatment: Ethical Challenges. Children in Crisis.* Hamilton: University of Waikato.

Dare, T., Vaithianathan, R. and de Haan, I. (2014) Addressing child maltreat-ment in New Zealand:is poverty reduction enough? *Educational Philosophy and Theory,* 46(9), 989–94. doi: 10.1080/00131857.2014.938450.

DCFS (2015) State of Illinois Contract: Rapid Safety Feedback Program. Department of Children and Family Services Contract number 5445089016.

de Haan, I. and Connolly, M. (2014) Another Pandora's box? Some pros and cons of predictive risk modeling. Children and Youth Services Review, 47(P1), 86–91.

Dencik, L., Redden, J., Hintz, A. and Warne, H. (2019) The 'golden view': data-driven governance in the scoring society. *Internet Policy Review,* 8(2). Available at https://policyreview.info/articles/analysis/golden-view-data-dr iven-governance-scoring-society (last accessed 5 January 2022).

Drake, B., Jonson-Reid, M., Gandarilla Ocampo, M., Morrison, M. and Dvalishvili, D. (2020) A practical framework for considering the use of predictive risk modeling in child welfare. *Annals of the American Academy of Political and Social Science,* 692(1), 162–81. doi: 10.1177/0002716220978 200.

Edwards, R., Gillies, V. and Gorin, S. (2021) Problem-Solving for Problem-Solving: Data Analytics to Identify Families for Service Intervention, Presentation British Sociological Association Conference. Available at https://journals.sagepub.com/doi/pdf/10.1177/02610183211020294 (last accessed 5 January 2022).

Eubanks, V. (2011) *Digital Dead End: Fighting for Social Justice in the Information Age*, Cambridge, MA: MIT Press.

Eubanks, V. (2018) *Automating Inequality*. New York: Macmillan.

Gandy, O. (2005) Data mining, surveillance, and discrimination in the post-9/11 environment. In K. D. Haggerty and R. V. Ericson (eds), *The New Politics of Surveillance and Visibility*. Toronto: University of Toronto Press, pp. 363–84.

Gangadharan, S. and Jedrzej, N. (2019) Decentering technology in discourse on discrimination. *Information, Communication & Society*, 22(7), 882–99.

Gillingham, P. (2015) Implementing electronic information systems in human service organizations: the challenge of categorization. *Practice*, 27(3), 163–75.

Gillingham, P. (2016) Predictive risk modelling to prevent child maltreatment and other adverse outcomes for service users: inside the 'black box' of machine learning. *The British Journal of Social Work*, 46(1), 1044–58.

Gillingham, P. (2019) Decision support systems, social justice and algorithmic accountability in social work: a new challenge. *Practice*, 31(4), 277–90. doi: 10.1080/09503153.2019.1575954.

Hoffman, A. (2020) Terms of inclusion: data, discourse, violence. *New Media & Society*, 23(12). doi: 10.1177/1461444820958725.

Jackson, D. and Marx, G. (2017) Data mining program designed to predict child abuse proves unreliable, DCFS says. *Chicago Tribune*, 6 December. Available at https://www.chicagotribune.com/investigations/ct-dcfs-eckerd-met-20171206-story.html (last accessed 5 January 2022).

Keddell, E. (2015) The ethics of predictive risk modelling in the Aotearoa/New Zealand child welfare context: child abuse prevention or neo-liberal tool? *Critical Social Policy*, 35(1), 69–88. doi: 10.1177/0261018314543224.

Kelly, D. (2017) Illinois drops rapid safety feedback, a predictive analytics tool. *The Imprint*, December. Available at https://imprintnews.org/politics/state line-illinois-drops-rapid-safety-feedback-predictive-analytics-tool/28913 (last accessed 5 January 2022).

Kitchin, R. and Lauriault, T. (2014) Towards critical data studies: charting and unpacking data assemblages and their work. The Programmable City Working Paper 2. Available at http://ssrn.com/abstract=2474112 (last accessed 5 January 2022).

Kjaer, J. S. (2018) The government has put its plan for monitoring families with children in the drawer. *Politiken*, 14 December.

Lyon, D. (2002) *Surveillance as Social Sorting: Privacy, Risk and Automated Discrimination*. New York: Routledge.

McIntyre, N. and Pegg, D. (2018) Councils use 377,000 people's data in efforts to predict child abuse. *The Guardian*, 16 September. Available at https://www.theguardian.com/society/2018/sep/16/councils-use-377000-peoples-data-in-efforts-to-predict-child-abuse (last accessed 5 January 2022).

Morozov, E. (2014) *To Save Everything Click Here: The Folly of Technological Solutionism*. New York: Public Affairs.

Mosco, V. (2014) *To the Cloud: Big Data in a Turbulent World*. New York: Routledge.

Munroe, E. (2010). The Munro Review of Child Protection. Part One: A Systems Analysis.Department for Education, Oct. 1. Available at https://www.gov.uk/government/publications/munro-review-of-child-protection-part-1-a-systems-analysis (last accessed 5 January 2022).

Oak, E. (2015) Methodological individualism for the twenty-first century? The neoliberal acculturation and remoralisation of the poor in Aotearoa New Zealand. *Sites: A Journal of Social Anthropology and Cultural Studies*, 12(1), 62–82.

Oak, E. (2016) A minority report for social work? The Predictive Risk Model (PRM) and the Tuituia Assessment Framework in addressing the needs of New Zealand's vulnerable children. *The British Journal of Social Work*, 46(5), 1208–23. doi: 10.1093/bjsw/bcv028.

OEIG (Office of the Executive Inspector General) (2017a) Final summary report to the Office of the Governor. 28 April. Available at https://www2.illinois.gov/oeig/investigations/documents/15-02309%20sheldon,%20anderson,%20and%20flach.pdf (last accessed 5 January 2022).

OEIG (Office of the Executive Inspector General) (2017b) Illinois Ethics Matters, OEIG Newsletter, 2 August. Available at https://www2.illinois.gov/sites/gov/transparency/OEIGMonthlyReport/OEIG%20Newsletter%20-%20August%202017.pdf (last accessed 5 January 2022).

O'Neil, C. (2016) *Weapons of Math Destruction: How Big Data Increases Inequality and Threatens Democracy*. New York: Crown Publishing.

Pasquale, F. (2015) *The Black Box Society: The Secret Algorithms That Control Money and Information*. Boston, MA: Harvard University Press.

Peckover, S., Hall, C. and White, S. (2008) From policy to practice: the implementation and negotiation of technologies in everyday child welfare. *Children & Society*, 23(2). doi: 10.1111/j.1099-0860.2008.00143.x].

Redden, J. (2020) Predictive analytics and child welfare: toward data justice. *Canadian Journal of Communication*, 45(1), 101–11. doi: 10.22230/cjc.2020v45n1a3479.

Redden, J., Brand, J., Sander, I., Warne, H., Grant, A. and White, D. (forthcoming) *Automating Public Services: Learning from Cancelled Systems*. Data Justice Lab and Carnegie UK Trust.

Redden, J., Dencik, L. and Warne, H. (2020) Datafied child welfare services:

unpacking politics, economics and power. *Policy Studies*, 41:5, 507–26. doi: 10.1080/01442872.2020.1724928.

Salganik, M. J., Lundberg, I., Kindel, A. T., Ahearn, C. E., Al-Ghoneim, K., Almaatouq, A. et al. (2020) Measuring the predictability of life outcomes with a scientific mass collaboration. *Proceedings of the National Academy of Sciences of the United States of America*, 117, 8398–403. doi: 10.1073/pnas.1915006117.

Sanders, M. (2020) Machine Learning; Now is a Time to Stop and Think, What Works for Children's Social Care. 10 September. Available at https://wh atworks-csc.org.uk/blog/machine-learning-now-is-a-time-to-stop-and-think/ (last accessed 5 January 2022).

Sheridan, E. (2019) Town Hall drops pilot programme profiling families without their knowledge. *Hackney Citizen*, 30 October. Available at https://www.hackneycitizen.co.uk/2019/10/30/town-hall-drops-pilot-program me-profiling-families-without-their-knowledge/ (last accessed 5 January 2022).

Vaithianathan, R., Maloney, T., Jiang, N., Dare, T., de Haan, I., Dale, C. and Putnam-Hornstein, E. (2012) *Vulnerable Children: Can Administrative Data Be Used to Identify Children at Risk of Adverse Outcomes?* University of Auckland, Auckland, New Zealand. Available at http://www.msd.go vt.nz/documents/about-msd-and-our-work/publications-resources/resea rch/vulnerable-children/auckland-university-can-administrative-data-be -used-to-identify-children-at-risk-of-adverse-outcome.pdf (last accessed 5 January 2022).

Vaithianathan, R., Maloney, T., Putnam-Hornstein, E. and Jiang, N. (2013) Children in the public benefit system at risk of maltreatment: identification via predictive modeling. *American Journal of Preventive Medicine*, 45(3), 354--9. doi: 10.1016/j.amepre.2013.04.022. PMID: 23953364.

White, S., Wastell, D., Broadhurst, K. and Hall, C. (2010) When policy o'erleaps itself: the 'tragic tale' of the integrated children's system. *Critical Social Policy*, 30(3), 405–29.

Wilson, M. L., Tumen, S., Ota, R. and Simmers, A. G. (2015) Predictive modeling: potential application in prevention services. *American Journal of Predictive Medicine*, 48(5), 509–19.

Wood, D. (2015) New Zealand crunches Big Data to prevent child abuse. *The Imprint*, 4 October. Available at https://imprintnews.org/featured/new -zealand-crunches-big-data-to-prevent-child-abuse/10824 (last accessed 5 January 2022).

Chapter 4

SEVEN STORIES FROM ALGORITHMWATCH

DUTCH CITY USES ALGORITHM TO ASSESS HOME VALUE,
BUT HAS NO IDEA HOW IT WORKS

by Nicolas Kayser-Bril
25 November 2020

In a seemingly routine case at the Amsterdam court of appeal, a judge ruled that it was acceptable for a municipality to use a black box algorithm, as long as the results were unsurprising.

The Magic of WOZ

In 2016, the municipality of Castricum, a seaside town of 35,000 in Holland, set the home value of an unnamed claimant at 320,000€ (in the Netherlands, property tax is paid based on a house's estimated resale value). Way too high, said the claimant, who promptly went to court.

The claimant argued that his property was damaged by an earthquake, so its resale value was much lower. Readers sitting on a seismic fault might laugh at the idea of earthquakes in Holland, but an earthquake did happen 10 km away from Castricum on 30 January 1997 – magnitude two. The municipality offered nine times to visit the house to assess the damage but the claimant declined, citing concerns over his freedom. The Amsterdam court of appeal logically upheld the municipality's assessment in a ruling last February.

The interesting part of the trial lies in the assessed value of a property at €320,000. Dutch municipalities have to estimate the value of properties every year, by law. The law in question is abbreviated to WOZ, leading the Dutch to speak of 'WOZ value' for the estimate. The valuation chamber oversees the processes that take place at the municipality level.

According to an official from the valuation chamber, almost all municipalities rely on tools from five companies to assess the WOZ value, which use clear statistical methods. While some municipalities experiment with artificial intelligence (AI), he was not aware that any such model was used to compute the actual WOZ values. The valuation chamber instructs municipalities to ensure that their models are explainable, and does not allow the use of black box models, the official added. But before the Amsterdam court of appeal, when the claimant demanded to be told how the valuation of €320,000 was arrived at, the municipality was unable to answer. Not because it did not want to, but because it could not.

Whitewashing the Black Box

Under Dutch case law and GDPR (General Data Protection Regulation), a public body must be able to provide the details and mechanisms that led to an automated decision. The court took note of the municipality's breach of the law and ordered them to pay the court costs.

Nevertheless, the court proceeded to explain why the €320,000 valuation was correct. Following the municipality's argument, the judge looked at properties that were sold around 2016 in the vicinity and found the price per square metre to match with the algorithmically generated value for the house of the claimant. The latter maintained that his house was in much worse shape and thus less expensive; the municipality answered that this information was already included in the computations (the main bone of contention was the extent of the earthquake damage).

A Dangerous Precedent

For Marlies van Eck, an assistant professor at Radboud University who specialises in the legal aspects of AI use, the Dutch supreme court set a principle that automated decisions should be explainable. Under this principle, the assessment of the municipality should have been annulled. 'We now learned that if the principle is not met, it has no legal consequences,' she added. The decision, which will not go to the Dutch supreme court, could set a precedent whereby judges accept results from black box algorithms as long as they seem reasonable, she told AlgorithmWatch.

While the ruling is unlikely to have serious consequences now (the complainant even belatedly invited the municipality to visit his house), it could hint at a dramatic turn in Dutch administrative law, Ms Van Eck said. Black box algorithms that have legal consequences are, in theory, prohibited under current law, but the approach of the Amsterdam court of appeal would make them acceptable.

IN FRENCH DAYCARE, ALGORITHMS ATTEMPT TO FIGHT CRONYISM

by Alexandre Léchenet
18 September 2020

In many French cities, it is unclear whose children can hope for a place in a public daycare facility. Algorithms could make the allocation of places more transparent, but not all politicians are happy.

For new parents in France, getting their newborn into the public daycare system can feel like a class in the dark arts. Cronyism, or simply the suspicion thereof, is rampant in a country where there are fewer than two daycare places per ten children under the age of three. In an (admittedly biased) poll conducted in 2013 by Maman Travaille ('Mum works'), a non-profit organisation that helps mothers in paid employment, French mothers cited luck, chance and pulling strings as the best way to get a spot in daycare.

An investigation by BuzzFeed News in 2016 in Boulogne-Billancourt, a city of 120,000 bordering Paris, revealed widespread cronyism. Several parents testified that they had to personally call the elected official in charge of daycare if they were to stand a chance of getting the coveted daycare slot.

In Paris itself, the regional court of auditors discovered in 2017 that in some districts allocation was made during meetings where elected officials shared handwritten notes. In some cases, officials wrote that the parents were not voters in the district, or described the family's situation ('two mothers' or 'undocumented father'). Such comments were probably not intended to speed up the parents' requests. The auditors recommended the use of a transparent allocation system based on the daycare management software already in use in other districts.

Dog Connection

In another town, parents were convinced that only dog owners could obtain a place, because the mayor was a veterinarian. This story is one of many collected by Elisabeth Laithier, the former deputy mayor of Nancy, a large city in eastern France. She wrote a report on daycare allocation in 2018 for the French mayors association (known as AMF).

In her report, she recommended that criteria for the allocation of daycare slots be made transparent, that the wishes of parents be given more weight and that the names of people sitting in committees deciding on daycare places be made public.

A few dozen cities acted upon these recommendations and are now more transparent. They publish a detailed list of the sorting criteria and give precise information about the allocation process. Most of them use a mix of variables related to the children, such as their age or their disabilities, and variables related to the parents (employment situation, income, address etc.). Each criterion is associated with a number of points, which allow city officials to rank the requests by order of priority and offer daycare slots accordingly. Half of Paris districts signed a transparency charter, stating that each parent should be informed of the allocation process, with transparent criteria.

Such decision making fits the definition of an algorithm: unambiguous instructions that produce a certain output from a given input. However, Ms Laithier notes, allocation committees always make the final decision because, she thinks, some situations require a human input (placing siblings in the same facility, for example).

Randomised Controlled Trials

In Valence, a city 100 kilometres south of Lyons, allocation of daycare slots went a step further. Researchers from the national agency for family welfare (CNAF) are studying the impact of daycare on child development. They wanted to make a randomised controlled trial, but giving places in daycare at random was not possible. Instead, they focused on the first children on the waiting list: random choices would be made for families with the same priority score.

The algorithm was developed in partnership with the municipality, and mostly involved converting criteria that were already in use into a computer program. The researchers then used the 'student optimal fair matching' algorithm, which ensures that no student who prefers a school to her outcome will be rejected while another student with lower priority is matched to the school. Because the allocation committee could not meet due to the pandemic, the allocation was done entirely by the machine, in May. The use of automated decision making, a first in France, was made transparent to families, as is required under French and European law.

Fear of Losing Grip

However, some city officials are concerned that the decision-making power is being taken out of their hands. This feeling can be stronger in small towns, where daycare management is already shifting from the municipality to the inter-municipality, a higher administrative level.

'The daycare allocation of places is in our scope. If computers sort out the demands, what are we going to do?', wonders Philippe Goujon, mayor for the 15th district of Paris, in defence of his old-fashioned, handwritten and opaque system. In her report published by the mayors' association, Ms Laithier warned against the use of computers. They 'are not able to grasp the specificity of each situation, and could leave out families that do not meet the required criteria'. Ms Laithier makes it clear: 'Even though elected officials keep deciding on the allocation criteria, there's a reluctance from the elected officials to see the political decision-making process being replaced by a machine.'

SUZHOU INTRODUCED A NEW SOCIAL SCORING SYSTEM, BUT IT WAS TOO ORWELLIAN, EVEN FOR CHINA

by Qian Sun
14 September 2020

A city of 10 million in eastern China upgraded its COVID-19 tracking app to introduce a new 'civility' score. It had to backtrack after a public outcry.

Suzhou is a city with a population of 10 million, located 100 kilometres west of Shanghai. It is well known for its classic Chinese gardens and now for one of the most Orwellian social scoring experiments to date.

The municipal government launched a pilot for a new social behaviour scoring system on 3 September 2020, also referred to as the 'civility score'. It is built on top of the current 'health code', a three-color scale used nationwide that decides whether or not an individual has the right to travel and enter public spaces (the health code is thought to be based on people's health condition and travel history, but the system is reported to collect more data than just health information and travel routes).

According to Suzhou's local media, the 'civility score' is the first in the country. The civility point system is constructed to form a 'personal portrait' of a citizen's social behaviours. It is reported by the state media CETV to be an attempt to advance the implementation of the social credit system – a comprehensive set of databases and initiatives to monitor and rate the trustworthiness of individuals. The social credit system is planned by the government to be rolled out by the end of 2020 (AlgorithmWatch published a report on the topic in October 2019).

A Criminal Record, for Non-Criminals

Several Chinese media outlets, like *thepaper.cn* and *Nanfang Metropolis Daily*, reported on Suzhou's new system. Individuals start with a score of 1,000 points. Violation of traffic rules and bad road manners can result in negative points and volunteer activities are rewarded with positive points.

Local officials said the score would increase social courtesy, civilised dining and online behaviour. According to an article published on the WeChat account of Suzhou's police department, the civility score could serve as a digital 'reference' for future warning or punishment. It is unclear what a 'reference' would be, and what it could be used for.

Worried that 'civility' was too loosely defined and that the system could lead to abuses of power, many took to the Internet to express their concerns. The initiative was criticised on Weibo (a Chinese microblogging platform and one of the few outlets where netizens can still vent their frustrations) as 'classifying people based on unquantifiable standards' or 'imposing public power in private and moral realms'. Xian-based lawyer Yang Hui drew comparisons with the 'good citizen certificate' (*liangmin zheng*) – a document that the Japanese army issued in occupied China during the Second World War.

Ramming Through Digitisation

It is not the first time that Suzhou authorities' attempts at digitisation have sparked controversy. In most parts of China, the 'health code' is a built-in function on WeChat and Alipay – two mobile phone applications that practically dominate the life of most Chinese. Some cities, like Suzhou, went one step further: they developed new mobile applications that combine the health code and other digital identities, such as the national ID, the resident's permit and the driver's licence.

According to the Suzhou municipal government, the aim of the 'Suzhou app' is to make the life of citizens easier by storing all digital credentials in one place. Use of the Suzhou app is supposed to be voluntary, but on Weibo, a search with the keyword 'Suzhou app' shows citizens reporting 'bad user experiences'. One said: 'I have to download the app and show the code from the app in order to pick up my kids from the kindergarten.'

Although the Suzhou app was met with moderate resistance from citizens, it was also accepted by many. A local resident from Suzhou, who wanted to be identified just as Quan, told AlgorithmWatch that the Suzhou app was a localised service provided by the government, and that it caters to the needs of different demographic groups compared to the apps from Alipay or WeChat. The Suzhou app also tracks where people have been, and individuals are occasionally required to show their travel route in order to access certain indoor amenities.

Suzhou App 2.0

The 'Suzhou app 2.0', with its new feature of 'civility score', has caused a much more public backlash. The trial was terminated after only three days. Local authorities explained in an interview that the system still required improvements, and that once it was rolled out, participation would not be mandatory.

Shanghai-based lawyer Shu Shengxiang commented on his social media account that no public consultation was made before the introduction of the 'health code', but that it was done in the context of an emergency (the pandemic). It is a short-term solution for the benefit of many, but it cannot become a widespread practice, he wrote.

Zhu Lijia, a public management expert at the Chinese Academy of

Governance in Beijing, said that the discussion of the civility score is a reminder of how far societal governance can go. 'I understand the reaction of the common people,' he said. 'The "civility score" exposes the privacy of the masses.'

SPAIN'S LARGEST BUS TERMINAL DEPLOYED LIVE FACE RECOGNITION FOUR YEARS AGO, BUT FEW NOTICED

by Naiara Bellio López-Molina
11 August 2020

Madrid's South Bus Station's face recognition system automatically matches every visitor's face against a database of suspects, and shares information with the Spanish police.

Around 20 million travellers transited last year through Madrid's South bus terminal, known as Méndez Álvaro Station to locals. Those 20 million persons had their faces scanned as they entered the station. They were tracked as they walked to the bay where their bus was parked, before leaving the Spanish capital – unless the station's face detection system produced an alert and they were arrested.

The terminal is a key transport exchange not only for Madrid, but for the whole country. It connects with subway stations and with Renfe, the national train service. Until 2010, the terminal did not have a security unit that was specifically tasked with coordinating the response to petty crime.

Running since 2016

The station is one of the few public buildings in Spain that has deployed a live face recognition system. Miguel Angel Gallego, the station's chief of security between 2010 and 2019, decided to deploy face recognition after he was contacted by a Spanish start-up organisation working with this type of software in 2016.

Mr Gallego faced an uphill battle. The Spanish police, who were not used to face recognition at the time, were not enthusiastic, and neither was Avanza ADO, the company that has been running the bus terminal since 2003. But he remained undeterred. The technology has been running for four years, without much scrutiny from privacy organisations or from the state.

A Question of Consent

I went to Madrid's South Bus Station. Not many people seemed aware of the face recognition system. Not even the people running small stores inside the station seemed to know that the face recognition system had already been operating for four years.

A jeweller, a person working in a profession that requires a keen sense of security, told me she did not know such technology was operating inside the building. She had been working at the store, which she owned, since 2014.

One of her neighbours, an older woman who has been selling pastries at the bus terminal for the past sixteen years, said she felt there were more security guards in the station, but she also said, while knocking on wood, that her store had always been free from theft.

Claiming Success

The firm behind the software that runs the bus terminal's face recognition system is Barcelona-based Herta Security, which has since expanded to Los Angeles, Montevideo and Singapore. Another company, Axis Communications, installed the hardware. Both companies are keen to stress that security at the bus station has improved since the system was deployed.

In 2019, Herta Security released a report, which AlgorithmWatch was given access to, detailing the 'successful case' that the station represented. According to the numbers provided by the operators of the station, incidents in its facilities have decreased by 75 per cent. A report by Axis Communications claims that the number of incidents went from 'five a day to five a month' after the system was deployed, but provides no detailed data.

Laura Blanc, Chief Marketing Officer at Herta Security, claims that cases of vandalism started to diminish when the face recognition system started in 2016. She considers that this kind of surveillance alone is effective at chasing away delinquents that mug and bother people at the station. Once experience tells you that you are getting caught in a specific place, it seems a good reason to reconsider if you still want to rob inside it or move on to the next building and commit crime in another place, Ms Blanc told AlgorithmWatch. The system is believed to act like a scarecrow in a garden, whether it gives positive results or not. (Ms Blanc did not provide an explanation for why shop owners had failed to see the scarecrow.)

Nine Cameras

Although the station has around 100 surveillance cameras, only nine are used by the face recognition system. They are deployed at strategic points in the facilities, such as entrance and exit points and connections with subway tunnels, Ms Blanc told AlgorithmWatch.

The cameras record constantly. The software analyses the video feed in real time, taking a snapshot of people's faces every time they enter the frame. The images are analysed in the operational centre, which was created between 2014 and 2016 as part of several improvements at the Méndez Álvaro station to increase safety, including changes to the building's layout and better lighting. In the centre, screens show the live video feeds from the surveillance cameras. One screen in particular is split ito two halves: the left side is constantly running the live recordings, displaying a column with snapshots of the faces of people that walk through the station. If there is a 'match' with one of the images stored in the database of suspects, an alarm pops up on the right half of the screen, alerting operators that an identification has been made.

Fifty Per Cent Certainty

The software gives a score from 0 to 100 to each match, indicating its reliability. In what seems a logical contortion, Ms Blanc says that a score of 50–60 per cent means that 'the system is sure about it'. Operators can adjust the percentage as they wish.

By raising the percentage threshold, operators limit the number of possible false positives that the system will generate (people who are mistaken for faces in the database). Conversely, this increases the number of possible false negatives (people who are in the database but are not matched). Human operators then decide whether or not to stop the person whose face produced a match.

Face Masks

Officials from the bus terminal did not comment on how the system currently works, as the COVID-19 pandemic limited citizens' movements and face masks limit face recognition technologies.

Even so, Ms Blanc insists on the system's efficacy: 'In March, we launched a new algorithm that allowed face recognition even though the person exhibited a big occlusion in the face, like a mask. We were already developing it before the coronavirus pandemic because we have clients in Asia, for example, where wearing one is usual. We also work in football stadiums, where people usually wear caps, scarfs, etc.'

She admits that working in such environments is 'difficult' because the less information you have in the video feed, the less accuracy you have for the identification. Nevertheless, she states that they managed to overcome this problem and, because the pandemic has made face masks compulsory in closed public spaces, there were 'even more reasons to commercialize it'.

City Transit Stops Face Recognition

Other operators of face recognition systems reacted differently to the pandemic. Madrid's city council suspended a pilot project where people were invited to pay using face recognition on some buses of the city's public transit network. It was announced in late 2019, but recent rules making face masks compulsory inside public transport in Madrid forced the authorities to call a halt to the project, claiming that the system is not yet perfected to recognise individuals when wearing a mask.

Operators at Madrid's Méndez Álvaro Station declined to provide AlgorithmWatch with precise data, or an audit, which would show that their system performs well with people wearing face masks.

A Private–Public Partnership

At the Méndez Álvaro Station, a pilot study was conducted before the system was deployed in 2016, in order to test its effectiveness. But a source with detailed knowledge of the operation, who asked not to be named, said the pilot had a second goal: training the program itself. Employees from the security department of Madrid's South bus terminal would upload pictures of themselves to the database of suspects wearing caps, glasses, scarfs and so forth in order to test the system and fine-tune it.

Despite their initial reluctance, both the company running the bus terminal and the police, who have a presence in the building, changed their minds about the system once it was installed.

The security team of Méndez Álvaro Station realised that cooperation with the national police was essential for the system to run properly. Law enforcement agencies provide the station's security centre with the details of people with outstanding warrants, and the station alerts the police when a match occurs. (This procedure is reserved for dangerous criminals or terrorists, whose pictures are sometimes made available by Interpol.)

However, the database holds more than pictures of suspects with outstanding arrest warrants. Some of the pictures it holds come from recordings from the surveillance cameras at the station itself. If a person is caught committing theft, he or she can be identified in video recordings and their face can then be incorporated to the database, so that the software can spot them across the station – even if the case has not been decided by a judge.

According to our source, in some cases a police officer comes to the station and asks for personal information about the people that the security department catalogues independently. In other words, the police can rely on matches obtained using biometric data that includes information on people selected with absolute discretion by a private company.

Lost Children

The surveillance system deployed at the Méndez Álvaro station works in real time, but it can also be used on past video footage.

This is how the security centre exploits the 'social' objective of automated surveillance, as Mr Gallego, the former head of security, described it. 'The face recognition system is not only used to prevent crime, but also with a social objective: looking for lost children, people with Alzheimer and other collaborations with the security forces in something that goes beyond common vandalism,' he said in a recorded interview for Herta Security in 2019.

A mother went to the police one day, saying that her daughter had disappeared from home and that there was a chance she had run to the station to catch a bus. The station's security told her to bring a picture of the girl. (Our source did not provide details such as the precise date of the event.)

Her image was introduced into the database and automatically scanned through the morning's video recordings. Even though they estimated that the girl could have arrived at the station at around 11 a.m., the system found her wandering in the building at 9:10 a.m. They virtually followed her trip through the facilities and saw which adults she had spoken to and what bus she had taken. The police were able to stop the bus she caught and bring the girl home. People who ran the system at the time said this would never have happened if they had had to check manually all the video recordings of that morning.

Security Justifies the Means

The system is based on the defence of public and legitimate interest, two grounds that count as special conditions in the General Data Protection Regulation (GDPR). This provides the station's operators with a large margin of discretion within which to act, according to Rahul Uttamchandani, a data protection lawyer working for the Spanish law firm Legal Army.

'If images used in the database are from people that are being pursued by the justice authorities, then they are protected by public interest,' he states. The fact that GDPR entered into force in 2018, two years after the system was started, did not make a huge difference, according to the people who built the system: they justify its use in maintaining 'public interest' in terms of security.

The use of personal data involved in surveillance made by law enforcement agencies is subjected to Directive 2016/680, which was approved in 2016 along with GDPR. But Spain has yet to transpose it into national law, although the deadline to do so was May 2018.

The main problem Mr Uttamchandani sees is that the snapshots that the cameras take of every single face that enters the station could be used to train the system. 'People need to know all the finalities of a treatment of their biometric data and when you pass by a surveillance camera you can think that you are being observed or they are recording, but you cannot know that the shape and points of your face are being used to build a better technological model,' he said.

Sources contacted by AlgorithmWatch said that the snapshots of people's faces who are not flagged as thieves are kept for thirty days with the original recordings and then erased, as is legally required.

Operating in the Shadows

Very few concerns have been raised since automated surveillance was first deployed at the South Station. AEPD, the Spanish Data Protection Authority, is not aware of any complaint on the matter, according to a statement to AlgorithmWatch.

The Méndez Álvaro Station kept silent for the whole period during which this article was written, alleging that the system is catalogued as a 'critical infrastructure' and that therefore no information about it can be disclosed. This argument is quite disingenuous, given that plenty of interviews and infomercials have been published in the media and in Herta's and Axis's official channels since 2016.

An infrastructure being 'critical' under Spanish regulation means that it is considered a strategic technological installation that functions as an essential service and that no alternative can achieve the same purpose. Therefore, its destruction or perturbation would lead to 'a great impact over essential services'. Citizen security is among 'essential services', according to the law.

Despite twelve days of practically daily calls to the Administration and Communication departments of the Méndez Álvaro Station and four emails, the station's personnel did not answer our questions. The head of station's administration repeatedly assured us that we would be attended to by the chief operator, which never happened. Instead, one of the operators called my number during his holidays to state that they would not disclose any information and that that was all he had to say to me. No further questions.

Face Recognition in the Supermarket

Just a few weeks ago, the supermarket chain Mercadona announced the installation of live face recognition in forty stores in three cities in order to keep suspected thieves from entering. The announcement provoked an immediate response. The media asked questions (few were answered), privacy experts openly wondered if the surveillance was legal and the Spanish data protection authority, AEPD, announced an inquiry into the issue.

Few details are available about Mercadona's face recognition system. Some media reported that Mercadona would build their own database of thieves based on the footage they captured in their stores.

ESTONIA: A CITY IS AUTOMATING HOMES TO REDUCE ENERGY CONSUMPTION

by Gerda Kelly Pill
26 May 2020

The city of Tartu installed automated systems in old housing blocks. Using nudges, sensors and automated decision making, it hopes to reduce energy consumption by two thirds.

SmartEnCity is a Europe-wide project that aims to transform cities to become carbon neutral. Tartu, a small campus town in Estonia, home to around 100,000 people, is one of the 'demonstrator cities' for this project, which it called Tark Tartu (Smart Tartu). As part of this project, the city introduced a public bike-sharing system, bought gas-powered buses and implemented automated LED streetlights that take into account local weather and traffic conditions to adjust lighting levels. They are also retrofitting Soviet-era 'khrushchyovkas' into 'smart-ovkas'. This means turning old concrete-panel apartment blocks into modernised, 'smart' living spaces.

Khrushchyovkas dot the cityscape of most former Soviet countries. In Estonia, they are an integral part of many neighbourhoods. They have housed several generations, although they were originally built to last fifty years – an estimate that was revised upwards by successive governments. The buildings are now thought to be fit for another half-century if properly renovated.

These concrete-panel apartment buildings were built between the 1950s and early 1970s, when Nikita Khrushchev was the first secretary of the Communist Party of the Soviet Union, hence their nickname 'khrushchyovkas'. They were easy and cheap to build, and millions of people still call them home.

In 1991, Estonia became independent from the Soviet Union, society moved on, the economy grew, cities developed, but the khrushchyovkas stayed. They are not without problems: heating is expensive because of sub-par insulation, poor ventilation and deteriorating plumbing. Many of these buildings have not been fully renovated since they were built.

Renovating a whole apartment building to bring it up to current standards is no easy task. It requires a lot of work and money, and the responsibility usually falls on the inhabitants. Khrushchyovkas house families of different sizes and types, people young and old from all walks of life. Some of them have been there since the beginning. Due to lack of funds, leadership or perhaps opportunity, khrushchyovkas are in less-than-prime condition although they sit on prime locations in Tartu.

Automated Homes

Taking the opportunity of European funding, some of these buildings were drafted to a pilot programme that promised to make them energy-efficient, high-quality living environments, with embedded, automated systems.

Taking a closer look, the reality is far from a futuristic ultra-modern automated smart home, but the project is a work in progress and the real results will become clearer in the years to come. The goal is to renovate and 'smart up' seventeen apartment buildings located in the centre of Tartu. The systems are still being developed and perfected.

There are already tangible results. 'Of course, I'm happy. The heating bills are lower, and I do not have to report my warm water and gas usage manually anymore,' said Anatoli, whose house was renovated as part of the project in the summer of last year. 'My home is finished, and everything works. But in some apartments, gas and electricity consumption indicators are still not showing,' he added.

Energy Efficiency

'The goal is to get the building's energy rating as good as possible, and for that the inhabitants have to contribute with their behaviour,' said Tõnis Eelma, who is one of the project's leads and the chairman of the apartment association of his building, which was the second block to be renovated as a part of the project.

'Every apartment has a tablet attached to their wall where they can monitor their consumption and we hope that, based on that information, people adjust their habits,' said Mr Eelma. The ultimate goal is to lower the building's yearly energy usage down from the current 270 kWh/m^2 to 90kWh/m^2.

'One of the most revolutionary things is our demand-driven central ventilation system. This means that the carbon dioxide levels are measured and the influx of fresh air to your apartment is regulated automatically,' said Mr Eelma. The solution is quite unique, as usually renovated apartment buildings get a certain amount of fresh air throughout the day regardless whether you are home. The other option is that there are set ventilation intervals, which only take into account people's nine-to-five working schedule, not the schedule of those who are at home all day, such as the elderly.

Raivo Raestik is the CEO of Enlife, the company that won the tender for developing the smart home systems for the 'smartovkas'. He explained that these tablets enable two main things for the inhabitants: monitoring information about themselves and controlling their indoor climate. The system records electricity, water and gas usage for each apartment and uploads it to a cloud environment, where it can be exchanged with various stakeholders, such as the city of Tartu.

Users can view their usage statistics, the current and desired inside temperature for all the rooms, CO_2 levels (measured in parts per million) and the outside air temperature. They can also check the time and greet guests through an intercom system. And if they previously had to state their hot water and gas usage to the utilities company, it is now read remotely automatically.

Ten out of the seventeen buildings opted to have their building upgraded with radio connections as opposed to cable connections, meaning that their sensors are all wireless. Smart home systems also allow the user to check battery levels for those remote sensors, such as the smoke alarm or thermostat. Users can control the temperature and ventilation and monitor their statistics through the tablet installed in the apartments, through a computer–web interface or a smartphone app. Control over ventilation was given to the inhabitants in case they are not happy with the level of fresh air input chosen by the system.

Nudges

Seeing statistics is part of raising energy consumption awareness. Tõnis Eelma said that in the future they would like to offer the option to compare an apartment's energy usage to that of the rest of the building. The building would then get an average, which in turn could be compared to the other renovated houses in the project, which could introduce an element of competition.

But it might not be so simple, due to people's different ways of living and thinking. 'We are still discussing what to compare and with whom,' said Mr Raestik. 'The first comparisons were made with the building's average,' he said. Those statistics were generated by the sum of all apartments' usage. 'But the apartments are very different. You can have an elderly person living alone or big families – that's apples and oranges. If you see that your usage is +156 per cent of the average, then that does not motivate you to save energy.' EnLife is, as an alternative, looking to develop a statistical comparison with the user's own past behaviour. 'But that also needs some thought because you cannot indefinitely lower your energy consumption – you still need some level for your basic activities. We do not want people to get discouraged when they cannot lower their energy usage levels anymore.'

However, the development is still in progress. Mr Raestik said that one of the next items on the list is to deliver automated scheduling for temperature levels, so that people can have lower temperatures during the night without having to manually change it from the system's interface.

In addition to the smart home system, the houses were fitted with solar panels, insulation for the walls and roof, a new heating and plumbing system, new windows and outside doors.

Unique Solution

There has never been a solution like this in the market. In Estonia, smart homes have the reputation of being expensive and complex, and not many people have these solutions in their home unless already built in by the developer. Retrofitting homes to become smart is not so common. The SmartEnCity project ordered a one-size-fit-all solution. EnLife started developing it for about 600 apartments. They designed everything in a way that allows for retrofitting all the apartments in case of future changes, because the smart home system is evolving together with the SmartEnCity project.

Comparing this smart home system to Apple Home, Samsung SmartThings or Google Nest, Mr Eelma said that there were two main differences: those solutions would have not fitted their budget and they do not focus on energy consumption. The goal of the project is to raise awareness among people about their habits and inspire them to change their behaviour to save energy.

Mr Raestik added that when you create a smart home system on such a large scale, you must consider technical support and continuous updates for as long as the building stands. 'In my experience with big players, as time goes by, tech-support for older versions gets discontinued,' he said.

The city's total investment to retrofit seventeen buildings is around €9 million, plus €400,000 to develop the smart home solution. The exact cost of each building's renovation depends on a tender. 'Our house had 32 apartments and the renovations cost over a million euros. We had to cover around half of that by taking out a loan,' said Mr Eelma. Using Horizon 2020 funds, the city of Tartu helped cover 25 per cent of the total cost and the rest came from a national renovation grant.

Reduced Costs

The first results show that, on average, heating bills have been cut in half. 'We were hoping that they come down to one third of the original cost, but we must consider that before heat was only used to warm up radiators in apartments. Now, in addition to that, it heats up water and air in the central ventilation system,' said Mr Eelma. 'But the monetary win is small, because while we can save from consuming less energy, the loan payments don't get any lower,' he said.

The renovations came with some conditions. For example, installing solar panels was mandatory in order to provide additional energy to the buildings. Additionally, while all the generated energy consumption data belongs to the inhabitants themselves, they have an obligation to share it (in an aggregated format) with the city of Tartu until 2021 to measure the effectiveness of the renovation programme.

'It is a great project; we are testing a lot of new things. But it is not ready yet – fine tuning the houses' systems to lower costs is still ongoing,' said Mr Eelma. With four years and some results already under its belt, this ambitious project hopes to prove that when you give people the opportunity to monitor their energy consumption behaviour, they will change their habits to save energy in the long run. You can only improve what you can measure.

UNCHECKED USE OF COMPUTER VISION BY POLICE CARRIES HIGH RISKS OF DISCRIMINATION

28 April 2020
by Nicolas Kayser-Bril

At least eleven local police forces in Europe use computer vision to automatically analyse images from surveillance cameras. The risks of discrimination run high but authorities ignore them.

Pedestrians and motorists in some streets of Warsaw, Mannheim, Toulouse and Kortrijk are constantly monitored for abnormal behaviour. Police in these cities, and many others, connected the video feeds of surveillance cameras to automated systems that claim to detect suspicious movements, such as driving in bus lanes, theft, assault or the coalescence of aggressive groups.

All automated surveillance techniques in use in the cities listed in Table 4.1 rely on machine learning. This approach requires that soft-

Table 4.1 At least eleven cities use automated surveillance in the EU.

Country	City	Vendor	Comment
Belgium	Brussels	One Télécom	Detection of illegal trash dumps, theft.
Belgium	Kortrijk	BriefCam	Null
Czech Republic	Prostejov	BriefCam	Null
Czech Republic	Prague	BriefCam	Tender in process.
Germany	Mannheim	Frauenhofer IOSB	Detection of body movements that constitute assault.
Spain	Marbella	Avigilon	Null
France	Nîmes	BriefCam	Null
France	Nice	Two-I	Not implemented yet.
France	Cannes	Datakalab	Detects if pedestrians wear face masks.
France	Roubaix	BriefCam	Null
France	Marseilles	Snef	Null
France	Toulouse	IBM	Null
France	Yvelines	null	Surveillance of high schools and one fire station.
Poland	Warsaw	BriefCam	Null

ware developers feed large amounts of scenes depicting normality, and others representing situations considered abnormal, to computer programs. The programs are then tasked with finding patterns that are specific to each type of situation.

Spurious Correlations

Machine learning has many applications that are now routinely used, such as reverse image search or automated translation. But the drawbacks of this technique are well known. The software does not understand a situation in the human sense; it only finds inferences in the data it has been given. This is why, after decades of controversy, Google Translate still renders the gender-neutral 'they are doctors' in German as 'sie sind Ärtze' (masculine) and 'they are nurses' as 'sie sind Krankenschwestern' (feminine). Google Translate was not programmed to be sexist. The corpus of texts it received happened to contain more instances of male doctors and female nurses.

What is true of automated translation is true of automated image recognition, known as computer vision. On 7 April 2020, AlgorithmWatch revealed that Google Vision, an image labelling service, classified a thermometer as a 'tool' in a hand that had a light skin tone, and 'gun' in a dark-skinned one (see Figure 4.1). (Google has since changed their system.)

Spurious correlations can have several causes, according to Agathe Balayn, a PhD candidate at the Delft University of Technology working on the topic of bias in automated systems, but most of them likely stem from the training datasets. Computer vision systems rely on the manual annotation of millions of images. This work is often done by workers paid a few cents for each task. They have strong incentives to be fast and to conform to the expectations of their clients, Ms Balayn wrote to AlgorithmWatch. Diversity and subtlety in the training dataset suffer as a result.

Misconceptions

AlgorithmWatch asked several vendors of computer vision solutions to police forces what training data they used, and how they ensured that their programs were not discriminatory.

A spokesperson for BriefCam, which is used by police forces from

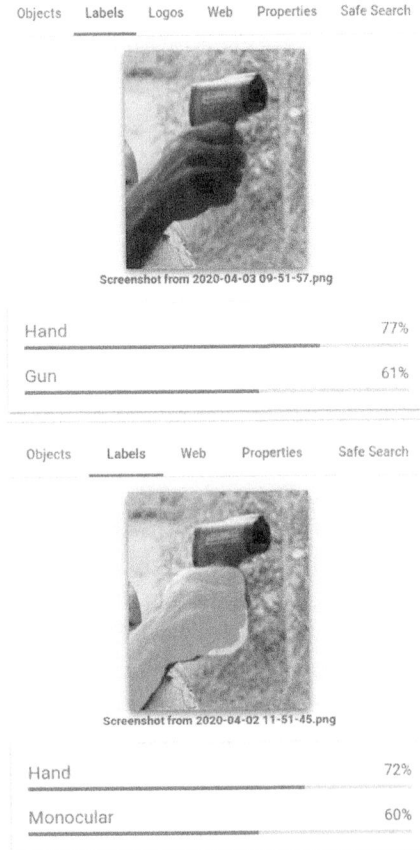

Figure 4.1 On 3 April 2020, Google Vision Cloud produced starkly different labels for a thermometer after an overlay was added

Warsaw to Roubaix, stated in an email that because the software did not use skin tone as a variable, it could not discriminate. This is a commonly held misconception. Machine learning software is designed to find patterns that are not specified by their programmers in order to achieve their results. This is why Google Translate produces sexist outcomes and Google Vision produces racist outcomes even though they were not explicitly programmed to take into account gender or skin tone.

BriefCam's spokesperson added that they used 'training datasets consisting of multi-gender, multi-age and multi-race samples without minority bias', but declined to provide any evidence or details.

The police force of Etterbek, in Brussels, uses computer vision to automatically spot illegal trash disposal. A spokesperson for the city wrote that the system did not take skin tone or any other individual trait into account, but failed to provide any information about the training dataset their software was built on.

A spokesperson for Frauenhofer IOSB, which powers the automated surveillance of Mannheim, Germany, claimed that their software could not be discriminatory because it relied on a three-dimensional modelling of body shapes. It analysed movements, not images, and therefore did not use skin tone, he added. Details on the training dataset and its diversity were not provided.

Avigilon declined to comment. One Télécom, Two-I and Snef did not reply to numerous emails.

Invisible Issue

Automated surveillance is hard to detect. Police forces have no obligation to disclose that they use it and the calls for tenders are rarely published. In Poland, for instance, AlgorithmWatch was told that any information on the issue was 'confidential'. The details of their automated surveillance operation were only available in an article in their internal publication, *Police Magazine*, which is available online.

This invisibility makes it hard for civil society organisations to weigh in. AlgorithmWatch spoke to several anti-discrimination organisations at the local and national level. While their spokespersons acknowledged the importance of the issue, they said they could not address it for lack of awareness among the population and for a lack of monitoring tools. Meanwhile, automated surveillance has the potential to dramatically increase discriminatory policing practices.

Unaudited

How much automated surveillance impacts discrimination in policing is not known. None of the vendors or cities AlgorithmWatch contacted conducted audits to ensure that the output of their systems was the same for all citizens.

Nicole Romain, spokesperson for the Agency for Fundamental Rights of the European Union, wrote that any institution deploying such technologies should conduct a 'comprehensive fundamental rights impact assessment to identify potential biases'. When it came to computer vision in policing, she was not aware that any such assessment had ever been made.

CENTRAL AUTHORITIES SLOW TO REACT AS SWEDEN'S CITIES EMBRACE AUTOMATION OF WELFARE MANAGEMENT

by Katarina Lind and Leo Wallentin
17 March 2020

Trelleborg is Sweden's front-runner in automating welfare distribution. An analysis of the system's source code brought little transparency – but revealed that the personal data of hundreds was wrongly made public.

Trelleborg is a city of 40,000 in Sweden's far south. Three years ago, it became the first municipality to introduce fully automated decision making in its social services. They named their robot Ernst and introduced it as a digital co-worker.

Sweden's social services are governed by local authorities. The 1992 Local Government Act gave decisionary powers to municipal committees, but this right can be delegated to an employee. With the exception of Trelleborg and their lawyers, all other instances assess that delegating decision making to an automated system is not allowed, and therefore automated decision making is not compatible with the law.

The same does not apply to state agencies. In 2018, automated decisions were allowed after a change in the Administrative Procedure Act (Förvaltningslagen), the law that regulates governmental agencies. Welfare payments such as parental benefits and dental care subsidies are now allocated without any human intervention.

Full Automation

Trelleborg uses a process known as robotic automation, or RPA, to handle applications for financial aid. The software is based on different rules that lead to a *yes* or *no* decision.

The first time Trelleborg residents apply for financial aid, they meet a caseworker in person. After that, they must reapply every month, and if they apply online, the decision will be made by a machine. They fill in details on their income and expenses, which the RPA compares with the previous month. It also pulls information such as tax and income statements and student loans from a database that gathers personal data from seven agencies, for controlling purposes. A decision is then made based on these data points.

Should the applicant's situation significantly change from one month to the next, the software stops and forwards the application to a human caseworker. Around one in three reapplications are currently handled by the software. The rest is treated by caseworkers because of circumstances the software cannot handle.

Because every beneficiary meets a caseworker the first time they apply and new circumstances are checked by a human being, there is always an individual assessment made, Ms Schlyter said.

Saving Time

The main reason for deploying RPA was to save time and relocate resources to meet people instead of handling documents, according to Ms Schlyter. It also shortens the time that beneficiaries have to wait to obtain a decision, as decisions that previously could have taken two days can now be reached in less than a minute.

The introduction of the RPA and the relocation of staff also led to lower payments for the municipality, she said.

During the last few years, many towns started using online applications for welfare distribution, a first step towards automating the process. A report by the Board of Health and Welfare (*Socialstyrelsen*), a national authority, showed that the number of municipalities that introduced online applications for welfare had more than tripled over the last three years, from 9 per cent in 2017 to 29 per cent in 2019.

Another report, published in November 2019 by the Swedish Association of Local Authorities and Regions (SKR), showed that the trend continued upwards, with 36 per cent of municipalities saying that they used online application systems.

However, few municipalities use automated processes. The SKR survey found that 8 per cent of the municipalities used some form of automation and only one (Trelleborg) used it for decision making. Things may change rapidly, as 40 per cent of the municipalities said they were planning to introduce automation of administrative work over the next few years.

Redefining Social Work

Most of the automated tasks, such as handling invoices, are uncontroversial. These programs are not especially 'smart': they are quite simple, rule-based algorithms. But introducing automated decision making into the welfare system sparked a discussion about the profession of social work and what social assistance should be.

'Financial aid is society's safety net, and has to be assessed individually by a professional social worker. When you replace these professionals with software, many social workers feel it is a threat to their profession,' said Lupita Svensson, a researcher at Lund University's School of Social Work.

Ms Svensson recently wrote a report about automating the welfare sector (*Technology Is the Easy Part*, published in November 2019). She said that, over the last twenty years, decisions about financial aid had moved away from individual assessments and towards more general, rule-based decisions:

> Initially, the legal text about financial aid gave social workers a great deal of room to manoeuvre, since the law was saying that you couldn't generalise. When this law is converted to code, it becomes clear that social work has changed. By converting law to software, the nature of financial aid changes, as you can't maintain the same individual assessments as before.

Ms Svensson is also concerned by the idea that an algorithm could be impartial:

> The municipal sector has a naive view of technological advances. They think a 'robot' will be impartial and objective. But how were these robots constructed? When I asked municipalities about this, they told me they followed the social workers' processes. This means there's a risk of copying in the norms, ideas and values that are already present in the system. There's very little critical discussion of this.

Mass Resignation

When Kungsbacka, a town of 20,000 inhabitants 300 kilometres north of Trelleborg, introduced the 'Trelleborg model', as it became known, in 2018, twelve of sixteen social workers left their work in protest. Some of them have returned to their jobs but the majority left for good.

Inger Grahn, a local representative for the Union for Professionals in Kungsbacka, said that the protest was about two things. First, the 'Trelleborg model', or at least its automated component, might not be legal. (Kungsbacka has not implemented full automation as of early 2020.) Second, implementing the Trelleborg model requires a major reorganisation of municipal services. It shifts responsibility for financial aid from the Department of Social Services to the Department of Work.

Kungsbacka's case workers said that this model might prevent them from getting the whole picture of a beneficiary. By focusing on getting beneficiaries directly into work, social issues such as children's welfare could be missed. Technology cannot solve everything, Ms Grahn said. 'As far as we know, there aren't yet any algorithms that take individual cases into account sufficiently to follow the law. Not when it comes to children with special needs, or any other kind of individual case,' she added.

Looking for Transparency

One central concern with automated decision making is transparency. How can automated decisions and the underlying algorithms be explained in a way everyone understands? And are algorithms official records that can be communicated to the public?

Simon Vinge, chief economist at the Union for Professionals (Akademikerförbundet SSR), has sought answers for over a year. In June 2018, he asked Trelleborg how the algorithm made decisions and how their system worked, but he did not receive satisfactory answers. After he sent a complaint to the Swedish Parliamentary Ombudsman (JO) in September 2019, he received some screenshots and a flow chart. Mr Vinge and the Union for Professionals argue that the information does not suffice to really explain how the program works, and he asked for 'meaningful information', in the sense of Article 15 GDPR, about how a decision is made. 'When it comes to automated decision making, no one knows what they have to share, or when you've received enough information to understand how an automated decision was made. I still don't know which parameters lead to a declined application, or what is being fed into the formula,' Mr Vinge said.

Trelleborg replied that they had given all the information they were asked for. The JO would make a decision on the case in the coming months. 'If it's difficult to explain how a simple rule-based algorithm works, how can we hope to explain more complex systems like machine learning?' Mr Vinge said.

Analysing the Code

Last fall, Freddi Ramel, a journalist, requested the source code of the software in Trelleborg under Sweden's Freedom of Information Act. When Trelleborg said it was not an official document, Mr Ramel lodged an appeal to the administrative court of appeal. Trelleborg argued that the code was a trade secret, but the court decided otherwise. The source code is an official document, judges said, and it was communicated to Mr Ramel (Figure 4.2).

The code that Trelleborg finally shared is made up of 136,000 lines of rules, spread out across 127 XML files. Some of the files seem to contain older, unused rule sets. Without access to the data used by the software, it is impossible to understand the rules with any certainty. The code interacts with other pieces of software, making the deciphering effort all the more difficult. But it is possible to (quite painstakingly) start outlining a general decision tree (Figure 4.3).

Without clear explanation from the municipality, the system remains a black box. 'Having the code does not change anything,' Mr Vinge of the SSR union wrote in an email.

```
<If Condition="[bErMedsøkendeIdentificeret]" sap2010:WorkflowViewState.IdRef="If_634">
  <If.Then>
    <Assign sap2010:WorkflowViewState.IdRef="Assign_2061">
      <Assign.To>
        <OutArgument x:TypeArguments="ui:GenericValue">[pCprNummer]</OutArgument>
      </Assign.To>
      <Assign.Value>
        <InArgument x:TypeArguments="ui:GenericValue">[row(13).ToString]</InArgument>
      </Assign.Value>
    </Assign>
  </If.Then>
```

Figure 4.2 An excerpt of the XML files made available by Trelleborg

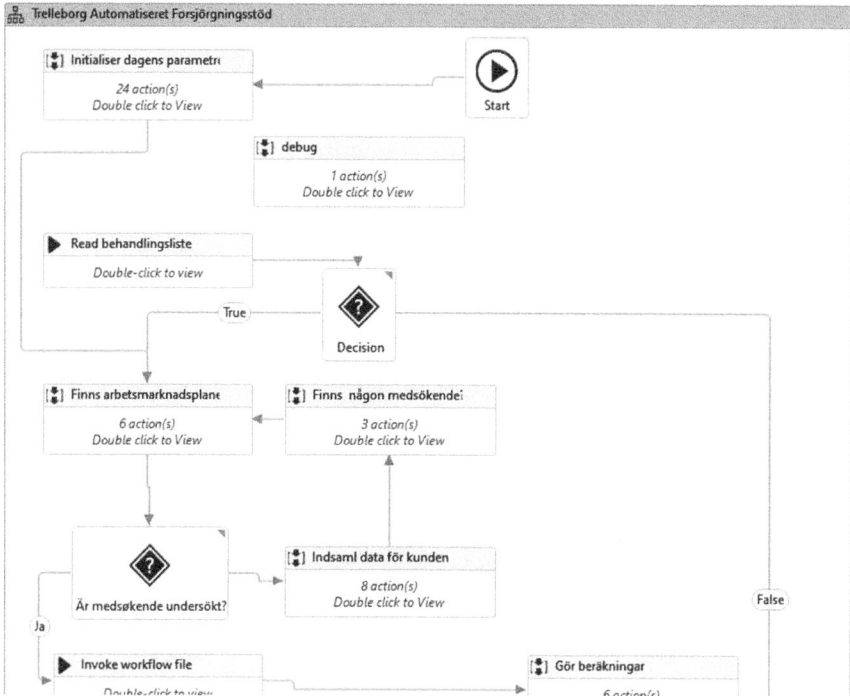

Figure 4.3 Tentative reconstruction of the Trelleborg algorithm

Personal Data Leak

The analysis of the code yielded not just some of the rules guiding the RPA. It also contained the names and social security numbers of approximately 250 people, seemingly citizens who had previously had welfare-related contacts with the municipality. This data seems to have been in the code since 2017 and is now visible for anyone who filed a FOI request to see the code, as well as the sub-contractors working on it. Trelleborg municipality is currently investigating why the personal data ended up in the code, and why the code was not screened before it was made public.

Even though Trelleborg introduced their 'robot' three years ago, the government has only just begun looking into this issue. In January, Stockholm ordered an investigation into the use of automated decision making by municipalities and regions. It will be published in March 2021.

ACKNOWLEDGEMENT

Content in this chapter is licensed under a Creative Commons Attribution 4.0 International license (CC BY 4.0): https://creativecommons.org/licenses/by/4.0/deed.en. The contents have been slightly modified by the editors for copyediting consistency.

Part II

Education

Dr Callum McGregor

This section, which approaches the relationship between data justice and the right to the city through an educational lens, is unique in that it features three chapters which can be read as critical interventions into a shared context – namely, the datafication of urban life in Scotland. To be sure, these critical interventions have different inflections, take a broad view of education and don't solely focus on Scottish policy and practice. Nevertheless, their common grounding in the particular Scottish context lends the collection an analytical cogency from which more universal tendencies and trajectories may be discerned.

In Scotland and the rest of the United Kingdom, data-led urban development manifests itself through large-scale public and private capital investment projects called City Region Deals. Authorial positionality (including my own) is significant here, since we are all located ambivalently within a Russell Group university that wields considerable influence over urban governance, mediating between local interests and global social and political-economic interests. On the one hand, the University of Edinburgh, via its interdisciplinary and ostensibly civic-facing Edinburgh Futures Institute, is the wellspring from which this very book emerged.[1] On the other hand, the University of Edinburgh arguably exercises disproportionate power over the production of the urban space in which it is rooted. An increasingly significant manifestation of the university's power to shape its urban surroundings is its vanguard role in the Data-Driven Innovation initiative (DDI), funded by the Edinburgh and South East City Region Deal. This positionality is a useful resource in so far as it is fundamentally about recognising and working through the ambivalence and contradictions of one's relationship to particular institutions in order to better understand possibilities for intervention. In this specific case, the University of Edinburgh can be conceptualised as one institution within a larger assemblage of private and public actors shaping the production of urban space through a narrative that aims to position the region as the 'data capital of Europe'. Indeed, as illustrated by all three authors, education is strategically deployed as a key policy instrument for realising this ambition.

A shared theoretical point of departure for this section is to be found in the contention that data justice must necessarily mediate any contemporary analysis of the relationship between education and the right to the city. Education is always an ideological endeavour in the sense that it is one of the primary means by which dominant discourses and practices of citizenship are reproduced and contested. We need scarcely rehearse the critique of neoliberal education that functions to produce citizens who are virtuous to the degree that they remain resilient entrepreneurs of the self who avoid making demands on the state. The right to the city presupposes a very different conception of citizenship, and thus of education – one that explicitly makes demands on the state and perhaps, above all, 'focuses on the question of who commands the necessary connection between urbanization and surplus production and use' (Harvey 2008: 40).

However, the answer to this crucial question isn't self-evident. Rather, it is an educational task involving the development of what Stuart Hall might have called a 'conjunctural analysis' – roughly meaning a mapping of the social terrain that aspires to clarify possible spaces for, and modes of, intervention. Cultural studies theorist Jeremy Gilbert argues that the present conjuncture is marked by the 'interaction of two key processes and tendencies: the overall change to the techno-social organisation of capitalism since the advent of platform capitalism in 2003, and the declining authority of the neoliberal political class since 2008' (Gilbert 2019: 34). The educational task then, is not only to understand these two processes and tendencies on their own terms, but to go further by developing an analysis of how they conjoin and interact. Since 2008 we have witnessed an explosion of emancipatory left-wing popular movements, including the Movement for Black Lives, various anti-austerity and economic justice movements, as well as climate action movements. However, we have also witnessed the global emergence of right-wing populism as a force capable of reasserting the authority of the nation-state amidst instability. In this latter context, the 'right to the city' has been increasingly articulated through racist ethno-nationalist discourse and realised politically through forms of 'welfare chauvinism' (Mudde 2013).

There is little doubt that the impact of contemporary social justice movements is partly a result of their astute use of digital technology, particularly social media platforms. In fact, such platforms function as vital and contested spaces of 'public pedagogy' (Sandlin, O'Malley and Burdick 2011) in their own right, for citizens concerned with social injustices. However, there is also little doubt that mass extraction of data through digital platforms has functioned as a key strategy for capital accumulation post-2008, for political surveillance and for manipulation of the democratic process by elites looking to weaponise racism, xenophobia and class division in order to consolidate their power and protect their wealth. Moreover, whilst the specific issue of 'dataveillance' has generated advocacy concerning data privacy and protection, there is evidence that these broader issues are under-played in the wider practices of social justice activists in the UK, who often perceive them as specialist rather than core concerns (Dencik, Hintz and Cable 2016).

Equipping citizens with the intellectual tools to cognitively map this conjuncture is an educational task. Education so conceived must be capable of marrying the widespread affective disavowal of the status quo with coherent analyses and political alternatives that refuse to trade in the complexity of reality for populist denunciation of folk devils, both on the right (as above) but also on the left. This, in turn, is an essential precursor for developing urban movements that avoid what Srnicek and Williams term 'folk politics', meaning 'a collective and historically constituted common sense that has become out of joint with actual mechanisms of power' (Srnicek and Williams 2016: 18).

Struggles over the right to the city are predominantly framed around the question of who has the power to produce urban space. Historically, this power has been codified in what Lefebvre (1991) named the 'abstract' or 'conceived' space of powerful technocrats, corporate developers, planners, architects and so on. In the current conjuncture, platforms such as Google 'wield massive aggregate power' in the abstract spatial representation of cities, thus influencing 'where people go, how and when they get there, what they do, the geography and characteristics of economic or social and political activities, and especially, the way in which some parts of the world are made visible or invisible' (Shaw and Graham 2017: 417). A frequent demand of right to the city activism is for popular sovereignty over key services and utilities. This is often expressed either through the concept of the urban commons, or state-mediated public ownership and control, that opposes relentless privatisation and commodification. But to the extent that entire areas of service provision in cities (health, environment, transport, energy, housing and so on) are increasingly mediated through data infrastructures, then perhaps we ought to conceptualise such data infrastructures as 'meta-utilities' requiring something like a demand for data sovereignty, without which other demands are rendered increasingly meaningless (Bria 2018: 166). Thus, if contemporary demands for right to the city are impoverished without an analysis of the monopoly tendencies of 'platform capitalism' (Srnicek 2017) and the anti-democratic tendencies of 'surveillance capitalism' (Zuboff 2019), then it follows that the development of critical data literacy must be a key tenet of education for the right to the city. Whilst this involves an integration of 'data justice' into data literacy, it also must also arguably involve a reflexive analysis of the way in which the discourse of social justice is incorporated by the nascent ideology of 'dataism' in contemporary social and educational policy.

If 'folk politics' describes rituals of resistance that constitute what we might call a 'fetishism from below' on the left, then the nascent ideology of dataism perhaps best describes one form of 'fetishism from above' currently driving urban planning and policy. Put simply, dataism is itself an ideology that fetishises Big Data by imagining it to be beyond ideology (Han 2017) – an apolitical panacea for myriad social and economic problems. Moreover, through the lens of 'dataism', social justice becomes a function of Big Data such that the horizon of social problems and solutions is increasingly only understood through this prism. In fact, radical urbanist Adam Greenfield (2017: 18) argues that data fetishism undergirds the core premise of the 'smart city' – that 'resource allocations and policy decisions can be made on the basis of evidence sieved directly from urban flows by a vast, distributed sensing apparatus reaching into every sphere of life'.

With this in mind, returning to the particular Scottish context provides us with a fruitful case study of the ambivalent educational and social possibilities that exist within a rapidly unfolding drive to restructure cities around data-driven innovation and growth. Implicitly or explicitly, the critique of 'dataism' animates each of the analyses in this section. To begin with, Nicolas Zehner critically analyses the University of Edinburgh's power to shape the production of urban space vis-à-vis a particular imaginary of 'smart urbanism'. Here, data (in)justice assumes a particular valence through Zehner's analysis of the 'unequal distribution of projective agency'. Zehner argues that the University of Edinburgh's power to effectively hegemonise the urban imaginary poses serious questions about democratic legitimacy. Drawing on Lefebvre and Geddes, Zehner reimagines the 'civic university' as a hub of authentic citizen participation in the collective imagination of alternative economic futures.

In the second chapter, Huw Davies analyses Scottish government policy on data literacy and presents an educational agenda for 'rescuing data literacy from dataism'. Whilst recognising that 'data economies need data skills', Davies contends that the Scottish government's vision of data literacy needs to extend beyond 'a technical skill intended to feed the tech talent pipeline with a side order of "data for good" values and ethics'. Although the Scottish government acknowledges that a 'digital first' strategy can compound existing inequalities, Davies nevertheless detects an apathy towards, if not embrace of, platform capitalism in practice. This analysis offers us a concrete example of how the discourse of social justice is itself a site of hegemonic struggle: by recognising the relationship between social (in)justice and datafication – particularly as it relates to educational inequalities and urban citizenship – the Scottish policy context leaves the door open for a progressive vision of data literacy. However, whereas a 'thin' vision of data justice in education represents the problem as unequal access to data education as a prerequisite for inclusion in the dominant narrative of datafication and digital disruption, a 'thick' vision of data justice in education is about disrupting 'disruption' itself, as if it were a natural and inevitable phenomenon rather than a socially constructed economic project.

At stake in these different inflections of 'data justice' in education are competing normative visions of citizenship. This is precisely what Ben Williamson focuses on in the final chapter through his examination of the ambivalent figure of the 'smart citizen apprentice'. Critically appraising 'educational smart city initiatives' in Milton Keynes, Glasgow and Edinburgh, Williamson examines the messy reality of policy discourse and implementation in order to highlight structural constraints as well as possibilities for agency and intervention. Williams identifies and analyses two dominant framings of citizenship in these initiatives – the 'civic' and 'economic'. Through a careful analysis of these framings,

Williams draws our attention to 'the ways dominant political logics of urban regeneration tend to constrain the inclusive, participatory and social justice aims of educational initiatives'.

To conclude, all three authors identify and problematise dominant trajectories in the contexts they analyse whilst also identifying in them the potential to develop affirmative visions of future education. To a certain degree, the dominant trajectory can be characterised by the entanglement of 'dataism' with what education theorist Gert Biesta calls the 'learnification' of social problems, meaning the social policy trend of reducing public 'structural' economic, social and political issues to problems of educational standards and attainment in schools, further and higher education as well as the learning deficits amongst 'excluded' individuals, communities and social groups. Countering the co-option of social justice into this dominant discourse will require educational and democratic processes that redistribute 'projective agency' itself to ordinary citizens rather than seeking to include and socialise them into the fetishistic urban imaginaries of policy elites.

NOTE

1. The Edinburgh Futures Institute funded and supported a week of interdisciplinary events on the theme of data justice between 20th and 24th May in 2019, organised by all three editors of this volume. This series of events provided the inspiration for a fully open-access book on the theme of Data Justice and the Right to the City, which is also funded by the Edinburgh Futures Institute, University of Edinburgh.

REFERENCES

Bria, F. (2018) A new deal for data. In J. McDonnell (ed.), *Economics for the Many*. London: Verso, pp. 164–3.

Denick, L., Hintz, A. and Cable, J. (2016) Towards data justice? The ambiguity of anti-surveillance resistance in political activism. *Big Data & Society* (July–December), 1–12.

Gilbert, J. (2019) This conjuncture: for Stuart Hall. *New Formations: A Journal of Culture/Theory/Politics*, 96, 5–37.

Greenfield, A. (2017) Practices of the minimum viable utopia. *Architectural Design*, 87(1), 16–25.

Han, B.-C. (2017) *Psycho-politics: Neoliberalism and New Technologies of Power*. London: Verso.

Harvey, D. (2008) The right to the city. *New Left Review*, 53, 23–40.

Lefebvre, H. (1991) *The Production of Space*. London: Wiley.

Mudde, C. (2013) Three decades of populist radical right parties in Western Europe: so what?' *European Journal of Political Research*, 52(1), 1–19.

Sandlin, J. O'Malley, M. P. and Burdick, J. (2011) Mapping the complexity of public pedagogy scholarship: 1894–2010. *Review of Educational Research*, 81(3), 338–75.

Shaw, J. and Graham, M. (2017) An informational right to the city. In Verso Editors (eds), *The Right to the City: A Verso Report*. London: Verso, pp. 402–81.

Srnicek, N. (2017) *Platform Capitalism*. Oxford: Polity Press.

Srnicek, N. and Williams, A. (2016) *Inventing the Future: Post-capitalism and a World Without Work*. London: Verso.

Zuboff, S. (2019) *The Age of Surveillance Capitalism: The Fight for a Human Future at the New Frontier of Power*. London: Profile Books.

Chapter 5

THE CIVIC UNIVERSITY AS KEY AGENT IN THE PRODUCTION OF URBAN SPACE

Nicolas Zehner

INTRODUCTION

Who has the power to reorganise urban life? Who gets to realise and hegemonise specific imaginaries of the datafied city? What role does higher education play in driving urban futures? Late capitalist economies are increasingly shaped by the advent of data-driven, information-led 'smart cities' (Karvonen, Cugurullo and Caprotti 2019). The twin forces of urbanisation and datafication (Mayer-Schönberger and Cukier 2013) hold the potential to revolutionise the way people live, shape the modes in which people think about society and, most importantly, how they imagine their futures. This chapter looks at how powerful urban stakeholders imagine and bring into being urban futures. Shedding light on the production and performance of a specific urban vision, I explore the notion of the right to the city in reference to higher education as a key mediator between the practico-material reality of the city and the urban social life that unfolds in it.

Taking the Edinburgh and South East Scotland City Region Deal[1] as an empirical case study, I argue that the University of Edinburgh constitutes a key agent in the production of datafied, urban space. In addition to its core missions – teaching and research – the University represents an urban planning agent responsible for driving the 'data capital of Europe' vision. Existing literature in sociology and science and technology studies (STS) demonstrates how the role of higher education institutions (HEIs) evolved from being a resource for policy and economy to being an engine of economic growth. In this chapter, I want to go one step further by suggesting that global HEIs such as the University of Edinburgh constitute powerful agents of urban transformation. This claim is rooted in an understanding of urban innovation

124

that recognises its inherently political nature and treats it as a locally constructed concept, which is simultaneously shaped by global reference points.

I begin by revisiting literature that examines the relationship between cities and universities. Particular emphasis will be put on tensions arising from the multi-scalar nature of higher education. Subsequently, a detailed description and analysis of the emergence of the 'Data Capital of Europe' vision will be provided. This includes an elaboration of Lefebvre's 'right to the city', a description of Edinburgh's innovation ecosystem and a critical engagement with the production of datafied urban imaginaries at the intersection of science and politics. This paves the way for a re-examination of the notion of the civic university by engaging with Patrick Geddes' notion of civics and pointing towards paths that allow Edinburgh University to fulfil its civic mission.

THE CITY AND THE UNIVERSITY

Examining the role of higher education as an urban stakeholder requires briefly unpacking how the city and the university relate to each other and, more importantly, how they shape wider processes of smart urbanism and regional development.

The future of the city is intimately tied to the future of the university. Cities and city regions are arguably the defining organisational units of our time (Amin and Thrift 2016). They constitute sources of innovation and novelty. They illustrate the fusion of speed and money (Simmel 2004). And their role is set to become even more important. According to the United Nations (UN), in 2016 an estimated 54.4 per cent of the world's population lived in urban settlements. This number is projected to increase. By 2030, 60 per cent of people globally and one in every three people will live in cities with at least half a million inhabitants (United Nations 2016). Cities drive global economic growth. According to the McKinsey Global Institute, by 2025, 600 cities will generate nearly 60 per cent of global GDP (Dobbs et al. 2011). Finally, cities are disproportionately responsible for environmental degradation and ecological and climate emergency. Burdett and Rode (2011: 10) emphasise that 'occupying less than 2 per cent of the earth's surface, urban areas concentrate . . . between 60 and 80 per cent of global energy consumption, and approximately 75 per cent of CO_2 emissions'. These figures underscore the importance of studying how cities are shaped, planned and reformed. Somewhat paradoxically, the increasing significance of cities does not come with a notable increase in the power of municipal authorities. Amin and Thrift (2016: 14) highlight that

> the world over, city governments are hampered by fiscal and juridical constraints, are often captured by vested interests or held back by shortages of resource, capability or commitment, while national governments – with far greater powers and resources – often remain largely blind to urban centrality.

It is other players – most prominently Silicon Valley tech companies – which shape urban development. In this chapter, I shed light on higher education institutions as powerful stakeholders of urban transformation.

(Global) universities are identified as central agents in emerging knowledge-based economies, driving data-driven innovation, providing human capital and acting as anchor institutions in local and regional economic governance networks (Charles 2003; Capello, Olechnicka and Gorzelak 2012; Goddard et al. 2014; Ransom 2015). One way of grasping the intimate relationship between cities and universities is to critically engage with the notion of the entrepreneurial university. Audretsch (2014: 314) points out that

> since the second world war, the university has evolved from a mandate and role characterised as the Humboldt model, with a primary emphasis on freedom and independence of scholarly inquiry . . . to being a source of knowledge that is requisite for economic growth and a strong economic performance.

This observation is confirmed by a whole body of literature which examines higher education's third mission, that is, its increasingly important role in regional and national economic development (see for instance Etzkowitz and Leydesdorff 1995; Etzkowitz 2002; Berman 2012; Barrioluengo, Uyarra and Kitagawa 2019). Etzkowitz and Leydesdorff's (1995) 'triple-helix model' of innovation seems emblematic for new institutional configurations amongst academia, government and industry, in which universities take up diverse development, innovation and regional leadership functions beyond their traditional teaching and research missions. Key knowledge exchange activities with societal and industry partners include collaborative research, consultancy work and intellectual property activities including shares, sales (patents and licences) and spin-offs.

The Multi-scalar Nature of Higher Education

The relationship between the city and the university, however, is much more tension-ridden than innovation models such as the 'triple helix' framework suggest. Undoubtedly, universities – as key civic institutions – can positively influence a wide range of urban issues. Examples include business support, human capital development or cultural production and consumption. Vice versa, there is a great incentive for universities to develop their public role, especially when it comes to dealing with major societal challenges such as climate change or the COVID-19 pandemic. However, it is important to take into account the multi-scalar nature of HEIs such as the University of Edinburgh. Goddard and Vallance (2013: 2) point out that universities constitute 'place-based institutions with connections into the different social and institutional spheres of [their] locality' and act as 'generative node[s] in national and international flows of knowledge and people (especially highly-mobile students)'. There seem to be at least two tensions emerging from the sociospatial differences prevailing between municipalities and universities. First, unlike city authorities, universities do not operate within bounded territories. As a result of their multi-scalar nature, universities' spatial interests might not necessarily be local. While universities certainly play a part in innovation, it is less clear how they contribute to urban-regional innovation (Power and Malmberg 2008; Addie, Keil and Olds 2015; Lee and Clarke 2019). In other words, innovations in artificial intelligence might change the world, but unless these innovations permeate regional industries they will not affect the lives of local residents.

A second concern refers to the unequal distribution of projective agency. Projective agency denotes 'the imaginative generation by actors of possible future trajectories, in which received structures of thought and action may be creatively reconfigured in relation to actors' hopes, fears, and desires for the future' (Emirbayer and Mische 1998: 971). In other words, who gets to imagine the future city? Who controls urban innovation? Universities – given their assigned role as drivers of innovation – form part of a new smart city epistemic community, that is, 'a network of knowledge and policy experts that share a worldview and a common set of normative beliefs, values and practices with respect to an issue and help decision-makers identify and deploy solutions to solve problems' (Kitchin et al. 2017: 3). This group of urban technocrats consists of local authority leaders and managers, chief data officers, consultants, change management civil servants and higher education officials (both academics and managers). They are united in the common mission to advance urban-regional economic growth. This, in turn, raises questions of democratic legitimacy – particularly with regard to including local communities in key decision-making processes. Put differently, it is not clear whether smart urban development actually leads to the mitigation of inequalities or whether it just reproduces issues such as labour polarisation and housing unaffordability.

The Civic University

One concept that seeks to break down barriers between universities and cities is the notion of the civic university (Goddard 2009; Goddard, Vallance and Kempton 2012). The latter indicates moving from the 'triple helix' (government, business, higher education) to the 'quadruple helix' (government, business, higher education, civil society). Transitioning from being in the city to being part of the city, the civic university is thought of as an organisation that places its research and education in the service of the community by engaging as a whole with its surroundings, partnering up with other local universities and using its location to form its identity (Goddard, Vallance and Kempton 2012). Moving from the entrepreneurial to the civic university also implies a transition from a focus on aggregate macroeconomic conditions and frameworks to place-based innovation. City and university leaders are supposed to act as 'place entrepreneurs' (Logan and Molotch 2007) in the pursuit of advancing inclusive city regional economic growth

The focus on city-regionalism and the reshaping of higher education as civic agents is reflected in the emergence of city region and growth deals in the UK. Rooted in the passing of the Localism Act in 2011, city deals constitute 'bespoke packages of funding and decision-making powers negotiated between central government and local authorities and/or Local Enterprise Partnerships and other local bodies' (Ward 2018: 4). In what follows, I will critically engage with the Edinburgh and South-East Scotland City Region Deal in order to shed light on the increasingly entangled private-public relationships that characterise data-driven social reforms.

CO-PRODUCING THE 'DATA CAPITAL OF EUROPE' VISION

Data-driven urbanism in Edinburgh is intimately tied to the Edinburgh and South East Scotland City Region Deal (CRD). The latter represents a £1.3 billion investment by the Scottish and UK governments and local partners over fifteen years, from 2018, which is designed to accelerate inclusive growth through the funding of infrastructure, skills and data-driven innovation. The University of Edinburgh's Data Driven Innovation (DDI) Programme sits at the heart of the Deal. Research, development and innovation are claimed to constitute the key means to ensuring inclusive growth. They take up more than half of the total budget (£791 million) and the vision is to transform the Edinburgh city region into the 'Data Capital of Europe' (The City of Edinburgh Council 2018). In many ways, the 'Data Capital of Europe' vision symbolises the multi-scalar nature of place-based innovation. 'Data' implies fluidity and mobility. 'Capital', in turn, signals place and steadiness.

The CRD illuminates the increasingly intertwined sociospatial interrelations between higher education and municipalities. The DDI Programme seems to allow Edinburgh University to leverage smart urban development 'to demonstrate [its] worth to society while also bolstering [its] reputation nationally and internationally' (Karvonen, Martin and Evans 2018: 107). Examples of practical DDI activity include the Global Open Finance Centre of Excellence[2] and the Wayra AI Blockchain Accelerator.[3] It follows that higher education in general and Edinburgh University in particular occupy centre stage in driving imaginaries of the datafied city. In addition to its core missions – teaching and research – the University of Edinburgh represents an urban planning agent – a key agent in the production of urban space. As a result, it appears highly relevant to analyse the co-constitutive and symbiotic relationships between higher education, regional innovation and the sociospatial dynamics of contemporary city regions.

The Right to (re-)Imagine the City

Reimagining the city – transforming it into the 'Data Capital of Europe' – requires actors to engage with time. Urban planning agents such as

Edinburgh University act in the present, yet their actions are determined by both the past and the future. Rewriting the city (Lefebvre 1996) entails linking past infrastructures, methods, regulations, buildings and ideas to desirable future outcomes. Importantly, the present is the only thing that exists. Both the past and the future are part of the present. It follows that urban planning agents must demonstrate an awareness of the conditions that allowed specific past futures to be mobilised and, at the same time, make credible claims with regard to future futures. Beckert's (2019) notion of 'promissory legitimacy' seems highly relevant in this context. The latter refers to 'the legitimacy that political authority gains from the credibility of promises with regard to future outcomes that political (or economic) leaders make when justifying decisions' (2019: 1). Put differently, urban planning or the production of urban space in Edinburgh requires the creation of credible promises, which lead key constituents – permanent residents, students, visitors – to follow the decision makers in their assessment of the future course of action. What threatens the city, therefore, is not only 'the departure of production' (Lefebvre 1996: 214) but also a lack of promissory legitimacy.

Invoking a Lefebvrian understanding of the urban, the city is conceived of as an imaginative space from which to envision and move towards a more equitable, collective and participatory process of urbanisation. Lefebvre (1996) points out that the right to the city implies and applies the knowledge of the production of space. Key to this conceptualisation is the distinction between the city and the urban. The former indicates a 'present and immediate reality, a practico-material and architectural fact' (Lefebvre 1996: 103). The latter describes 'a social reality made up of relations which are to be conceived of, constructed or reconstructed by thought' (ibid.). The urban is inseparable from the city. Edinburgh University embodies and affects both. It only works with the city since it forms an essential part of it. Founded by the City of Edinburgh Council in 1582, the University of Edinburgh is now the biggest landowner of the city and one of the largest employers in the city region.[4] It functions as an anchor institution coordinating Edinburgh's innovation ecosystem. Doing so, it shapes both the practico-material and social reality of Edinburgh. It sets up 'innovation hubs' such as the Bayes Centre[5] or the Edinburgh Futures Institute[6] and acts as key narrator in Edinburgh's drive for smart sociality (Rose 2020). It produces space, which, in turn, 'commands bodies, prescribing and proscribing gestures, routes and distances to be covered' (Lefebvre 1991: 143). In the next section, I will shed light on the construction of the 'Data Capital of Europe' vision and the role of Edinburgh University in coordinating the innovation ecosystem.

The Edinburgh Innovation Complex

In order to gain a better understanding of the emergence of the 'Data Capital of Europe' vision in Edinburgh, it appears crucial to briefly engage with at least three key contextual factors that help explain the rise of the innovation economy in the UK. First, digital technology changed. The development and diffusion of smartphones – particularly the release of the first iPhone in 2007 – changed the way people and organisations move and transact in cities. Second, the global financial crisis of 2007/8 and the ensuing financial damage and cutbacks in jobs led to new strategic vision for economic growth based around innovation and entrepreneurship (Zukin 2020). Finally, cities and city regions were identified as key drivers of national economic growth. Following the passing of the Localism Act in 2011, the UK government aimed to facilitate the devolution of decision-making powers form central government to individuals and communities. Since then, city region and growth deals have become the preferred model of subnational economic development (Waite et al. 2018).

The Edinburgh and South East Scotland City Region Deal and its focus on innovation confirm the emphasis on cities and city regions as dynamic centres of a growing tech economy. Data-driven urbanism in Edinburgh seems emblematic for what Sharon Zukin (2020) calls 'urban innovation complex'. She points out that 'building a city's "innovation complex" requires material structures of buildings and land, social structures to train a workforce, and financial mechanisms to integrate public- and private-sector capital investment and direct it toward tech production' (Zukin 2020: 7). There are at least four key factors shaping Edinburgh's innovation complex. First, there exist networks of institutional and private investors. The CRD is funded by the two national governments contributing £300 million each, by six local councils providing £303.2 million and regional partners contributing £426.9 million (Audit Scotland 2020). Second, higher education plays a key role, with two entrepreneurial universities (University of Edinburgh; Heriot-Watt University) leading on the DDI Programme. Third, the

City of Edinburgh Council takes an activist approach to business development. Having to deal with shrinking budgets on the one hand and a growing population on the other, it takes an entrepreneurial view of public services and sources key themes such as innovation out to actors in the private and higher education sector. This approach is best exemplified by Edinburgh City Council's collaboration with the Canadian ICT services provider CGI. Seeking to lower costs and become 'one of the world's smartest capital cities', Edinburgh City Council recently extended its partnership with CGI until 2029. At the heart of the agreement is the creation of a smart city operations centre which promises to bring together real-time data flows from transport, policing, health and other service areas into one centre.[7] Finally, tech companies are ready to move into the city region. One example of Edinburgh's growing recognition as a tech hub was Deliveroo's decision in April 2020 to launch its first UK tech office outside of London.

The University of Edinburgh as Key Agent in the Production of Space

The University of Edinburgh acts as a key agent in the production of urban space. More specifically, it functions as an anchor institution linking discourses, organisations and geographical spaces. Key to coordinating Edinburgh's innovation complex is the 'Data Capital of Europe' vision. The latter depicts what Jasanoff and Kim (2015) call a 'sociotechnical imaginary' – a 'collectively held, institutionally stabilized, and publicly performed vision of [a] desirable future, animated by shared understandings of forms of social life and social order attainable through, and supportive of, advances in science and technology' (2015: 4). Having gained sufficient 'promissory legitimacy' (Beckert 2019) among key decision makers, the 'Data Capital of Europe' vision seems capable of stabilising actors' expectations about the future city.

Originally put forward in an internal university audit in 2014, the notion of the 'Data Capital of Europe' first officially appeared in a Science and Innovation Audit (SIA) report in 2017 by a local consortium of higher education officials and council managers, who identified data-driven innovation as key driver of economic growth in the Edinburgh city region. Building on the Shakespeare Review (2013), which concluded that a second wave of economic and societal value will be generated by the 'capacity to process and learn from data' (2013: 5), the consortium envisioned the Edinburgh city region becoming 'a global destination of choice by 2025 for organisations powering services through the application of data science' (UK Government 2017: 217). The findings of the SIA subsequently formed the basis for the emergence of the DDI Programme. The latter seeks to enhance the data capability of the city region across ten key industry sectors through five areas of activity: talent, research, adoption, data and entrepreneurship (TRADE).

Lefebvre (1996: 131) points out that the urban 'is a quality born from quantities (spaces, objects, products)'. The 'Data Capital of Europe' imaginary is performed through discourses, organisations and geographical spaces. First, there is a practico-material dimension. Setting up the five innovation hubs,[8] Edinburgh University is actively remaking the city around it. It is literally building the future. The innovation hubs represent materialised imagined futures. Particularly noteworthy is the Edinburgh Futures Institute (EFI), which will be based in the former Royal Infirmary of Edinburgh (RIE). Opened in 1879, many if not most Edinburgh natives were born here. Seeking to move in by 2022, the EFI depicts the University's attempt to live up to the ideal of the 'civic' or 'porous' university, that is, engaging with local residents and placing its research and education in the service of the community. Second, there is a discursive dimension. The 'Data Capital of Europe' imaginary is performed through narratives and consciously embedded in existing imaginaries, which are linked to Edinburgh's historic role during the Scottish Enlightenment. Characterising Edinburgh as a 'city of ideas', data-driven innovation is framed as the next step in intellectual and scientific progress.

Lack of Inclusion and the Role of Legitimacy

Surprisingly, 'inclusion' does not feature in the 'TRADE' framework. The DDI Programme appears to reflect what Evgeny Morozov (2013) calls 'technological solutionism'. That is, the idea that given the right code, algorithms and robots, technology can solve highly complex social phenomena such as education and social justice. Agency is assigned to Big Data and artificial intelligence rather than human beings. Little focus is put on the environmental and social impact of data-driven innovation and there do not seem to be avenues for citizen and third sector participation beyond the fact that representatives form part of governance bodies. There seems to exist a discrepancy between 'innovation in discourse' and 'innovation in reality': while the notion of data-driven innovation has successfully captured university officials' imagination, it is far less clear how 'the woman in the street' can actually benefit from it.

Seeking to grasp the disconnect between vision and reality more effectively, it appears useful to apply three forms of democratic legitimacy to the construction and implementation of the 'Data Capital of Europe' imaginary: input legitimacy (Scharpf 1970), throughput legitimacy (Schmidt 2013) and promissory legitimacy (Beckert 2019). Studying the interlinkages between these three forms of democratic legitimacy allows one to grasp the unequal distribution of projective agency that characterises data-driven social reforms in the Edinburgh city region. The first form of legitimacy invokes the ideals of participatory democracy and refers to citizens expressing demands institutionally and deliberatively through representative politics (Scharpf 2003). Studying the emergence of the Edinburgh CRD, it becomes clear that local communities were not involved in crafting Edinburgh's economic futures. One high-ranking third sector representative describes the emergence of the CRD as 'like a spaceship that landed'.[9] This observation was confirmed by an Audit Scotland report (2020) which concluded that communities have had very limited direct involvement in the development of deals. Put differently, there was no room for early public consideration of alternatives to this chosen pathway of urban-regional economic development.

On the contrary, the CRD was negotiated at the intersection of science and politics with Edinburgh University officials playing a key role in defining and structuring power relationships. The emergence of the CRD demonstrates that the politics and the science of the future are closely intertwined. The future of the city region is closely tied to the future of Edinburgh University. Wenger, Jasper and Dunn Cavelty (2020: 229) point out that 'the oftentimes parallel processes of creating and assembling future knowledge and the integration of this knowledge into public policy-making and governance bring policy-makers and scientific experts from within governments, private industry, and academia in close contact with each other'. This, in turn, raises questions of legitimacy and accountability since the alleged separation between science and politics can no longer be upheld. Higher education officials – or more aptly, managers – engage in 'boundary work' (Gieryn 1999) by claiming that science is merely providing evidence-based research, which politics then transforms into policy. Studying urban planning at the intersection of science and politics in the Edinburgh city region, however, shows that the process of creating and assembling future knowledge (here: data-driven urbanism) is increasingly organised in a transdisciplinary, fluid and unbounded fashion. Boundaries between science and non-science (governments, civil society, tech ecosystem) are drawn and redrawn in a very flexible way. As a result, normative standards such as legitimacy, transparency and accountability are called into question. One way of grappling with the unbounded nature of city-making is the attempt to create and preserve throughput legitimacy.

Following the official signing of the CRD in August 2018, key decision makers attempted and still attempt to correct the lack of input legitimacy by ensuring adequate throughput legitimacy. The latter 'demands institutional and constructive governance processes that work with efficacy, accountability, transparency, inclusiveness and openness' (Schmidt 2013: 8). The governance structure of the Edinburgh CRD is built around the Joint Committee – the key decision-making body – which is predominantly comprised of political leaders from the six local authorities. Furthermore, decision makers attempted to ensure better throughput legitimacy by establishing the Regional Enterprise Council (REC). The latter is comprised of business and third sector representatives and is designed to advise the Joint Committee on the implementation of the Deal. Given the lack of input legitimacy in the first place and the fact that key budget decisions were taken before the establishment of the REC, it remains to be seen whether it fulfils more than a token role.

Underlying both input legitimacy and throughput legitimacy is promissory legitimacy. The Edinburgh CRD was officially signed in August 2018 and spans fifteen years. Given the early implementation stage, the Deal, first and foremost, denotes the promise of accelerating inclusive growth through the funding of infrastructure, skills and data-driven innovation. The promise of becoming the 'Data Capital of Europe' aligns individuals, organisations, discourses and geographic spaces. Keeping in mind the lack of input legitimacy and the attempt to ensure throughput legitimacy, two questions emerge: Are citizens in the Edinburgh city region aware of the CRD and its ambition to transform the city region into the 'Data Capital of Europe'? If so, does this promise appeal to collective imaginations and lead citizens to follow decision makers in their assessment of the future course of action?

To sum up, the University of Edinburgh constitutes a key agent in the production of urban, datafied space. It coordinates Edinburgh's innovation complex and links the practico-material to the social reality of the urban by performing the 'Data Capital of Europe' imaginary. Its officials act as narrators by imagining a 'landscape of innovation' (Zukin 2020) where digital technology leads to innovative research, more efficient public services, the transformation of businesses and, most importantly, the creation of new jobs. The apparent lack of inclusion and the disconnect between decision makers' imagined futures and citizens' lived experience, however, call for a re-examination of the civic university. The next section will take a look at how Edinburgh University can rethink its role as a civic university and promote a more equitable form of data-driven urbanism.

REIMAGINING THE CIVIC UNIVERSITY?

The previous sections have shown that higher education in general and Edinburgh University in particular occupy centre stage in driving imaginaries of the datafied city. Given its prominent role in coordinating 'Edinburgh's Data Revolution',[10] higher education must redress the uneven distribution of projective agency. Edinburgh University is uniquely positioned to rethink its role as an urban stakeholder and to engage with local communities by promoting more inclusive forms of urban development. In what follows, I will engage with Patrick Geddes' notion of civics and examine how research and education can serve local communities, thereby allowing for the possibility of imagining alternative economic futures.

Seeing Like a Citizen

But a city is more than a place in space, it is a drama in time.
Geddes, 1904, p. 107

Ensuring data justice and the right to the city means studying the city. This implies listening to, observing and interpreting the city from both distance and in detail rather than imposing social action from the top down. Similar to Henri Lefebvre, Scottish sociologist Patrick Geddes perceived cities as constantly changing and adapting organisms that hold the promise of reaching higher forms of living. Central to Geddes' work was the notion of civics. Encouraging close observation and exploration, Geddes (1904: 104) defined civics as the 'application of social survey to social service'. Civics, understood as 'applied sociology' (ibid.), can be grasped by Geddes' distinction between two different kinds of seeing the city: the synoptic and the detailed view. The synoptic view depicts an 'over-arching vision that synthesises everything into a single image' (Lesser 1974: 320). The detailed view, on the other hand, implies the immersion of the urban planner into particular characteristics of neighbourhoods by conducting street-by-street surveys. Following Fourcade and Gordon's (2020) analysis of the changing role of the state in the digital age, I suggest that in order to ensure data justice and the right to the city, Edinburgh University must see like a citizen. This implies promoting and adopting both a synoptic and detailed view of the city by 'identifying social problems . . . from the perspective of those affected' (Fourcade and Gordon 2020: 96).

One place that is aiming to live up to Geddes' notion of civics is the Edinburgh Futures Institute – one of the five innovation hubs underlying the DDI Programme. Similar to Geddes' Outlook Tower and its camera obscura on the top floor, which projects a real-time image of the city, the EFI seeks to be open to all and to be a place to study and learn about the city.[11] The high-level vision of the EFI is to 'support humanity's navigation of complex futures' (McAra 2019: 49) by promoting co-production in research and education. Given the early stages of the Edinburgh CRD, it remains to be seen whether the EFI is able to tackle technological, or, more aptly, data determinism and provide a platform for citizens and higher education to interact. The COVID-19 pandemic presents a unique opportunity to rediscover the power of urban communities. If anything, it has triggered different sensorial experiences of the city. Sound, smell, emotion and movement of everyday urban life has changed. The lockdown has created a city where cars are absent and nature (plants, animals) returns. As a result, the city looks and smells differently. Novel forms of (digital) solidarity, most notable by the emergence of mutual aid groups,[12] provide fertile ground for the EFI to learn from and study the city.

Key to making sense of the datafied city is an acute awareness of the limitations of the tools of Big Data analysis. Complex social problems will never be solved through data alone. Instead, it is important to advance the 'right to the smart city' (Cardullo, Di Feliciantonio and Kitchin, 2019). That means complementing predictive methods such as risk assessment, cost–benefit analyses and climate modelling with 'technologies of humility' (Jasanoff 2003). These social technologies seek to expose the distributive implications of data driven innovation by including factors such as personal experience, place, history and social connectedness (Jasanoff 2012). HEIs such as Edinburgh University must engage with mutual aid groups to learn about urban experiences, for instance in the context of the COVID-19 pandemic. Living up to the ideal of the civic university involves an honest engagement with the normative implications of humanity's lack of perfect foresight. Seeing like a citizen necessitates a conceptualisation of human beings as active, knowledgeable and imaginative agents. It requires HEIs to follow Geddes' ideal of civics: that is, embracing observation and experimentation as well as creating an environment that encourages citizens to bring in their knowledge and actively contribute to the resolution of common problems.

Imagining Alternative Economic Futures

The right to the (smart) city also involves the right to (re-)imagine it. Lefebvre (1996: 211) points out that 'what threatens the city today is the departure of production'. Embracing the ideal of the civic university, higher education must not only ensure access to future-imagining practices but also allow for the possibility of imagining alternative economic futures. Urban futures can not only be imagined with digital technologies and Big Data. They can also be imagined with art, food, fiction, music and theatre. Edinburgh University – as key driver of the sociotechnical imaginary of the 'Data Capital of Europe' – must work actively towards a more even distribution of projective agency. The University of Edinburgh is the oldest university in the English-speaking world to be established on a civic foundation. As such, it is uniquely positioned to distribute projective agency across the city region. In its community plan 2020–25, Edinburgh University emphasises that it strives to 'be a university of, with, and for Edinburgh and the wider region' (The University of Edinburgh 2020: 2). Given the initial lack of both input legitimacy and transparency and the apparent disconnect between key decision makers and local communities, two aspects seem particularly important for fulfilling its civic mission: first, an inclusionary process of knowledge production and, second, a critical engagement with Scotland's journey as a digitising nation.

The first aspect relates to the idea 'that future-imagining practices have future-making consequences' (Lindner and Meissner 2019: 17). As a result, it appears crucial for a civic university to provide citizens with access to future-imagining practices. Keeping in mind the exclusionary nature of scientific expertise in the creation of the DDI Programme, it is important to broaden the understanding of expertise and design avenues for participation. Eyal (2019: 4) observes that there exists an 'unprecedented reliance on science and expertise coupled with increased suspicion, skepticism, and dismissal of scientific findings [and] expert opinion'. Dealing with this 'crisis of expertise' means confronting the tension between the 'problem of legitimacy' and the 'problem of extension' (Collins and Evans 2007). In other words, how can the civic university tackle growing distrust and alienation on the one hand but ensure effective decision making and consensus on the other?

Trying to find the right balance between increasing and limiting citizen participation, Edinburgh University must identify social problems from the perspective of those affected (Fourcade and Gordon 2020). That means embracing observation and listening through the use of both tools of Big Data analysis and individual lived experiences. One way of dealing with this crisis of confidence is a stronger reliance on lay people in the production and dissemination of scientific knowledge. Importantly, it is not enough to just install formal mechanisms that allow citizens to participate in knowledge making. Instead, it seems important to introduce cultural change by promoting 'more meaningful interaction among policy-makers, scientific experts, corporate producers, and the public' (Jasanoff 2003: 238). A concrete example of living up to the 'co-production of knowledge model' (Callon 1999) would be to encourage citizen science projects such as the issuing of small grants to conduct data-gathering experiments. Importantly, this should not invoke an entrepreneurial understanding of publicness, in which residents are involved in creating services and economic value (Cowley, Joss and Dayot 2018), but rather enhance a modality of publicness that encourages citizens to politicise urban innovation.

The second aspect refers to the national impact of the civic university. Urban and regional imaginaries are always linked to and embedded in national and global imaginaries. Edinburgh University constitutes the most powerful higher education institution in Scotland and significantly contributes to the implementation of the Scottish government's digital[13] and AI[14] strategy. Doing so, there exists an opportunity to shape Scotland's journey as a digitising nation based on the experiences other countries have made with regard to data-driven innovation. Riding on the 'second wave of data-driven innovation', Edinburgh University can contribute to finding the right balance between unrestrained, experimental models of data-driven innovation, such as those in Silicon Valley, and authoritarian, top-down models, as can be found in China.

One theme that appears particularly promising is the debate around 'algorithmic accountability' (Pasquale 2019). Whereas the first wave of algorithmic accountability stressed the importance of empowering individuals to both access and control their own surveillance, advocates of the second wave challenge the basic existence of current systems and suggest more collective forms of governance (Fourcade and Gordon 2020). Seeking to become a civic university, Edinburgh University must advance this latest form of data justice by encouraging the decentralisation and democratisation of data. One way of translating the notion of the civic university into the digital realm could be the support of 'technological sovereignty', which denotes citizens' capacity to have a say and participate in how the technological infrastructure around them operates and what ends it serves (Morozov and Bria 2018). One of the most prominent examples of this alternative approach to smart urbanism is Barcelona's digital agenda,[15] which, amongst other things, advances the notion of 'city data commons'. The latter enables groups of people to pool and leverage their data, for instance in data cooperatives, in order to improve public services.

In sum, reimagining the civic university implies rejecting and actively debunking two widely held ideas about the relationship between technology and society: data determinism and technocracy. More and better data will not necessarily lead to better solutions to complex social problems. Similarly, the management and control of data-driven innovations should not be limited to specialist scientific knowledge; it also requires experiential knowledge. In attempting to see like a citizen, the civic university is uniquely positioned to provide access to future-imagining practices and to ensure the possibility of imagining alternative urban futures.

CONCLUSION

Future visions have powerful consequences. Those whose stories and imaginaries count exhibit power. In this chapter, I have argued that science and the city are co-produced. The future of the city region is intimately tied to the future of the University of Edinburgh. Not only does the city constitute a key context in which scientific practices unfold, but science must be regarded as an urban practice. Studying the emergence of the Edinburgh and South East Scotland City Region Deal and its ambition to transform the city region into the 'Data Capital of Europe', I have demonstrated that the University of Edinburgh constitutes a key agent in the production of urban space. The University represents an extremely powerful actor in the drive for 'smart urbanism' and regional economic development by shaping the 'politics of urban imagination' (Lindner and Meissner 2019).

Highlighting tensions emerging from the sociospatial differences prevailing between municipalities and universities, this chapter has shown that urban planning in the Edinburgh city region is characterised by an uneven distribution of projective agency. Not only was there a lack of input legitimacy in the creation of the CRD but there still appears to be a significant mismatch between decision makers' imagined economic futures and local communities' lived realities. If Edinburgh University wants to live up to its civic mission and transform intself into a civic university, it must see like a citizen, that is, ensuring access to future-imagining practices and allowing for the possibility of imagining alternative economic futures. This includes rethinking the role of scientific expertise in city-making and encouraging the decentralisation and democratisation of data.

NOTES

1. CRD, Edinburgh CRD or Deal subsequently.
2. For more information, see https://www.globalopenfinance.com.
3. For more information, see https://www.ed.ac.uk/bayes/our-community /past-collaborations/wayra-uk.
4. This information was gained in interview research conducted with more than fifty individuals involved in the CRD as part of my doctoral study.
5. For more information, see https://www.ed.ac.uk/bayes.
6. For more information, see https://efi.ed.ac.uk.

7. For more information, see https://www.edinburgh.gov.uk/news/article/12 962/council-extends-partnership-with-cgi-as-it-aims-to-become-one-of -the-world-s-smartest-cities-.
8. Edinburgh Futures Institute, Bayes Centre, Usher Institute, National Robotarium, Easter Bush.
9. This quote is taken from interview research conducted with more than fifty individuals involved in the CRD as part of my doctoral study.
10. This phrase was recently used by Peter Mathieson, vice chancellor and principal of the University of Edinburgh, at the Scotsman Data Conference 2020.
11. Particularly interesting is the 'Data Civics Programme' led by Liz McFall. For more information, see https://efi.ed.ac.uk/closes-and-opens-a-screen -test-for-efis-data-civics-programme/.
12. For more information, see https://covidmutualaid.org.
13. For more information, see https://www.gov.scot/publications/realising-scotlands-full-potential-digital-world-digital-strategy-scotland/.
14. For more information, see https://www.scotlandaistrategy.com.
15. For more information, see https://ajuntament.barcelona.cat/digital/en.

REFERENCES

Addie, J. P. D., Keil, R. and Olds, K. (2015) Beyond town and gown: universities, territoriality and the mobilization of new urban structures in Canada. *Territory, Politics, Governance*, 3(1), 27–50.

Amin, A. and Thrift, N. (2016) *Seeing Like a City*. London: Wiley.

Audit Scotland (2020) *Scotland's City Region and Growth Deals*. Available at www.audit-scotland.gov.uk/about-us/auditor-general (last accessed 7 January 2022).

Audretsch, D. B. (2014) From the entrepreneurial university to the university for the entrepreneurial society. *Journal of Technology Transfer*, 39(3), 313–21.

Barrioluengo, M., Uyarra, E. and Kitagawa, F. (2019) Understanding the evolution of the entrepreneurial university: the case of English higher education institutions. *Higher Education Quarterly*, 73(4), 469–95.

Beckert, J. (2019) The exhausted futures of neoliberalism: from promissory legitimacy to social anomy. *Journal of Cultural Economy*, 13(3), 318–30.

Berman, E. P. (2012) *Creating the Market University: How Academic Science Became an Economic Engine*. Princeton, NJ: Princeton University Press.

Burdett, R. and Rode, P. (2011) Living in the urban age. In R. Burdett. and S. Deyan (eds), *Living in the Endless City*. London: Phaidon.

Callon, M. (1999) The role of lay people in the production and dissemination of scientific knowledge. *Science Technology & Society*, 4(1), 81–94.

Capello, R., Olechnicka, A. and Gorzelak, G. (2012) Introduction: Cities, regions and universities as knowledge and innovation creators. In R. Capello, A. Olechnicka and G. Gorzelak (eds), *Universities, Cities and Regions: Loci for Knowledge and Innovation Creation*. London: Routledge, pp. 1–10.

Cardullo, P., Di Feliciantonio, C. and Kitchin, R. (2019) *The Right to the Smart City*. London: Routledge.

Charles, D. (2003) Universities and territorial development: reshaping the regional role of UK universities. *Local Economy*, 18(1), 7–20.

Collins, H. and Evans, R. (2007) *Rethinking Expertise*. Chicago, IL: University of Chicago Press.

Cowley, R., Joss, S. and Dayot, Y. (2018) The smart city and its publics: insights from across six UK cities. *Urban Research and Practice*, 11(1), 53–77.

Dobbs, R. et al. (2011) Urban world: mapping the economic power of cities. Available at https://www.mckinsey.com/featured-insights/urbanization/urban-world-mapping-the-economic-power-of-cities (last accessed 7 January 2022).

Emirbayer, M. and Mische, A. (1998) What Is Agency? *American Journal of Sociology*, 103(4), 962–1023.

Etzkowitz, H. (2002) The triple helix of university – industry – government: implications for policy and evaluation. Working paper, 11, pp. 1–17. Available at http://www.donorth.co/appurtenancy/pdfs/etzkowitz_triple_helix.pdf (last accessed 7 January 2022).

Etzkowitz, H. and Leydesdorff, L. (1995) The triple helix – university–industry–government relations: a laboratory for knowledge based economic development. *Easst Review*, 14(1), 14–19.

Eyal, G. (2019) *The Crisis of Expertise*. Chichester: Wiley.

Fourcade, M. and Gordon, B. J. (2020) Learning like a state: statecraft in the digital age. *Journal of Law and Political Economy*, 1(1).

Geddes, P. (1904) Civics: as applied sociology. *The Sociological Review*, 1(1).

Gieryn, T. F. (1999) *Cultural Boundaries of Science: Credibility on the Line*. Chicago, IL: University of Chicago Press.

Goddard, J. (2009) Reinventing the civic university, NESTA Working paper. Available at https://media.nesta.org.uk/documents/reinventing_the_civic_university.pdf (last accessed 7 January 2022).

Goddard, J. et al. (2014) Universities as anchor institutions in cities in a turbulent funding environment: vulnerable institutions and vulnerable places in England. *Cambridge Journal of Regions, Economy and Society*, 7(2), 307–25.

Goddard, J. and Vallance, P. (2013) *The University and the City*. London: Routledge.

Goddard, J., Vallance, P. and Kempton, L. (2012) Chapter 2: The civic university: Connecting the global and the local. In R. Capello, A. Olechnicka and

G. Gorzelak (eds), *Universities, Cities and Regions: Loci for Knowledge and Innovation Creation*. London: Routledge, pp. 43–63.

Jasanoff, S. (2003) Technologies of humility: citizen participation in governing science. *Minerva*, 41, 223–244.

Jasanoff, S. (2012) *Science and Public Reason*. London: Routledge.

Jasanoff, S. and Kim, S.-H. (2015) *Dreamscapes of Modernity: Sociotechnical Imaginaries and the Fabrication of Power*. Chicago, IL: University of Chicago Press.

Karvonen, A., Cugurullo, F. and Caprotti, F. (2019) *Inside Smart Cities. Place, Politics and Urban Innovation*. London: Routledge.

Karvonen, A., Martin, C. and Evans, J. (2018) University campuses as testbeds of smart urban innovation. In C. Coletta, L. Evans, L. Heaphy and R. Kitchin (eds), *Creating Smart Cities*. Abingdon: Routledge, pp. 104–18.

Kitchin, R., Coletta, C., Evans, L., Heaphy, L. and Mac Donncha, D. (2017) Smart cities, urban technocrats, epistemic communities and advocacy coalitions. The Programmable City Working paper 26.

Lee, N. and Clarke, S. (2019) Do low-skilled workers gain from high-tech employment growth? High-technology multipliers, employment and wages in Britain. *Research Policy*, 48(9), 103803.

Lefebvre, H. (1991) *The Production of Space*. London: Wiley.

Lefebvre, H. (1996) *Writings on Cities*. Oxford: Blackwell.

Lesser, W. (1974) Patrick Geddes: the practical visionary. *Town Planning Review*, 45(3), 311.

Lindner, C. and Meissner, M. (eds) (2019) *The Routledge Companion to Urban Imaginaries*. London: Routledge.

Logan, J. and Molotch, H. (2007) *Urban Fortunes: The Political Economy of Place*. Berkeley: Univerity of California Press.

Mayer-Schönberger, V. and Cukier, K. (2013) *Big Data: A Revolution That Will Transform How We Live, Work, and Think*. Boston, MA: Houghton Mifflin Harcourt.

McAra, L. (2019) Positive contagion: what universities are for. In *The Evergreen: A New Season in the North*. Edinburgh: The Word Bank.

Morozov, E. (2013) *To Save Everything, Click Here: Technology, Solutioism and the Urge to Fix Problems That Don't Exist*. London: Allen Lane.

Morozov, E. and Bria, F. (2018) Rethinking the smart city. Available at https://rosalux.nyc/rethinking-the-smart-city/ (last accessed 7 January 2022).

Pasquale, F. (2019) The second wave of algorithmic accountability – LPE Project. Available at https://lpeproject.org/blog/the-second-wave-of-algorithmic-accountability/ (last accessed 7 January 2022).

Power, D. and Malmberg, A. (2008) The contribution of universities to innovation and economic development: in what sense a regional problem. *Cambridge Journal of Regions, Economy and Society*, 1(2), 233–45.

Ransom, J. (2015) *Future of Cities: Universities and Cities*. Available at https://assets.publishing.service.gov.uk/government/uploads/system/uploads/attachment_data/file/477295/future-cities-universities.pdf (last accessed 7 January 2022).

Rose, G. (2020) Actually-existing sociality in a smart city: the social as socio-logical, neoliberal and cybernetic. *City*, 24(3–4), 512–29.

Scharpf, F. W. (1970) *Demokratietheorie zwischen Utopie und Anpassung*. Druckerei u. Verlagsanst. Universitätsverl. Available at https://kops.uni-konstanz.de/handle/123456789/34455 (last accessed 7 January 2022).

Scharpf, F. W. (2003) Problem-solving effectiveness and democratic account-ability in the EU'. MPIfG working paper 03/1. Available at http://www.mpifg.de/pu/workpap/wp03-1/wp03-1.html#1 (last accessed 7 January 2022).

Schmidt, V. A. (2013) Democracy and legitimacy in the European Union revis-ited: input, output and 'throughput'. *Political Studies*, 61(1), 2–22.

Shakespeare Review (2013) *An Independent Review of Public Sector Information*. Available at https://assets.publishing.service.gov.uk/government/uploads/system/uploads/attachment_data/file/198752/13-744-shakespeare-review-of-public-sector-information.pdf (last accessed 7 January 2022).

Simmel, G. (2004) *The Philosophy of Money*. London: Routledge.

The City of Edinburgh Council (2018) *Edinburgh and South East Scotland City Region Deal*.

The University of Edinburgh (2020) *Community Plan 2020–25*.

UK Government (2017) Enabling a world-leading regional digital economy through data driven innovation. Available at https://www.ed.ac.uk/files/atoms/files/edinburgh_science_and_innovation_audit_mainreportoct16.pdf (last accessed 7 January 2022).

United Nations (2016) *State of the World's Cities 2016: Urbanization and Development: Emerging Futures, United Nations Human Settlements Programme (UN-Habitat)*. United Nations Human Settlements Programme (UN-Habitat).

Waite, D. et al. (2018) The emergence and evolution of City Deals in Scotland. Available at https://www.semanticscholar.org/paper/The-emergence-and-evolution-of-City-Deals-in-Waite-Maclennan/0417ec722e6e544c3c3cd2eca7338098eae963f5 (last accessed 7 January 2022).

Ward, M. (2018) City deals. Available at https://www.gov.uk/government/collections/city-deals (last accessed 7 January 2022).

Wenger, A., Jasper, U. and Dunn Cavelty, M. (2020) *The Politics and Science of Prevision: Governing and Probing the Future*. London: Routledge.

Zukin, S. (2020) Seeing like a city: how tech became urban. *Theory and Society*, 49, 941–64.

Chapter 6

RESCUING DATA LITERACY FROM DATAISM

Huw C. Davies

INTRODUCTION

The Scottish government is transmitting mixed messages. On the one hand it wants data-literate citizens whose lives are improved by data and recognises that the dominance of the giant technology companies from Silicon Valley (the platform capitalists; Srnicek 2016) is problematic, while on the other hand it is outsourcing its digital services and infrastructure to other corporate technology companies and doing little to address platform capitalism's expanding monopolies. The government is therefore promising citizen empowerment through data while creating structural and systemic inhibitors to its realisation. This unacknowledged contradiction exists because the government has bought into a form of hype about what data can deliver – called dataism – that suggests data itself has some catalysing properties of its own that are independent of the political implications of ceding control to corporate tech.

The Scottish government is operationalising dataism in public policy by promising each citizen's digital footprint will be an expression of how they want to see their cities designed and governed. This creates the 'illusion of inclusion' (Saliternik 2019: 717) by marginalising or erasing altogether those who are unwilling and unable to represent themselves digitally, and it summons forms of power that diminish prospects for democratic accountability. This is because many sources of data that modern cities produce now are owned and monetised by Silicon Valley companies such as Airbnb, Uber and Google (Shaw and Graham 2017; Kitchin, Cardullo and Di Feliciantonio 2018). And, in Scotland, the data infrastructures such as cloud computing to run smart cities are outsourced to private corporations such as CGI, Capita

146

and Amazon (Chief Digital Officer 2018; City of Edinburgh Council 2020; UKAuthority 2020; CGI 2021). The Scottish government therefore recognises problems with corporate technology companies, such as their harvesting and hoarding of personal data and allergy to taxes (The Scottish Government 2017), while simultaneously outsourcing its services to them. Consequently, it is unclear if access to and control of the data – or the data commons – will be available to the public for its own benefit or enclosed or removed from the public domain and privatised. The government's open data strategy, for example, has not been updated since 2015 and contains no mention of tech monopolies or outsourcing (The Scottish Government 2015).

Partly as a response to Silicon Valley's hegemony, the Scottish government wants its citizens to be data literate (The Scottish Government 2017), but, given the context, it is uncertain if this means it wants its citizens to be better consumers of the data that hasn't been privatised or just better trained employees in the corporate-dominated digital economy.

While data economies need data skills, the version of data literacy suggested in Scottish policy circles – a technical skill intended to feed the tech talent pipeline with a side order of 'data for good' values and ethics and supplementary training in evaluating sources – is inadequate for Scotland's reckoning with platform capitalism. An alternative form of data literacy that operationalises and combines the concepts of data justice (Dencik et al. 2019) and the right to the city (Kitchin et al. 2018) could truly empower citizens by equipping them with ways of mobilising data and participating in the data economy but simultaneously raise awareness of platform capitalism (and other unaccountable commercial interests) and help ensure vulnerable groups and the digitally disenfranchised aren't forgotten or exploited.

Scottish Government's Subscription to Dataism

Prominent cultural commentators describe dataism as a powerful ideology. For example, David Brooks, the conservative political commentator, in his 2013 *New York Times* article about dataism, said:

> We now have the ability to gather huge amounts of data. This ability seems to carry with it certain cultural assumptions – that everything that can be measured should be measured; that data is

a transparent and reliable lens that allows us to filter out emotion-
alism and ideology; that data will help us do remarkable things –
like foretell the future. (Brooks 2013: n.p.)

The popular historian Yuval Noah Harari, in his 2016 book *Homo
Deus*, calls dataism a new form of religion that treats 'Beethoven's Fifth
Symphony, a stock-exchange bubble and the flu virus' all the same, as
'three patterns of data flown that can be analyzed using the same basic
concepts and tools' (Harari 2015: 174). In Alex Garland's short form
science fiction series *Devs*, dataism is imagined through a tech bil-
lionaire's secretive project to develop a quantum computer that, given
enough data about the universe all the way down to the behaviour of
subatomic particles, can perfectly reconstruct the past and predict the
future (BBC 2020).

Dataism is an overestimation of data's affordances that suggests data
has its own transformative properties: that if more data is produced and
made accessible, and more people are taught to analyse it, then more
ambitions will be realised. A subscription to dataism in public policy
means the process of dispelling ignorance about the society becomes
a simple transaction involving ubiquitous sensors, endless quantification, super-forecasters, colossal datasets, machine learning, stats,
graphs and visualisations (van Dijck 2014). Dataism assumes a 'self-
evident relationship between data and people, subsequently interpreting aggregated data to predict individual behaviour' (ibid.: 199). Silicon
Valley's dataism tells us that, given the right data in the sufficient
amounts, we can be healthier, have better housing and medicine,
more efficient transport, reverse ecological breakdown and species
extinction, improve our educational outcomes, gain psychological and
bodily self-knowledge, find our perfect partner, improve our sleep
and sex-lives, find our ideal job and become more productive at work
(Levina and Hasinoff 2017). Commercial vendors of dataism tell governments they can forecast policy outcomes, defeat bureaucracy and
institutionalised inertia, eliminate human bias, and, last but not least,
increase GDP (Fourcade and Gordon 2020). Dataism 'declares that a
society consists of data flows, the state's responsibility is to collect and
process that data, and a well-governed society is one in which events
are aligned to the state's models and predictions, no matter how dis-
orderly in high-modernist terms' (ibid.: 81). Given its promise, and its
relatively low cost as by-product of everyday habits and transactions, it

is unsurprising that governments are interested in public–private partnerships that mobilise data: particularly to manage cities.

DATAISM AND THE SMART CITY

Dataism is influencing city policy because from contactless payment systems and CCTV cameras to our fitness wearables and smartphones, modern cities contain millions of sensors and data points to supply data about our sleep, travel, work, exercise, consumption, education, leisure, civic engagement, politics and transgressions. This data, we are told, can be used to make cities, in the lexicon of dataism, 'smart'. Defined generally, smart cities are urban areas that exploit such 'operational data to optimize the operation of a city' (Harrison et al. 2010: 1). Smart city policy 'seeks to improve city life through the application of digital technologies to the management and delivery of city services and infrastructures and solving urban issues' (Kitchin et al. 2018: 2). Advocates of smart cities argue that maximising the utility of all the data a city can produce can transform the city into an 'intelligent infra-structure' that realises 'the value of a smart economy, smart environmental practices, smart governance, smart living, smart mobility, and smart people' (Cohen 2012: 1). The city becomes a 'self-aware' urban environment capable of diagnosing and curing its dysfunctions such as crime, traffic congestion, pollution, homelessness and educational inequalities. The city and its citizens are imagined unified in a Möbius strip of free-flowing and mutually reinforcing benefits between consumers and service providers (Kitchin et al. 2018).

Equipped with self-knowledge through data *and* data about others, the logic of dataism tells us people will make better, more informed choices that help themselves and increase the city's prosperity. For example, a resident looks at data provided by the smart city about the cheapest, most efficient and environmentally friendly journey to work. They see where the areas of high air pollution and congestion are, the difference between off-peak and peak fares, journey times, availability of Wi-Fi and so on, and, on balance, decide it would be better for their personal health data-informed health goals and, by extension, the city, if they cycled to work. However, they find that during their commute their route lacks cycle lanes. Fortuitously, the smart city is monitoring cycle journeys, recognises that this route is in demand and has accident blackspots so sets about building a cycle lane that is guided by the data.

The idealised smart city evolves into a healthier place to live and consequently becomes more attractive to businesses who want to locate there. Data becomes the lifeblood of the city, improving its economy and environment and incentivising its citizens to become better people.

Within this fantasy, the smart city would also monitor the job market, job adverts and recruitment services within its boundaries to provide data about skills shortages within the city's business sectors. Learning providers could use this data to align their provisions including infrastructure such as labs, educators and course content with what the skills market is demanding. They could also collect data about learners to diagnose their educational deficits, abilities and weaknesses and decide which educational technologies they can use to personalise educational content. Assessors could use data to identify achievement and excellence, and learners could use data to audit their educational needs relative to which skills are in demand within the city. To remain employable or fill a vacancy, citizens of the smart city could take new courses and acquire credentials in skills that the city needs to grow. Clearer pathways would emerge for graduates between degrees and jobs in industry; their job might even be a data scientist analysing data about the city. Described like this, the smart city is attractive to policy makers who see opportunities to completely reinvent urban living for the better.

Brooks, Hari and Garland are right: there are problems with excluding or downgrading alternative ways of interpreting and evaluating the world, not least because data is only ever a partial representation of the world through sampling. As such, dataism has become a powerful discursive construct that marginalises or excludes other epistemologies and ways of seeing and thinking. When operationalised in policy dataism, political decisions based on 'the data' or the value of data become objective technocratic truths unavailable to challenge. When data and data science is co-opted into public policy, such as smart city programmes, it is depoliticised, when dataism is anything but political. Garland memorably draws on poetry as an antidote to dehumanisation through data. However, in the instance of smart cities the danger here is less one of cultural disenchantment and more about how it conceives of citizens and citizenship, who and what it marginalises and the forms of power that dataism mobilises. Dataism is more than a faith in the power of data; it also makes assumptions people's subjectivities, how they behave or should behave, and systematises normative ideas about how society works as an aggregation of people's consumer choices.

DATAISM'S IDEA OF THE CITIZEN

The smart city model assumes citizens can and will be incentivised or coached into better behaviours. Dataism regards people as willing participants in this apolitical datafication because self-knowledge through data is a prerequisite of self-improvement: self-improved health, educational attainment and employment prospects. This model operationalises a form of behaviourist psychology that helped platforms such as Google and Twitter become successful (Fourcade and Gordon 2020). It addresses people as consumers whose (for example) political needs are translated into commercial choices such as 'liking' a political advert. These platforms' engineers and data scientists become choreographers of live behaviourist experiments designed to make choices that are in the company's commercial interests (ibid.). The most desirable outcomes are the ones that represent the largest aggregation of individual choices. In smart cities, such consumer choices become a proxy for civic engagement. Dataism 'understands governing to be about dispositifs that guide individuals to make desirable choices regarding their health, behaviour, and personal finances' and 'frames governance as a design problem: takes slices of individual behaviours as the most pertinent unit of analysis' (ibid.: 86).

But as Saliternik (2019: 720) argues, 'public decision-making must represent something more than the simple aggregation of individual interests or preferences', especially when the authenticity of digital choices is undermined by their external and commercially motivated manipulation. Those living in poverty, the disabled, the elderly or anyone who produces few digital traces may be excluded from data-informed policy decisions because their 'voice' goes unheard:

> Their health problems do not affect public health programs, their commuting patterns do not affect the planning of urban transportation, their energy consumption habits do not affect governmental energy policies, and their educational needs do not affect schools' curricula. While other people's practices and preferences increasingly shape public policies, theirs remain untraceable and therefore irrelevant. (Saliternik 2019: 731)

Hence, governmental reliance on data analysis might create an 'illusion of inclusion', while actually entrenching inequality (p. 717). In smart cities, individuals who aren't contributing to the flow of data or insisting on analogue services such as libraries suddenly become problematic. In her analysis of Milton Keynes's drive to become a smart city, Rose (2020) observed how older people with no digital footprint were problematised, often feminised, and described as technologically incompetent.

The Scottish government acknowledges that a 'digital first [*sic*] strategy could further marginalise already disconnected communities and groups' (The Scottish Government 2020: 30). Yet, questions about where the power lies, who else benefits from the smart city's existence, who owns the data and why, and alternative ways of organising cities are all also relegated or ignored by the logics of dataism. As scholars of race, gender and class tell us – particularly where their discussions converge on the history and understanding of empires – data can reinforce the forms of structural power that dataism ignores (Benjamin 2019).

The scale, quantity, ubiquity and velocity of data is new but dataism's ancestry can be traced through ledgers of the empires that counted, valued and processed the slaves they captured and traded (Nieboer 2011). The natural resources empires extracted from colonialised countries, and the administration and violent suppression of colonised peoples was all recorded in data (Richards 1993). During the Enlightenment, data such as physiological measurements were used to design racial hierarchies that could be used to 'predict' social traits such as trustworthiness and criminality (Fairchild 1991). Data also enabled the scientific management of crime, disease and poverty in industrialised cities (Bulmer, Bales and Sklar 2011). We therefore know from history that data flows through the contours of social stratification, accumulates at sites of power and creates and solidifies asymmetries between groups and institutions that own the data and those of us who are datafied.

The goal of some modern progressive governments is to make sure these days are behind us. Yet when dataism malfunctions, it begins to disclose its darker origins and potential for discriminatory outcomes. For example, facial recognition systems used by surveillance cameras to in public settings such as stations and shopping centres can operationalise pseudoscientific profiling metrics that can lead to targeting of ethnic groups (Zou and Schiebinger 2018). However, within dataism these problems too are treated as isolated and fixable governance failures: bugs rather than features of the system (ibid.). Dataism tells that such structural problems in society such as social injustice can be addressed with technical data-led solutions in ways that operationalise commercial incentives and invite powerful corporate actors to participate in public spaces and institutions (Fourcade and Gordon 2020). Datafied vulnerable groups may have resources 'triaged their way', but often at 'the expense of attacking the underlying problem' in ways that 'subject the entire population to invasive surveillance' (ibid.: 87). By reducing people to consumers who can be manipulated to make better choices, the answer to the rat race becomes a smarter maze; the reasons for the maze or its ownership's legitimacy are never troubled. This provides an open invitation for the corporate takeover the digital economy.

DATAISM'S INVITATION TO CORPORATIONS

Dataism, especially operationalised within the smart city, is packaged within optimistic descriptions of modern mixed digital economies that imply trickledown economic effects will benefit all. We are told that from the tech companies the state gets cutting-edge infrastructure such as full fibre broadband and 5G, investment and expertise (PricewaterhouseCoopers 2021). From the state, the tech companies get positive publicity and opportunities to develop their technology, expand their customer bases and collect data about the city and its residents that they can monetise. Their involvement, it is argued, generates jobs for the local economy, and produces tech hubs around which expanding ecosystems of services and suppliers coalesce that all have a multiplier effect to increase the spending power of the local community (ibid.). The state's role here is seen as a facilitator: to bring together stakeholders, incentivise and organise their participation in realising this vision, and provide the public infrastructures, standards, and legal and ethical frameworks to enable the fast, frictionless flows of data (Fourcade and Gordon 2020). This opens up new business opportunities for 'big ICT, consultancy firms and utilities' (March and Ribera-Fumaz 2016: 826). The result is that, with very little public knowledge or scrutiny, often the most valuable data individuals and societies produce is collected and owned by commercially aggressive, self-interested, monopolistic and relatively unaccountable private companies. While they may create jobs for the local economy, they are also in the business of defeating their competition and, where profitable, outsourcing jobs.

These companies include the UK government's preferred suppliers of technology services and infrastructure, such as the international business process outsourcing and professional services company Capita, which has been tasked with continuing to help Scottish Wide Area Network deliver digital transformations until 2023 (Capita 2019). The multiple contract renewals are worth a total of £11 million to supply digital services to, among others, the Scottish Government, Scottish Natural Heritage, Scottish Qualifications Authority, and Skills Development Scotland. Over 6,000 sites have been connected to the network, including schools, hospitals, GP surgeries, pharmacists and local council offices (ibid.). Edinburgh City Council's IT services, including its smart city programme, are owned by a Canadian supplier and consultancy firm called CGI (CGI 2021). Foreign tech giants such as Amazon that often seek to minimise their tax liabilities are increasingly becoming part of government infrastructure. Amazon Web Services hosts the Scottish Social Security Agency's data (Chief Digital Officer Division 2018). Research by the Data Justice Lab shows that fifty-three local authorities in the UK are in commercial partnerships that use predictive analytics systems to predict and modify human behaviour as a means to produce revenue and market control (Dencik et al. 2019).

Many existing smart cities are mixed economies – private and public sector services in co-dependent relationships (Shaw and Graham 2017). The distinction is often invisible to the public (ibid.). Companies such as Capita are assemblages of partners and subsidiaries that share data for commercial purposes that they have collected in public settings. Such companies in the business of smart cities and education seek to monopolise their data-led markets. The primary interest of such commercial stakeholders is to monetise data by targeting consumers with the most disposable income, sometimes at the expense of social justice (Srnicek 2016). If the data is collected and owned by private technology companies, it becomes one of their protected assets rather than something to be shared for better health outcomes and city living. Therefore, data drives are not progressive, inclusive or innovative by default.

Smart city policy also suggests either a tolerance or embrace of platform capitalism (Srnicek 2016). Platforms are companies such as Airbnb that combine servers, apps and websites to create an enclosed digital ecology within which businesses and users can make transactions (ibid.). In exchange for hosting the transaction, the platform monetises the transaction and the data the transaction generates and data about the business and the users (ibid.). Within such so-called peer-to-peer markets, where platforms bring together clients and services in smart cities, being a first mover and leveraging network effects are crucial to success. The more people using these systems, the more desirable and effective they are; to boost reputation, service providers need more reviews, for example, which in turn fortifies trust in a mutually reinforcing relationship (ibid.).

Such platforms, supported by venture capital, can often afford to operate at loss in a city in order to be the first to market and grow their networks before any potential competition scales up its operation (ibid.). This is part of the success story of Airbnb and other platforms such as Uber. Once dominance is achieved, these companies begin to influence a city's economy and character in ways smart city initiatives can't ignore. They also minimise their taxes by declaring their profits abroad (Standing 2016). These companies have monopolies on patents, technologies and data that make it almost impossible for competition on equal terms. They are globalised, so can subsidise enterprises in different regions in order to finish off local competition (ibid.). Because there is no viable alternative, local businesses and workers are forced to operate on these platform's terms, and accept their working conditions and algorithmically mediated judgements about them and their city (Shaw and Graham 2017). The data about the city's inhabitants and visitors that these companies collect therefore becomes one of their company assets to monetise internally or sell on.

This business model needs to be understood within the context of monetary responses to the 2008 financial crisis, such as quantitative easing and low interest rates which produced a stagnation in wages and growth in the value of assets such as land and data (Adkins, Cooper and Konings 2020). Whether it's property to rent out, your own car for hire, or petabytes of data, platform capitalism rewards the ownership of assets (Srnicek 2016). An increase in the value of assets means young people earning less than their previous generation in real terms cannot afford their own assets, such as a home (Standing 2016). A driver who rents a car from Uber or a freelancer whose reputation reviews belong to a platform such as Upwork is locked into this relationship within which they supply labour to those who own assets. A fulfilled and frictionless data economy can produce wealth but also, in the current structural conditions, disempowerment and dependency for others including an underclass of digital freelancers who are dependent on platforms for work but cannot afford to buy a home (Wood 2020).

While such companies would argue that they increase economic growth, governments and their citizens have little no access to or control of the data that these companies collect about our movements, behaviour, choices, habits and views: all the data that represents society in action as the taxable proceeds from monetising this data are sent to offshore accounts (Shaw and Graham 2017). Dataism is therefore also a delivery system for the monopolisation, accumulation and exploitation of data about people: it sustains platform capitalism.

The Scottish Government wants to ensure that taxes due from digital activity are collected, 'because taxes exist to provide public goods within a jurisdiction, the rise of online retailing is causing tax revenues to be diverted from places where people live and work to the jurisdictions where head-offices are located is becoming increasingly problematic' (The Scottish Government 2020: 6). Moreover, the fact that 'two thirds of the world's privately owned newer companies valued more than $1bn are based in just two countries' tells us it is important for 'the wellbeing economies that principles of fairness be brought to bear more closely on the taxation of large digital corporations' (ibid.). This undermining of the Scottish tax base is compounded further when Scottish companies that could challenge big tech's market dominance in Scotland are 'bought out by international competitors and global technology companies before they have had a chance to grow' (Schmalkuche, Marshall and Swamy 2019: 22). Yet, the ability to raise corporation tax is not a power that has been devolved to Scotland. Therefore, companies that millions of Scots use, such as Amazon, Facebook, Uber and Airbnb, pay the minimum of tax in Scotland and there is little the Scottish government can do about it. Instead, given its 'small tax base', the Scottish government is emphasising that 'skills are crucial for recovery' from the COVID-19 crisis (The Scottish Government 2020: 30), led by data literacy.

Given the Scottish government's commitment to a progressive agenda, we would expect it to take opportunities to alert citizens to this incessant and all-pervasive encroachment of technology monopolies in the digital economy and their conception of citizenship. Yet, there is no indication of this in its calls for data literacy.

SCOTTISH CALLS FOR DATA LITERACY

Scotland wants its citizens to be data literate. The Scottish Government chaired a roundtable meeting on 'Improving Open Data and Data Literacy' in Edinburgh, 26 April 2019, that sought to 'to address how it can give people access to the information that describes the country and communities that they live in, and how can we make it more understandable' (Cassidy, Hardie and Lord 2019: 5). The meeting cited 'functional data literacy' (more instrumental data analysis skills directed to perform elementary data visualisation of spreadsheets, for example) and 'more importantly', 'critical data literacy' that 'helped citizens to understand what happened with their personal data on social media, for instance'. Attendees discussed 'the appropriate level of data literacy required for citizens to have', from 'elementary competencies' to 'advanced data sciences skills', and described initiatives that 'seek to explore ways of embedding data literacy to empower citizens and communities and in policy making and curriculum design'. The consultation concluded that 'data literacy is not the same as numeracy. It includes skills needed to find data, to evaluate the quality of sources of information, and assess whether information is appropriate for the task you are trying to achieve' (ibid.: 5). To produce these skills at a 'societal level', delegates said Scotland needs to 'build data literacy into school curriculums' (ibid.: 8). This follows a report by Digital Scotland (2017) that called for data literacy that 'makes young people to be aware of their data rights and responsibilities, and helps them use and interpret data critically and ethically to inform decision-making'. To facilitate this the report said that any data literacy curriculum should be underpinned by 'the values of "data for good" and uses real-world data sets and problems, scenarios' (ibid.: 26). These definitions of data literacy voiced in Scottish policy circles therefore hint that dataism could be a problem; that data can be flawed, biased or discriminatory; and that the current data bonanza may not live up to its expectations and it may not always be a means to an end.

Sociological evidence suggests 'data literacy' may not even deliver the economic benefits it promises. Expertise in data or 'data literacy' is not a stand-alone asset in the job market. To have genuine value it has to be accompanied by other skills, resources and habits that signal competency and reliability and 'cultural fit' to employers (Cedefop 2020). The more data scientists or people advertising data literacy enter the jobs market, the more these other mechanisms of differentiation come into play (ibid.). Within the broader digital economy, holding a degree from a 'high-tariff' university, being geographically mobile, and having an internship and parental capital supporting you are also valuable assets in the competition to land a well-paid career (Shadbolt 2016). Skills in data science do not therefore transcend class inequalities (Davies and Eynon 2018). Moreover, the job market in data skills is now transnational. The expansion of two-sided digital freelancer markets on platforms such as Fiverr, Upwork, Twago and People Per Hour means employers can source skills online without having to pay the overheads associated with physical workplaces and permanent employees, such as office space and sick pay (Cedefop 2020).

This more or less depoliticalised form of data literacy discussed in Scottish policy circles could just help preparing people to be better consumers of digital services, but little else. It is intended to make people become 'an "effective" citizen able to cope in a fast changing and disrupted new world of work and leisure' (Emejulu and McGregor 2016: 3). However, 'constructing technology as innocent or neutral misunderstands the social relations of technology and its very real material consequences in our social world' (ibid.).

AN ALTERNATIVE DATA LITERACY

It is beyond the scope of this chapter to envisage how an alternative form of data literacy that includes data justice and the right to the city can be operationalised within formal educational systems and settings, as well as within programmes for lifelong learning. The purpose of this chapter is to articulate it, in principle, as the antidote to dataism. Like usual forms of data literacy, it begins with an understanding of maths and English: how to read data and its attendant technical terms and explanations. Then learners can be taught about forms of data collection, data cleaning and rendering and visualisation: how flawed sampling techniques, mistakes in formatting and in equations, restricted access to data, a lack of transparency, and its selective or misleading representation can undermine or even invalidate data. But this should then be should be developed into a social scientific critical analysis of strengths and weaknesses of quantitative data that dominates our understanding of data. Data-literate citizens should know that often one form of quantitative data, no matter how statistically sophisticated or voluminous, sometimes won't tell the full story until it is critiqued, synthesised, triangulated or compared with other forms of understanding the world such a qualitative data and theory. Understanding ourselves and society involves synthesising an array of data sources and research techniques, from fMRI scans to GPS data to focus groups and interviews – that each have their strengths and flaws. This would build the knowledge to begin to understand dataism as an ideology that overestimates the power of digital data. However, we do live in a datafied society. So how is dataism debunked while data's utility is retained? The concepts of data justice and the right to the city, integrated into a social scientific framework for data literacy, becomes a fully fledged counterbalance to dataism.

Data justice has 'emerged at the intersection of activism and technology in which data is seen as an avenue to revert or challenge dominant understandings of the world, (re)creating conditions of possibility for counter-imaginaries and social justice claims to emerge' (Dencik et al. 2019: 875). 'Data justice pays particular attention to structural inequality, highlights the unevenness of implications and experiences of data across different groups and communities in society' (ibid.) and reorientates the design process and the conditions within which data infrastructures emerge, to institutionalised participatory design practices that emphasise the involvement of communities and that seek to build alternative bottom-up infrastructures to empower rather than oppress marginalised groups (ibid.). This form of data literacy would:

> require us to stipulate how society is and ought to be organized in relation to digital infrastructures – on social, political, economic, cultural and ecological terms – that can consider and develop the meaning of justice in this context. This would include questions of how to think about notions such as security, autonomy, dignity, fairness and sustainability in a data-driven society and make us ask what, for example, the implications are for workers' rights, or for community cohesion and discrimination; for welfare and inequality; or for the environment, for poverty, and for conflict. Most importantly, advancing this agenda would transform surveillance from a special-interest 'issue' into a core dimension of social, political, cultural, ecological and economic justice, and thus respond to the central position of data-driven processes in contemporary capitalism. (Dencik, Hintz and Cable 2016: 9)

Let us imagine, for example, that a key social and community service is outsourced to a large technology company. The design and development jobs are given to external contractors. The users aren't consulted in the design process, their needs or circumstances aren't considered, the service's terms and conditions are long, esoteric and obfuscatory, the users' data is removed from their control, commodified and monetised elsewhere within the company's subsidiaries and partners. The company releases little or no reusable data into the public domain. It provides its customers with only call centre, email or chat bot support. The company pays only lip service to environmental commitments and minimises its local taxes – all beyond the reach of Scottish legislators. By the time it has become crucial to digital infrastructures and has accumulated legacies in data and knowledge, it is too expensive and impracticable to replace the company with a competitor, so it becomes a de facto monopoly supplier. Data justice seeks to challenge and provide an alternative to this gradual concretisation of corporate power that takes place at the expense of the communities that government is intended to serve. The strength of data justice can also be compounded by operationalising the right to the city within data literacy.

For Isin (in Kitchin et al. 2018: 18), the right to the city is 'the right to wrest the use of the city from the privileged new masters and democratise its space': it is the right of the excluded, the distressed and the alienated to demand and receive the material (e.g. a living wage, shelter) and non-material (e.g. recognition, respect, dignity) necessities of life (Marcuse 2012). The 'new masters' are companies that collect and privatise data. The 'excluded, the distressed and the alienated' are those who are unwilling or unable to participate in their corporate datafication, who can't express their needs through their data avatars, or who don't benefit from dataism with lucrative jobs in the data economy.

Data justice and the right to the city are not just rallying calls; they are constructive concepts that can be used to build prosperous yet fairer societies and institutions that are more accountable to their citizens. If we want software developers, entrepreneurs, business leaders and public servants to develop effective and emancipatory technologies that don't reproduce systemic inequalities, we need all the structures and institutions across society to be synchronised in the pursuit of data justice and a critically informed citizenship to hold them to account when they fail. This would involve operationalising data justice and the right to the city with what Mazzucato (2018) calls 'mission-driven innovation': a totalising and systematic approach to data literacy – everything from governance of data, including data transparency and data release standards, right down to lesson plans in the classroom and programmes for lifelong learning is required. If Scotland's citizens are to be truly empowered by data in ways that challenge dataism and the corporate actors it summons into being, they need a government that is going to make this form of data literacy its mission.

REFERENCES

Adkins, L., Cooper, M. and Konings, M. (2020) *The Asset Economy*. Cambridge: Polity Press.

BBC (2020) *Dev.* UK. Available at https://www.bbc.co.uk/programmes/p087 gjmw (last accessed 7 January 2022).

Benjamin, R. (2019) *Race After Technology: Abolitionist Tools for the New Jim Code*. Cambridge: Polity Press.

Brooks, D. (2013) The philsophy of data. *New York Times*, 4 February. Available at https://www.nytimes.com/2013/02/05/opinion/brooks-the-ph ilosophy-of-data.html (last accessed 7 January 2022).

Bulmer, M., Bales, K. and Sklar, K. K. (eds) (2011) *The Social Survey in Historical Perspective, 1880–1940*. Cambridge: Cambridge University Press.

Capita (2019) Delivering a smart, connected Scotland. Available at https://www.capita.com/our-work/delivering-smart-connected-scotland (last accessed 7 January 2022).

Cassidy, N., Hardie, A. and Lord, J. (2019) Open Government Partnership roundtable on open data and data literacy. Available at https://blogs.gov .scot/open-government-partnership/2019/06/19/roundtable-on-open-data -and-data-literacy/ (last accessed 7 January 2022).

Cedefop (2020) Developing and matching skills in the online platform economy. Available at https://www.cedefop.europa.eu/en/publications /3085 (last accessed 7 January 2022).

CGI (2021) *Smart Cities & Connected Communities*. Available at https://www .cgi.com/uk/en-gb/SmartCities (last accessed 7 January 2022).

Chief Digital Officer Division (2018) *Hosting Build Support: Statement of Requirements*. Available at https://www.gov.scot/binaries/content /documents/govscot/publications/foi-eir-release/2020/07/foi-2020000406 30/documents/foi-202000040630---information-released-a/foi-202000040 630---information-released-a/govscot%3Adocument/FOI-202000040630 %2B-%2BInformati (last accessed 7 January 2022).

City of Edinburgh Council (2020) Council extends partnership with CGI as

it aims to become one of the world's 'smartest cities'. Available at https://
www.edinburgh.gov.uk/news/article/12962/council-extends-partnership
-with-cgi-as-it-aims-to-become-one-of-the-world-s-smartest-cities- (last
accessed 7 January 2022).

Cohen, B. (2012) What exactly is a smart city? *Fast Company*, 19 September.
Available at https://www.fastcompany.com/1680538/what-exactly-is-a-sm
art-city (last accessed 10 February 2022).

Davies, H. C. and Eynon, R. (2018) Is digital upskilling the next generation our
'pipeline to prosperity'? *New Media & Society*, 20(11), 3961–79.

Dencik, L. et al. (2019) Exploring data justice: conceptions, applications and
directions. *Information, Communication & Society*, 22(7), 873–81.

Dencik, L., Hintz, A. and Cable, J. (2016) Towards data justice? The ambiguity
of anti-surveillance resistance in political activism. *Big Data & Society*, 3(2),
1–12.

Dencik, L., Redden, J., Hintz, A. and Warne, H. (2019) The 'golden view':
data-driven governance in the scoring society. *Internet Policy Review*, 8(2),
1–24.

Digital Scotland (2017) *Realising Scotland's Full Potential in the Digital World:
A Digital Strategy for Scotland*. Available at https://www.gov.scot/pub
lications/realising-scotlands-full-potential-digital-world-digital-strategy
-scotland/ (last accessed 7 January 2022).

Emejulu, A. and McGregor, C. (2016) Critical studies in education towards a
radical digital citizenship in digital education. *Critical Studies in Education*,
60(1).

Fairchild, H. H. (1991) Scientific racism: the cloak of objectivity. *Journal of
Social Issues*, 47(3), 101–15.

Fourcade, M. and Gordon, B. J. (2020) Learning like a state: statecraft in the
digital age. *Journal of Law and Political Economy*, 1(1), 78–108.

Harari, Y. N. (2015) *Homo Deus*. London: Harvill Secker.

Harrison, C. et al. (2010) Foundations for smarter cities. *IBM Journal of
Research and Development*, 54(4), 1–16. doi: 10.1147/JRD.2010.2048257.

Kitchin, R., Cardullo, P. and Di Feliciantonio, C. (2018) Citizenship, Justice and
the Right to the Smart City. (October). doi: 10.31235/osf.io/b8aq5.

Levina, M. and Hasinoff, A. A. (2017) The Silicon Valley ethos: tech industry products, discourses, and practices. *Television and New Media*, 18(6),
489–95.

March, H. and Ribera-Fumaz, R. (2016) Smart contradictions: the politics
of making Barcelona a self-sufficient city. *European Urban and Regional
Studies*, 23(4), 816–30.

Marcuse, P. (2012) Whose right(s) to what city. In N. Brenner, P. Marcuse and
M. Mayer (eds), *Cities for People Not for Profit: Critical Urban Theory and the
Right to the City*. London: Routledge, pp. 24–41.

Mazzucato, M. (2018) Mission-oriented innovation policies: challenges and opportunities. *Industrial and Corporate Change*, 27(5), 803–15.

Nieboer, H. J. (2011) *Slavery as an Industrial System*. Cambridge: Cambridge University Press.

PricewaterhouseCoopers (2021) The global forces shaping the future of infrastructure. Available at https://www.pwc.com/gx/en/industries/capital-pro jects-infrastructure/publications/infrastructure-trends/global-infrastructure -trends-developments-in-technology.html (last accessed 7 January 2022).

Richards, T. (1993) *The Imperial Archive Knowledge and the Fantasy of Empire*. London: Verso.

Rose, G. (2020) Actually-existing sociality in a smart city: the social as sociological, neoliberal and cybernetic. *City*, 24(3–4), 512–29.

Saliternik, M. (2019) Big Data and the right to political participation. *Journal of Constitutional Law*, 21(3), 713–60.

Schmalkuche, N., Marshall, P. and Swamy, R. (2019) *AI and Data Strategy*. Brisbane: Strategic Architects, pp. 1–40.

Shadbolt, N. (2016) Shadbolt review of computer sciences degree accreditation and graduate employability. Available at https://www.gov.uk/gover nment/publications/computer-science-degree-accreditation-and-graduate -employability-shadbolt-review (last accessed 7 January 2022).

Shaw, J. and Graham, M. (2017) An informational right to the city? Code, content, control, and the urbanization of information. *Antipode*, 49(4), 907–27.

Srnicek, N. (2016) *Platform Capitalism*. Oxford: Polity Press.

Standing, G. (2016) *The Corruption of Capitalism: Why Rentiers Thrive and Work Does Not Pay*. Biteback Publishing.

The Scottish Government (2015) *Open Data Strategy v1.2*. Available at https:// publications.qld.gov.au/dataset/7a7149ee-d4a1-4f1e-a795-b1b8d719ea4c /resource/5085e683-d31c-4495-8f90-13ee837cb5d7/download/opendatastr ategy201516.pdf (last accessed 7 January 2022).

The Scottish Government (2017) *Realising Scotland's Full Potential in a Digital World: A Digital Strategy for Scotland*. Available at http://www.gov.scot /Resource/0051/00515583.pdf (last accessed 7 January 2022).

The Scottish Government (2020) *Towards a Robust, Resilient Wellbeing Economy for Scotland*. Available at https://www.gov.scot/publications/towa rds-robust-resilient-wellbeing-economy-scotland-report-advisory-group -economic-recovery/ (last accessed 7 January 2022).

UKAuthority (2020) City of Edinburgh sets out smart ambitions. Available at https://www.ukauthority.com/articles/city-of-edinburgh-sets-out-smart -ambitions/ (last accessed 7 January 20212).

van Dijck, J. (2014) Datafication, dataism and dataveillance: Big Data between scientific paradigm and ideology. *Surveillance & Society*, 12(2), 197–208.

Wood, A. J. (2020) *Despotism on Demand*. Ithaca, NY: Cornell University Press.

Zou, J. and Schiebinger, L. (2018) Design AI so that it is fair. *Nature*, 559, 324–6.

Chapter 7

SMART CITIZEN APPRENTICES: DIGITAL URBANISM AND CODING AS TECHNO-SOLUTIONS TO THE CITY

Ben Williamson

INTRODUCTION

Projects to develop 'smart cities', urban 'open data' programmes, and other projects of 'digital urbanism' often focus on developing the figure of the empowered data citizen, an apprentice data analyst and computational coder who can mobilise data analysis to solve city problems. Drawing on a study of explicitly educational initiatives in urban reform programmes, and on an examination of the wider configuration of student subjectivities through coding and data skills initiatives, this chapter characterises the subject of the 'smart apprentice'. The smart apprentice is an emerging configuration of the ideal inhabitant of the 'actually-existing smart city' (Shelton, Zook and Wiig 2015), educated to 'learn to code' and perform data analysis in order to become an 'actually-existing smart citizen' (Shelton and Lodato 2019). Urban education programmes are intended to school individuals' capacities, skills and literacies to participate in the future city itself. From a social justice perspective, the educational focus on smart apprentice subjectivities raises key questions, such as: How is the idealised data citizen constructed and conferred with 'rights to the city' as an educated coder, techno-solutionist and digital urbanist-in-the-making? Do educational programmes for smart city development produce and reproduce gendered and racialised hierarchies of technological expertise? And could alternative rights to inclusive citizen engagement and participation produce more equitable urban reform? (Cardullo and Kitchin 2019; Lynch 2020).

The aim of the chapter is to highlight the particular role of education in digital urbanism programmes, and in the making of apprentice digital subjects as idealised smart citizens. The chapter is organised, first, to delineate recent scholarship on smart cities and smart citizenship; second, to examine a series of UK programmes dedicated to educating smart citizens with skills in computer code and data analysis; third, to trace out the wider social, economic and political resonances of urban educational coding and data skills programmes; and fourth, to identify the implications of emerging forms of smart citizenship from an explicitly social justice and rights perspective.

SMART CITIES AND CITIZENS

Discourses of 'smart cities' and 'digital urbanism' often conjure up images of high-tech urban landscapes and vast environmental sensor networks. The vision of the highly instrumented city involves the deployment of sensors to measure the activities of people and things; the collection and analysis of vast swathes of Big Data; use of data dashboards for urban decision making; automation of key services; increasing involvement of multinational technology corporations in urban governance; and, often, the creation of 'open data' portals enabling a range of stakeholders to participate in urban data analysis (e.g. Crang and Graham 2007; Batty 2013). At its most idealised, digital urbanism is presented in epochal terms as a technological transformation to the entire urban infrastructure:

> The old city of concrete, glass and steel now conceals a vast under-world of computers and software. Linked up via the Internet, these devices are being stitched together into a nervous system that supports the lives of billions in a world of huge and growing cities. . . . This digital upgrade to our built legacy is giving rise to a new kind of city – a 'smart city'. (Townsend 2013: xii)

In digitalised and data-intensive cities where 'machines run the world on our behalf' (ibid.), urban managers can conduct real-time diagnostics of the city – using the results from digital data to allocate resources, manage traffic and transportation, and monitor energy use – and even monitor social media to gather insights into public sentiment expressed about certain urban locations, services and events. As Mattern (2018: n.p.) details, these 'visionary' smart urbanism projects tie together computational approaches to the measurement of human behaviours – using large-scale data extraction from smartphones, web and app usage, and administrative data – with environmental monitoring and analysis, including citizens acting as 'participatory sensors' and urban 'citizen scientists' in order to collect data from the city at mass scale and engage in 'problem identification, data interpretation, and problem-solving'. Such approaches to both the quantification and analysis of humans and environments treat urban citizens as 'databodies' and cities as 'codespaces' (ibid.).

More critical urban research from geographical and sociological perspectives has critiqued the high-tech imaginary and enactment of the smart city. For critics, the smart city is characterised by technocratic governance and forms of technological solutionism; intensification of neoliberal urbanism; devolution of urban governance to multinational technology corporations; simplistic one-size-fits-all smart-city-out-of-the-box models; creeping surveillance and control; erasure of citizens' lived experiences or the political and cultural complexity of different urban settings; and reproduction of power asymmetries (e.g. Kitchin 2014).

Moreover, most smart city developments in practice involve a much more messy and pragmatic mix of retrofitting and modification rather than ground-up urban reconstruction. Shelton et al. (2015: 14) refer to the 'actually-existing smart city' where 'smart city interventions are always the outcomes of, and awkwardly integrated into, existing social and spatial constellations of urban governance and the built environment'. Indeed, as high-profile smart city construction projects have faced criticism and public resistance, one key shift in smart city development has been away from top-down models of urban reconstruction to ostensibly bottom-up participatory forms of citizen engagement in urban redevelopment. For example, Vanolo (2016: 28) refers to 'citizens' re-subjectification in smart city imaginaries' as 'active smart citizens', though notes various forms of inclusion and exclusion emerging from this categorisation as certain prescribed and proscribed forms of participation are designated as appropriate to being a smart citizen:

Here, there is a shift from citizens having defined civil, social and political rights and entitlements, who are disciplined to act in prescribed ways, to consumers with autonomy to choose from a suite of public service options dependent on desire and budget, who

gain rights through acting responsibly, and are nudged to act in
the interests of state and capital. (Graham et al. 2019: 5)

In this context, citizens with advanced digital skills are conferred with
enhanced capacity for participation in urban reform. For example,
Townsend (2013: 243) emphasises the role of 'civic hackers' and 'civic
laboratories' in the creation of citizen-centred urban services, where
'knowing how to code will be an important skill for civic improvement'.
The imagined citizen of such digital urbanism initiatives is a 'computational operative' in cities that are characterised as 'datasets to be
manipulated' (Gabrys 2014: 38). As such, smart citizenship represents
a form of consumer empowerment for those individuals and groups
able to deploy or 'upgrade' their computational capacities to participate in programming and hacking urban systems and processes, while
reproducing a particular gendered, classed and racialised configuration
of technological expertise that persists across both smart city developments (Lynch 2020) and digital citizenship education (Emejulu and
McGregor 2019).

Recent analysis by Shelton and Lodato (2019: 35) of 'actually-
existing smart citizens' casts doubt on claims that citizens may be
unproblematically enrolled into smart city participation, as 'the universal and unspecified figure of "the citizen" is discursively deployed to
justify smart city policies, while at the same time, actual citizens remain
largely excluded from such decision and policy-making processes'. In
their empirical analysis of ongoing smart city and citizenship initiatives
in Atlanta, USA, Shelton and Lodato (2019: 36) have identified how
the citizen plays a 'much messier and more ambivalent role in practice
– both as this figure gets deployed discursively in the everyday practices of smart city-making, as well as in the actually existing practices
of citizens participating (or not participating) in such efforts' – than
is presupposed by many corporately backed urban governance programmes. In smart city programmes, they argue, lines of inclusion and
exclusion are drawn both discursively and materially in the framing of
citizen participation and in the very social, political and technical infrastructures designed to enable or constrain, include or exclude, certain
modes of citizenship.

The forms of citizen inclusion noted by Shelton and Lodato (p. 48)
lead to the conclusion 'that, in practice, the "actually existing smart
citizen" might not actually exist at all', or at least 'that the smart citizen

does not exist outside of the discourse of the smart city, nor outside the material constraints of the neoliberal city more generally':

> Both the smart city and smart citizen always already exist within a much broader set of assumptions related to the centrality of cities in the global economy . . ., information technology as fundamentally 'disruptive', and the necessity of both the private market and responsibilized volunteer citizens to the provision of public services. Both the discourse and practice of smart citizenship exists within the same power geometry that produces the smart city more generally, with their seeming opposition to one another belying both their common grounding in market- and technology-centric ways of approaching contemporary urban problems, as well as their divorce from the actual practices of democratic citizenship and city-making. (p. 49)

Likewise, in their study of the ways citizens and citizenship are framed within a major European Commission smart cities programme, Cardullo and Kitchin (2019) identify a pervasive neoliberal governance rationality that presupposes a model of citizenship based on market values of choice, competition and entrepreneurship, which systematically excludes the majority of citizens or leads to tokenistic forms of participation, whilst 'operationalising' limited forms of citizenship:

> citizen participation is often synonymous with 'choice' and the market, with the predominant citizen roles being: 'consumer' or 'user', selecting which services to acquire from the marketplace of providers; 'resident', if they can afford the exclusive access to a smart district; or 'data product', creating data through their use of smart city technologies that companies can then incorporate into products and extract value from. (Cardullo and Kitchin 2019: 814)

In the European framework, 'citizens occupy a largely passive role, with companies and city administrations performing forms of civic paternalism (deciding what's best for citizens) and stewardship (delivering on behalf of citizens)', while promoting 'a technologically led neoliberal model of urban growth' characterised by marketisation, innovation, entrepreneurship, competition and economic growth (pp. 814–15). Consequently, 'despite attempts to recast the smart city as "citizen-focused", smart urbanism remains rooted in pragmatic, instrumental and paternalistic discourses and practices rather than those of social rights, political citizenship, and the common good' (p. 813).

Vanolo (2016: 33), too, identifies the 'invisibility' of citizens in many smart city imaginaries and instantiations, but highlights examples where active smart city citizens are imagined as 'inhabitants-as-sensors', 'participating in computational sensing and monitoring practices'. As such, 'the citizens that are expected to live in a smart city are supposed to be rather homogeneous: s/he is digitally educated, s/he possesses a smartphone and a PC, s/he constantly generates data and feedback about everything in her/his daily life. Non-digital citizens have apparently little room and a limited voice in the city of the future' (pp. 33–4). Even more strongly, Gabrys (2014: 38) has described smart citizenship as a form of enforced passivity rather than empowered participation:

> The actions of citizens have less to do with individuals exercising rights and responsibilities, and more to do with operationalizing the cybernetic functions of the smart city. Participation involves computational responsiveness and is coextensive with actions of monitoring and managing one's relations to environments, rather than advancing democratic engagement through dialogue and debate. The citizen is a data point, both a generator of data and a responsive node in a system of feedback.

As these critical perspectives attest, the figure of the smart citizen is contested, inhabiting diverse characterisations as an economic, political and civic actor, as well as passive roles as containers of data for extraction by both the state agencies and technology corporations that are responsible for urban governance. In the most idealised form of many smart city imaginaries, smart citizenship confers special rights of participation on digitally educated individuals to participate in urban reform reprogrammes through expert computational practices of coding, hacking and digital making. In other words, smart cities require the education of smart citizens through pedagogic and curricular forms of training and apprenticeship into programming practices. The rest of the chapter examines a number of UK-based urban data education programmes, revealing the specific role of education in shaping forms of smart digital citizenship.

SMART APPRENTICES

Education has been positioned in a range of high-level policy documents and on-the-ground initiatives as a key component of smart city development and related forms of digital, data-driven urban regeneration. For example, a 'Charter of Smart Education for Smart Cities and Smart Regions' was produced by the New Education Forum of the European Parliament with the Centre for Innovative Education. It aimed to produce new milestones and indicators of educational innovation aligned to European smart city development objectives, including aims to promote technical skills such as computer programming alongside capacities of active citizenship (New Education Forum 2017). Likewise, in the UK, the civil society organisation Nesta (National Endowment for Science, Technology and Arts) has played a significant role in attaching educational agendas to smart cities policies. During a spell of agenda-setting work on open data and digital urbanism, the chief executive of Nesta claimed that it was 'promoting digital making of all kinds in cities', particularly through its educational programmes (Mulgan 2014). These educational programmes included after-school coding clubs, advocacy for computing and programming to be introduced to formal school curricula, a nationwide campaign around 'digital making', and the production of promotional reports, thought leadership and policy briefs dedicated to the benefits of digital and data skills to policy, industry and individuals alike.

In parallel, Nesta also extensively promoted smart cities thinking, in particular advocating citizen participation in smart cities. Its manifesto for 'Rethinking Smart Cities from the Ground Up' described how citizens might 'shape the future of their cities' through 'collaborative technologies', 'citizen sensing projects' and 'civic crowdfunding'; it promoted 'people-centred smart cities' which use 'open data and open platforms to mobilize collective knowledge', 'take human behaviour as seriously as technology' and 'invest in smart people, not just smart technology' (Saunders and Baeck 2015). An accompanying Nesta report analysing forty smart city governments from around the world detailed how the city might act as a 'digital governor' to 'foster high-quality, low friction engagement with citizens' – by enabling citizens to interact with city services and input into urban policy making through digital interfaces – and to turn Big Data into 'smart data' to 'optimize city services' by allowing citizens and businesses alike to access and build services (Gibson and Robinson 2015). The capacity of the smart city to become a 'digital governor', in Nesta's conceptualisation, was dependent upon educating citizens to become digital producers and smart people – a task delegated to programming clubs for young people and continued through civic coding projects where those individuals who have learned to code could contribute to the production of new digital interfaces to city services. The core claim of such initiatives is that the economic, cultural and political functioning of smart cities will rely on smart people that can help contribute to the monitoring and management of the city itself.

An early example of how learning to code and civic coding might connect in practice to UK smart city and urban data programmes was provided by the Milton Keynes smart city programme. A collaboration between the local government and the Open University known as MK:Smart, it included a major educational initiative called the Urban Data School. The aims of Urban Data School were to teach young people 'data literacy' to access and analyse urban datasets; to create tools and resources to 'bring data skill education into the classroom'; and to encourage new forms of 'active citizenship' through using data 'to design and evaluate Urban Innovation Projects' and to devise 'effective solutions on the local, urban and global level'. Initially piloted within the MK:Smart initiative, Urban Data School was positioned and framed as a nationally pioneering approach to data skills education, developing an online learning platform for urban data analysis and 'seeking partnerships with city councils and businesses wanting to promote and provide schools with the necessary resources to support students gain data literacy skills' (https://www.mksmart.org /education/).

The Urban Data School was also part of an Open University programme on 'Smart City Learning and Education', which combined ideas about urban managers learning from each other and educational approaches being innovated to enhance smart city functioning:

> For smart cities to be effective they need to engage a broad range of people. Key to this is education, so that people better understand what smart cities are, and how they can participate and shape them. Education courses are needed to support smart city decision making; for example, cities need to learn how to assess the social, economic and environmental value of different smart

solutions and choose the best one for their city. (OpenLearn n.d.)

As such, these twinned initiatives sought to enlist young people into the coding and data practices associated with forms of computational urbanism that assume city services can be optimised by enrolling citizens into civic coding practices. A similar US initiative called MakerCities encouraged people to 'hack the future of your city', transforming commercialised smart cities into maker cities crafted by 'civic coders': 'Makers are starting to reimagine the systems that surround them. They are bringing the "maker mindset" to the complex urban challenges of health, education, food, and even citizenship. Makers will make the future of their cities' (Institute for the Future 2014). The 'civic coder' with a 'maker mindset' perceives technology development as a non-political means of intervening in urban issues, applying technical solutions to problematic effects whilst eliding the underlying social causes of such problems. 'Maker cities' as a consequence demand the technical expertise of programming and computational thinking that learning to code initiatives are designed to teach.

Similarly, the Future Makers programme, part of Glasgow's Future City initiative in the UK (a £24 million government-funded smart cities showcase project), emphasised the 'literacies' required to 'empower and educate people in using city data' and the 'knowledge and skills to participate, understand or contribute to the Future City' (Open Glasgow 2014: 4–9). In order to promote these smart city literacies, the Future Makers programme provided an 'innovative coding education programme' to develop programming and coding skills among young people (Open Glasgow 2014: 14). Future Makers consisted of coding clubs and workshops all aimed at enabling young people to help shape and sustain the Future City. Related activities in the Glasgow Future City included 'Hacking the Future' events and 'hackathons' putting citizens, programmers, designers and government staff together in teams to focus on coding citizen-centred solutions to urban problems. Future Makers was intended to ensure young people were equipped with the relevant technical expertise of coding and computational urbanism to help 'hack' or code the future of the city – although it had little long-term impact, according to final evaluations of the Future City programme (mruk 2016).

These initiatives exemplify the positioning of smart citizens as human augmentations to the expanding digital infrastructures of urban space and management. They require citizens to learn to code and analyse open data in order to help reprogramme, debug and optimise the smart city and its urban services. As Vanolo (2014: 893) argues, 'citizens are very subtly asked to participate in the construction of smart cities' and 'implicitly considered responsible for this objective. This means that the citizen is re-subjectified in the form of an active citizen', enabled and 'invested with a moral obligation' to participate in the programming of apparently non-political solutions to problems of urban governance. Similarly, Gabrys (2014: 38) argues that in this context the actions of citizens have less to do with exercising rights, responsibilities and democratic engagement and more with operationalising computational processes 'so that smart cities will function optimally'. However, as Shelton et al. (2015: 21) note, other 'education and digital literacy programming' established as part of smart city initiatives are evidence of how citywide urban policy 'often narrows its focus onto much smaller deliverables that may have minimal effect'. As such, educational coding and data skills initiatives can be understood as narrow, short-term, tokenistic attempts to enrol citizens into highly specific forms of smart city citizenship that privilege technical upskilling and the inculcation of literacies for urban optimisation – a form of smart citizen 'upgrading' that treats citizens as optimisable in similar ways to the computational infrastructures of smart city environments.

While these early initiatives in Glasgow and Milton Keynes overtly deployed the imaginary of the smart city, and identified specific (short-term) educational programmes for inculcating smart citizens into the skills and literacies of coding and data analysis, other cities have adopted subtly different designations. The city of Edinburgh, for example, launched a major Data-Driven Innovation (DDI) programme with a range of initiatives and partnerships focused on the areas of industry, government, academia and education, all animated by the city's proclaimed aim to become the 'data capital of Europe' (https://ddi.ac.uk/about-us-data-innovation/data-capital-of-europe/). As part of a major ten-year, £1.3 billion City Region Deal investment led by the Scottish and UK governments, formally launched in 2018, the DDI Programme is led by the universities of Edinburgh and Heriot Watt and 'aligned to the City Region Deal's Skills and Employability component, which will improve our citizens' digital skills through working with schools, further and higher education, employers, and training providers' (https://ddi.ac.uk/about-us-data-innovation/eses-city-regio nal-deal/).

Enabling citizens to participate in the future 'data capital of Europe' is a key aim. DDI emphasises the significant growth of the 'data economy' and the 'tech sector' in the Edinburgh region, and aims to ensure the continued development of 'data talent' for ongoing growth:

> The City Region's tech sector has seen impressive growth in recent years, but it needs more people with the right skills to meet demand. We're aiming to help 100,000 people gain data science-related qualifications over the next 15 years. This will help our tech industries but also benefit many other businesses and organisations, as data skills become increasingly important in a wide range of jobs. (https://ddi.ac.uk/data-talent-for-industry/our -growth-plan/)

To achieve these ambitious targets for educational data science quali-fications, DDI has initiatives focused on 'data talent for industry' and 'data talent for people'. Its citizen-focused data talent for people ini-tiatives aim to promote digital skills in computer programming and data science. One of its initial showcase projects is a 'Data-Driven Innovation Skills Gateway', overtly promoted as a citizen-centred, life-long learning approach to 'inclusive growth', 'increased prosperity' and 'greater equality' to 'share the social and economic benefits of data-driven innovation in the city and surrounding region':

> The DDI Skills Gateway has been set up so that the whole popu-lation can benefit from the opportunities of the new economy. It creates the potential for everyone to sharpen their data skills and exploit their digital talents.
>
> That includes girls in school who might be put off by the fre-quently male-dominated image of the technology sector, people returning to the workforce after a break, or anyone who com-bines work with caring for family members or friends. It also includes people whose roles are changing and who may now face redundancy.
>
> It covers teaching and skills at all stages, from early years to adult learning. It includes people of all backgrounds and social groups,

people with disabilities and other challenges, and people with all levels of previous education. (https://ddi.ac.uk/data-talent-for-people/data-driven-innovation-skills-gateway/)

The DDI Programme evidences a shift in discourse away from the smart city or future city imaginary to a more overtly 'inclusive' framing animated by aims to promote equality and social justice in the city and region. At the same time, however, it is continuous with the imagining of citizenship in terms of a form of apprenticeship into the data economy and as a form of participation in the regeneration of the city and the surrounding region itself. This is not meant to downplay the aims of the data skills programme itself, but to draw attention to the ways dominant political logics of urban regeneration tend to constrain the inclusive, participatory and social justice aims of educational initiatives through industry-facing, technology-led and economy-driven demands, while limiting participatory input (also see Chapter 5, in this volume).[1]

As with educational smart city programmes in Glasgow and Milton Keynes, the political and economic framing of data-driven innovation in Edinburgh is primarily focused on an imagined digital citizen who can develop skills for economic participation in the new techno-economic context of the city's urban governance strategy. While certainly laudable on the grounds of increasing participation and aspiring to greater equality, as well as attending to issues of data ethics, DDI also, however, configures the 'data economy', 'data talent' and 'data skills' as urban, political and economic imperatives. In this sense, it appears entangled within, and reproductive of, a particular set of technological, political and economic logics that have dominated and come to characterise the approach to digital, coding and data skills programmes at a much wider scale than urban regeneration programmes, as examined below.

SMART CITIZENSHIP

Educational data and coding initiatives within UK city regeneration schemes such as those outlined above need to be understood as the outcomes of a number of intersecting genealogical threads over recent years. The various rationales and instantiations of coding and data skills initiatives include political, economic, technical and civic aspects, often in complex and contradictory combinations. Here, it is possible to characterise two dominant framings of citizen participation and the forms of apprenticeship they entail: (1) techno-economic apprentice-ship for work, economy and urban growth, and (2) civic technology apprenticeship to solve social problems and optimise urban regenera-tion. The pedagogies and curricula of coding and data skills initiatives in cities are not just pedagogies of technical craft but rather they act to model and sculpt particular forms of participation that have been deemed by a variety of commercial, political and civic authorities to be appropriate to contemporary digital, urban citizenship.

In the first framing, educational coding and data skills initiatives are situated as a form of apprenticeship into the technical occupa-tions and sectors that are considered politically expedient to economic growth. This framing flows through the urban initiatives outlined above, perhaps most notably in emphases on 'data talent' for the 'data economy'. These emphases on developing technical skills for economic productivity are, of course, long standing in education policy, and are wrapped up in historical attempts to create structural isomorphism between education and industry, learning and earning, personal skills and the 'knowledge economy' (Ball 2008). Indeed, past efforts to embed computer programming, coding and computer science in edu-cation, in the UK and beyond, have often been connected to economic imperatives, such as the development of smart workers for the technol-ogy sector, the cultivation of entrepreneurial qualities, and demands of value production across various industries. Smart city education programmes can thus be understood as a commingling of education policy agendas focused on 'human capital' development for advanced digital industries and economies with smart urbanism programmes that promote 'a technologically led neoliberal model of urban growth' (Cardullo and Kitchin 2019: 815).

At the same time, initiatives for coding and data work have also been positioned as pedagogic relays for developing the capacities considered necessary for citizens to participate in the computational dynamics of an increasingly digitised social and political order, as represented in pro-totypical smart city programmes. In this second framing, educational coding and data skills are characterised as a form of civic apprentice-ship, inculcating socially conscious technical skills that are ostensibly fit for problem identification and resolution in urban contexts. In this framing, urban educational programmes align with recent emphases on 'technology for good', 'data for good' or 'AI for good', as well as associated ideas about 'civic coding', 'DIY citizenship' and other calls for citizens to participate in hackathons (Green 2019). The overarching logic of such approaches is that urban problems require citizen participation, not just as participatory urban sensors providing data from their smartphones during their everyday interactions with city amenities and services, but as active computational operatives and experts who have learned to code and to handle data in order to participate in the creation of new services. In this sense, the smart city is a model for emerging forms of digital governance that require citizens to be 'upskilled' for participation in economic growth, and the inculcation of the digital and data talent required for the smooth deployment and enactment of government digital services and other related forms of 'smart' governance. As the examples above indicate, digital urbanism requires apprentice digital urbanists and other 'smart people' to be educated in relevant code and data skills to design, use and maximise future city services.

However, as with the techno-economic framing, the civic apprenticeship framing assumes technology solutionist approaches that obscure the complex social, political and economic causes of many urban problems (Kitchin 2014). It assumes many social, scientific, governmental and human problems can be treated as technical problems to be solved or optimised through the application of code, algorithms and data, twinned with the necessary expert techniques of programming, algorithm design and software development. Such approaches emphasise a particularly instrumentalised form of digital citizenship 'which reduces digital citizenship to mere skills acquisition for navigating a digital world' while 'operating to obscure the material inequalities and socially exploitative relations upon which the proliferation of digital technology is premised' (Emejulu and McGregor 2019: 132). As Emejulu and McGregor note,

> thinking about digital citizenship only in the context of technological change renders digital citizenship as an unproblematic and instrumental process of becoming an 'effective' citizen able to cope in a fast changing and disrupted new world of work and leisure. Constructing technology as innocent or neutral misunderstands the social relations of technology and its very real material consequences in our social world. (2019: 133)

Such approaches also privilege certain groups and subjectivities as active citizens, and reproduce 'gendered and racialized hierarchies of technological expertise':

> In contemporary technocapitalism particular privileged subjects – overwhelmingly white, middle-class and wealthy men with formal technical training – are positioned as leaders of the 'digital revolution' making key decisions about the future direction of technological development. The remainder of the population is positioned as 'users' or consumers, the grateful beneficiaries of innovation anxiously awaiting the next 'big thing,' whose personal data feed new forms of algorithmic governmentality and control. (Lynch 2020: 1–2)

This is civic tech participation and digital citizenship within the political and technical constraints established by both political bodies and commercial technology companies, through which the possibilities of citizenship are shaped in ways reproductive of existing contours of race, gender, class and other forms of social stratification and inequality.

The emerging forms of citizenship represented by educational coding and data skills initiatives also reflect a wider reorientation of notions of citizenship that are now possible through digital technologies. Isin and Ruppert (2015: 9), for example, note that the emerging figure of the 'digital citizen' has become 'a problem of government: how to engage, cajole, coerce, incite, invite, or broadly encourage it to inhabit forms of conduct that are already deemed to be appropriate to being a citizen'. They highlight how the lives of digital citizens, as 'political subjects', are 'configured, regulated and organized by dispersed arrangements of numerous people and things such as corporations and states but also software and devices as well as people such as programmers and regulators' (Isin and Ruppert 2015: 4). Learning to code or developing digital data skills are thus enmeshed in existing political, technical and economic arrangements and priorities, and serve to reproduce notions of digital citizenship that are premised on ostensibly depoliticised technological solutionism rather than participatory engagement in struggles over political representation, rights and justice.

SOCIAL JUSTICE AND RIGHTS TO THE CITY

Recent coding and data skills initiatives in UK urban development and smart city programmes simultaneously promote economic growth through technical 'upskilling', and new forms of citizen participation that require dedicated skills and capacities to manage computer code and data. However laudable and ambitious their aims, these initiatives tend towards attenuated configurations of digital citizenship that focus either on instrumentalist skills development or forms of participation that demand enrolment into existing social, political and technical arrangements.

These issues are increasingly foregrounded by critical appraisals of 'smart citizenship' policies and practices, although the specific role played by education in the production of digital citizenship within urban reform programmes remains backgrounded by such studies. For example, Vanolo (2016) argues that many smart cities lack any firm grounding in aims to promote citizens' empowerment and capacity for engagement and participation in urban renewal. Likewise, for Shelton and Lodato (2019: 49),

> even though the smart citizen represents a scalar shift within discussions of technological solutions to urban problems, this way of approaching the challenge represented by smart cities is still situated within the same overarching discourse: both the smart city and smart citizen always already exist within a much broader set of assumptions related to the centrality of cities in the global economy, citizenship as a trans-local, transactional, or performative process, information technology as fundamentally 'disruptive', and the necessity of both the private market and responsibilized volunteer citizens to the provision of public services.

As such, smart citizen programmes tend to obscure actual practices of democratic citizenship or city-making, instead leaving citizens on the periphery of existing 'structures of power and decision-making processes, revealing the limits to the smart city and its ability to reckon with disparate voices and political claims' (p. 48). Likewise, while so-called 'civic tech' initiatives aimed at promoting digital citizenship 'are important in the democratisation of digital technology knowledge, they seek to include the so-called digital have nots in the prevailing logic of exclusion and capitalist consumption' rather than promoting alternative forms of participation, rights and justice (Emejulu and McGregor 2019: 140).

The technology-centred, neoliberal recasting of citizenship runs counter to what Cardullo and Kitchin (2019: 819) articulate as 'rights to the digital city', rights which confer 'more inclusive forms of citizen engagement and participation'. They identify five alternative rights to the smart city aimed at bringing 'citizens and civility' to 'the core of smart city initiatives, rather than capital and the market':

- reflecting and serving the interests of citizens, rather than these continuing to be subservient to the interests of state and market;
- more inclusive and deliberative framing of citizen participation in the smart city beyond consumerism and tokenistic civic engagement, including more extensive public consultation, collaboration and co-production, and roles such as creators, members and leaders;
- a shift back from citizenship grounded primarily in market principles to a framework underpinned by a set of civil, social, political, symbolic and digital rights and entitlements;
- public assets would form commons to be protected and leveraged for the common good;
- rather than smart city initiatives being directed principally at instrumental issues, more normative concerns such as fairness, equity, democracy, and social justice would become centre-stage. (Cardullo and Kitchin 2019: 825)

Likewise, in a study of contests over 'technological sovereignty' in the reimagining of Barcelona as a digital city, Lynch (2020: 2) highlights how grassroots groups, activists, community initiatives and activists have 'focused on decentralized control, ownership, and decision-making' and on 'claiming community control over the vital systems of everyday life'. This reflects what Emejulu and McGregor (2019: 131) have articulated as a 'radical digital citizenship', through which 'individuals and groups: (1) critically analyse the social, political, economic and environmental consequences of technologies in everyday life; and (2) collectively deliberate and take action to build alternative and emancipatory technologies and technological practices'.

A radical smart citizenship would, then, need to start from a more overtly political position with regard to alternative technologies and practices than many of those practices and technologies presupposed by current educational coding and urban data skills initiatives. Writing specifically on the related framing of 'data for good' or 'AI for good',

Green (2020: n.p.) argues that projects 'purporting to enhance social good without a reflexive engagement with social and political context are likely to reproduce the exact forms of social oppression that many working towards "social good" seek to dismantle'. Elsewhere, he elaborates, 'rather than presuming that algorithms provide an appropriate solution for every problem, the field must evaluate algorithmic interventions against alternative reforms. This also means finding new types of algorithmic interventions that better align with long-term pathways of social change' (Green 2019: n.p.). His proposal is that data science needs to commit to directly addressing social issues and developing new practices and methods that orient data science around a mission of social justice. Such a commitment to using digital technologies and data science for long-term social change would invigorate educational coding and data programmes with a more radical politics of social justice, rather than apprenticeship into forms of citizenship predicated on existing hierarchies of technical expertise and techno-solutionist assumptions that complex social problems can be fixed 'for good' with code and data analysis.

As in Shelton and Lodato's (2019) analysis of 'actually-existing smart citizens', in educational programmes aimed at promoting citizen participation in cities through coding and data skills, we find the idea of digital urbanist participation to be part of a powerful set of discursive and material arrangements that, despite their commitments to civic and participatory co-production, continue to reproduce existing forms of inclusion and exclusion – between technical experts with the right data and coding skills to enact the neoliberal, digital city, and otherwise 'absent' citizens whose participation is largely only sought in short-termist or tokenistic ways. A more social justice-oriented approach to citizenship in smart cities would need to engage fully with direct social issues in their immediate political and economic urban contexts, and, rather than educating young apprentices in coding and data science skills as solutions to those problems, would seek citizens' active engagement in consultation and co-production of city services. A transformational smart apprenticeship model for urban regeneration would start from issues of inclusion, equality, rights, democracy and social justice, educating young citizens' capacities for engagement and participation by mobilising coding and data science towards the diverse political, economic, technical and cultural problems restricting many citizens from urban participation.

NOTE

1. Disclosure: I am affiliated to the DDI Programme at the University of Edinburgh: https://ddi.ac.uk/chancellors/ben-williamson/.

REFERENCES

Ball, S. (2008) *The Education Debate*. Bristol: Policy Press.

Batty, M. (2013) *The New Science of Cities*. London: MIT Press.

Cardullo, P. and Kitchin, R. (2019) Smart urbanism and smart citizenship: the neoliberal logic of 'citizen-focused' smart cities in Europe. *Environment and Planning C: Politics and Space*, 37(5), 813–30.

Crang, M. and Graham, S. (2007) Sentient cities: ambient intelligence and the politics of urban space. *Information, Communication & Society*, 10(6), 789–817.

Emejulu, A. and McGregor, C. (2019) Towards a radical digital citizenship in digital education. *Critical Studies in Education*, 60(1), 131–47.

Gabrys, J. (2014) Programming environments: environmentality and citizen sensing in the smart city. *Environment and Planning D: Society and Space*, 32, 30–48.

Gibson, J. and Robinson, M. (2015) *CITIE: City Initiatives for Technology, Innovation and Entrepreneurship*. London: Nesta.

Graham, M., Kitchin, R., Mattern, S. and Shaw, J. (2019) How to run a city like Amazon. In M. Graham, R. Kitchin, S. Mattern and J. Shaw (eds), *How to Run a City like Amazon, and Other Fables*. London: Meatspace Press, pp. 1–12.

Green, B. (2019) 'Good' isn't good enough. Paper presented at AI for Social Good workshop at NeurIPS, Vancouver, Canada. Available at https://www.benzevgreen.com/wp-content/uploads/2019/11/19-ai4sg.pdf (last accessed 10 January 2022).

Green, B. (2020) Data science as political action: grounding data science in a politics of justice. arXiv. Available at https://arxiv.org/abs/1811.03435v3 (last accessed 10 January 2022).

Institute for the Future (2014) MakerCities. IftF.

Isin, E. and Ruppert, E. (2015) *Being Digital Citizens*. London: Rowman & Littlefield.

Kitchin, R. (2014) The real-time city? Big Data and smart urbanism. *GeoJournal*, 79, 1–14.

Lynch, C. R. (2020) Unruly digital subjects: social entanglements, identity, and the politics of technological expertise. *Digital Geography and Society*, 1, 1–8.

Mattern, S. (2018) Databodies in codespace. *Places Journal*, April. Available at https://placesjournal.org/article/databodies-in-codespace (last accessed 10 January 2022).

mruk (2016) *Building a Future City. Future City Glasgow Evaluation*. Future City Glasgow. Available at https://futurecity.glasgow.gov.uk/reports/128 26M_FutureCityGlasgow_Evaluation_Final_v10.0.pdf codespace (last accessed 10 January 2022).

Mulgan, G. (2014) Smart cities: what we're doing and why. Nesta blog, 23 January. Available at http://www.nesta.org.uk/blog/smart-cities-what -were-doing-and-why (last accessed 10 January 2022).

New Education Forum (2017) *Smart Education in Smart Cities and Smart Regions*.

Brussels: NEF/CIE. Available at https://www.neweducationforum.com/docu ments/Report-NEF-Brussels2017.pdf (last accessed 10 January 2022).

Open Glasgow (2014) Engagement and Literacy Programme. Open Glasgow.

OpenLearn (n.d.) Available at https://www.open.edu/openlearn/ocw/mod/ou content/view.php?id=67889&section=2.1 (last accessed 10 January 2022).

Saunders, T. and Baeck, P. (2015) *Rethinking Smart Cities from the Ground Up*. London: Nesta.

Shelton, T. and Lodato, T. (2019) Actually existing smart citizens. *City*, 23(1), 35–52.

Shelton, T., Zook, M. and Wiig, A. (2015) The actually existing smart city. *Cambridge Journal of Regions, Economy and Society*, 8(1), 13–25.

Townsend, A. M. (2013) *Smart Cities: Big Data, Civic Hackers and the Quest for A New Utopia*. London: W. W. Norton.

Vanolo, A. (2014) Smartmentality: the smart city as disciplinary strategy. *Urban Studies*, 51(5), 883–9.

Vanolo, A. (2016) Is there anybody out there? The place and role of citizens in tomorrow's smart cities. *Futures*, 82, 26–36.

Part III

Gig, Platform and Crowd Labour

Dr Jeremy Knox

This section focuses on labour in the contexts of data justice and the right to the city (RTTC), specifically as it is understood through so-called 'gig', 'platform' or 'crowd' work. These terms, as elucidated in chapters by Cailean Gallagher, Karen Gregory, and Alex J. Wood and Vili Lehdonvirta, refer to an increasingly common and much-debated restructuring of the labour market around the provision of paid work without formal contracts of employment, a valorisation of freelance work, and the increasing provision of 'on-demand' services facilitated by data- and algorithmically driven software platforms. This restructuring has attracted significant attention in recent years: on the one hand, for the ways such systems ostensibly offer increased flexibility and autonomy for workers, as well as potentially higher incomes for some, but on the other, for significant concerns over the status and rights of employees, alongside 'social isolation, lack of work–life balance, discrimination, and predatory intermediaries' (Graham et al. 2017: 1). Brewing legal debates over the regulation of gig work and the exploitation of workers continue, with ride-hailing firm Uber, after many years of resistance, finally consenting to union recognition in the UK (see BBC 2021), but also continued protests from Deliveroo workers as the company began trading on the London stick market (Butler and Jolly 2021).

Such concerns for justice in this shifting labour market might be usefully seen in the context of emerging relationships between platform technologies, data, cities and capital, for which this section offers a contribution to a growing area of research, often at the intersection of urban geography and critical data studies (for example, Graham et al. 2019; Graham and Shaw 2017). Particularly in the case of delivery riders (as Gallagher's and Gregory's chapters examine), such labour appears explicitly linked to the spatial (re)configurations of the data-fied city, as Deliveroo and Uber Eats workers are hailed by algorithmic systems to navigate urban space. As these chapters highlight, delivery riding is often promoted in terms of the supposed autonomy and flex-ibility that it provides, not only in terms of scheduling work, but also in the sense of the assumed liberty of cycling (as opposed to driving) through the urban landscape, that might be easily mistaken for the notions of agency, participation and ownership that the RTTC suggests. However, such promotion of delivery riding overlooks the significant issues of risk and precarity that seem to contradict notions of worker empowerment, as riders experience not only the hazardous terrains of city cycling but also the insecurities of tenuous rights as employees.

Such an explicit production of the urban landscape, rendered through the grinding of pedals and the exertion of bodies as well as through an increasing infiltration of digital infrastructures and mobile applications, is contrasted with Wood and Lehdonvirta's examination of 'remote' platform work. This usefully foregrounds questions of presence, par-ticularly where urban public spaces, and opportunities for communal, co-located experiences, appear to be diminished in the workings of the platform economy. While delivery riders toil the very streets and thor-oughfares of the city, other platform workers are just as present in con-temporary renditions of urban space and time, conditioned to reside in particular neighbourhoods by prevailing economic conditions, but often also engaged in transient working in shared inner-city offices, all while producing the kind of labour seen as intrinsic to the supposedly creative economies of the metropolis – advertising, marketing, graphic design and coding. One might, therefore, see this section as reformu-lating the question of what it means to be present in a city – not only to dwell or reside, but also to participate as an agent – in terms of the profound restructuring of urban space engendered by the rise of data-fication and the platform economy.

In contrast to the rational, data-driven and algorithmically ordered renditions of work (and urban life in general) envisioned in the pro-motion of platforms, this section foregrounds the day-to-day lived experience of workers as they negotiate the nexus of urban existence, employment and study. Despite the individualising, and often isolat-ing, influence of the ways 'gig' work is structured (Graham et al. 2017), the contributions in this section highlight continued efforts of workers to socialise, create communal spaces, share experiences, and protest. It is through engagement with such 'on the ground' practices and experiences that one might locate an alternative vision of the (re)making of contemporary cities, and the struggle for participation and agency within them, as opposed to the neatly arranged futures assumed in the doctrines of 'dataism'.

Gallagher's and Gregory's chapters in this section focus on delivery riders, and the specific context of the city of Edinburgh. As such, these chapters might be read not only as complementary within this section, but also in conjunction with the Education section of this book (Part II), which shares an explicit focus on the datafication of urban life in Scotland, and its capital city in particular. As also discussed in the introduction to the Education section, this local emphasis provides a coherence from which more general tendencies in the data-driven (re)structuring of cities and resulting social (in)justices might be distinguished and contrasted. Gallagher's contribution provides an important historical perspective to the current fascination with 'gig' work, examining the case of the eighteenth-century 'Society of Cadies', which attempted to organise and exercise control over courier work in the city of Edinburgh. A key aspect of Gallagher's analysis here focuses on the temporal dimensions of gig work, where, under the promotional discourse of flexibility (also discussed by Gregory), platforms seek to appropriate workers' time outside of usual working hours, particularly where consumer demand for deliveries peaks during evenings and weekends. Thus, platform work is suggested to trouble established urban regulations of labour and leisure time. Gallagher's underlying contribution is to focus on the capacity for collective organisation, and how such practices might evolve in response to growing data-driven surveillance, management and control, for which the eighteenth-century cadies offer some productive insights.

Gregory's chapter examines the formative role of gig work in young people's initiation into, and understanding of, employment and labour. Drawing on interviews with delivery riders, Gregory focuses on perceptions and experiences of workers and their work, rather than the specific functioning of the platform technology that has garnered significant attention elsewhere. In particular, the chapter charts a key relationship between gig work and the university, where increasingly neoliberal institutions are implicated in wider urban structures which facilitate both the desire for on-demand services, and the provision of labour to sustain it. Edinburgh provides a productive context for examining this context of the 'university city', where a relatively small urban space is populated by five institutions of higher education. Gregory thus shows students to be foundational sources of labour for delivery riding, and, through rich accounts of experience, examines how such populations comprehend and rationalise such work. Of clear concern here is the way such views appear to align with a long-established 'cultural script' that accepts risk and precarity as normal and necessary elements of work. On the one hand, delivery riders emphasise a sense of agency in the form of the work, and thus a presumption of a kind of ownership of urban space. Yet, such perceptions are ultimately conditioned by underlying data-driven systems focused on private profit, from which delivery riders are largely excluded. While the university is implicated in supporting the conditions through which gig work is presented as viable labour, Gregory sees higher education as simultaneously able to raise awareness and critical understanding amongst young people about the exploitative practices of platform economies, and the datafied cities into which they are situated.

Wood and Lehdonvirta, while continuing the attendance to lived experiences of labour in the datafied city, shift the discussion to a study of the 'remote' gig economy, comprised of geographically dispersed and often isolated freelance workers undertaking 'crowdwork' through online platforms. Drawing on interviews conducted across five city contexts, such platforms are shown to exploit workers, not only through the provision of low wages, but also by calculated abuse of their monopoly power. Far from being irrelevant to contemporary understandings of the city due to their online labour, 'remote' gig workers are shown to be critically important to the ways urban space is being economically, spatially and politically reconfigured. Without physical co-location or common space for protest (and indeed many such workers are shown to be excluded from urban living explicitly because of the insecurity of their income), 'remote' gig workers turn to online environments to build a sense of community, and in some cases even repurpose the platforms provided by employers for such action. These examples offer valuable insights into the ways practices of occupation and subversion persist underneath the slick facades of the platform economy, and the capitalist organisation of urban space. Wood and Lehdonvirta ultimately suggest that, rather than the idea of community-owned 'platform cooperatives' which have been proposed in some areas as alternatives to the corporate power of large-scale platform companies, collective organisation and unionisation tend to be perceived as more tangible routes to justice in the emerging platform economy. In this sense, it is perhaps continued contestation and struggle for participation, rather than solutionism, that continues to characterise the datafied city.

REFERENCES

BBC (2021) Uber recognises union for first time in landmark deal. BBC, 26 May. Available at https://www.bbc.co.uk/news/business-57254962 (last accessed 10 January 2022).

Butler, S. and Jolly, J. (2021) Deliveroo workers protest as shares rise on first day of open trading. *The Guardian,* 7 April. Available at https://www.theguardian.com/business/2021/apr/07/deliveroo-workers-strike-as-shares-rise-on-first-day-of-open-trading (last accessed 10 January 2022).

Graham, M., Kitchin, R., Mattern, S. and Shaw, J. (eds) (2019) *How to Run a City Like Amazon, and Other Fables.* London: Meatspace Press.

Graham, M., Lehdonvirta, V., Wood, A., Barnard, H., Hjorth, I. and Simon, D. P. (2017) *The Risks and Rewards of Online Gig Work at The Global Margins.* Oxford: Oxford Internet Institute.

Graham, M. and Shaw, J. (eds) (2017). *Towards a Fairer Gig Economy.* London: Meatspace Press.

Chapter 8

CADIES, CLOCKS AND THE DATA-DRIVEN CAPITAL: INCORPORATING GIG WORKERS IN EDINBURGH

Cailean Gallagher

These are a set of men who are called in this country Cadies, and who have been formed many years into a society for their own emolument and the public good – a society which is probably as useful and extraordinary as ever existed. To tell you what these people do is impossible; for there is nothing, almost, which they may not do. . . . A certain number of them stand all day long and most of the night at the top of High Street waiting for employment. Who-ever has occasion for them has only to pronounce the word 'Cadie', and they fly from all parts to attend the summons. Topham, *Letters from Edinburgh*, 1775

INTRODUCTION

In Edinburgh, as in every city, gig workers have always been subject to changing systems of control. Gig workers have responded to that control with various degrees of success, sometimes managing to take control of their own work. Data-driven technology is providing corporations with new ways to control workers with the aid of apps, platforms and other digital systems. Platforms and apps are enabling companies to scatter workers across the city, to embed new patterns of working time that respond to the market, and to prevent any need for workers ever to assemble, in some cases by actively discouraging their assembly. These new forms of control are affecting the experiences of many worker cohorts, including those who perform a series of tasks or gigs at different points across a city, such as couriers, delivery drivers and home carers. City authorities are eager to support these developments and Edinburgh is quite typical in its efforts to promote companies that deploy digital technologies, to integrate data-driven technologies into their industrial plans and policies, and to encourage schools to educate future workers in skills that these companies desire. Various aspects of data-driven platforms and of algorithmic management make it difficult for workers to develop the common aims, spaces and understanding necessary to establish collective agency. As data-related developments lead to deteriorating working conditions, and as new systems of control disrupt stable patterns of working time and working life, 'data justice' increasingly becomes a framework for workers to critique power asymmetries and to pinpoint where and how to challenge data-driven control (Dencik et al. 2019). In this so-called data revolution, as in every period of industrial development, new technologies pose obstacles and hazards for workers. But there is nothing new about task-based work and the challenges of organising within it, and historic instances of gig work incorporations are instructive for platform workers in our own time.

In 'The Right to the City', Henri Lefebvre suggested that as long as the city is the space across which workers are controlled, it may also be regarded as the space in which to resist and to take back control (Lefebvre 1996). But for gig workers in cities today, a lack of information about their work, unstable and irregular working-time regimes, and the challenges of associating inhibit their capacity to make 'right to the city' demands. Some of these challenges are similar to those described by E. P. Thompson, when clocks and other new time-based technologies were introduced in the early industrial period (Thompson 1967). Others resemble those which were overcome by the Society of Cadies, Edinburgh's eighteenth-century couriers, in their efforts to organise and assert control over work in the city. After exploring these conceptual challenges and historical precedents of gig worker organising, this study reaches a promising conclusion. While gig workers lack power when embedded in national or even global systems of technological control, there is great potential for workers to gain power at a more local and regional level, building associations with the capacity to gather information, collectively monitor changing work regimes, and win collective rights over their work in the city.

THE RIGHT TO THE DATA CAPITAL

In 1968, the sociologist and philosopher Henri Lefebvre presented his study of how urban planners embrace and encourage new systems of control in the city economy. 'The Right to the City' describes how urban planners shaped an ideology that saw the city 'as a network of circulation and communication, as a centre of information and decision-making' (Lefebvre 1996: 98), which 'intensifies by organizing the exploitation' of the working classes (p. 109). From the planners' perspective, the city is a space of sale and exchange, much more than a place which social groups use in their own way and time. Under this ideology, orders are issued in and by the city. These orders manage life and regulate time – including working life and working time – and function to preserve embedded hierarchies of place, occupation and people (p. 117). In modern times, an impulse of 'neo-capitalism' has given rise to a centralised decision-making system that 'no longer gathers together people and things, but data and knowledge', incorporating the whole 'into an electronic brain, using the quasi-instantaneity of communications' to harness information and prevent unemployment in an efficient economy (p. 170). 'The Right to the City' provides a useful way to understand issues of control that emerge from the economic powers and priorities of modern cities. Yet as we shall see, his schema has limitations when it comes to the current experience of platform workers. It does not anticipate the use of worker-generated data to command and control platform work. It encourages workers to *appropriate time* in which they might live life most fully, such as evenings and weekends, but does not address how new systems of control affect and adjust workers' sense of having to work at that time. Nor does it consider the challenges of forming bodies through which to assert and protect their interests when companies and cities are keen to keep control.

While it is a commonplace that platform companies use data to monitor and manage workers, less attention is paid to the initiatives of cities to control the workforce in the city through data-driven innovation. Cities like Edinburgh are investing in enormous programmes to increase their information and maintain their decision-making power. They are creating infrastructure to gather masses of data, to monitor the allocation and distribution of jobs, and to avoid unemployment by matching workers to work. Edinburgh is one of thirty-one UK cities that has negotiated a City Deal, granting it funds and powers to generate growth in the city and region. The Edinburgh City and Region Deal (hereafter 'the Deal'), which involves a £1.3 billion investment, is unique among City Deals both for its emphasis on data-driven innovation (DDI) and the digital economy, and for the core role the University of Edinburgh has assumed to advance DDI.[1] It is therefore an ideal subject for studying the way that DDI affects labour across a major city. The Deal's architects aim 'to establish the region as the data capital of Europe', involving stakeholders in business, civil society, and the academy. 'With the University of Edinburgh at its centre,' a news report explained, 'the City Deal's data-driven innovation (DDI) programme aims to give businesses and people in the region and its surrounding areas maximum advantage in the data revolution' (Scotsman 2018). Besides providing support, skills development and subsidies for data capitalists who choose to invest in the city, a major chunk of this funding will help the city to gather data and knowledge through the development of '[d]ata storage and analysis technology that will allow large datasets to be brought together, in a secure environment, from public and private sector organisations', to 'allow the development of new products and services within key sectors' (Office of the Secretary of State for Scotland 2017: 2).

As well as gathering and controlling knowledge, the Deal is helping companies to change the way that labour is employed and orders are issued in the city. The City of Edinburgh Council, in its Economic Strategy, projected that the Deal's programmes 'will support the good growth ambitions of the city by widening access to the skills and employment opportunities created within the data economy' (City of Edinburgh 2018: 21). These skills directly relate to new systems of work and discipline, as well as task substitution by automated systems. A report on the proposition for the 'Data Driven Innovation (DDI) Skills Gateway Project' prepared for the Deal's committee declared that 'the data worker is in demand', helping to justify its programme to equip local people with skills for data worker roles. Its two examples of such roles are work in *care* and *delivery/distribution*:

the importance of data skills is being recognised in a large number, and diverse range, of job roles. For example, care workers are likely to be required to provide more patient-centred care using telemedicine to connect with doctors and coordinate care activities, and drivers, threatened by the increasing prevalence of autonomous vehicles, may be required to develop new skills so that they can carry out tasks using data management to co-ordinate and supervise a convoy of autonomous vehicles. The data worker is in demand. The DDI Skills Gateway aims to equip local people, working across all sectors, with these skills, training them for changing roles and preparing them for the jobs of the future. (City Deal 2019: 206)

If the *roles* that these workers perform are to deliver goods or provide care, the *requirements* involve working under new digital systems, and the *skills* they require include the ability to use data-driven interfaces, apps and platforms. By providing these skills through education, the city is providing companies with workers who can maximise the rate of sale and exchange, and work as and when they are required, rather than for set hours in the way that traditional contracts require. With this skills agenda, the city is organising the employment – or, in Lefebvrian terms, the exploitation – of the classes of workers who will deliver data-driven services in the city.

Meanwhile, the city has a parallel objective to fit out Edinburgh for the 'data revolution' by seeking to inspire data capitalists to invest in the city. The city is proud to be host to the travel search company Skyscanner, a 'unicorn' that was sold in 2016 for £1.4 billion, and many of the start-up's initial staff remain in the city. Firms like Deliveroo have offices in Edinburgh, while at Codebase ('the largest technology incubator in the UK and one of the fastest growing in Europe') a host of platforms are hatching. One, Caresourcer, plans to be 'the first comparison and matching site for older people care'. The free service founded by former Skyscanner staff is accruing masses of data in an effort to control market flows, and at the time of writing it had over 27,000 registered providers across the UK, and employed over forty people in Edinburgh. In 2019, as part of the 'largest ever Series A funding round by a digital tech company in Scotland', it received £1.5 million investment from Scottish Enterprise (Scotland's public agency to fund and support businesses) to create seventy more jobs (Scottish Enterprise 2019). As well as offering care providers ways to increase custom, it features a free support service for care workers, equivalent to aspects of a union service, offering guidance about workplace issues, insurance and health advice.

But what connects the effort to amass data about the economy, to upskill the workforce, and to attract and support tech companies to pioneer new ways of organising delivery and care work? Certainly, Lefebvre's schema helps to interpret these dynamics as an integrated ideology. The Deal, rather than an agreement with companies to develop a new planned economy, expresses the city's declaration that it will smooth the ground for companies to build a new 'network of circulation and communication' (Lefebvre 1996: 98). It perhaps reflects a concern to sustain the 'centre of information and decision-making' in the city (ibid.), as platforms become increasingly able to control goods and labour flows in the market, and to gather and privatise data about the city. But as the City Deal strains to synchronise the different elements of its plan, the power of the city itself is brought into question. Official documents emphasise that the Deal will be the tugboat to a bulksome barge of integrated bureaucratic agencies (including education agencies like Skills Development Scotland, the Scottish Qualifications Authority, employability authorities like Joined Up for Jobs, third sector partners like Into Work, research centres like the Data Lab, and training schemes like the Workforce Development Fund; City Deal 2019). With respect to data gathering, while managers have ambitions to pool data from private and public sources and are embarking on expensive work to build the infrastructure to do it, it remains unclear whether these agencies will be able to access the data, or whether they will have the capacity to understand, process and use it. And if the aim is to enable such agencies to improve the allocation of work in the city, platform corporations have tended neither to require information or data from cities about workers, nor to hand to cities the data that would allow local agencies to monitor and control the labour market. If the objective is for public services to be monitored and controlled by data-driven systems, will the city develop these systems itself and deliver them through its agencies and departments, or hand the information and licences to private platforms? With respect to employment and skills, care and delivery companies require workers on a city level, but what stake does this really give the city? Are the urban planners offering the city as a kind of guinea pig, which different stakeholders can experiment with? Does the city aspire to be a broker between companies and workers? Is the proliferation of an app-pliant proletariat really what companies look at when they consider where to open an office? Certainly, there is little direct contact between a Deliveroo rider in

Edinburgh and a member of its tech staff, except when a rider delivers a pizza to the door of the office. The city cannot make decisions about corporations.

If its impact on the development of data-driven companies seems limited, still, the Deal will impact workers through promoting new kinds of work and skills in ways already described. The Deal has involved no process of worker consultation. It has not called on representatives of platform workers to help shape policy, let alone explored what kind of collectives would give workers a voice or a stake in their data-driven future. In 400 pages of core documentation, there is one passing mention of unions.[2] Explicitly 'citizen and employer-centric' (p. 255), it treats employers as having discrete interests but collapses those of workers into those of citizens. It plans a scheme for citizens to 'learn about data citizenship; how personal data is stored and used, as well as their legal rights and privacy implications' (p. 221) but proposes no equivalent opportunity for workers to learn about data justice at work. In this bright new digital revolution, the asymmetry of power between classes is not only embedded in algorithms. It is coded into policy.

CLOCKING THE NEW RHYTHMS OF THE CITY

For scattered workers, working in isolation under the illusion of flexibility, the city is the common ground. Even if platforms operate internationally, above the level of any city policy, the city is the space across which gig workers operate, and it may also be regarded as a space of potential control. In Lefebvre's concepts, this may develop through *encountering* one another in the city, and establishing *fluid spaces* – such as clandestine and changeable assembly points – for meeting and plotting, that are not arranged by apps or by civic authorities. It may mean *reading the city* in ways that the apps cannot, judging the attitudes of business owners and customers in different parts of the city, and spotting hazards and opportunities that a good eye can detect in the streets and open spaces. And it may mean making efforts to take control of working time, allowing them to *reclaim the time* in which they would live the urban life most fully, such as at evenings and weekends.

Gig workers face organising challenges because they are dispersed across the city. The automatic deployment of workers across cities often puts workers in hazardous situations that are undetected by apps, increasing workers' risk of bodily harm (Gregory 2020), but accidents are not recorded or known in ways that enable workers to identify common hazards. Apps command and constrain workers to work alone, and in certain cases prohibit contact between them (van Doorn 2017). Isolated workers struggle to meet other workers and make companions. Companies have operational tools to undermine attempts to create common cause and solidarity. Both algorithms that reward the best performers, and the self-employment contract model, encourage competition rather than cooperation. The 'algorithmic despotism' of delivery platforms constrains freedoms over schedules and activities (Griesbach et al. 2019). Tracking and monitoring impair workers' ability to meet privately, while the need to chase periods of high demand and structure their lives according to the market makes an illusion of the notion that workers have control of their own time (Jamil and Noiseux 2018).

During 2020, gig workers in Edinburgh launched the 'Workers' Observatory', a research and organising initiative to monitor work in the city. Its website includes testimony from workers highlighting the ways in which these Lefebvrian approaches are all made more difficult by the changing character of work. Encounters with other workers tend to become less frequent in the context of gig work. To take the example of couriers, one Deliveroo rider explained that couriers used to gather at certain points to pick up shifts, but that is no longer the case. Whereas Deliveroo once required riders to gather at certain fixed points, the logic has now changed. You are now always making decisions about how to get away from other riders, since you do not want there to be a high availability of workers in a certain area. It is often in the interest of a rider to get away from other riders, and to be as isolated as possible. This means that fluid gathering spaces may only emerge if they are intentionally organised, rather than springing organically from the hidden channels through which workers flow. Even when workers do meet together, the lack of fixed breaks or schedules can result in the interruption of these encounters, sometimes by business owners:

> I was going out [of a restaurant] with the meal [to deliver], and I'd been chatting for one minute with another rider who was coming. He was Spanish as well, and we were chatting for one minute, one minute, and then the boss came and said something like 'Are you ok? Do you have the order? Yeah?' It was really disgusting, the sensation. (Workers' Observatory 2020)

For care workers, too, encounters are difficult. According to one care worker, the allocation of work means that she 'rarely get[s] to meet other care workers' (ibid.). The COVID-19 lockdown exacerbated this, so that workers appreciated even wordless encounters in the street. While the pandemic was 'very isolating', one said, 'Care workers can see care workers, and that's what I like when I'm out and about. There's a glance that we can pass to each other, "how's it going?"' (ibid.).

The capacity to read the city is also affected by gig work. The lack of encounter may make collective interpretation and observation more difficult, but the roaming nature of gig work and the view of businesses and customers in their commercial or private domains gives workers insights into the circumstances of different classes of people, and their attitudes and approaches to work and life. Alongside the example of the rude, and possibly drunk, employer shooing the Deliveroo rider out of the shop, that same rider described the strange effect of serving unseen customers and seeing the attitude and atmosphere of the homes of the rich:

> At a house near the Meadows, in Morningside [an affluent area], a big terrace house that you have to go down a little path to get to, the deal was that I had to leave the bag, and I don't ring the bell, I just say that the order is complete, and I leave . . . It's something I'll remember all my life. (Ibid.)

The requirement for workers to encounter customers in their homes, and to be constantly aware of the contrast in manners and attitudes between neighbourhoods and classes within the city, does lay the city more open to the gaze of workers, even if the lack of communication and encounter with other workers makes it more difficult to share these observations and to organise on the basis of what is seen and known.

Algorithmic management also alters the tempos and rhythms of work. While there is a tendency to regard platform work as irregular and unsteady, with Deliveroo there is some level of seasonality, as well as spikes at certain times of the day and week. While these are relatively predictable, they do mean that riders have to constantly adjust their working regimes and to take risks about when and how much to work. You may work one Saturday night because you expect it to be a period of high demand, then find it to be barren. You may plan to work during a festival like the Edinburgh Fringe, then find a drought of work because too many extra couriers signed up to work. Riders are of course aware that patterns of working time are based on consumer demand which changes throughout the days, weeks and years. The regularity of certain working times and patterns 'exposes the lie' of flexibility, in the words of one courier, since consumer demand means that work is, in fact, fairly steady. Riders become used to the inflxible pressure to work when others socialise:

> Nobody, honestly, nobody loves to work on a Friday night. 9 o'clock, everybody's hanging out, and you are out cycling, going here and there, and then you finish at like 11 o'clock and you have a shower and then you go with your friends . . . that's the situation all the Saturdays and Fridays of your life. (Ibid.)

The Lefebvrian demand to *appropriate time* applies clearly to situations where time is not yours, such as when a manager schedules you to work on a Friday night. That sense is being replaced with an expectation that you will obviously, voluntarily, spend your time working on a Friday night, even at the risk of not earning what you expected to earn. Technologies are enabling this changing sense of working time, complicating the idea of reclaiming time appropriated by companies. Food delivery apps reward a worker for working at times traditionally reserved for leisure and punish those who do not. But still, at least the time is their own.

There is nothing new about the measurement of time by piece, tasks or gigs rather than hours and shifts. But the sense of working time is changed by technology in that each piece of work is no longer worth a fixed amount. The app user sells their work on the market as if they are self-employed. In work such as that offered by Deliveroo, you do not *really* need to work Friday night, you *could* go to the pub, but your decision about working time is personal: you *choose* to work. The choices and considerations leading up to this decision are based on the information that is given to the rider by data-driven technologies, not on predetermined hours or steady rates. If you are a Deliveroo or Uber rider, you can see how much you will be paid for every piece of work, but you can only take informed guesses as to what times are going to be more or less well paid. You do not *know*. And without this knowledge, you can only learn over time from your own experience and from sharing hints and insights with others. In this way, data-driven technology is changing the rhythms of work. Just as the clock super-seded the old tempos of labour provided by nature, and gradually altered the pace and pattern of working time, so the application to work of algorithmic computation and data collection has begun to sup-plant older systems of time discipline. A factory worker could not tell the time for work from the rising of the sun, and nor can an app-based worker necessarily check her watch to discover the duration of her shift or the wage she can expect.

When clocks were introduced to factories, one way that workers resisted the control that the new system of time management afforded to bosses was by attempting to monitor and understand the new time systems (Thompson 1967). Another was by establishing the times and rates at which they were prepared to work, through association and collective negotiation. Workers at first resisted the new time systems, but as they became accustomed to the new rhythms of working time, they 'accepted the categories of their employers and learned to fight back within them' (p. 86). Fighting back within the new forms of time measurement might be part of what is required in order for workers to *reclaim the time* as Lefebvre proposes. Efforts to reclaim the time by preserving the eight-hour working day, or attempting to force compa-nies to revert to fixed piece-rates, appeal to older forms of working time that are enshrined in law, or established in working culture. They are ways of fighting back against the categories of the employers, not ways to fight back within them. But workers understand that the time of their work depends on the market demand for a service, and that apps are an effective and efficient way of matching workers with demand. Data-driven technologies allow companies to change the sense of working time, in order to match it more directly with the market. These markets can be analysed digitally, and they can also be understood locally. Resisting the changing sense of time may result not from legal or traditional demands, but by gathering or demanding information about data and its use. As platforms gather extensive information about workers, workers may be capable in turn of exerting a form of 'techno-normative' control over their time of work, and their real-time movements (Gandini 2019). The Workers' Observatory aims to support workers' efforts to monitor and even measure the factors affecting their time of work in the city, such as market dynamics, the number of active workers, and the logic of automated management (Gallagher 2020), in order to articulate their own time-related demands. Organising to gather information that helps workers understand new rhythms of work-time may form part of the effort to obtain both rights and justice as workers in the city.

INCORPORATING GIG WORKERS IN THE EIGHTEENTH CENTURY

In order to pursue any such strategy, however, workers must overcome their isolation and create collective unity, identity and organisation, under conditions that make such incorporation difficult. Just as Lefebvre's scheme says little about the significance of changing tempos of working time, it also offers few clues about the way that workers whose work takes them across the city can come to form associations, have their work regulated by the city, and ultimately achieve autonomy to set their terms of work collectively. Eighteenth-century gig workers in Edinburgh provide a vivid case of how to assume control in work that depended on timely, punctual and trustworthy service delivery. Like modern couriers, the cadies were ready to run errands in every corner of the city. Their piece work had inconstant prices depending on the market and consumer demand. And both public and private authorities were always eager to monitor and manage their work. As we shall see, their process of gradual incorporation through the course of the eighteenth century sprang from a natural tendency to share knowledge of the city. From this emerged a common awareness that the basis of the trust they established in their service depended on their timeliness and reliability, rather than the system of control under which they worked. Since their work could just as well be organised by themselves as by an external authority, they built the power, identity and common interest they needed to overcome competition between themselves, demand autonomy and obtain the right to be sole providers of the service in the city.

The Society of Cadies was an association of couriers in eighteenth-century Edinburgh whose members took messages around the city, acted as guides and escorts, delivered parcels, distributed pamphlets, and carried out other odd jobs. More formally known as *running stationers*, they would be stationed at the town cross, and would 'execute suddenly and well whatever Employment is assigned them' (Burt 1754: 27). Largely consisting of highlanders who, though they were not foreign in status, were quite foreign in culture, their expansive and indefinite function made them in some respect the archetypal gig worker – not constrained to particular tasks, but hireable for whatever the hirer wished. There were some demarcations: they could not, for instance, taxi people around the city in sedan chairs, which was the prerogative of the Chairmen, and they were distinct from the Porters who made their bread 'carrying burdens fastened to their backs by ropes and creels' (Jamieson 1916: 215). With such exceptions, their 'whole office [was] to do any thing that any body can want, and discharge any kind of business' (Topham 1780: 106).

Cadies saw the city and knew its streets forensically. Until 1790, the names of courtyards and closes in Edinburgh were not painted, so for a visitor to find a friend, service or a place to stay was difficult without a cadie, while residents relied on them for cross-city communication. They knew 'every body in the Town who is of any kind of Note', making it 'impossible at Edinburgh to be concealed or unknown' (Burt 1754: 26). Their knowledge surpassed that of the city authorities, and indeed the cadies were relied upon by Edinburgh's Council to prevent crime and enforce law – to be 'tutelary guardians of the city' (Topham 1780: 106) – even while they provided clandestine support for prostitution and other nefarious trade. By escorting visitors, running errands and observing inhabitants, the cadies gathered and pooled masses of information: 'They are the only persons who may truly be said to have attained universal knowledge, for they know everything and everybody; they even know sometimes what you do, better than you yourself' (pp. 216–17).

Alongside knowledge, the cadies' other most valuable virtues were their reliability and punctuality. They were, an observer remarked, 'considerably trusted, and, as I have been told, have seldom or never proved unfaithful' (Burt 1754: 27), including with large sums of money which, on rare occasions when they were lost, would be reimbursed to the hirer under a kind of liability insurance provided by their society, while those who delayed in delivering a parcel were rebuked and reprimanded. It was of course in the cadies' *interest* to be timely and trusted. A tourist remarked that one needed not to assume in them 'any idea of moral obligation, beyond what is inspired in this way by the immediate feeling of self-interest' (Morris 1819: 244). In a court case involving the detainment of an errant cadie who had taken more than his share for finding a lost dog in the city, the integrity of the society was the central thrust in prosecuting for his internment. Cadie-ship was 'not properly a *trade*, but an office of *trust*' (Hope 1788: 15). It was in the individual interest of a cadie to be trustworthy, and in the collective interest of the Society of Cadies to enforce the trustworthiness of each of its members.

Although cadies carried out their tasks independently, their shared knowledge, and common yet distinctive sense of timekeeping and timeliness, bound them together as a group of workers. Their knowledgeability and reliability, so vital to their reputation, by extension secured their institutional status as public servants. But with this public role came public regulation, and the discipline it entailed. The extent of the cadies' autonomy varied throughout the lifetime of the society. At first, cadies were compelled to act as eyes and ears of the council and faced serious penalties for refusing tasks. As they grew in strength, the society regulated and governed itself. Three phases of the Society's development chart the gradually increasing degree of control and autonomy that the cadies achieved by pooling and sharing information, and illustrate the significance of the moment when cadies broke free from external authority and established themselves as a free association. Each of these three moments in the Society's history offers lessons regarding the contemporary gig economy.

During the first phase in the development of the society, from their earliest appearance until their incorporation in 1714, cadies were at the mercy of external controllers appointed to enforce duty and discipline (Marwick 2021: 3). At the turn of the century, in 1699, the city council restricted the company to twenty members and required them to wear a uniform of 'a kind of Apron of Blew-Linnen made in the Form of a Bag' (Jamieson 1916: 220). It stipulated that everyone who became a cadie should give security of the large sum of ten pounds Scots, for honesty, and pay into the Company's box which was opened and dispersed in the summer to those in need. The council laid down regulations for their good behaviour, religious obedience, education and, importantly, a system of task allocation and workplace discipline:

> When one is called to go on an Errand, or to sell a Paper, where two or more are present, he who cometh first to the Person who called him, shall have the Benefit of what is sold or had for going the Errand, unless the Person who called otherways determine it. And when they are sent an Errand, if the Business wherein he is instructed, or thing committed to him, be miscarried through his Default, he shall lose his Privilege and be further punished. (NLS, MS/1.22, 201)

The regulation of the cadies at this stage was not so dissimilar from modern forms of licensing and regulating black cab drivers. Observance of the rules was ensured and enforced by an independent inspector, hired by the council. In ensuing decades, cadies had other rules and duties added to their role. Under these external commanders, the cadies were in a state of competition with one another, facing negative incentives to complete their tasks, and having 'no Manner of Government among them' (Maitland 1753: 326).

They remained under this external authority until their incorporation in 1714. During their second significant phase, as an incorporated body, cadies secured a degree of self-governance, and rights to set their own rules and systems of discipline. But they still needed to appeal to the council to enforce their privileges. When others pretended to be cadies, reducing the amount that they could charge, and risking the security and reputation of their work, they had to seek external help. In 1739, the society felt the need to petition the council to intervene in securing its privileges due to an influx of people 'tak[ing] upon themselves to act in the character of running stationers or cadies' (NRS, RH9/14/131). The council agreed to enforce the closed shop, but simultaneously introduced new systems of discipline. A cadie now had to wear a numbered badge, or else would face a hefty fine and 48 hours in prison. Refusing an errand without a reasonable excuse, or charging above the scale of fees, also warranted a pecuniary penalty and a stint in the Guard-house. Prices and rates for errands were fixed, preventing the cadies from setting their own rates. Later, in 1759, the council likewise saw fit to 'bring in proper Regulations for preventing the frequent and just Complaints made against the cadies' (ECA, Moses Bundles, 1759). They restricted the society to sixty members, and reiterated a list of unacceptable behaviours, from swearing and pimping, to neglecting their duties and over-charging customers.

The third significant phase of the cadies began when their security and status changed in 1771. After another petition from the society, a Seal of Cause was granted them, elevating the society into 'a Fraternity or Body Corporate' (ECA, SL1/1/87). By this change, the now-autonomous society was better able to manage its own funds and administer welfare to sick workers, and pay for the burial of the dead. Cadies were still required to abide by most of the rules and regulations laid down in 1759, but rather than having to appeal to the city to police the trade, they were given the right to 'exerc[ise] the business of cadees within the city of Edinburgh and libertys in all time coming [*sic*; the liberties are the areas immediately around the city]' (ibid.). They now had won 'power to make bye-laws for their own government, to elect office-bearers, and to admit such persons as they shall think proper to become members' (Hope 1788: 14). They had obtained the right to regulate their own work in the city, and they maintained the information and institutional structures to practise it.

Throughout the century, the cadies sustained a sense of autonomy and, despite the ebbs and flows that followed the course of economic development in a period of massive growth, they shifted from a situation of being a scattered, unincorporated body at the mercy of an agent hired by the council, to demanding and assuming the right of self-governance and incorporation. The initial stage saw a kind of regulator in command of the cadies, pushing them to compete and punishing them with arbitrary rules. The second phase saw a degree of regulation, but inadequate measures to prevent them being undercut by an influx of new workers; and when they appealed to the city, they were forced to accept a degradation in their working arrangements and autonomy. The third phase saw the elevation of the incorporated society into an autonomous body with the right to self-regulate, the information to do so, and common agreement as to their working time and rates.

Their extent of incorporation was, in short, about information and control. Their incorporation allowed them to monitor and influence the numbers of cadies in the city, the rates at which wages and prices were set, the system by which orders were dispensed, the way that discipline was maintained and trust was sustained, and the way that the knowledge, information and data on which their work depended was collected, pooled and shared within the society. The right to the city for these workers was the right to be in control of their work in the city, not a right to work at the behest of the city, or the right to work under a supervisor appointed by the city. In its earliest form, the society had little or no control, but over the course of decades these gig workers formed into a strong and independent association, able to regulate their own conditions. Throughout the century, the Edinburgh cadies consistently maintained the desire to develop an incorporation that had rights at the city level, rather than to be externally regulated or endure rules enforced by a private agent.

Many analogies can be drawn between the cadies and the current situation of delivery riders and other gig workers. Under modern working arrangements, workers are commanded by apps, through which they compete with one another and are punished for falling below the standard set by algorithms. Algorithmic systems make it challenging for workers to gather and share information about their work arrangements. But like the cadies, couriers can begin by gathering information about the private agencies and the policies they work under, sharing this information when they encounter one another in the city, and recognising that even if their working time is unaligned with many workers in society, it is still capable of being brought under their control. This information can inform collective demands to regulate conditions, to prevent an influx of labour from harming rates and conditions, and to be recognised and consulted as a collective of workers providing a valued public service. This recognition, in turn, could become the basis for gathering further information and building infrastructure to enable a society or guild to achieve the right to work in the city on their own terms.

Encouraging initiatives are springing up across the world to equip platform workers in the data-driven economy. Some initiatives focus on gathering and sharing information. The Fairwork research project on platform work has developed models for rating platforms by pay, conditions, contracts, management and representation (Fairwork 2021); Turkopticon gives online Mechanical Turk workers a way to share information about clients and task givers (Irani and Silberman 2013); and Worker Info Exchange helps workers to access and gain insight from data they have generated at work (Athreya 2021). Other initiatives enable workers to monitor their working time, such as WeClock and Workerbird, both applications allowing workers to track their working day (Uniglobal 2020; Herman 2019). Others still provide workers with ways to build networks and form communities. Union Platform, an Argentinian app, allows workers to exchange information securely in forums (Friedrich Ebert Stiftung 2020), while the Industrial Workers of the World union has developed Wobbly, a communication and coordination tool and workplace organising platform (Evans 2018). While most of these initiatives provide tools for workers who are working across different cities, regions or localities, other projects are exploring how such tools can be used to equip groups of gig and freelancers in particular locations and circumstances. In Belgium, the United Freelancers union, an offshoot of the CSC trade union confederation, is developing a tailored service for Belgian platform workers with common needs. At a still more local level, the Workers' Observatory is exploring how platform and gig workers in the city of Edinburgh might develop and deploy various tools at the same time as developing guilds or associations that can assert control over their work, and develop collective autonomy and agency in the city.

CONCLUSION

For as long as workers have been paid for discrete tasks or gigs, those workers have organised. As the digital revolution unfolds, the process of collective organising will certainly involve new tools and technologies that equip workers to challenge data-driven surveillance, management and control. Since these are developed and commanded by platform companies operating across the globe, many gig organising initiatives tend to frame the gig economy as a recent global phenomenon with national particularities. But as a detour to Edinburgh's eighteenth-century high street demonstrates, many of the conditions and challenges of city-based gig work are centuries old. The cadies' story helps to illuminate the obstacles facing gig workers today, who labour under unstable conditions set by private agencies. The local authorities of Enlightenment Edinburgh, not unlike the City Dealers of today, sought to control the cadies and to limit their ability to shape their own conditions. The challenge, then, for platform workers dominated by private and city corporations is to create corporate bodies of their own that can establish rates, set routines and enforce collective rights. This is not the same as forming a traditional trade union, by way of organising models designed to respond to twentieth-century employer–employee relations, stable working days and bargaining rights. The alternative is complicated, and it is still developing. It involves workers gathering information about the systems under which they work, sharing knowledge about changing patterns of work, and forming new associations that give them collective agency. And since the city is the site of their experiences and encounters, is it not also the best stage on which to act?

ACKNOWLEDGEMENTS

I would like to thank Dr Amy Westwell, Xabier Villares, Boyan Karabaliev, Alice Barker, Gemma Moncrieff, Dr Karen Gregory and Dr Wenlong Li for their invaluable interviews, comments and insights. I am also grateful to

Sandra Marwick for allowing me to cite her excellent account of the Society of Cadies' development, based on research at the Edinburgh City Archives. Some of my ECA references are reproduced from her paper. Marwick started to investigate the cadies in her research for the People's Story Museum in the Canongate which opened in 1989. She has subsequently updated the paper so suggested that I use the date of access as its date of publication.

NOTES

1. Documents relating to the City Deal can be accessed at http://esescity regiondeal.org.uk/, while information about the cluster of 'innovations hubs' forming the University-based Data-Driven Innovation project can be found at https://ddi.ac.uk/.
2. 'The Data Skills Journey is a framework that will be developed for the region's workforce with employers, unions, and professional bodies' (City Deal 2019: 246).

ARCHIVES

ECA, Moses Bundles (1759): Edinburgh City Archives, Moses Bundles, vol. VI, No. 6604, Act of Council containing Regulations for Cadies, 14 February 1759.

ECA, SL1/1/87: Edinburgh City Archives, SL1/1/87 (7 November 1770), quoted in Adam Fox, *The Press and the People: Cheap Print and Society in Scotland: 1500–1785* (Oxford: 2020), p. 204.

NLS, MS/1.22, 201: National Library of Scotland, MS/1.22 (201), Rules and Instructions by the Town Council of Edinburgh to be observed by All who are permitted to cry Gazettes and other Papers, or to sell Roses and Flowers, or to Carie Links upon the Street of Edinburg, (Noblemen and Gentlemen's Servants excepted) (Edinburgh: [1700]).

NRS, RH9/14/131: National Records of Scotland, RH9/14/131, Petition of George McLaren, 30 June 1739.

REFERENCES

Athreya, B. (2021) With One Huge Victory Down, UK Uber Driver Moves on to the Next Gig Worker Battlefront. Inequality.org, 5 April. Available at https://inequality.org/research/uk-uber-drivers/ (last accessed 11 January 2022).

Burt, E. (1754) *Letters from a Gentleman in the North of Scotland to His Friend in London; Containing the Description of a Capital Town in that Northern Country*. London.

City Deal (2019) Edinburgh and South East Scotland City Region Deal Joint Committee, 1 March 2019, Data Driven Innovation (DDI) Skills Gateway Project Proposition. Available at https://democracy.edinburgh.gov.uk/do cuments/s9936/Full_Meeting_Papers___Edinburgh_and_South_East_Scot land_City_Region_Deal_Joint_Committee___01.03.19.pdf (last accessed 11 January 2022).

City of Edinburgh (2018) *Edinburgh Economy Strategy: Enabling Good Growth.* June 2018. Available at https://www.etag.org.uk/wp-content/uploads/20 19/10/Edinburgh_Economy_Strategy___June_2018.pdf (last accessed 11 January 2022).

Dencik, L., Hintz, A., Redden, J. and Treré, E. (2019) exploring data justice: conceptions, applications and directions. *Information, Communication & Society,* 22(7), 873–81.

Evans, J. (2018) An introduction to Wobbly: an app for 21st century workers' power. Notes from Below, 16 August. Available at https://notesfrombelow .org/article/an-introduction-to-wobbly (last accessed 21 January 2022).

Fairwork UK Ratings (2021) *Labour Standards in the Gig Economy.* Available at https://fair.work/wp-content/uploads/sites/131/2021/05/Fairwork-UK-Re port-2021.pdf (last accessed 11 January 2022).

Friedrich Ebert Stiftung (2020) #UNION PLATFORM el sindicato en tu bol- sillo. Friedrich Ebert Stiftung blog, 17 November. Available at https://argen tina.fes.de/e/union-platform-el-sindicato-en-tu-bolsillo/ (last accessed 11 January 2022).

Gallagher, C. (2020) Why workers' observatories can help empower gig workers. Brave New Europe. 19 November. Available at https://bravenew europe.com/cailean-gallagher-why-workers-observatories-can-help- empower-gig-workers (last accessed 31 January 2022).

Gandini, A. (2019) Labour process theory and the gig economy. *Human Relations,* 72(6), 1039–56.

Griesbach, K., Reich, A., Elliott-Negri, L. and Milkman, R. (2019) Algorithmic control in platform food delivery work. *Socius,* 5, 1–15.

Gregory, K. (2020) 'My life is more valuable than this': understanding risk among on-demand food couriers in Edinburgh. *Work, Employment and Society,* 35(2), 316–31.

Herman, J. (2019) How can tech be designed to support workers? RSA blog, 4 September. Available at https://www.thersa.org/blog/2019/09/tech-desig ned-support-workers (last accessed 11 January 2022).

Hope, C. (1788) Information for Alexander Walker, one of the late Magistrates if Edinburgh . . . Against John McGlashan, late Running Stationer in Edinburgh. . . . Edinburgh.

Irani, L. and Silberman, S. (2013) Turkopticon: interrupting worker invisibil- ity in Amazon Mechanical Turk. CHI 2013. Available at http://crowdsour

cing-class.org/readings/downloads/ethics/turkopticon.pdf (last accessed 11 January 2022).

Jamieson, J. H. (1916) The sedan chair in Edinburgh. In *The Book of the Old Edinburgh Club*, vol. 9. Edinburgh.

Jamil, R. and Noiseux, T. (2018) Shake that moneymaker: insights from Montreal's Uber drivers. *Papers in Political Economy*, 60.

Lefebvre, H. (1996) *Writings on Cities*, Part II: Right to the City. Oxford: Blackwell.

Maitland, W. (1753) *A History of Edinburgh from its Foundation to the Present Time*, Book V. Edinburgh.

Marwick, S. (2021) The Society of Running Stationers or Cadies – 'useful and intelligent servants of the public'. Umquhile Edinburgh. Available at https://063a6ba4-2815-4034-83a6-f472820bf481.filesusr.com/ugd/1dc3b2_311ba8c2b0a6490fb2f6a8fc9ef02529.pdf (last accessed 11 January 2022).

Morris, P. (1819) *Peter's Letters to his Kinsfolk*, vol. 1. Edinburgh.

Office of the Secretary of State for Scotland (2017) City Deal: Heads of Terms for Edinburgh and South East Scotland. Available at https://www.gov.uk/government/publications/city-deal-heads-of-terms-for-edinburgh-and-south-east-scotland (last accessed 11 January 2022).

Scotsman (2018) Can Edinburgh become data capital of Europe? *The Scotsman*, 28 September. Available at https://www.scotsman.com/news/can-edinburgh-become-data-capital-europe-571667 (last accessed 11 January 2022).

Scottish Enterprise (2019) Scottish Enterprise grant targets over 70 new high value jobs at Care Sourcer (news release). 28 August. Available at https://www.scottish-enterprise-mediacentre.com/news/scottish-enterprise-grant-targets-over-70-new-high-value-jobs-at-care-sourcer (last accessed 11 January 2022).

Thompson, E. P. (1967) Time, work-discipline, and industrial capitalism. *Past & Present*, 38(1), 56–97.

Topham, E. (1780) *Letters from Edinburgh, Written in the Years 1774 and 1775: Containing Some Observations on the Diversions, Customs, Manners, and Laws, of the Scotch Nation, During a Six Months Residence in Edinburgh*, vol. II, pp. 217–18. Dublin.

Uniglobal (2020) New app for workers to fight wage theft. Uniglobal news release, 8 July. Available at https://www.uniglobalunion.org/news/new-app-workers-fight-wage-theft (last accessed 11 January 2022).

van Doorn, N. (2017) Platform labor: on the gendered and racialized exploitation of low-income service work in the 'on-demand' economy. *Information, Communication & Society*, 20(6), 898–914.

Workers' Observatory (2020) Insights of a courier: we don't need the company. Available at https://workersobservatory.org/delivery-guild/ (last accessed 31 January 2022).

Chapter 9

THE STUDENTS ARE ALREADY (GIG) WORKERS

Karen Gregory

INTRODUCTION

The title of this chapter is a reference to Marc Bousquet's *How the University Works: Higher Education and the Low-wage Nation* (2008). That book was then, and continues to be, a guide for understanding the shifting relationship between education and the world of work. I taught his chapter 'The Students Are Already Workers' in my Sociology and Labour Studies courses at the City University of New York to undergraduate students who saw themselves on the page. Many of these students arrived for class exhausted, coming from or attending classes between a range of caring obligations and jobs like baggage handling and retail work at JFK Airport, which required students to work through all hours of the night. Bousquet's chapter opens with a quote from a similar student-worker named Kody who says:

> I know that I haven't updated in about two and a half weeks, but I have an excuse. UPS is just a tiring job. You see, before, I had an extra 31 hours to play games, draw things, compose music . . . do homework. But now, 31+ hours of my life is devoted to UPS. I hate working there. But I need the money for college, so I don't have the option of quitting. My job at UPS is a loader. I check the zip codes on the box, I scan them into the database, and then I load them into the truck, making a brick wall out of boxes. (Bousquet 2008: 125)

The remainder of the chapter explores how the delivery company was able to turn students like Kody into a standing reserve of cheap and indebted labour by forging close links with local community colleges

211

through an 'earn and learn' programme that enticed undergraduate students to take up physically exhausting, over-night, part-time jobs in exchange for tuition support. As Bousquet shows, while UPS benefited from this cheap labour, these jobs resulted in fragmented, unsustainable work schedules and financial precarity for students.

Today, Kody might work for Deliveroo or another on-demand delivery platform. Such platforms do not even need to entice students through earn and learn programmes. Rather, as this chapter shows, the platform economy has been, in part, fuelled by dovetailing with the broader financialised regimes of higher education and urban development. These regimes simultaneously enlist students as both consumers and standing reserves of labour. In both regards, students produce valuable data that flows back to only the platform. As this chapter shows, platforms such as Deliveroo sit comfortably in the broader financialisation of student life. As consumers, on-demand services offer convenience and care. As sites of work, platforms offer accessibility, flexibility and the promise of relatively high wages, as well as the option to 'get fit while working' (Malin and Chandler 2017). The promise of flexible work that fits around student schedules, as well as the possibility of relatively high wages (relative to other work available such as retail or hospitality work), are valuable to students who increasingly find themselves working to stave off costs, debts and stress associated with their degrees. As this chapter shows, students often dismiss their own platform labour as 'temporary work' or 'not real work' that they will abandon once they complete their studies. Yet, for some students, Deliveroo becomes their full-time work even after the degree, raising serious questions about student mobility, the risks of on-demand work while studying, and the role that platforms play in relation to the university more broadly.

Drawn from interviews with twenty-five on-demand food couriers in Edinburgh, Scotland, this chapter has two aims. The first is to explore the relationship between on-demand, platformed courier work, the University and the city, taking the city of Edinburgh as a case study. The second turns to interview material to explore how and why students take up this work and examines the ways that students minimise the risks associated with on-demand courier work. Taken together, this chapter shows that students are already gig workers and that such work requires deeper attention if we are to understand the extent to which platform labour and 'data work' are shaping student work trajectories.

As such, this chapter hopes to add nuance to the narratives that we tell about the gig economy. As Pasquale (2016) has suggested, platforms enter into new locales and markets, bringing opportunities, particularly for flexible work and small-scale entrepreneurialism. Along with this, they enable new streams of personal income and the creation of new social networks. Yet, platforms enable deep exploitation – turning local populations into standing reserves of labour, while extracting value, often in the form of data, from existing assets and resources such as homes, roads and worker bodies (Gregory and Sadowski 2021). Student-workers sit within these narratives, and their experiences may help us to see that fights over the future of work are deeply entangled in fights over rights to the city.

GLOBAL PLATFORM: LOCAL, DATAFIED LABOUR

Deliveroo is a global company that operates across twelve countries and more than 800 cities and towns. In Edinburgh, the company has scaled rather quickly, from a core group of riders in its first two years of operation to over 600 riders in the city (BBC Scotland 2018). The company's business model, which affords the quick delivery of meals from a range of restaurants, requires a fleet of riders who deliver by bicycle, scooter, motorcycle and car. This fleet of riders is essentially a local, skilled workforce who must be capable of translating the platform's delivery services into an urban environment with speed and efficiency. In the case of Edinburgh, these workers must be able to handle inclement weather, rough and elevated terrain, and dangerous traffic conditions (Gregory and Paredes Maldonado 2020). While not all university students are able to do this work, higher education students –particularly those who have experienced a middle-class culture of cycling and who have childhood histories of cycling in the city – present an ideal pool of delivery workers for the company, which markets itself with distinct cycle and bike messenger culture imagery.

I interviewed Deliveroo riders in Edinburgh as part of a research project to explore the nature of risk in on-demand courier work. The majority of those interviewed were students or former students. Eleven interviewees were currently students at the University of Edinburgh, Edinburgh Napier University or Stirling University. Another five are former students who remained in the city after their studies in the area. Nine individuals are not current or former students and are attempting to work full time as on-demand couriers, or are combining courier work with other part-time jobs. The majority of those interviewed in this research currently work via the food delivery platform Deliveroo, although almost half of riders also acquire work via other platforms such as Uber Eats or Beelivery. The majority of those interviewed for this project relied on their own bicycles to complete the work and, overall, the use of bicycles skews heavily towards student workers. Early in the recruitment of interviewees, student social networks were used and on two occasions an entire suite of student flat-mates arrived to be interviewed, having recommended each other to Deliveroo; they, in turn, recommended my research project to one another.

The ages of those interviewed ranged between 18 and 45, and the group was skewed towards male respondents (72 per cent male; 28 per cent female). This age and gender breakdown resonates with RSA (2017) findings, which reported that over half a million young people (16 to 30 years old) had taken part in some form of 'gig work'. The RSA (2017: 18) went so far as to suggest that gig work may have become an 'entry point' to self-employment in young people's lives. In the case of Deliveroo, the RSA also found that these couriers tend to be under 25 years old and mostly men. However, my interviews (and the RSA study) were conducted before the COVID-19 pandemic, and it is likely that these numbers would need to be updated as more individuals have turned to platforms such as Deliveroo for financial support during the crisis.

As Huws et al. (2017) note, surveys of the gig economy have often asked individuals to identify as either student or worker, which means that we may underestimate the overlap of these categories. As such, determining the exact number of student-workers using Deliveroo is difficult, but it is fair to say that students account for a considerable portion of the on-demand courier workforce in Edinburgh, where the presence of five campus-based universities means that the city is seasonally populated by valuable and lucrative flows of local and international students. As Bousquet noted (2008: 27), the term 'student' can easily refer to a type of worker 'who can be put to work but does not enjoy the rights of labor'. For Bousquet, this insight allows him to theorise the structural value and function of graduate labour in the university, but we might also see that such a classification parallels developments in the gig economy, which puts individuals to work as self-employed contractors rather than employees or workers. In this way, student-workers easily mingle with formally recognised working populations and tend to be discounted in assessments of the labour market.

On-demand platforms enjoy a dual relationship with local university-enabled markets, where students arrive as both consumer and potential worker. As Ross (2012) shows, flows of local and international students do not simply arrive in a city like Edinburgh, but rather are the product of what he calls 'the business of growth'. This does not only mean that universities expand (they do, often geographically and in terms of student numbers), but that universities play a unique and powerful role in shaping the development of cities. Already themselves highly financialised institutions with deep relationships to finance and their own debt, universities sit in a nexus of public and private funding and governance and are capable of funnelling monies into a range of profit-making (and often privatised) projects, primarily in the realm of real estate development. On the one hand, 'growth' is the necessary mechanism for the circulation of financialised capital. On the other, 'growth' lays the groundwork for the branded experience of student life which is sold to students, who are increasingly conceived of, and addressed, as consumers. However, what this means in practice is that the university is increasingly drawn into the business of housing and feeding students, even while it outsources this necessary work to various companies. As Ross (2012) writes of New York University (NYU), the university is one of New York's largest landowners and is perpetually buying, selling and leasing buildings – so much so that

> an administrator once remarked to me that he feels as if he is running a hotel and restaurant chain – given how many beds and cafeteria seats NYU caters to on a daily basis. It is difficult to operate at that kind of that volume without favoring a tidy list of clients and contractors. (Ross 2012: n.p.)

In the case of Deliveroo, its business model depends on consumption and accommodation markets generated by flows of local and international studies of urban areas. On-demand platforms directly enter into both of these markets, aiming to skim profit from student needs for housing and food. In Edinburgh, where the rental market moves quickly, platforms such as Airbnb function as directories of available short-term rentals, and companies such as Deliveroo hope to, and do, dovetail nicely into this privatising housing market, supplementing both the university's accommodation racket and offering what Richardson (2019) has called a 'flexible arrangement of the delivered meal' to students. Much in the same way that on-demand food delivery offers to step into the busy schedule of urban families, providing ready-made lunches and dinners, these platforms offer students convenience, as well as some semblance of healthy meal options delivered from local establishments. In Edinburgh, on-demand food delivery supplements universities' food services, which are outsourced to private companies. Here, on-demand food offers a branded 'value-added' service to university accommodations, which are also privately owned and operated by a range of companies. For example, companies such as 'Prime Student Living', which simply broker student private accommodations, often partner with platforms such as Deliveroo to offer incentives and perks to would-be student renters. In the case of Edinburgh, student dorms offer a reliable source of delivery orders. In my own interviews conducted with local riders, workers mentioned a direct and reliable flow of orders from Uber Eats and McDonalds to dorms, which raises the deeper questions about the role the university and students play in the supply chain logistics of food delivery pipelines.

In students, however, Deliveroo also finds a relatively stable and continuous supply of eager, and able, labour. As Jacob, Gerth and Weiss (2020) show, students now spend a considerable amount of time looking for work, and their ability to find work is limited by the overall availability of work and the quality of jobs. In Edinburgh, the work that students find tends to skew towards hospitality and retail, both of which can be physically demanding and poorly remunerated. Hospitality work, in particular, can be accompanied by harassment and unstable scheduling. As Canny (2002) has documented, shifts in the nature of work have meant the younger workers are increasingly faced with zero-hours contracts, low wage work and 'flexible' employment. Yet, student-workers increasingly make up a significant portion of the general labour market. These shifts in the nature of work have been mirrored by shifts in the experience of the university where rising tuition fees, the requirements to take on debt in order to complete a degree, and the rising costs of living and accommodation are now the norm. This means that students increasingly combine work with their studies. In many respects, on-demand platforms like Deliveroo actually offer what appears to be a 'good' job to students, relative to other jobs on offer, and, as I show below, on-demand work fits around student schedules and appears to offer slightly better than minimum wage.

Additionally, many students in the UK are international students, who make up a considerable portion of all students in the market for higher education. As Reilly (2013) shows, international students not only contribute to the consumption of education, but they form a pool of 'mostly semi-skilled' yet unprotected labour. As the pandemic has exposed, these students are often financially vulnerable and unqualified for state-based support. However, as UK universities increasingly rely on international students, particularly at the post-graduate level, to pay full tuition fees and exorbitant accommodation costs, these students turn to platform work because of its accessibility, the lack of regulation and a desperation for income. As a graduate student writing on Medium attests:

> I started my masters at International Institute of Social Studies (ISS) The Hague, University of Rotterdam in September, 2016 with students almost all continents. I was on full scholarship by Netherlands which at that time called Netherlands Fellowship Program (NFP) and has changed to OKP. While there were students who were either working at restaurants or doing dog keeping or taking care of children. There was only one student, Pablo my best friend, who was working for Deliveroo. He was one of the first riders on contract working for Deliveroo in The Hague. In late 2017 when students arrived after completing their field work, many of them started working for Deliveroo. (Turi 2020: n.p.)

The author goes on to simply state, 'We used to joke around in the school that Deliveroo is mandatory internship after graduating from ISS' (ibid.).

UNIVERSITY LIFE: LEARNING TO GIG

That students take up gig work, however, is not new. As MacDonald and Giazitzoglu (2019) show, there is a rich social history of youth work and student work at play in the gig economy – a history that platforms step into and extend, drawing in those in education and those with degrees. As they write, 'even young adults who are heavily loaded with educational capital (to PhD level), and who occupy the heights of successful youth transitions, are not protected from pre-carious, casualised work' (MacDonald and Giazitzoglu 2019: 734). Students that I spoke with have already learned that 'good' work is relatively difficult to find and, as we see in the interview material below, students want their work to be feasible, to be self-directed, and to support a healthy lifestyle. Additionally, students do take pleasure in on-demand courier work – they enjoy the work itself, they actively want to be, and enjoy being, part of a community of couriers, and they enjoy learning to master the city and its shortcuts. Turning to the interview data, we can see that students learn to gig, as well as learn to minimise risk.

Student Schedules

Fundamentally, the flexibility of platform-based gig work appeals to student-workers. As Thomas, a Deliveroo rider and current student, suggests, on-demand couriering fits in and around his study schedule:

> I have worked in a lot of different places but that, particularly I just did not enjoy it. I found it a lot to have the set hours plus uni work because there's no flexibility, whatsoever, I think was the worst thing in terms if you've got deadlines coming up or whatever, but you have to go, as well. I thought with Deliveroo in terms of com-bining it with university, it's a lot more flexible. That's one of the main attractions.

The appeal of flexibility is echoed in the words of Iain, a Deliveroo and Uber Eats rider who also sees the work as 'not restricted to any hours at all'. He went on to say:

> I love cycling and then it was in the second year of uni, so two and a half years ago it started to really grow in Edinburgh and I was one of the first riders to be put on the Edinburgh North section . . . I was the first one to do that and I thought that was a great way to earn money while doing something that I enjoy and being physi-cally active.
>   Also retail work I really wasn't that interested in, just spending eight hours a day in this big warm box and it was, yes, it didn't

quite suit me personally . . . I mean, yes, getting paid to cycle is my dream job, like dream, dream job definitely.

For Iain, this work is a dream because it is an innovation in the realm of work – work that you enjoy and work that can be considered healthy. In comparison to the retail job that Iain previously held, this is truly an improvement as he does not have to spend all day on someone else's schedule, is paid for physical mobility, and is able to do what he 'loves', which is cycling. The promise of earning money appears to Iain as almost too good to be true, and he spoke of using the platform's incentive system as inspiring 'healthy' breaks from studying, saying, 'I might be sitting in the library and I get a message twenty minutes before this promotion to earn an extra £20, I'm like, "Yes, go,"' totally.' Overall, what Iain is describing sounds 'great' but in his last statement we can see that he is being conditioned to work on demand and to be continually ready for work, to the extent that he will allow it to interrupt him from his studies.

Students find this work so appealing that they do turn to one another and recommend the job. As Jonathan, a part-time rider and full-time medical student said:

My flatmate had a friend who was doing it, and there was the incentive of the bonus sign-up scheme. He said, 'Me and my friend are doing it, we'll split the bonus so if you want to do it, it's only 20 deliveries, you can do it and then we'll split the bonus.' Then he started doing it and said, 'It's actually really quite good, because it's good money for just getting out on your bike. It's quite fun, it's a nice wee break from studying and such.'

The idea that delivery is 'quite fun' and a 'nice wee break' is a theme that ran throughout the interviews and that is picked up again later on, as students talk about this work as temporary and 'not real'. This, however, is the first part of the dismissal of broader working conditions for couriers, where work is often risky, dangerous and what Kidder (2006) has called 'dirty' work.

In tandem with this dismissal of work as 'fun', the idea of the dream job came up again in conversation with Andreas, a part-time rider and full-time student, who said:

> I wanted to work as a bike delivery agent for a while, because I watched this movie, I forgot what it's called, it's about a guy in New York who rides a bike and he's doing some fun job to save some kids in a container . . . I'm like, that seems so fun, and I really like cycling. I felt like making money with that was kind of a dream of mine, and I used to see all the backpacks going around, so I just Googled it and applied.

Here can we see that students imagine this work as part of a broader culture of messengering. The movie the student is referencing is *Premium Rush* (Koepp 2012) and tells the story of a heroic and speedy bike messenger whose advanced cycling skills enable him not only to defeat criminals, but also to stay alive while cycling in the city. Such an imaginary does two things. First, it attracts students and younger workers to the idea of on-demand work. Second, it helps workers to feel that they are joining a broader and bigger community of messengers, something which is deeply valuable to younger workers. Still, the idea that delivery work can be a respite from the stress of university work was echoed throughout interviews with students. As Andreas said:

> No, I don't think if I would do less Deliveroo I would study more, because I know, like, all the time outside Deliveroo is not 100 per cent study, and Deliveroo helps me relax. I usually study a bit, and my brain gets clogged with information, so I go out and ride, and that helps empty it.

His words are echoed by Sandra, also a full-time student and part-time rider, who also says that the work is 'just a space to have some exercise, make money at the same time, so you feel like you're being really productive, but, also, a bit of alone time, and time and space to clear your head a bit, yes'. It may be the case, as it is for many who work or study in the contemporary university, that time away from the institution is valuable as it lets them breathe, think and clear their heads.

Tuition Fees, Debt and Money

While school work can be demanding and stressful on its own, students also find themselves in a nexus of pressures, which are well articulated by Bethany, a student who left the university to work full-time as an on-demand courier. She says:

> I was doing my undergrad at Edinburgh full-time, and then I started to work . . . I was also finding that in order to pay for my fees I was having to work a lot, and any time off that I had I was trying to study, but I was so tired that neither really worked. I just ran out of, I don't know, space in my head as well because studying, it's not just a case of reading a book and relaxing, it's really intensive as well. Yes, so I started to just work more in a kind of transition from studying, and I decided that I would take a suspended study break and work more.

As Bethany explains, the pressure to pay tuition fees means that she must work in order to attend university, but as work and study compete for her attention and energy, she has found the coupling exhausting. For Bethany, the combination eventually became too much and she felt that her overall well-being was being reduced. She chose to suspend her studies, in part, because cycling seemed like a healthier and more lucrative choice. While many working students feel the pull of work over study, on-demand work draws them bit by bit. At first, flexible work seems manageable, as we saw above, purporting to fit into a study schedule, but for students who rely on working wages to pay for university (or rent or accommodation), the pressures to manage flexible work can be difficult. As Jonathan said:

> I enjoy cycling and it's like a wee mission when you get your 'pick up from this place and take to this place'. It's quite nice to do that, and it's really good money, especially for students I feel it's excellent . . . but I think as a reliable source of income I would be wary, because it's one of these zero hour contracts things and you can't rely on – or I feel personally I couldn't trust myself to rely on a zero.

As long as cycling stays within the realm of 'good money', students enjoy and recommend the work to each other, but once a student (or any individual, as other research has shown – see Gregory and Sadowki 2021) begins to depend on this income, the pressures mount and the quality of the job decreases. Yet, given that students can often earn more from on-demand work more quickly than compared to other jobs, it is not uncommon for students to prioritise courier work or to turn down other forms of work. As Victor, a full-time student, said:

> I used to work a little bit for this company that would have party every two weeks or so, and I would get £20 for doing stuff there, and when I got into Deliveroo, I started accepting less of those offers, because it was more profitable to work for Deliveroo.

Just a Job, Not a Real Job

Beyond the appeal of the work and the potential for students to earn better money relative to other work available, a key theme across interviews with students was a dismissal of on-demand food couriering as 'work'. Phrases such as 'not a proper job', 'only temporary' and 'not that complicated' were used frequently. As Aaron, a current student and part-time rider said:

> I see Deliveroo as a kind of contingency until I can find another job, because, I'm not entirely sure if I'm going to stay in Edinburgh, but I think if I am going to be in Edinburgh, I will definitely do Deliveroo until I find a job that is, I don't know, like a proper job, I guess!

For Liam, a current full-time student and part-time rider, the work is reduced to fitness and leisure, saying:

> You go round cycling, improve your fitness. I wouldn't say anything about the traffic. I don't think the traffic's that bad . . . It's just a leisurely cycle around Edinburgh.

For Anna, also a full-time student and part-time rider, Deliveroo is something she might always pick up, even after graduating from University:

> *Interviewer*: Do you think you'll do anything after Deliveroo?
> *Anna*: I think it's an ongoing thing. Whatever else I'm doing, if I'm living somewhere where they're operating, then I'll probably still hang onto the bag and do the odd shift here and there.

As Anna goes on to say, even though her parents have been concerned about her doing this type of work, those concerns were minimised through recourse to the 'good money' narrative, saying:

> Yes, it was quite funny when I told them! My mum said, 'Why are you doing that for? Isn't it horrible?' I think, because they'd heard a lot of stories about how badly Deliveroo treats their employees, and things like that, they were quite concerned, I think, and, in general, they're quite concerned about safety. My mum's quite worried about me being on the road a lot, and stuff, but, yes, I kind of said, 'Oh, well, it's a good way for me to make money. I can be on my bike.' I think they were convinced after I'd told them my reasons for it, but, at first, they were definitely shocked.

As Gregory (2020) shows, there is good reason for concern as the work is inherently risky. At the time of these interviews, a Deliveroo rider and student in Edinburgh, Daniel Smith, was hit by an oncoming car while on his bicycle en route to a delivery pickup. Daniel suffered a cracked spine and minor head injuries. The dismissal of on-demand couriering as 'pay for leisure' or 'not a proper job' or 'fitness' minimises the very real risks that riders face. Almost all the riders I spoke with in these interviews told me the job was 'not that complicated' or only required 'common sense' or that 'I just do what the app tells me'. This minimisation of the work is particularly troubling as it means that students may not be fully aware of the risks they assume as self-employed contractors before they take up this work. This should raise the question: are universities exploring these risks with students in any capacity?

CONCLUSION

As recent work done in the field of platform urbanism illustrates (Plantin et al. 2018; Barnes 2020; Fields, Bissell and Macrorie 2020; Sadowski 2020), on-demand work requires us to map evolving relationships between technology, capital and cities. These platforms draw our attention to the ways in which urban environments, assets and bodies are enrolled into proprietary data production. In the case of on-demand food couriering, platforms such as Deliveroo not only aim to scale or enrol students as customers or 'users', but their stated company vision aims to monopolise the urban food delivery market and to become a pipeline for food preparation, delivery and consumption (Panja 2018). This pipeline leads directly to and from the neoliberal university. For places like Edinburgh, whose university has a large economic and geographic footprint, the right to the city will as a result need to account for these interconnections between higher education and the platform economy.

In these interviews with students, descriptions of gig work echo what others have written about with respect to post-Fordist culture more broadly (McRobbie 2016; Sandoval 2018; Simpson and Smith 2019), which is a call to do what one 'loves' in spite of broader risks, working conditions or structural precarity. In this regard, these interviews echo a cultural script that has been playing out for years across many industries. Students now encounter the script as routine and even an expected part of their university experience and career trajectories. The notion that one might study and work around the clock, and use gigging as a way to take a break from that work, is also being normalised. As Richardson (2018) has shown, platform labour fundamentally extends the place and locations of work and intensifies the experience of work – or rather, it demands that workers be ready or are able to work at any time of the day. The blurring of work and fitness here only feeds this machine.

In turn, the ideal worker for Deliveroo specifically is an able-bodied individual who can not only work under the conditions, but who is able and willing to assume all risk – from physical harm to mobility to navigating the stress of an algorithmic boss. In practice, this looks like someone who doesn't need the job to pay their bills or someone who can socialise risks (in the case of students, that might be parents who pay rent or tuition). However, as we can also see, the university more broadly plays a role in this socialisation of risk. Much like a private home that can be opened to Airbnb or a private car that can be rented out to Uber, the financialised, growth-driven university can be seen as an asset to be sweated – both for workers and for their data. As such, the university is a key site for raising awareness of working conditions in the gig economy – for, as you might find, if you raise this topic in your class, the students are already gig workers, bearing the brunt of risk, exhaustion and a future of work without clear trajectories or protections.

REFERENCES

Barns, S. (2020) *Platform Urbanism: Geographies of Media*. Singapore: Palgrave Macmillan.

BBC Scotland (2018) Deliveroo reveals big rise in rider numbers. BBC, 10 December. https://www.bbc.co.uk/news/uk-scotland-scotland-business -46496070 (last accessed 12 January 2022).

Bousquet, M. (2008) *How the University Works: Higher Education and the Low-wage Nation*. New York: New York University Press.

Canny, A. (2002) Flexible labour? The growth of student employment in the UK. *Journal of Education and Work*, 15(3), 277–301. doi: 10.1080/1363908022000012058-2.

Fields, D., Bissell, D. and Macrorie, R. (2020) Platform methods: studying platform urbanism outside the black box. *Urban Geography*, 41(3), 462–8. doi: 10.1080/02723638.2020.1730642.

Gregory K. (2021) 'My life is more valuable than this': understanding risk among on-demand food couriers in Edinburgh. *Work, Employment and Society*, 35(2), 316–31.

Gregory, K and Paredes Maldonado, M. (2020) Delivering Edinburgh: uncovering the digital geography of platform labour in the city. *Information, Communication & Society*, 23(8), 1187–202. doi: 10.1080/1369118X.2020.1748087.

Gregory, K and Sadowski, J. (2021) Biopolitical platforms: the perverse virtues of digital labour. *Journal of Cultural Economy*, 14(6), 662–74. doi: 10.1080/17530350.2021.1901766.

Huws, U., Spencer, N. H., Syrdal, D. S. and Holts, K. (2017) *Work in the European Gig Economy*. Brussels: Foundation for European Progressive Studies.

Jacob, M., Gerth, M. and Weiss, F. (2020) Social inequalities in student employment and the local labour market. *Kölner Zeitschrift für Soziologie und Sozialpsychologie*, 72(1), 55–80. doi: 10.1007/s11577-020-00661-8.

Kidder, J. L. (2006) 'It's the job I love': bike messengers and edgework. *Sociological Forum*, 21(1), 31–54.

Koepp, D. (2012) *Premium Rush*. Columbia Pictures.

MacDonald, R. and Giazitzoglu, A. (2019) Youth, enterprise and precarity: or, what is, and what is wrong with, the 'gig economy'? *Journal of Sociology*, 55(4), 724–40. doi: 10.1177/1440783319837604.

Malin, B. J. and Chandler, C. (2017) Free to work anxiously: splintering precarity among drivers for Uber and Lyft. *Communication, Culture & Critique*, 10, 382–400. doi: 10.1111/cccr.12157.

McRobbie, A. (2016) *Be Creative: Making a Living in the New Culture Industries*. Cambridge: Polity Press.

Panja, S. (2018) Deliveroo plans to make its own food and replace chefs and riders with robots. London Eater, 29 March. Available at https://london .eater.com/2018/3/29/17175482/deliveroo-future-plans-robots-profits-in vestors (last accessed 12 January 2022).

Pasquale, F. (2016) Two narratives of platform capitalism. *Yale Law & Policy Review*, 35(1), 309.

Plantin, J.-C., Lagoze, C., Edwards, P. N. and Sandvig, C. (2018) Infrastructure studies meet platform studies in the age of Google and Facebook. *New Media & Society*, 20(1), 293–310. doi: 10.1177/1461444816661553.

Reilly, A. (2013) Protecting vulnerable migrant workers: the case of international students. *Australian Journal of Labour Law*, 181–208, University of Adelaide Law Research Paper no. 2013-08.

Richardson, L. (2018) Feminist geographies of digital work. *Progress in Human Geography*, 42(2), 244–63. doi: 10.1177/0309132516677177.

Richardson, L. (2019) Platforms, markets, and contingent calculation: the flexible arrangement of the delivered meal. *Antipode*, 52, 619–636. doi: 10.1111/ anti.12546.

Ross, A. (2012) Universities and the urban growth machine. *Dissent*, 4 October. Available at https://www.dissentmagazine.org/online_articles/universities -and-the-urban-growth-machine (last accessed 12 January 2022).

RSA (Royal Society for the Encouragement of Arts, Manufactures and Commerce) (2017) Good gigs: a fairer future for the UK's gig economy. 26 April. Available at https://www.thersa.org/discover/publications-and -articles/reports/good-gigs-a-fairer-future-for-the-uks-gig-economy (last accessed 12 January 2022).

Sadowski, J. (2020) Cyberspace and cityscapes: on the emergence of platform urbanism. *Urban Geography*, 41(3), 448–52. doi: 10.1080/ 02723638.2020.1721055.

Sandoval, M. (2018) From passionate labour to compassionate work: cultural co-ops, do what you love and social change. *European Journal of Cultural Studies*, 21(2), 113–29. doi: 10.1177/1367549417719011.

Simpson, J. and Smith, S. (2019) 'I'm not a bloody slave, I get paid and if I don't get paid then nothing happens': Sarah's experience of being a student sex worker. *Work, Employment and Society*, 33(4), 709–18. doi: 10.1177/0950017018809888.

Turi, H. (2020) Deliveroo diary of migrant worker in The Hague. Available at https://medium.com/@turirebel/deliveroo-diary-of-a-migrant-worker-in -the-hague-7fff6bc7ac24 (last accessed 12 January 2022).

Chapter 10

DATA (IN)JUSTICE, PROTEST AND THE (RE)MAKING OF SPACE AMONG FRAGMENTED PLATFORM WORKERS

Alex J. Wood and Vili Lehdonvirta

INTRODUCTION

In 2016, dramatic strikes by London Deliveroo workers brought platform work to the world's attention. But other, less visible platform workers had already been protesting for a long time. They were remote platform workers, and they were protesting against online gig platforms like Amazon Mechanical Turk, Upwork and Fiverr. In this chapter, we examine how spatially fragmented platform workers in the remote gig economy, also commonly referred to as crowdwork, attempt to (re)make the digital and physical space of global cities and envision a more just economy. These freelance workers mainly work from their homes, using their own computers to undertake the digital labour of advertising and marketing, modelling and graphic design, administration, customer service and copywriting – and thus appear as possibly the most fragmented, atomised and isolated segment of workers in the gig economy. By taking a broadly ethnographic approach to study these workers in five global cities, we uncover new injustices that otherwise lay hidden in the economies of our datafied cities. Yet we also document how these workers form online communities, support collective organisation and reconfigure platforms to enable protest.

REMOTE PLATFORM WORK

Over the past decade, labour platforms have enabled a new type of self-employment, known as the gig economy, to emerge and grow dramatically around the world (Kässi and Lehdonvirta 2018; Pesole et

227

al. 2018). This type of labour can be divided into local gig work, which includes transport and delivery work, and remote gig work, which consists of tasks that can be delivered over the Internet, such as data entry, graphic design and content writing. Remote gig work can be further broken down into 'microwork' (or digital piecework; Lehdonvirta 2018) and 'macrowork', consisting of larger projects paid on an hourly or per-deliverable basis. In all these segments of the gig economy, issues such as low earnings, insecurity and perceived unfairness have led to the emergence of collective actions (Irani and Silberman 2013; Lehdonvirta 2016; Wood, Lehdonvirta and Graham 2018; Cant 2019; Tassinari and Maccarrone 2020).

By bringing together two or more distinct user groups, in this case workers and clients, platforms create new opportunities for exchange. Srnicek (2016: 48) defines platforms generally as 'a new type of firm; they are characterised by providing the infrastructure to intermediate between different user groups'. In economics and management literatures, platforms are often theorised as multi-sided markets (Evans 2003; Rochet and Tirole 2003; Eisenmann, Parker and Van Alstyne 2006). Via these platforms, workers individually contract a multiplicity of clients, and, to varying degrees, are able to choose the clients and jobs they take, how they carry out those jobs, and, in a majority of cases, the rates they charge. However, the agency of workers is in reality shaped and constrained by platform rules and design – an important theme of our research that we discuss in detail below.

An important characteristic of multi-sided markets is that demand across both sides is interdependent (Rochet and Tirole 2003): the more clients there are, the more useful the platform is for workers, and vice versa. These positive network effects can cause a platform market to tip towards a single near-monopolistic platform. At the same time, more users on one side of the platform also means more competition for projects or workers on that side, creating so-called same-side negative network effects. Platform strategy thus involves coordinating growth across the sides, for instance by subsidising one side with fees charged from the other side. On online labour platforms, there tend to be more workers signing up than there are gigs, with the result that the worker side is highly competitive, and the platform company's efforts are directed more towards growing the client side.

A complementary literature analyses platforms from the perspective of transaction costs (Malone, Yates and Benjamin 1987; Oyer 2016;

Lehdonvirta et al. 2019). Platforms reduce search costs by providing search engines and algorithmic suggestions for clients to identify suitable workers and vice versa. They reduce information costs by displaying digital skill certificates, reputation scores and other statistics concerning participants' past history on the platform. They also provide cheap, standardised and partly automated means to form contracts, monitor performance, invoice, pay, and raise disputes in case of non-performance or non-payment and thus act as market organisers that maintain the necessary social order for transactions to take place (Kirchner and Schüßler 2019, 2020). The relative coordination cost and complexity of controlling labour power outside of formal employment has previously acted as a barrier to the wider use of self-employed labour. By significantly reducing this barrier, platforms contribute to a growth of self-employed work (Davis 2016).

It is the growth of this new platform-enabled self-employment that we explore in this chapter, paying particular attention to how the platform and its two-sided dynamics can generate new sources of injustice. Our study is based on semi-structured interviews with seventy remote gig economy workers – workers engaged in macro-remote gig work who frequently identify as 'freelancers' (Wood et al. 2018) – and therefore we also interviewed eleven advocates and activists for the rights of self-employed freelancers and undertook participant observation at fifteen freelancer community events in San Francisco, Los Angeles, New York, Manila and London.[1] Below we describe the sense of injustice that platform workers feel about their situation and their concerns about the monopolistic practices of their employers. We ask how labour organising tactics – including the right to local spaces where workers could organise – might help workers resist the current relations structuring their platform labour.

INJUSTICE AND THE POWER OF PLATFORMS

The process by which injustice is experienced at work is central to the sociological and industrial relations theory known as 'mobilisation theory' (Kelly 1998) and has consequently been widely studied in these fields (Gall 2018; Gall and Holgate 2018). According to this research, individuals hold something to be an injustice when a 'breach of legal or collective agreement, rights or of widely shared social values' has taken place (Kelly 2005: 66). Blame for this breach of socially accepted values, rules or rights must also be attributed to a tangible external agency, normally the employer or the government, rather than being seen as resulting from an inevitable and impersonal force such as 'the market' or 'global competition', so that a sense of personal efficacy is possible (Kelly 1998). This sense of injustice is strengthened when shared by a substantial number of peers, as its normative basis is reinforced through a process of collective legitimisation (Kelly 1998, 2005; Wood 2020).

A major theme of our interviews was how the power that platforms wielded over the ability of workers to make a living often generated a sense of injustice among remote platform workers. The most evident manner in which the power of platforms over workers provoked a sense of injustice was that platform firms made their profits by charging workers a fee for using the platform. This fee was usually 10–20 per cent of the workers' earnings for each gig they undertook via the platform. While some workers accepted the platform fee as the price of using their service, a far more important theme of the interviews was how platforms were seen to be exploiting workers. An example is Earl's (copywriter; Manila) dissatisfaction:

> They [are] taking pay, 10% out of my take-home pay . . . which is really unfair.

Karen (digital marketing; Birmingham, UK) exemplified another common concern – that the platforms would use their power over workers to engage in price gouging (unfairly increasing the amount workers had to pay the company to gain access to the platform):

> They are in it to benefit themselves and . . . it gets to a point where it . . . stops feeling fair and it just becomes a little bit frustrating because the risk is that people like GigOnline can just monopolize because they'll . . . become so dominant that people won't have a choice but to use GigOnline.

The sense of injustice became crystallised for some workers after one of the major platforms doubled the fees it charged for many gigs from 10 per cent to 20 per cent. Gabe (digital marketing; Manila) used the idioms of slavery and sweatshops to express this concern about price gouging by platforms:

You don't have to charge them an arm and a leg . . . we're earning less and less . . . because the platform that we're using is taking away twenty percent from us . . . if it stays this way, the freelancing industry . . . [will] turn into slavery or a sweatshop.

The power of platforms also provoked a further sense of injustice as the platforms were often seen as having an interest in driving down pay. In particular, the global nature of the platforms, along with some of their design features, such as highly competitive bidding wars, were seen to undermine workers' ability to earn a decent living. As Kelly (digital marketing; San Francisco) explained:

Most of the things I get there is just offensive like just offensively low . . . I'm not gonna write an article for you for $8.

Workers in Manila, where the cost of living was lower, were also concerned about the degree to which they were exposed to market competition. For instance, Earl (copywriter; Manila) explained his frustration with the platform he used:

I don't know why . . . GigOnline is . . . letting these people come in and just, you know, do whatever they want to their freelancers . . . it's horrible . . . Even if . . . the project's really good . . . you are fighting . . . against . . . copywriters who are charging $5 per hour, how are you supposed to win? . . . Outside [the platform] you can . . . dictate your price . . . [but you] can't do that in GigOnline.

Nevertheless, these concerns tended to lead to greater outrage among workers in the high-income countries where the issue had a more immediate impact on their livelihoods. This sense of injustice was particularly evident where platforms were seen as having a wider effect by undermining locally accepted industry pay norms. Julie (writing; Los Angeles) exemplified these concerns:

[Platforms] are undermining the industry. You know, if you're telling someone I'm getting paid 30 bucks . . . for this blog post, then who's gonna wanna pay our living wage?

Paul (advertising, content creation, logo design; Los Angeles) echoed them:

[The platform] was quite hard because it would list the project and then it would list the bidders . . . it's just appalling . . . because of the nature of the platform . . . [clients] believe they're gonna get a bargain . . . I'm not just giving you a 300-word sales letter, I'm giving you 20 years of experience in sales and marketing . . . So, what you're getting for your $349 probably is a hell of a bargain.

A further source of injustice was the sense that the powerful platforms cared little for the well-being of workers. Gabrielle (translation; London) could not understand why the platforms cared so little for their freelancers when it was freelancers' labour which generated their profits:

I think they're more focused on the clients than they are on the freelancers, which is weird because they get the money from the freelancers . . . we the translators are the ones paying the fees, but they tend to focus more on the client.

That the power platforms wielded over workers' livelihoods provoked such perceived injustice raises the question of whether workers accepted this situation and, if not, how they sought to challenge it.

Monopoly and Resistance

Traditionally, feelings of injustice among self-employed freelancers have been considered unlikely to trigger protests. This is due to self-employment being understood as involving purely market relations, rather than consisting of a managerial relationship (Sisson 2008). The absence of an employment relationship limits the potential for antagonism to be structured into this economic exchange (Edwards 2003) as dissatisfied individuals can easily exit working conditions that they find objectionable. According to Hirschman's (1970) 'exit, voice, loyalty' framework, voice (protest) is unlikely when actors, such as the self-employed, can easily exit a relationship and instead vote with their feet. However, an important theme of our interviews was that workers tended to rely on a single labour platform, which they could not easily exit. There were three principal reasons for this. The first reason is that positive network effects result in most of the high-quality clients in a certain sector being on a particular platform, so that workers had little option but to use it. As Holly (digital marketing; Los Angeles) explained:

> GigOnline really has a monopoly on it . . . they truly do . . . I don't wanna say it's the best one, it's the only one . . . I think a monopoly is always bad.

In fact, one of the major platforms used by our informants had recently merged with its major competitor:

> Most people I know dislike it [GigOnline] . . . you use them because you have to . . . they purchased platform X . . . [and] platform Y and consolidated . . . no one has any other option. I tried to get [in] to FreelanceOnline but that sucks even more. So they got me back on GigOnline. (Chris, digital marketing; Los Angeles)

The second reason for reliance on a single platform was data lock-in. Srnicek (2016) points out that by placing themselves as an intermediator, platforms are able to collect data on their users' behaviours. This data can be highly valuable, and, in the case of the gig economy, what is particularly valuable to the worker is their online reputation. This platform reputation is created from customer feedback on the workers' performance. Without a good platform-based reputation it was very difficult to get clients. It also represents an important source of bargaining power, since the only way to build a reputation on a new platform is to accept a much lower rate, as Casey (UX and graphic design; Los Angeles) explained:

> Any time you sign up for a new platform there's just a big barrier to entry because you have to have those reviews . . . I just don't want to start at that $15 per article again . . . I'm glued to GigOnline.

Reputation data is trusted because the platform takes efforts to guarantee its integrity (Lehdonvirta et al. 2019). As a result, the data cannot simply be copied from the platform and presented outside of it without compromising its value; this locks the worker into using the platform. As Raymond (programming; Manila) explained:

> I was so close to deactivating . . . then I realised, oh, no, all those, all those good feedbacks are going to be deleted . . . and so, I said,

'Okay, I just won't do it' 'cause I won't get any new jobs . . . I need that [reputation].

The third source of platform dependence derived from the ways that the platforms ensured that contractual restrictions and limited access to information about the clients made it difficult for workers to connect with clients outside of the platform. Such tactics included not displaying users' full names, and automatically screening communications to block out links to other websites and contact information. These techniques were buttressed by exclusivity clauses in the platforms' terms and conditions, which prohibited workers and clients from undertaking business together outside of the platform.

Community and the (Re)making of Space

Since remote platform workers could not easily exit their main platform, could they instead use voice (protest), as per Hirschman's (1970) framework? To generate protest, feelings of injustice must transform into a sense of shared collective interests through group social identification (Kelly 1998; Wood 2015). But platform workers are spatially fragmented, which may impair the formation of shared identities (Lehdonvirta 2016). Our surveys with Asian, African and European remote platform workers highlight the extreme spatial fragmentation and social isolation that these workers experience as a consequence of being spread across cities that are themselves geographically dispersed around the world while working remotely from their own homes via the Internet (see also Wood et al. 2019). Around 80 per cent of those we surveyed rarely or never engaged in face-to-face communication with other remote platform workers (Wood et al. 2018, 2021). As a consequence, loneliness was a common theme of our interviews. Some workers attempted to overcome their social isolation by joining co-working spaces or attending meet-ups. However, denied a right to shape and design their urban environment to meet their needs, these workers found that their efforts were blunted by the social relations imprinted onto the city by capital. Workers expressed disappointment that co-working spaces generally did not cater for freelancers and instead focused on attracting start-ups with financial backing. As Alicia (writing, SEO, social media marketing; Manila) explained:

I've tried a few. The environment is okay, but you still don't get to talk with other freelancers . . . they're probably business people.

These glistening steel and glass co-working spaces with their free kombucha on tap were usually aimed at start-ups with significant financial backing, often in the form of venture capital. As a result, membership fees for most co-working spaces presented too great a financial burden for most freelance platform workers. An alternative means of meeting other platform workers was to attend freelancer co-working days, in most cases organised on the platform meetups.com or by the Freelancers Union (in the US), and usually hosted by a co-working space for free. While workers were often keen to attend such events, as they saw them as opportunities to forge friendships, learn new skills and feel part of a community, a common barrier was travel and the frequent problems with traffic that it entailed. As a result of their spatial fragmentation, workers were dispersed across these sprawling major cities, meaning it could take hours to get to an event from one's home – and usual place of work. This was especially the case in Los Angeles and Manila, where public transport was limited. Since workers were paid hourly or per gig, the time spent travelling had a significant opportunity cost. Indeed, in one instance, when observing a co-working meetup in Los Angeles, the first author was the only attendee to show up. Our data was collected before the COVID-19 pandemic, which has no doubt made in-person meet-ups even less viable.

Denied the right to the city in terms of access to existing urban resources or influence over the design and reimagining of urban space (see the Introduction to this book), workers were left spatially fragmented and with limited opportunities to meet physically. Workers therefore turned to the creation of an informational commons. In what Castells (2012) terms the 'space of flows', workers created places on the Internet where they could meet other platform workers, learn new skills, ask for help and discuss how to deal with clients. These groups tended to be Facebook groups, but could also take the form of forums and message boards (see also Wood et al. 2018). Indeed, around half of the one thousand Asian, African and European workers we have surveyed elsewhere indicated that they communicated with other platform workers via social media or online forums at least once a week.

However, it is not only workers that create online spaces in which they can congregate and aggregate their fragmented experiences.

Gerber (2021) and Gerber and Krzywdzinkski (2019) point out that remote gig platform companies themselves invest in creating online communities as a means to indirectly enhance their control over workers' performance. But in the context of the injustice and dependence elucidated above, we find that workers sometimes engage in the remaking of these spaces of control into places of resistance. During our research, one of the largest remote gig economy platforms, which we refer to as 'GigOnline', used its power to unilaterally double its fees for many gigs from 10 per cent to 20 per cent of the gig's value. In response, thousands of workers voiced their opposition via social media. This included more than a thousand workers taking to the platform's own Internet forum. Thirty-five of our informants had directly participated in this protest. The informants explained how posting on the forum was driven by feelings of outrage at the perceived injustice of the platform's behaviour:

> My blood was boiling . . . It just made me see red because they were taking us for fools . . . they thought we were stupid. (Gemma, writer and script editor; Liverpool, UK)

> I was reading through a lot of the responses . . . it's probably pretty charged . . . people [were] getting angry on forums, 'No, we don't like this!' 'It's not fair!' (Karen, digital marketing; Birmingham, UK)

This anger was heightened by the platform's poor communication and the perception that they were trying to mislead the workers:

> I thought that they were full of shit . . . I didn't think it was right. I thought they were abusing their [position] . . . it was greed. (Nick, video and audio editing; London)

The informants made clear that their posting on social media was not simply a form of individual voice. Instead, they explained how this event was experienced as a collective one undertaken collaboratively with their virtual co-workers:

> You read all the . . . posts and you, you feel, you see all the anger that's building up in each freelancer that's posting. (Raymond, programming; Manila)

In fact, the informants themselves often used the idiom of a 'protest' to describe this online event:

> Just adding a voice to them . . . million other voices. The same way people did on a tax march last week. Tax march doesn't mean much if there's only ten people, when there's a million people, people notice so I didn't think it would get responded to or read but I thought if I added one to those thousands, then it would help . . . It was a way of protesting. (Chris, digital marketing; Los Angeles)

These efforts to remake the labour platform's own digital infrastructure as a place of protest were short lived and ultimately unsuccessful in that, perhaps unsurprisingly, it lacked the bargaining power necessary to force GigOnline to change its behaviour.

Platform Cooperativism?

If workers could not successfully hijack platform companies' spaces, then perhaps they could create their own platforms? One suggestion for how platform workers could bypass the unaccountable power of existing platforms and create a more just data ecosystem is through 'platform cooperatives' (Scholz and Schneider 2016; Scholz 2017). According to Scholz (2017: 180–1), platform cooperatives would be owned by the users who produce most of their value – in this case workers, who would also be involved in the platform's design. Platform cooperatives thus constituted would seek to ensure workers received decent pay, income security and benefits, had good communication channels, data transparency and data portability, and were protected from arbitrary punishment via rating systems while limiting digital surveillance. However, only two of our informants had heard of this notion of platform cooperatives. Once the concept was explained, our informants expressed lots of enthusiasm for this potential alternative means for organising the remote gig economy. This enthusiasm was rooted in feelings of economic injustice towards existing 'greedy capitalist' platforms, which were seen as exploiting workers with little regard for their welfare. For example, Isaac (graphic design and web programming; Manila) stated:

It will be positive, unlike GigOnline which is privately owned and . . . just taking money [from us].

Likewise, Raymond (programming; Manila) argued that while existing platforms are only interested in

justifying their increase in rates what it's missing is taking care of freelancers. Co-owning part of the business that would be a pipe-dream but it would be really great.

However, while supporting the ideals of platform cooperativism, there was also significant scepticism at its practical potential to solve the actual issues they faced. Indeed, the worker who had heard of plat-form cooperatives explained that:

It's academics that are trying to create a utopian society. It's just not necessarily addressing the needs of low-income people. (Manish, writer, PR and marketing; San Francisco Bay)

Other workers raised the concern that the international and highly competitive nature of this sector meant that, in reality, cost competition would render platform ownership irrelevant:

I'm not sure what difference it would make, platforms being coops and run by the freelancers . . . [It's] just the free market. It's irrel-evant who owns the platform. (Gemma, writer and script editor; Liverpool, UK)

Or that this would render democratic governance impossible due to the cultural barriers and weak ties that existed between the geographically fragmented workforce:

Freelancing is very large industry internationally, I don't know how harmonious the discussions would be. How would all these different cultures [come together]? So it could be not the best dealings and relationships between the people in the co-op. (Javier, training and online marketing; Manila)

We don't know each other so there's a trust issue. (Jean, e-commerce, website consulting, design; Los Angeles)

For these reasons one worker even stated that they would prefer to be governed by their existing platform than by one run by workers. Even among those workers who were less sceptical about the possibilities of cooperative governance there was a realism that their platform use would ultimately be determined by market dominance not ownership. As clients trust existing platforms, workers recognised that they too would have to remain on those same platforms due to the interdependence of demand on multi-sided markets (Rochet and Tirole 2003). As Andray (lead generation and customer service; Manila) explained:

> We don't want to leave because we need a job. Some clients only trust GigOnline [so] even though 80% or 60% of freelancers leave, clients will still remain on the platform.

Therefore, even putting to one side worker scepticism regarding cooperative governance, the market dominance, interdependence of demand, and monopoly tendencies of platforms – which workers are all too aware of – makes cooperatives unlikely vehicles for reducing injustice in the remote gig economy (see also Srnicek 2016). Any potential for platform cooperativism to offer a viable alternative, in this sector at least, seemingly hinges on the provision of state financial and regulatory supports that could enable platform cooperatives to overcome the market dominance of existing platforms (see also Sandoval 2020).

Platform Unions

Our informants suggested that instead of alternatives to existing platforms, what would be of greater benefit for addressing the injustices they faced was collective organisation. This, they argued, would enable them to counter the power of platforms and overcome their fragmentation, something which Paul (advertising, content creation, logo design; Los Angeles) highlighted particularly clearly:

> If the road that we're all on is increased fragmentation, there's gotta be some collective something that looks out for the interests [of freelancers]. I mean I realise that freelancers have had to . . . lookout for themselves . . . But wouldn't it be a better place if you had a number of people that had similar interests that were looking out for each other.

Likewise, Julie (writing; Los Angeles) explained how a collective organisation that could increase freelancers' visibility and rights was central to her vision of the future for freelancing:

> What I'd like to see for freelancing in the future is like definitely more community, more visibility, more rights.

Karen (digital marketing; Birmingham, UK) further elaborated on this theme by highlighting the importance of an organisation that would be able to represent freelancers to the platforms:

> I think it would be more useful to have some sort of other ways of communicating with these companies because . . . they are so important to so many people making a living, and that's only going to . . . grow . . . Like a conference where you can go and . . . speak to a board . . . Or people to represent us as a group, so that we can have some sort of protection and representation.

As suggested by the findings reported thus far, our informants often had similar experiences of injustice, despite the multiplicity of platforms that they use and the widely different tasks that they undertake. Even in the face of geographic fragmentation, these similar experiences could lead to a sense of shared interests. As Thomas (programming; Ipswich, UK) explained:

> Everybody have the same struggle. Everybody have same experience and we as a community can, I don't know, use our force for instance, to . . . enforce some changes, so at least spread discontent and in that way . . . one thousand might try acting in a way that will . . . benefit everybody.

We found that among our informants there was in fact widespread support for unions, despite the fact that almost none of the informants had any previous experience of them, and that the informants had little certainty as to how unions could function in a gig economy. Nevertheless, a clear theme was the hope that a union could rebalance the freelancers' unequal relationship with the platform. Laura (digital marketing; San Francisco) explained how a union could benefit freelancers if large numbers of high-end workers joined:

[If] the higher-cost freelancers, all or a great majority, joined a union . . . I can imagine . . . [that] helping towards reduced fees and other . . . things that are of interest to freelancers.

Jean (e-commerce, website consulting, design; Los Angeles) believed that even with a membership of a few thousand workers, a union could apply pressure on platforms:

If there was a way for us to talk to each other and organise . . . even if it was just a thousand of us . . . 'look, we're not going to work anymore until you change this'. Maybe a thousand, a few thousand we'd have more power.

Raymond (programming; Manila) explained how such a union could be built around the shared experiences of undertaking labour through a platform:

A union . . . [for] freelancers must first unite and . . . agree on several certain common things that are immutable . . .whatever your job is, whether you're a web developer or a graphic designer.

Other workers, particularly in the Philippines, where there is less history of trade unionism, were not as hopeful, but still supportive in principle. For example, Gabe (digital marketing; Manila) explained:

GigOnline I don't think they're going to allow [a union]. Yeah. It's not going to work . . . [But] if there is I'd join.

Workers in the Philippines were also fearful of government repression. Bernadette (virtual assistance, SEO; Manila) summed this up particularly clearly when she responded that being in a union:

takes a lot of my time and it's very dangerous . . . here in the Philippines, in the street, it's not safe.

Despite having no previous union experience or formal knowledge of industrial relations, Karen (digital marketing; Birmingham, UK) even articulated a desire for industry-level bargaining:

I wouldn't say [the union should be only] GigOnline-focused 'cause I know there are other companies like them, you know . . . Getting some . . . representatives of these people and these companies in the same room and saying 'How can we work together now for the next five years' to, you know, grow what we're doing but also, it's so we could work for both sides.

This union support is perhaps surprising, as the informants overwhelmingly identified as freelancers rather than as employees of clients or platforms. Many of those who identified as freelancers saw themselves as constituting a 'business' or at least aspiring to be one with regard to their relationship with their clients. For example, Karen (digital marketing; Birmingham, UK) explained:

the conversations and meetings I have with my clients is, it's like business-to-business, because, you know, I am my business.

Likewise, Laura (digital marketing; San Francisco) emphasised the importance of seeing oneself as a business when interacting with clients:

I like to consider myself a business that's interacting with their business. I think it puts us more on a level field. I don't consider myself an employee because well, I'm technically . . . Well, I'm not an employee . . . It is a business. It's a business-to-business relationship.

It seems that this identification as a business was rooted in the experience of formal autonomy in their relations with clients. As Danica (customer service, virtual assistance; Manila) highlighted:

I do business . . . I'm removing my employee mentality, 'cause I am able to do business . . . I market myself . . . I handle everything . . . I do negotiations and all. So I'm leaning in the direction of doing business . . . I still see myself as a freelancer, but I would like to evolve to business.

However, despite this identification with business, they saw no contradiction with also being a member of a union. This situation reflected the power that platforms were perceived to hold over freelancers' livelihoods. As exemplified by Marcus (digital marketing; London), many of the informants could not comprehend why it might be considered a contradiction to be both a business and a member of a union:

> What you would hope for is an established authority that you feel has your best interests at heart ... Where would the contradiction [between being a freelancer and a member of union] be? ... You're likely going to be self-employed for a longer time, and I think those people deserve support or some sort of [protection as workers], some sort of union.

Even when the informants were aware of this potential contradiction, they explained how it was the power of platforms which meant that contemporary freelancers needed a union:

> You have to stand up and go we're not gonna do this anymore. So I'm surprised there isn't a union as such for freelancers which sounds [like] an anomaly. You know a freelancing union. But there should be because it needs to be regulated more. In a way, it's slave labour. It's slave labour every day for freelancer writers, fighting, trying to find work through platforms like GigOnline and OnlineGigs because it's just is not a fair market place at all. (Gemma, writer and script editor; Liverpool, UK)

CONCLUSION

In this chapter, we have drawn on ethnographic research to highlight the perceived injustices faced by platform workers in the remote gig economy. In particular, powerful platforms are seen to exploit workers through the fees that they charge them and the low rates of pay that they encourage. Anger towards these platforms is heightened when they are seen to use monopoly power to engage in price gouging or to undermine local industry pay norms. Traditionally, injustice among self-employed workers was seen as unlikely to generate protest, as such workers could easily utilise exit in response. However, platform network effects, data lock-in, lack of access to information and restrictive contractual terms all limit platform workers' ability to exit.

Unable to easily exit platforms, workers turn to protest. However, as a result of being denied 'the right to the city', they also find themselves spatially fragmentated across vast sprawling metropolises by an urban environment which does not meet their needs. This fragmentation creates a barrier to protest. Yet we find that workers overcome physical barriers to interaction by creating commons in the space of flows through the making of Internet-based communities and the repurposing of virtual spaces created by platform firms themselves. Specifically, we illustrate how in response to a fee rise, workers essentially took over a leading platform's forum and, briefly, transformed it into a place of protest in which they could aggregate their discontent. Nevertheless, this attempt to remake the digital infrastructures created by platforms proved ineffective, and did not cause the company to change its behaviour.

As an alternative, we considered worker-run platform cooperatives as a possibility for creating a more just data ecosystem in this sector. While workers were enthusiastic about the anti-exploitation principles underpinning such initiatives, they also displayed scepticism regarding the governance of such a platform. Workers highlighted the international and competitive nature of the sector as limiting the potential for collaborative and democratic governance. Therefore, this form of economic organisation may be more suitable for local sectors of the digital economy, where face-to-face interaction leads to the generation of stronger bonds of trust. Workers also highlighted that cost competition in the remote gig economy would render platform ownership largely irrelevant. Moreover, workers highlighted that their platform use was a function of client demand rather than worker choice. As clients trust existing platforms and these platforms have achieved market dominance, workers have little choice but to continue using these platforms. State financial and regulatory support would be necessary to overcome these economic barriers. Nevertheless, the support we find for the underlying principles of platform cooperatives suggests that this concept could act as a mobilising ideal for the platform workers' movement, much like Owenite cooperativism did during the early labour movement (Polanyi (2001 [1944]: 176).

Informants felt that collective organisation and even the formation of unions had the greatest potential for addressing their immediate concerns over the power that platforms wielded over their lives. Interestingly, as a result of their dependence on platforms, these self-employed workers saw no contradiction between being a 'business' and belonging to a trade union, suggesting that organising may be a pertinent route for achieving justice as the platform economy grows ever more pervasive.

NOTE

1. This chapter is based partly on Wood and Lehdonvirta (2021). This research conducted in 2017 and 2018 included 70 interviews with workers in the remote gig economy and 11 with non-platform worker activists and advocates. We also undertook participant observation at four co-working days (Los Angeles, Oakland CA, London × 2), three meet-ups for freelancers or digital nomads (Manila, San Francisco and Freemont CA), three events organised by a freelancer union (Los Angeles and New York City × 2) and a platform co-op conference (New York City). An online meet-up of freelancers in the Philippines was also attended, via video conferencing, while the first author was carrying out fieldwork in Manila.

REFERENCES

Cant, C. (2019) *Riding for Deliveroo: Resistance in the New Economy*. Cambridge: Polity Press.

Castells, M. (2012) *Networks of Outrage and Hope: Social Movements in the Internet Age*. Cambridge: Polity Press.

Davis, G. F. (2016) *The Vanishing American Corporation: Navigating the Hazards of a New Economy*. San Francisco, CA: Berrett-Koehler.

Edwards, P. K. (2003) The employment relationship and the field of industrial relations. In P. K. Edwards (ed.), *Industrial Relations: Theory and Practice*, 2nd edn. London: Blackwell, pp. 1–36.

Eisenmann, T., Parker, G. and Van Alstyne, M. (2006) Strategies for two-sided markets. *Harvard Business Review*, October.

Evans, D. (2003) Some empirical aspects of multi-sided platform industries. *Review of Network Economics*, 2, 191–209.

Gall, G. (2018) The uses, abuses and non-uses of *Rethinking Industrial Relations* in understanding industrial relations and organised labour. *Economic and Industrial Democracy*, 39(4), 681–700.

Gall, G. and Holgate, J. (2018) *Rethinking Industrial Relations*: Appraisal, application and augmentation. *Economic and Industrial Democracy*, 39(4), 561–76.

Gerber, C. (2021) Community building on crowdwork platforms: autonomy and control of online workers? *Competition & Change*, 25(2). doi: 10.1177/1024529420914472.

Gerber, C. and Krzywdzinkski, M. (2019) Brave new digital work? New forms of performance control in crowdwork. In S. Vallas and A. Kovalainen (eds), *Work and Labor in the Digital Age: Research in the Sociology of Work*, vol. 33. Bingley: Emerald, pp. 121–43.

Hirschman, A. O. (1970) *Exit, Voice, and Loyalty: Responses to Decline in Firms, Organizations, and States*. Cambridge, MA: Harvard University Press.

Irani, L. and Silberman, M. S. (2013) Turkopticon: interrupting worker invisibility in Amazon Mechanical Turk. *Proceedings of the ACM Conference on Human Factors in Computing Systems (CHI)*, Paris, France.

Kässi, O. and Lehdonvirta, V. (2018) Online labour index: measuring the online gig economy for policy and research. *Technological Forecasting and Social Change*, 137, 241–8.

Kelly, J. (1998) *Rethinking Industrial Relations: Mobilisation, Collectivism and Long Waves*. London: Routledge.

Kelly, J. (2005) Social movement theory and union revitalisation in Britain. In S. Fernie and D. Metcalf (eds), *Trade Unions: Resurgence or Demise?* London: Routledge, pp. 62–82.

Kirchner, S. and Schüßler, E. (2019) The organization of digital marketplaces: unmasking the role of internet platforms in the sharing economy. In G. Ahrne and N. Bunsson (eds), *Organization outside Organizations: The Abundance of Partial Organization in Social Life*. Cambridge: Cambridge University Press, pp. 131–54.

Kirchner, S. and Schüßler, E. (2020) Regulating the sharing economy: a field perspective. In I. Maurer, J. Mair and A. Oberg (eds), *Theorizing the Sharing Economy: Variety and Trajectories of New Forms of Organizing: Research in the Sociology of Organizations*, vol. 66. Bingley: Emerald, pp. 215–36.

Lehdonvirta, V. (2016) Algorithms that divide and unite: delocalisation, identity and collective action in 'microwork'. In J. Flecker (ed.), *Space, Place and Global Digital Work: Dynamics of Virtual Work*. London: Palgrave Macmillan, pp. 53–80.

Lehdonvirta, V. (2018) Flexibility in the gig economy: managing time on three online piecework platforms. *New Technology, Work and Employment*, 33, 13–29.

Lehdonvirta, V., Kässi, O., Hjorth, I., Bernard, H. and Graham, M. (2019) The global platform economy: a new offshoring institution enabling emerging-economy microproviders. *Journal of Management*, 45, 567–99.

Malone, T. W., Yates, J. and Benjamin, R. I. (1987) Electronic markets and electronic hierarchies. *Communications of the ACM*, 30, pp. 484–97.

Oyer, P. (2016) *The Independent Workforce in America*. Stanford, CA: Stanford University Graduate School of Business.

Pesole, A., Urzí Brancati, M. C., Fernández-Macías, E., Biagi, F. and González Vázquez, I. (2018) *Platform Workers in Europe*. JRC Science for Policy Report, Brussels, European Commission.

Polanyi, K. (2001 [1944]) *The Great Transformation: The Political and Economic Origins of Our Time*. New York: Farrar & Rinehart; Boston, MA: Beacon Press.

Rochet, J. C. and Tirole, J. (2003) Platform competition in two-sided markets. *Journal of the European Economic Association*, 1, 990–1029.

Sandoval, M. (2020) Entrepreneurial activism? Platform cooperativism between subversion and co-optation. *Critical Sociology*, 46(6), 801–17.

Scholz, T. (2017) *Uberworked and Underpaid: How Workers are Disrupting the Digital Economy*. Cambridge: Polity Press.

Scholtz, T. and Schneider, N. (eds) (2016) *Ours to Hack and to Own: The Rise of Platform Cooperativism, a New Vision for the Future of Work and a Fairer Internet*. New York: OR Books.

Sisson, K. (2008) Putting the record straight: Industrial relations and the employment relationship. Warwick Papers in Industrial Relations No. 88 April, Coventry, Industrial Relations Research Unit, University of Warwick.

Srnicek, N. (2016) *Platform Capitalism (Theory Redux)*. Cambridge: Polity Press.

Tassinari, A. and Maccarrone, V. (2020) Riders on the storm: workplace solidarity among gig economy couriers in Italy and the UK. *Work, Employment and Society*, 34, 35–54.

Wood, A. J. (2015) Networks of injustice and worker mobilisation at Walmart. *Industrial Relations Journal*, 46(4), 259–74.

Wood, A. J. (2020) *Despotism on Demand: How Power Operates in the Flexible Workplace*. Ithaca, NY: Cornell University Press.

Wood, A. J., Graham, M., Lehdonvirta, V. and Hjorth, I. (2019) Good gig, bad gig: autonomy and algorithmic control in the global gig economy. *Work, Employment and Society*, 33, 56–75.

Wood, A. J and Lehdonvirta, V. (2021) Antagonism beyond employment: how the 'subordinated agency' of labour platforms generates conflict in the remote gig economy. *Socio-Economic Review*, 19(4), 1369–96.

Wood, A. J., Lehdonvirta, V. and Graham, M. (2018) Workers of the Internet unite? Online freelancer organisation in six Asian and African countries. *New Technology, Work and Employment*, 33, 95–112.

Wood A. J, Martindale, N. and Lehdonvirta, V. (2021) Dynamics of contention in the gig economy: Rage against the platform, customer, or state? New Technology, Work and Employment, doi: 10.1111/ntwe.12216.

Part IV

Art and Activism in the Datafied City

Dr Morgan Currie

As previous chapters have shown, data-intensive technologies, just like older computer networks and state statistical systems, are part of the basic functions of city governments and commerce, imposing various 'structures of domination' on the political and economic systems that shape citizens and communities (Downing et al. 1991: 2). But a focus on these more top-down relations of domination and control through data infrastructures does not tell the full story.

Grassroots activists and community organisations have also long used data to demand policy change, hold authorities to account and counter authoritative numbers and official knowledge systems. Historian Alain Desrosieres documents how, in the 1970s, France's largest union produced statistics to challenge official national price indexes, making a case for lowering the costs for goods to the advantage of the working class (2014). In 1980s-era America, the environmental movement pressed for statistical indicators to bring accountability to dangerous polluting industries, demanding the federal government create the Toxic Release Inventory, one of the first US government datasets released to the public in digital form. Appadurai (2001) describes how early 2000s grassroots censuses of informal settlements helped housing advocates in Mumbai demand housing rights for the poor and gave them greater political visibility and voice. These practices are not specific to the twentieth century – they recall older legacies of activist statisticians in nineteenth-century Europe who were among the first to track and count indicators of poverty to call for welfare reforms (Desrosieres 2002).

Today's activists draw on a variety of data practices and tools to address long-standing problems of human rights violations, economic inequality, criminal justice disparities and climate change. Human

Rights Watch mobilises volunteers to analyse online satellite images to create evidence of human rights atrocities in sub-Saharan Africa. Police accountability efforts in the US are building grassroots, participatory and journalist-led digital databases to trace police brutality. And environmental activists use cheap, accessible sensing technologies to bring about greater awareness of pollution and environmental reforms in Eastern Europe (Making Sense n.d.).

Yet while activists make use of data processes to create counter-epistemologies, they continue to face challenges of data-intensive systems. Community organisations rely on social media platforms and online services in their basic communications and advocacy, navigating the complex trade-offs of these systems. Activists face new forms of visibility on these platforms and through data flows between governments and the technology sector. Minorities and low-income populations are particularly visible to these systems, as chapters in this book, along with several important studies, have shown (Browne 2015; Eubanks 2017; Buolamwini and Gebru 2018; Noble 2018). Milan and van der Velden (2016) describe forms of activism that reactively resist these data-driven systems, to challenge and ultimately refuse commercial and government digital infrastructures. Here, the work of projects such as the Algorithmic Justice League, which explores the harms and biases of artificial intelligence (AI), and Our Data Bodies, a grassroots research project that works with local communities to understand digital data collection, among others, lead the way in developing critical public literacies around algorithmic systems.

Art can also play a role in making datafication and algorithmic surveillance more visible. Through her feminist dataset, British artist Caroline Sinders uses her art practice to shed light on the AI pipeline, from data collection and labelling to the design of the algorithm that goes into developing chat bots, exposing the power-laden and potentially discriminatory structures such systems can perpetuate. At each step, Sinders asks if the design is informed by feminist, intersectional principles. James Bridle's Drone Shadow project likewise is about creating visibilities: it draws on city streets the outlines of unmanned aerial vehicles at a 1:1 scale, making drones – which are so often invisible, and their operators, therefore, unaccountable – a point of public focus.

In this section, contributors offer insights into the role that activists and artists play in pressing for human rights and social justice in the city in a time of heightened datafication. Jessica Feldman's research –

which spans a decade and multiple continents – vividly describes the tensions activists face, tracing how activists in cities across the globe confront the limitations and dangers of using platforms that do not have civic or social justice values as foremost concerns. In her encounters with social organisers in cities around the Middle East, Europe and the US, Feldman finds activists repurposing or designing alternative communication technologies, both in efforts to avoid surveillance by local authoritarian governments and to create tools that reflect the radically democratic values of their movements. Benedetta Catanzariti similarly looks at harms to civil society by dataveillance, but with a focus on facial recognition software in public space; she builds on Judith Butler's reflections on public assembly politics to ask how infrastructures of facial recognition – including the classification choices embedded in underlying face datasets – shape new forms of public assembly politics and public visibility. This infrastructural lens, Catanzariti argues, should inform anti-facial recognition interventions and critiques.

In Paris et al.'s chapter, the authors consider changes made to local data collection of police-officer involved homicides in the US since the 2014 murder of Michael Brown in Ferguson, Missouri, by police. Several major cities, the authors find, have passed policies requiring greater transparency around police shooting incidents in efforts to lead to reforms around police violence. At the same time, statistics show that little has changed in subsequent years, as the rate of police shootings and brutality stays the same. Data transparency has not had the widespread structural effects reformists had supposed they would. The authors call for de-emphasising data comprehensiveness in police reform, and instead for supporting efforts that place radical structural change – rather than better data collection for reform – at the centre of police brutality activism.

Finally, artist Pip Thornton explores how art in public spaces can press people to consider the power of data-driven technologies and digital technology companies. Thornton's chapter presents several projects and prototypes that defamiliarise the mechanisms behind Google's search engine, giving search results new forms – such as ticker tape – to highlight the construction of their economic values. Thornton discusses the possibilities of using public space for art outside the confines of the gallery, to break down complex and hidden technical and economic processes for general audiences, and she concludes with critical reflections on what worked best in these settings. Here, art illuminates opaque algorithmic systems while building new critical literacies among urban publics.

REFERENCES

Appadurai, A. (2001) Deep democracy: urban governmentality and the horizon of politics. *Environment and Urbanization*, 13(2), 23–43. doi: 10.1177/095624780101300203.

Browne, S. (2015) *Dark Matters: On the Surveillance of Blackness*. Durham, NC: Duke University Press.

Buolamwini, J. and Gebru, T. (2018) Gender shades: intersectional accuracy disparities in commercial gender classification. *Proceedings of Machine Learning Research*, 81, 77–91.

Desrosières, A. (2002) *The Politics of Large Numbers: A History of Statistical Reasoning*. Cambridge, MA: Harvard University Press.

Desrosières, A. (2014) 'Statistics and social critique', Partecipazione e conflitto. *The Open Journal of Sociopolitical Studies*, 7(2), 330–41, doi: 10.1285/i20356609v7i2p330.

Downing, J., Fasano, R., Friedland, P. A., McCullough, M. F., Mizrahi, T. and Shapiro, J. J. (1991) Computers for social change: introduction. *Computers in Human Services*, 8(1), 1–8. doi: 10.1300/J407v08n01_01.

Eubanks, V. (2017) *Automating Inequality: How High-Tech Tools Profile, Police, and Punish the Poor*. New York: St. Martin's Press.

Making Sense (n.d.) Making sense: the toolkit. Available at http://making-sense.eu/publication_ categories/toolkit/ (last accessed 12 January 2022).

Milan, S. and van der Velden, L. (2016) The alternative epistemologies of data activism. *Digital Culture & Society*, 2(2), 57–74. doi: 10.14361/dcs-2016-0205.

Noble, S. U. (2018) *Algorithms of Oppression: How Search Engines Reinforce Racism*. New York: New York University Press.

Chapter 11

THE STREET, THE SQUARE AND THE NET: HOW URBAN ACTIVISTS MAKE AND USE NETWORKED TECHNOLOGIES

Jessica Feldman

Urban activists all over the world wrestle with the need for – and limitations of – digital communications and data storage – often with rather creative and hopeful results. This chapter outlines these struggles through ethnographies of activist groups in the United States, European Union (EU) and Middle East and North Africa regions, through a values-in-design analysis of their tools. Drawing on interviews and participant observation with progressive-left activist and community organisations, over the years 2011–21, the chapter gives an overview of the ways in which digital tools have helped or troubled these groups differentially, focusing on new technologies designed by or for these groups to better serve progressive, participatory politics. I pay special attention in the coda to recent challenges presented to organising by the COVID-19 pandemic and the mandate to move many group activities online.

PUBLIC SPACE, MEDIATION AND THE RIGHT TO THE CITY

Henri Lefebvre (1996 [1968]) suggests that we think of the city as an oeuvre. Like a work of art, it is not simply a material product; its 'work' is rather a 'production and reproduction of human beings' and their relations, within historical contexts (p. 101). Mediation is key to forming these relations and the power structures that subtly act upon them. Moreover, this project of the city is forever a work in progress, and remains the metaphorical terrain on which the order of state and capital attempt to inscribe their logics in social relations. The right to the city is therefore a grounded, immediate (what Lefebvre calls 'near order'[1]) and creative struggle to reclaim the mediation of this terrain for other purposes – for social justice and human flourishing.

Urban activism makes clear the co-construction of technological mediation and actual, material space. Much urban activism is situated in and addresses public space – through occupations of squares, open-air assemblies and protests. For climate justice, housing rights and migration rights activists, the terrain (sidewalks, tents, buildings, borders, soil and water) is more than just a platform on which to air grievances, but is the very subject of those concerns. As discussed throughout this chapter, communication tools, data and connectivity are key means by which this oeuvre forms itself – by which groups organise, publicise, discuss and plan. These technologies are core to how political and social order are imagined and how the city is reclaimed – not just as a site of mediation, but also as a place of survival.

THE MOVEMENTS

This chapter anchors itself on a selection of 'the movements of the squares', a term that describes a recent (2010–16) flourishing of protest movements taking place in – and often occupying – public city squares worldwide. The movements can be traced to the 2010 Tunisian revolution, which was followed quickly by the 2011 Egyptian revolution. Shortly thereafter came a rash of public protest movements in Portugal, which inspired the 15-M movement in Spain, starting on 15 March 2011. Greek anti-austerity protestors soon occupied Syntagma Square in Athens, starting on 27 May 2011, establishing a people's assembly and communicating via Skype with the assembly in Madrid (Dalianis and Katsakos 2011). In September of that year, Occupy Wall Street (OWS) began in New York City, and spread internationally. Also included in this list is the 2013 occupation of Gezi Park in Istanbul, the 2014 Umbrella Movement in Hong Kong and finally Nuit Debout, a modified Occupy of France, which happened in 2016 (Feldman 2018).

These movements of the squares all had in common demands for 'real democracy',[2] frustrations with government corruption and a rejection of economic austerity policies implemented in the wake of the 2008 housing and stock market crash. The particular groups that are the subject this chapter – the 2011 Tahrir Square encampment in Cairo (leading to the Egyptian revolution), 15-M in Madrid, Occupy Wall Street in the US, the Gezi Park encampment in Istanbul, and Nuit

Debout in Paris – were chosen because of their relationship to public space and communication *technics*. These groups all set up camp in public space, occupying a square in the heart of their cities; they all had to develop their own communications protocols in order to enact their politics, which placed a heavy emphasis on direct democracy and assembly; and they all experienced failure or surveillance of corporate- and state-run communications infrastructures and platforms, leading them to create their own digital tools.

These cases are particularly interesting to study because, to greater or lesser degrees, their method of addressing their grievances was to attempt to practise direct democracy within their occupations, along-side acts of protest or revolution. As such, they must be understood as much more than protest movements – many were invested, simultane-ously with their critiques, in more productive and creative processes of prefigurative[3] political practice of reimagining the governance and sharing of the city, which eventually demanded a related design practice.

Many of these movements have morphed into or had strong influ-ences on current groups, such as self-governing neighbourhood assem-blies in Spanish cities, citizens' assemblies throughout France and new waves of social movements that share their values and practices, including recent climate justice, anti-fascist and anti-austerity protest movements. As such, this chapter also draws on more recent fieldwork (2018–21) and interviews with climate justice groups, housing rights activists and activists involved in movements for racial justice and against police violence, mainly in Europe and the US.

The sudden need to move online during the COVID-19 pandemic and its related confinements challenged urban activism and assembly in general. While the need for activism and mutual aid became even more pronounced in this moment of democratic, health and economic crises, the capacity to come together in dense, shared urban space was greatly diminished. This situation has put a fine point on the need for digital tools that serve progressive values – for the near-term need of organising and care at all levels, and, eventually, for a longer-term need to syndicate and scale up practices of collectivity and social justice across global distances (Feldman 2020).

FROM VALUES-IN-DESIGN TO VALUES-DRIVEN DESIGN

This chapter draws on a multi-sited case study involving long-form interviews and participant observation with democratic social movements and activist groups in New York City, Madrid, Istanbul, Paris and Cairo. More recent (2018–21) research includes participation and interviews with individuals and groups involved in open source design collectives, movement tech groups and in social movements and community groups in Lebanon, France, Spain, Los Angeles, New York City and Brussels. The activists I spoke to are involved in general progressive-left groups, as well as issues-based groups focused on climate justice, housing rights and on combating racist policing or working towards police abolition. Overall, I carried out seventy-eight interviews, mostly in person, while some were performed over encrypted voice or video calls, or email exchanges. Subjects included activists, journalists, engineers and human rights workers affiliated with these movements; their names have been pseudonymised in this chapter.

I couple this fieldwork with a values-in-design analysis of the code and protocols of the technologies that were built by participants in these movements in order to serve their politics. I have focused on a few example cases of recurring types of designs from a larger sample of technologies. Values-in-design is a broad term for a range of analytical frameworks for articulating the ethical and political values that are (or should be) 'baked in' to an object's design. This analysis generally involves looking closely at (or, in the case of values-driven design, being part of the process of) the design itself, by reading code, describing circuits and discussing the political and ethical choices provided and foreclosed by certain design decisions. My analysis of these tools asks to what extent their design creates possibilities for certain political practices, and forecloses others. Flanagan, Howe and Nissenbaum (2008: 322) advocate 'a pragmatic turn from this largely descriptive posture' in order to 'set forth values as a design aspiration, exhorting designers and producers to include values, purposively, in the set of criteria by which the excellence of technologies is judged'. The activist groups discussed here often practise this pragmatism, and a description of their innovations can lay the groundwork for further design practice in this direction.

NETWORKS – AS WE NOW KNOW THEM – ARE NOT PUBLICS

Much research at the intersection of social movement studies and new media considers how movements use existing networked tools (usually social media platforms, such as Twitter and Facebook) to organise and to publicise. A first phase of optimism about 'Twitter revolutions' and 'mass self-media' (Castells 2009) has been followed by critiques, either of these technologies or these movements. Tufekci's (2017) study of Gezi Park and Tahrir Square focuses on the ways in which corporate and state-owned platforms and networks failed civil society by permitting surveillance, while simultaneously facilitating the growth of the movements at an unprecedented rate. Tufekci concludes by criticising the social movements themselves for relying too heavily on these tools rather than on more traditional, analogue and longer-range forms of movement building, such as political parties. Other work focuses instead on problems with the centralised and individualised nature of these digital platforms (Fenton and Barassi 2011), causing bitter fights within movements over passwords (Gerbaudo 2017) and group decision making (Kavada 2015).

Ethnographic research on these movements reminds us that the relationship between technology and politics is not fully deterministic in either direction (Treré 2019). For example, as Aouragh and Alexander's study of the use of the Internet in the 2011 Egyptian revolution shows, it is reductive to attribute the revolution to Western-designed social media, such as Twitter, overlooking long local, regional and national histories of in-person organising and social movements, while it is also reductive to claim that these tools were not used for both productive and repressive purposes. Aouragh and Alexander (2011: 1353) write that the Internet 'empowers and disempowers. What seems to be a paradox is actually the normal contradiction of capitalist society, precisely because the Internet is not a subject with independent characteristics but an object shaped by the social environment in which it is embedded'.

This chapter elaborates on the alternatives that arise when this paradox is no longer sustainable for progressive politics. This research found that tools such as Facebook, Instagram and Twitter have been useful – *but only to a point*. These platforms allow for mobilising certain activities such as large public protests, and can be helpful for publicising issues- or identity-based advocacy campaigns (since the networks are designed to recommend activities and groups that match a user's political and demographic preferences). As Paulo Gerbaudo's research with these same movements of the squares eloquently argues, social media have been 'chiefly responsible for the construction of a choreography of assembly', which brought together in public space dispersed individuals (2012: 5). These platforms were useful for mobilising, organising and framing practices of assembly.

Once it is realised, however, public, assembly-based activism that practises direct democracy and seeks to open itself to strangers quickly finds that different digital tools are needed. And, once protests become large enough to challenge the existing order, the mainline Internet becomes less available, and somewhat dangerous. Three sets of problems arise. First, social media platforms are heavily surveilled, and, in some cases, states and corporations are responsible for throttling or altogether shutting down certain platforms, or entire Internet and SMS services (Access Now 2021). Second, social media, which is designed to recommend 'more of the same', is just not particularly useful for a political practice focused on public inclusivity. Finally, the conversations enabled by such platforms are designed more for publicity and sound-bites than for deep discussion or decision making. For these reasons, some rather old analogue communication and decision-making methods have been used by these movements, and some very new, alternative communication technologies are being designed by activists and sympathetic engineers to expand and supplement these methods.

DESIGN SOLUTIONS FOR A DEMOCRATIC PUBLIC

In this section of the chapter, I discuss three types of technologies that emerged in these groups: decentralised network infrastructures, techniques for distributed and localised data sovereignty and algorithms for inclusive deliberation and decision making. By focusing on detailed descriptions of a few examples, I articulate through these cases recurring values across the technologies designed by and for these movements.

Decentralised and Localised Infrastructures –
Mesh and Local Networks, Alternets

Many of these movements began to develop alternative network infra-structures in order to provide connectivity to participants in response to blocking and shut-downs; to address concerns about surveillance; and to mirror the non-hierarchical and autonomous values of the move-ments. Mostly, these projects were smaller scale, localised and short term – meant to serve the squares and neighbourhoods where they were needed – although their designers and users often had visions for larger-scale or more enduring versions. And, as they were erected rather hastily to meet a failure of existing structures, many were not fully adopted, nor were they fully realised in their ideal forms. At the end of the section, I will touch on more enduring projects that have been built outside of movements by engineers and artists who share and expand upon these visions.

Mesh networks are networks in which each device (mobile phones, laptops, etc.) can serve as a node to route data. Such networks do not return to a centralised antenna and therefore have the potential to avoid both corporate service providers and the surveillance and block-ing of centralised chokepoints (Abdul 2017). A fully distributed mesh, in which no one node has more routing or receiving power than any others, mirrors the structure and ideology of horizontal democracy, which aims to give equal voice, power and access to any member of the assembly (see Figure 11.1). Meshes also are capable of operating inde-pendently of mainline telecom providers, and they therefore put this infrastructure in the hands of the users. Mesh networks are also very resilient, as the failure of one device will not affect the whole network, due to their redundancy in transmission. If one node drops out, trans-missions continue through the many other paths made available by all other nodes. While centralised telecom can struggle – or refuse – to transmit signals from too many devices through one single antenna (a common problem during assemblies, protests and other large gather-ings), in the case of a mesh network, more devices make more trans-mission nodes, and the network becomes harder to take down as more people join.

This design in some ways echoes analogue transmission methods used in assemblies, like 'the people's mic'. The people's mic was a method of transmitting speech through crowds at Occupy Wall Street,

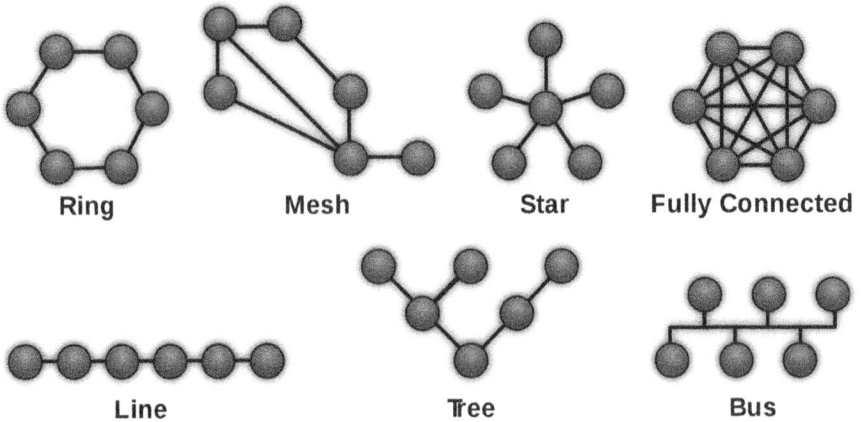

Figure 11.1 Network topologies. The mainline Internet and cellular telecom are closer to a hybrid of multiple tree models. Source: https://commons. wikimedia.org/wiki/File:NetworkTopologies.svg

which was subsequently adopted by other Occupies around the globe. As the protestors in New York City did not have permission to use amplified sound, they instead used a technique of concentric circles of vocal repetition, extending the range of the speaker throughout the crowd. The practice requested that everyone within earshot of the speaker repeat everything that they heard, thereby making it audible to those near them, who then repeated what they heard, and so on. In such a model, the consent and support of the group is required to share a message, and the larger the group is, the farther the message can travel. The growth of the group becomes a strength and security rather than a challenge.

Fully distributed mesh networks, much like the people's mic, are difficult to implement and can be slow, because each device is both sending and receiving all communications. A common solution to this problem is to build a local area network (commonly called LAN, or WLAN for a wireless one) with one or a handful of more powerful nodes, which handle routing, and which are still autonomous from corporate Internet service providers (ISPs). Even still, a hybrid mesh can be used to distribute a connection to the global Internet: one or a few key nodes pay for access to the 'capital I' Internet, and distribute that access by connecting other devices in the neighbourhood, who then serve to route the signal on to still other devices.

In Madrid, at least one mesh network originated during 15-M to provide free localised Internet access in a neighbourhood in the red belt, a working-class area in the south of the city, where assemblies were held in the neighbourhood squares and a number of activist-occupied social centres. From the top of a tall building in the neighbourhood, a Wi-Fi signal was able to reach nearby squats and assemblies, connecting users to the Internet for free, and allowing other buildings nearby to serve as nodes to route signals. In this area, where many activists lived in squatted communal social centres[4] without basic infrastructure and utilities, a hybrid mesh was a way to provide that access without having to buy into (or pay for) a lease, cables and corporate services.

Similar projects to the Madrid mesh appeared in Occupy camps throughout the United States some months later. These projects served multiple purposes: providing local or global network access in public squares, protecting against external surveillance and mirroring the non-hierarchical and autonomous values of the movement.

The Freedom Tower network, which originated at Occupy Wall Street, distributed connections to the global Internet through a localised network. The first Freedom Towers were built by Isaac Wilder and Charles Wyble, two occupiers and computer scientists, who had recently formed a group called the Free Network Foundation (Cook Network Consultants 2012). The camp – a collection of tents, tarps and assemblies in a public square – had no reliable Internet access, yet needed to be able to communicate both internally and externally: with the press, with human rights observers and with other activists elsewhere.

To solve this problem, Wilder and Wyble built a small-scale Internet connection to serve the camp. The core of the network is a tall pole on which a number of Wi-Fi radio units are mounted, which distribute access to the Internet and receive local signals. The network connects to the Internet through a traditional upstream radio or modem of some sort, and a lower power laptop (or a number of these) to act as routers to send connections to the radio units on the tower. Instructions for setting up the hardware and installing the software for the laptop and router were all available on the Free Network Foundation's website. The laptops ran an open source program that made it possible for the users to do their own network administration (Free Network Foundation 2012). Freedom Towers were soon in use at Occupy Austin and Occupy LA, providing Internet access to the encampments in a space where no other infrastructure existed; they also have the capacity to create autonomous networks, separate from the global Internet. A secure connection was built between Austin and New York City, but further developments were stymied in November 2011 when police raided and shut down the Occupy Wall Street camp, and the hardware was confiscated and never recovered (Cook Network Consultants 2012).

While the Freedom Tower project began by plugging into the global Internet, a second project was born during Occupy Wall Street, called occupy.here, created as an offline message board for people in the vicinity of the camp. Described as a 'tiny, self-contained darknet' (Phiffer 2013), occupy.here consists of a Wi-Fi router and a Linux distribution for building applications and software for the occupy.here website. Instructions for setting up a router and code for the website are available, free to download, from the occupy.here GitHub. Once running, the system creates a LAN that allows users within its Wi-Fi broadcast range to connect to this network and access the occupy.here website, which provides a message board and file sharing. Those beyond the vicinity of the router cannot access the website (see Figure 11.2).

The localised and autonomous nature of this project was a result of a desire to 'create a technology out of Occupy', according to Dan Phiffer,

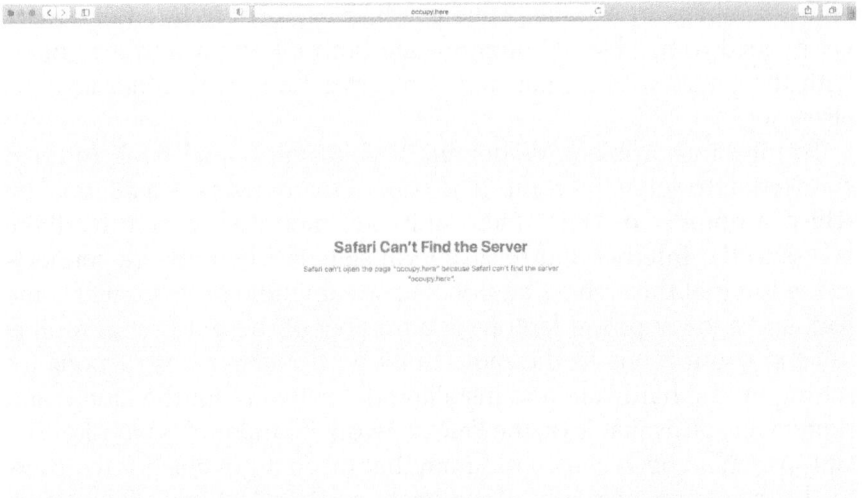

Figure 11.2 Screenshot of failed attempt to access occupy.here from a remote location. Source: http://www.occupyhere.org

the founder and lead developer, who spoke to me in 2017. Phiffer's interest in a localised dark network was twofold: to create something resistant to surveillance, and to create a place where strangers could meet. 'The thing I really appreciated about Occupy,' Phiffer said, 'was that people could encounter people they wouldn't normally and have a conversation. [occupy.here] filters by proximity and not by previous association, unlike other social media.'

Like Freedom Tower, occupy.here also had (as yet unrealised) ambitions to create a larger scale network of autonomous local networks. The project's website explains this vision: 'building up a collective network infrastructure that is owned and controlled by its users can lay the groundwork for other uses and applications' (Phiffer 2013). Phiffer later focused on developing a similar tool but for SMS texting, in the interest of accessibility for those without smartphones. Phiffer says he doesn't think of occupy.here as prefigurative in the way that Occupy Wall Street was, because 'prefigurative implies that this is how I think things should be and I'm not sure that's the case. Having control over the stack, owning the physical data, for sure. The offline of it, I'm not so attached to anymore.'

An SMS system was in fact built, months before OWS, in the Tahrir Square protest camp in Cairo. The 2011 shutdown of Internet and cell phone service went hand in hand with physical violence against protestors. As Ziad explained to me in a 2016 interview in Cairo:

> In my experience, when they do this, shut off the internet, this is combined with bullets and tear gas. I was shot two times, they tried to kidnap me. There is not any space for communication. You aren't tweeting, you are mainly concerned with physical safety at this point.

Alternative communications infrastructures were urgently necessary to coordinate care, protection and publicity, and were therefore quickly adopted in Tahrir Square. Human rights workers who were involved with the communications committee in Tahrir Square have remarked that they did not have the time to develop horizontally governed tools or to engage in drawn-out discussion processes; instead they were focused on creating workarounds to the shutdown in the midst of a violent revolution.

An ad hoc, localised SMS hub was successfully established within

the square in order to connect lawyers, doctors, researchers and journalists to protesters and frontline activists in the midst of the occupation. The system filtered text messages sent to a certain number based
on a keyword, and then forwarded them to either the legal support
team, the medical team or researchers and trusted journalists, who
were then sent to the GPS location of the SMS. This solution allowed
those in most urgent need to connect with help and support, while preserving their privacy, and allowed the communications group to push
online the most important documentation, independent of the state's
attempt to shut down communications.

While the hub was clever and successful, the centralised nature
of this design went against the values of the team. Organisers were
careful to be clear that this way of working was a result of their limited
resources, and not in line with their values; as Ziad said, 'This set-up
was not political, it was pragmatic. This was the initial plan. We would
have changed it if it [the revolution] succeeded.'

Similar projects have developed more slowly over the past decade;
these are mostly open source projects, built by civic tech and movement tech groups to promote values of democratisation and data
sovereignty or to support local communities. Some of these projects,
like the community-run guifi.net mesh project in Spain, provide infrastructure to a broader community – a neighbourhood or village – based
on values of open and equal access and self-governance.[5] Tools like the
Briar project[6] – a messaging app that connects devices when they are
in proximity, without storing anything in the cloud – were built explicitly for activists and journalists who need to be mobile and to protect
their safety. Briar is increasingly adopted by urban activists and crisis
responders. Qaul.net,[7] a decentralised and open ad hoc mesh network,
designed to work with mobile phones, was originally designed by a
German–Swiss artist team in 2011 and has since gathered funding and
support for development from a number of American and European
non-governmental organisations (NGOs). International activists are
using Qual, as are local communities in France.

Distributed and Localised Data Sovereignty – Servers and Security

Overall, less work has been done *within* movements at the layer of
privacy and security design and data archives; more often, these movements make use of existing tools and code, cobbling together solutions

that work for them or finding ways to work around vulnerabilities.[8] A few innovations, and a few unsolved problems, demand attention here.

Local and Federated Servers

In addition to alternative infrastructures, storage and access to the data sent through these networks also required rethinking. In many of the examples discussed above, localised servers and hard drives are key to maintaining autonomy and security over data. Some groups store messages, emails and archives on local servers owned by a member of the group. Other groups use services like RiseUp,[9] an encrypted email and server space run by a movement tech collective, or an international server that is in the hands of the group. Sometimes, however, the physical security of these servers is at risk: for example, the RiseUp servers have been repeatedly seized by the FBI, two interviewees told me in 2019 (Fakhoury 2012). Similarly, when the Occupy Wall Street camp was evicted by police, local servers and other hardware were seized, leading to a lawsuit against the City of New York by Isaac Wilder and the Free Network Foundation (Wilder vs City of New York 2021).

Alternative, non-commercial and open source social networks, such as N-1, originating in Spain and Northern Morocco (Cabello, Franco and Haché 2013), and diaspora, which started as a student project at New York University (diaspora* foundation 2013), also emerged and gained traction in many of these movements. These platforms offered social networking capabilities similar to Facebook but prioritised privacy and autonomy. As such, these platforms did not harvest metadata for advertising income, nor did they store data in a centralised server. One interviewee told me that at the core of N-1 was Lorea, 'a software for self-managed social networks', which allowed users to run a social network off federated, decentralised servers. Unlike fully distributed peer-to-peer architectures, federated severs involve 'installing software on a trusted server application that communicates with other trusted servers', allowing multiple networks to connect to each other while each maintains its own local servers and data sovereignty therein (ibid.). As Marta, a 15-M activist involved with Lorea, explained, 'the idea with Lorea was to develop the software so that collectives could get it and install it on their server and have protocols so that different networks could communicate among each other. Some collectives managed to get their own server and set up the server'. While the project preceded 15-M by a few years, it grew hugely during the movement – too much so, in fact. Said Marta, 'It had 3000 users and then it suddenly had 40,000. The project died; we weren't ready for so many users. It finished in 2013. One year after 15M it was more or less over because we had a lot of problems keeping the server up.' In some ways, Lorea was a victim of its own success – the syndicated, decentralised model flourished politically and required communications tools that mirrored these political goals, only the tools could not be scaled up as quickly.

Encryption
When the physical security of the data is uncertain, encryption becomes important. All of these groups included members who were vigilant about data privacy, to a greater or lesser degree; they often used different, already existing, tools and protocols for encrypted SMS and emails and encrypted their hard drives and computers. Such groups were early adopters of encrypted messaging apps such as Signal and Telegram, which are now widely used by activist groups as well as the general public (Kharpal 2021). Larger-scale internal communications and most public-facing communications are implemented using email clients such as Gmail and RiseUp, websites or social media accounts on Facebook. Concerns over surveillance and data sovereignty have led these activists increasingly to use open source and encrypted tools. Tools like jitsi[10] for video conferencing, mattermost,[11] element[12] and etherpad[13] are becoming more widely used by community organisers and activist groups, particularly since many meetings moved online during the COVID-19 pandemic – although, as discussed at the end of this chapter, open source tools often meet with resistance within these groups because they are less easy to use for some members.

Practices of encryption have repeatedly given rise to internal power struggles within many groups over use of passwords and access to archives and mailing lists, a phenomenon that seems to occur more often in cases of commercial communications platforms than physical hardware. Questions such as who has access to the email list, who can post on the Facebook page or who can use the Twitter account have led to bitter fights and even lawsuits within some groups, including those which attempt to self-govern without centralised authorities. The bottlenecking of power that comes with a single password and authorship has exacerbated already existing power struggles within organisations, or moved them from decision-making groups to communications teams. Methods such as distributed passwords have only been implemented at the industrial or military level or remain in the realm of theoretical computer science.[14] While discussions arose within these groups over more equal distribution of password rights (Kavada 2015), my research has found no example of digital designs which have surfaced to implement a solution. Further research and development is required here.

Inclusive Deliberation and Decision-Making Algorithms

Beyond problems of security and connectivity, many of these groups struggle to implement directly democratic self-governance. The more bodily mediated listening and consensus protocols practised at in-person assemblies bring with them classic participatory democracy problems, including access (who can be present in the assembly), exhaustion (who can stay present) and scale (Polletta 2002). One of the main means of addressing these issues, especially since the COVID-19 confinements, has been the use of online digital tools for group deliberation and decision making, including a number of voting and consultation algorithms.

Richard Bartlett, one of the founders of the Loomio project, an open source collective decision-making platform, explained to me in a 2018 interview that it arose in part to address inclusion problems that the founders experienced in activist assemblies:

> Over time we started to realise that actually, there's a lot of people here that are not having a great time. And we started to appreciate: it's not just like a random group of people who are not having a good time. The more different you are from being a straight, male, wealthy, confident, native-speaking-English, the more different you are from those categories, the less of a good time you're having here, the less safe you feel here, or the less it feels like your movement. Bit by bit, we started to see some of the shadows around the utopia.

These feelings of exclusion were aggravated by the long, drawn-out nature of the deliberation process, which enabled those with disposable time to 'dominate by waiting everyone else out'. Pablo, an ICT engineer who was active in 15-M from the beginning, agreed, telling me

We should ban Marmite!

POSITIONS

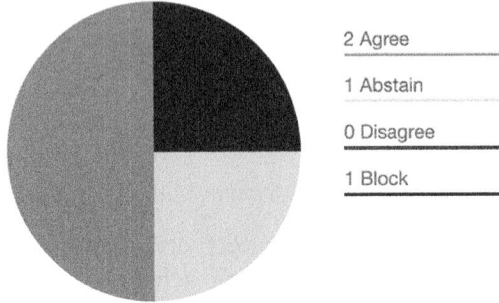

2 Agree

1 Abstain

0 Disagree

1 Block

21% of members have stated their position (4/19)

👍 **Richard D. Bartlett** agreed: Sounds like a good plan

Figure 11.3 Feedback interface example from Loomio (rdbartlett 2016).
Source: https://blog.loomio.org/2016/02/09/
spreading-the-contagious-idea-of-collaborative-decision-making/

in 2016 that '[demonstrations] are good, but you can't do it every day, because people get tired. In my opinion, consultation is better because your voice counts for years.' Pablo also articulated problems of scaling: assembly politics works for small to mid-sized groups, but technology is required to coordinate larger groups like municipalities or nations.

The designers of Loomio sought to streamline the decision process in a way that included everyone equally, while still holding fast to the consensus system. In Loomio, groups gather together through initiations by the group moderator and discuss a topic online in a thread, in which anyone in the group can comment. In the thread, you can start a proposal and ask for responses from the group. Instead of just yes and no responses, the designers allow four responses, based on the hand signals used to make decisions in Occupy assemblies: agree, abstain, disagree and block (Figure 11.3).

A space also exists for deliberation, and Loomio's website features a guide on how to facilitate discussions, which echoes many activist values, such as the establishment of working groups, the promotion of quieter or marginalised voices, using clear language and maintaining a safe environment (Alanna 2021). According to Clara, whom I interviewed in 2021, this software is currently used quite widely, by climate activist groups such as Extinction Rebellion as well as by community groups and NGOs concerned with horizontal democracy, including ouishare[15] and the P2P Foundation[16] (Loomio 2015a, 2015b).

Tensions exist, however, between deliberation and scale: it is hard to sustain a conversation in person or in an online thread with a larger number of participants. Groups have used run-off voting and sortition as solutions to this problem. During 15-M, people successfully used appgree,[17] a pre-existing, free, but not open source, application and website for collective decision making, which combines sortition and run-off voting, based on the theory that 'the opinion of a random sample from a big group of people considerably represents that of the whole group, and the bigger the sample size, the more accurate the representation will be' (Material for journalists and bloggers 2016). The app collects proposals from participants in a community, and each proposal must be worded so that it can be answered with a 'yes' or 'no' vote. Participants are broken into equal-sized groups that are random samples of the larger group, each of which votes on one proposal. The most popular proposals are then selected for a second round of voting, with increasingly larger voting groups due to the smaller number of proposals. This process continues until one proposal emerges. Podemos, a political party that developed out of 15-M, subsequently used the tool in its Congress meetings.

Users within the movement appreciated this tool but noted that it lacked the space for conversation or deliberation: there is no way to edit or synthesise proposals. More flexible alternatives were quickly developed. Paolo was part of a tech working group within 15-M that designed algorithms for referenda in Madrid, leading to the free, open source software called CONSUL (Figure 11.4). The software is now used internationally, perhaps most notably by cities throughout Spain for referenda and participatory budgeting, and by New York City for its participatory budgeting initiatives (Organizations using consul 2021). The CONSUL software allows citizens to vote online about various local issues, with rankings rather than only yes/no decisions. Pablo managed the database for this site so that people could see the votes in real time, which he believes produced a snowball effect. The first referendum vote he automated was a vote against the privatisation of water in Madrid, which was successful. According to Pablo, on the first day 60,000 people voted, and on the next day 170,000 people had

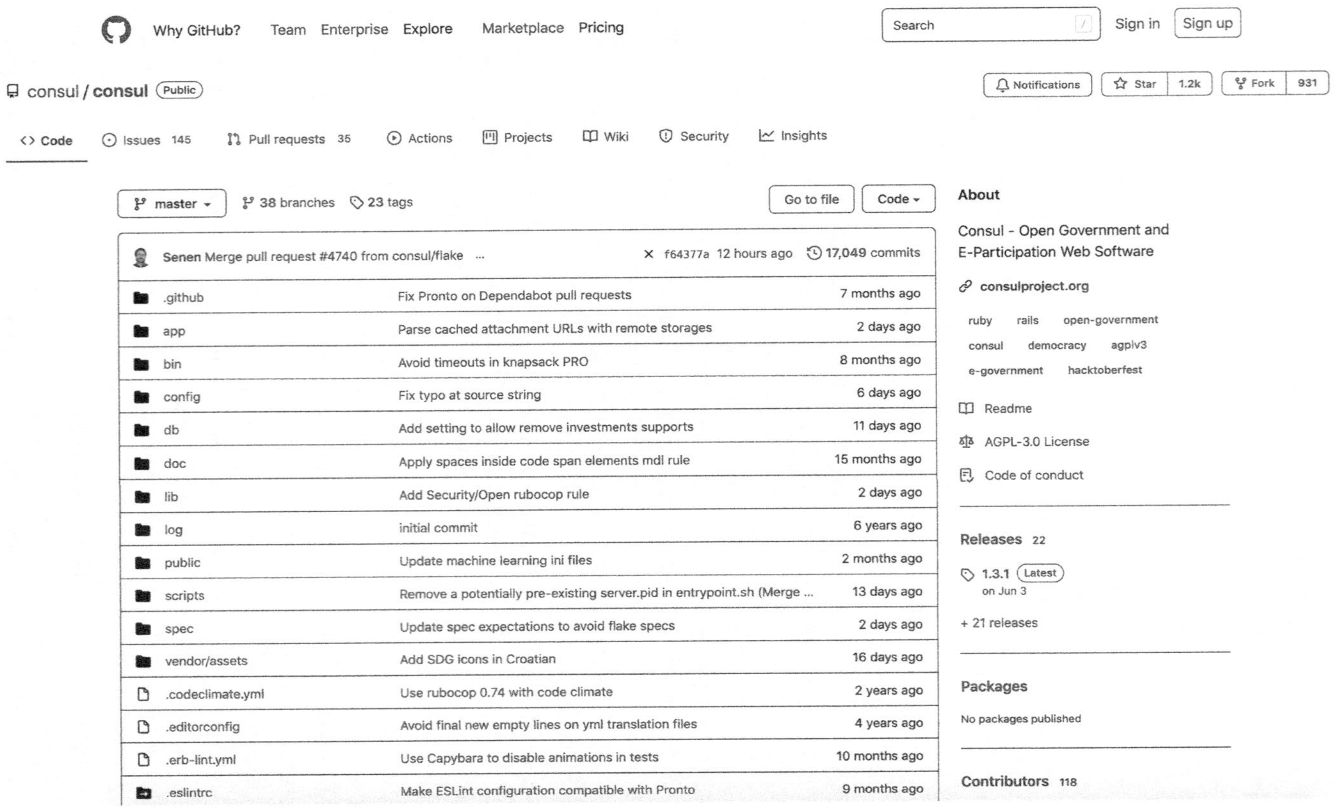

Figure 11.4 Github page for CONSUL (Consul 2017). Source: https://github.com/consul/consul

participated. In the next vote, on health care, 1 million people voted on the site. This vote stopped the privatisation of five or six hospitals.

Ideally, Pablo says, a tool would ask a question, have a space for open answers, condense these into proposals, facilitate votes on the proposals, then have a means for going through cycles of improvements on the proposals: 'The perfect tool in deliberative democracy we don't have yet. It is difficult. Now automatic synthesis is impossible, but people are working on it.' Recent preliminary research has used Natural Language Processing (NLP) to automatically sort proposals on the CONSUL platform to help users find their interests (Nesta 2021). However, scholars of digital democracy have also warned that automated recommendation systems that encourage homophily can be detrimental to the plurality of opinions and diversity needed for inclusive democracy. The Desegregating Digital Neighborhoods project in the Digital Democracies Institute at Simon Fraser University is working to design platforms that deliberately go against such homophily (Digital Democracies Institute 2021).

Others are not so sure that AI is the best solution. Juan, an activist from 15-M whom I interviewed in 2016 and who is currently involved with Kurdish rights groups, agrees that these kinds of tools are necessary 'for coordination of big organisations and decisions'. However, he feels that in order to really 'make work', he needs to work in person with a close group of people he trusts. 'I like to always have protocols, but to be able to change them.'

In recent years there has been a flourishing of digital democracy tools throughout the world, and a tentative adoption by municipal and even national governments (Research Center of Citizen Participation 2021). In practice, many of these tools have been implemented through cycles of online voting and in-person deliberation, as is the case in many municipal assemblies throughout Spain – for example, the Citizen Participation processes organised by the city of Barcelona, which incorporate in-person deliberation with the use of the Decidim software program (Ajuntament de Barcelona and Decidim Barcelona, 2021).

Empathy and trust are key to consensus-based decision making: participants must feel connected to the struggles and needs of others within the community – including strangers – and make choices with the common good in mind. Questions arise as to whether these connections can truly be built remotely. Some experts on deliberative democracy argue that this hybrid model of in-person and online deliberation is a more ideal way to integrate empathy, discussion and scale (Chwalisz 2021).

CODA: COVID-19, ONLINE ASSEMBLY AND CRISIS COMMUNICATION

Such a hybrid model was difficult to test in 2020–1; the COVID-19 pandemic brought with it a huge reduction in face-to-face group meetings and public activism such as protests. At the same time, the pandemic exacerbated many of the inequities and precarities that such meetings try to circumvent for their participants and that are also often the subject of their activism in the streets. As groups began working from home, it became increasingly clear that not all homes are equal (Winkler 2020). Issues of housing justice, domestic violence, access to connectivity and digital hardware, digital literacy and gender inequality in domestic labour have all come to the fore during confinement, and these have also differentially affected activists' ability to participate in their groups, while at the same time somewhat shifting the priorities of some activists. In this coda, I focus mainly on more recent groups that identify as responding to specific issues, particularly crises of police brutality, climate change, food and housing insecurity and domestic violence. While some of these groups are organised using values of horizontality and direct democracy, others are less concerned with process and more focused on immediate outcomes. These are certainly not the only types of activists who have organised in recent years (see, for example, growing groups like Democratic Socialists of America, which focuses on systemic economic change, or the Gilets Jaunes movement in France, which, while not particularly cohesive politically, has been a reaction against austerity politics and often advocates for and practises direct democracy). However, activists organising around issues of response to crisis and violence provide an important, and increasingly substantial, counterpoint to *prefigurative* groups. Their perspectives and needs are important to consider vis-à-vis the design and adoption of emerging technologies.

The groups discussed earlier in this chapter all embraced a position vis-à-vis technology that saw it as constructive of their political possibilities and thought that their tools had to be carefully selected and built to align with their values. In some ways, the increasing use of open source and alternative tools by these groups is a tentative success story: activists and designers recognised an ideological and grounded need for such tools, and some of these tools – mainly those which were able to secure a more sustained situation of funding and workers – are slowly being developed and increasingly (although still quite marginally) adopted.

However, the design, selection and onboarding required for new members to become comfortable with alternative tools all take some time and are difficult in moments of crisis. This practice is generally not one that had been important to groups that focus more heavily on in-person meeting – particularly those less focused on systemic change and more focused on the very urgent provision of social services or defence of the most vulnerable people. Localised, near-order community-facing organisations that address housing justice, migrant protection or food aid have always been more 'boots on the ground' in their practices: meeting in person, providing material resources such as blankets, meals and physical defence from police sweeps. For groups like these, publicity and advocacy are less of a priority, and internal decision making, while important, was not so much the focus of their time. According to an interviewee, Anna, whom I spoke to in 2021, the groups mainly care about providing aid and defence for the neediest, and this generally was not datafied or digital.

The sudden onset of the COVID-19 pandemic, and the ensuing amplification of many forms of crisis – food insecurity, homelessness, domestic violence, as well as more generalised political crises of racist policing and anti-immigrant policies – have pushed together the need to organise online with the need to communicate quickly and effectively, especially for such organisations. This raises issues that are both technical and organisational. Smaller organisations, especially those that operate locally and rely heavily on in-person meetings and conversations, often struggle the most to reconfigure their internal communications and decision-making methods.

Disruption of Decision-Making and Power Structures

With the sudden move online, decisions had to be made first about who was responsible for making choices about which platforms to use, when to move to a platform and for which purposes. In moments of crisis, decision making often fell by default to those who were the most tech savvy or to those who had the time and enthusiasm to work on these questions. This way of working is certainly not new to remote working, but it is exacerbated by it. Power issues, such as those mentioned above around passwords, author-level control of data and access to online forums, became increasingly common and disrupted or complicated dynamics within many of these groups. One activist in a climate justice group explained to me in 2021 that, when they were meeting in person, it was easier to identify unofficial power structures, but that these became even more oblique and amplified once moving online: 'It's very visible in person,' she told me, 'because the very experienced stay together and know each other . . . online, I don't even know who these people are.'

Security versus Usability Debates

In the process of choosing platforms, debates arise in many groups around the security versus usability dichotomy. Mainline, commercial tools like Zoom, WhatsApp and Facebook have invested a great deal of time and development into making their user interface friendly and, in fact, addictive (Madrigal 2013). Their services are already very widely adopted, and almost always easy for new users, making access much broader and faster and operations smoother. This usability is a priority for many groups that are responding to urgent needs and who involve demographics who tend to use tech less – especially older activists (interview with Clara, 2021) or people from economic demographics which do not permit them to own a lot of hardware or to spend a lot of free time with digital tools.

However, these profit-driven tools compromise user privacy to a much greater extent because their business models rely on the harvesting and selling of user data to advertisers. Open source tools such as Mattermost or Signal are less well funded and generally do not sell or even collect user data. These platforms are much more privacy-preserving, but the lack of funding also means they are often more 'bare bones' because they have less time and resources to put into user experience design, and fewer options developed for accessibility.

These constraints raise huge debates around inclusion and alienation of those populations whom these groups are most committed to welcoming. As Anna, a housing justice activist in Los Angeles, told me in an interview in 2021, 'There is so much drama and chaos around involving older folks, especially monolingual, non-English speakers. . . . The tenants work is where we really see that a lot.' For Anna, the most accessible tool is the best one – in this case, Zoom, as it is the only video conferencing tool that provides channels that allow simultaneous translation. 'Anything that helps people access, I think is a wonderful thing.' Mon M, a member of an anti-racist group working against police violence, offered a more ambivalent view of this situation, explaining that the move online led to a huge and sudden problem, with racist Zoom-bombing happening so often that the group had to spend a lot of time training in how to screen for it and handle it when it occurred (DARN It 2020).

This very dichotomy is a dangerous and challenging one, especially for associations that work with vulnerable populations who are most in need of privacy protections, including queer communities, migrants, victims of domestic violence and anti-racist groups, and it points to a need for more accessible and secure design (Feldman and Oxley 2021).

Missing Connections: Drop Off and Exhaustion

Overall, the move online also differentially affected movements versus organisations. Larger, newer groups that were just forming or that were more public-focused (meeting in assemblies and focusing on public protest actions) got much smaller with the move online. An activist involved in Extinction Rebellion France explained, 'last year we had 2000 people [at the National Assembly] and this year we are just 300'. Mon M (DARN It 2020) also noticed that although meeting online made the activism accessible to different people, these weren't always the people who most needed the movements. 'The best thing about assembling online . . . is that people can come who can't normally come. . . . But I realize it was a very limited form of assembly – we didn't reach the people who most needed to be reached and brought into the campaign.' Two interviewees I spoke to in 2021 reflected on how groups that are older and smaller and had core members who had known each other for years tended to continue meeting more successfully; even so, they discussed the problems of Zoom fatigue and missing the connection of offline meeting.

Particularly for groups such as citizens' assemblies, whose mandate is to share stories and work towards understanding of different perspectives, the move online has been challenging as it disrupted the connections built through face-to-face meetings. The most successful stories of this move are those that devote time, resources and coaches to training, providing technology and facilitations. For example, the French Convention Citoyenne pour le Climat (Citizen's Assembly for the Climate) – which, in some ways, was a response to the demands and complaints of the Gilets Jaunes movement – was well funded by the French government. In this case, a group of participants were semi-randomly selected from throughout France in order to be sure to represent a range of ages, genders, income and education levels, and locations (rural versus urban), and were paid for their time in the Convention. In order to accommodate this diversity, the organisation had to be sure to introduce tools that were accessible across this range of demographics. As one interviewee told me in 2020, the organisation in charge of facilitation had trainers, outreach personnel and facilitators to make sure that all members were comfortably connected and attended to in the online meetings. Although much less well funded and institutionalised, Anna explained to me that the Los Angeles tenants' association with whom she worked was also 'much more open to providing members with the tech they need to be organisers and interpreters', compared to other, larger left groups; she attributed this to the group's demographic – unlike some organisations wherein it might be considered 'uncool' to reveal that you cannot afford or understand a technology, this group was explicitly made up of 'people in struggle, working class, poor people'.

CONCLUSION

The global pandemic only drew attention more strongly to the need for urban activism to syndicate itself across issues and inequalities, requiring communication technologies that can successfully bridge the gap between the near-order, on-the-ground work in the streets and the square, and the globalised, longer-term nature of cyclical crisis and structural oppression. The need is not a new one, but it is an accelerated one. Urban activists have used network tools to coordinate, make decisions and protect their data for decades. However, as outlined in this chapter, mainline, corporate tools only help to a point – when protests grow large because coordination is successful, when users' privacy becomes more crucial and when decision making and messaging needs to be democratically shared, corporate, mainline platforms and infrastructures often (sometimes deliberately) do not work. Once groups require more resiliency, security or less hierarchical and individualised structures for their politics, new tools need to be made. The tools and solutions discussed in this chapter can offer promising models and templates for designs and practices worthy of larger-scale implementation, built around core values of distribution, decentralisation, inclusion and participation. Going forward will require some structures of support and sustainability to carve out the time, support the labour and source the materials needed to scale up and make such visions broadly useable.

ACKNOWLEDGEMENTS

This research was supported in part by a doctoral fellowship from the National Science Foundation, Center for Interdisciplinary Studies in Security & Privacy, Information Security & Privacy Interdisciplinary Research and Education, by the Ford Foundation and Alfred P. Sloan Foundation Digital Infrastructure Fund, and by l'Institut français du Monde associatif, under the aegis of the Foundation for the University of Lyon, and by l'Institut National pour la Jeunesse et l'Éducation Populaire (France).

NOTES

1. Lefebvre (1996 [1968]: 101) defines the 'near order' as 'relations of individuals in groups of variable size, more or less organized and structured and the relations of these groups among themselves' and juxtaposes this with the 'far order' of distant institutions of power and regulation (church, state, legal codes, etc.), which attempt to operate on the near order.
2. For example, the Spanish organisation ¡*Democracia Real YA!* (Real Democracy Now!) was instrumental in organising the 15-M movement.
3. By 'prefigurative', I draw on Carl Boggs's term to describe a political movement or group that embodies 'those forms of social relations, decision-making, culture, and human experience that are the ultimate goal' within its 'ongoing practice' (Boggs 1977: 100)
4. A CSO (Centro Social Okupado – 'occupied social centre') or CSOA (Centro Social Okupado Autogestionado – 'self-managed occupied social centre') is a neighbourhood building that has been squatted and turned into a community social centre. These centers generally host a range of activities such as youth groups, political and union meetings, workshops, art exhibitions, conferences and solidarity canteens. Such spaces are very common throughout Spanish cities. See https://15mpedia.org/wiki/Lista _de_centros_sociales_de_la_Comunidad_de_Madrid.

5. Many other community mesh projects exist, such as NYCMesh (New York City), Freifunk (Germany), Sarantaporo.gr (Greece). While these projects are not all specifically designed to serve activists, they are often conceived of by engineers or users with political values close to anarchism or, sometimes, libertarianism. (In fact, some projects have members on both ends of that spectrum.)
6. https://briarproject.org/
7. https://qaul.net/
8. Many of the hacktivists and engineers involved in these movements are also involved in digital security projects (Signal, etc.), and those designs indeed emerged from or were informed by their work in these movements, although they do not necessarily emerge from a participatory design process within these groups (which is why they are not discussed in this chapter).
9. https://riseup.net/
10. https://meet.jit.si/
11. https://mattermost.com/
12. https://element.io/
13. https://etherpad.org/
14. See 'Shamir's Secret Sharing Algorithm', which breaks a password up across a group, and requires multiple parties to agree to collaboratively assemble it in order to authorise access (Shamir 1979).
15. https://www.ouishare.net/
16. https://p2pfoundation.net/
17. https://www.appgree.com/appgree/en/

REFERENCES

Abdul (2017) Network topology types with diagrams. Telecom Hub, 2 November. Available at https://telecom-hyb.blogspot.com/2017/11/network-topology-types-with-diagrams.html (last accessed 13 January 2022).

Access Now (2021) Internet shutdowns and elections handbook. Access Now. Available at https://www.accessnow.org/keepiton/#problem (last accessed 13 January 2022).

Ajuntament de Barcelona and Decidim Barcelona (2021) Guies pràctiques de la participació ciutadana a Barcelona: els processos participatius [Practical guides to citizen participation in Barcelona: Participatory processes]. decidim.barcelona. Available at https://www.decidim.barcelona/processes (last accessed 13 January 2022).

Alanna (2021) The facilitator's guide. Loomio Help. Available at https://help.loomio.org/en/guides/facilitators_guide/index.html (last accessed 13 January 2022).

Aouragh, M. and Alexander, A. (2011) The Egyptian experience: sense and nonsense of the internet revolution. *International Journal of Communication*, 5, 1344–58.

Boggs, C. (1977) Marxism, prefigurative communism, and the problem of workers' control. *Radical America*, 11–12, 99–122.

Cabello, F., Franco, M. and Haché, A. (2013) Towards a free federated social web: Lorea takes the networks! In G. Lovick and M. Rasch (eds), *Unlike Us Reader: Social Media Monopolies and Their Alternatives*. Available at https://www.networkcultures.org/_uploads/%238UnlikeUs.pdf (last accessed 13 January 2022).

Castells, M. (2009) *Communication Power*. Oxford: Oxford University Press.

Chwalisz, C. (2021) The pandemic has pushed citizen panels online. *Nature*, 589, 171. Available at https://www.nature.com/articles/d41586-021-00046-7 (last accessed 13 January 2022).

Consul (2017) 'Consul – open government and e-participation web software. github.com. Available at https://github.com/consul/consul (last accessed 13 January 2022).

Cook Network Consultants (2012) *Peer to Peer User Owned Communications Infrastructure: The Free Network Foundation and Building an Inter-occupy Network*. Ewing, NJ: The Cook Report on Internet Protocol. Available at https://www.yumpu.com/en/document/read/25286943/peer-to-peer-user-owned-communications-infrastructure-public- (last accessed 25 January 2022).

Dalianis, V. and Katsakos, P. (2011) 'Δεν υπάρχουν αρχηγοί, είμαστε όλοι μαζί' Κυριακή 5 Ιουνίου 2011: Έμεινε στην Ιστορία! ('"There are no leaders, we are all together" Sunday, 5 June 2011: Stay in History!'). Protothema online, 6 June. Archived from the original on 7 June 2011, accesed 10 May 2021, https://web.archive.org/web/20110607021837/http:/www.protothema.gr/greece/article/?aid=126165.

DARN It (2020) Online conference, Stanford University Digital Assembly Research Network, 23 September. DARN It #1: Digital Assembly, social media and elections, online conference. Conversation with Mon M (pseudonym).

'diaspora* celebrates one year as a community project'. diaspora* foundation. Available at https://blog.diasporafoundation.org/1-diaspora-celebrates-one-year-as-a-community-project (last accessed 13 January 2022).

Digital Democracies Institute. Desegregating network neighbourhoods. Available at https://digitaldemocracies.org/research/desegregating-network-neighbourhoods/ (last accessed 13 January 2022).

Fakhoury, H. (2012) Update: With May First/Riseup server seizure, FBI overreaches yet again. EFF.org, 3 May. Available at https://www.eff.org/fr/de

eplinks/2012/04/may-firstriseup-server-seizure-fbi-overreaches-yet-again (last accessed 13 January 2022).

Feldman, J. (2018) Strange speech: structures of listening in Nuit Debout, Occupy, and 15M. *International Journal of Communication*, 11, 1840–63.

Feldman, J. (2020) Listening and falling silent: towards *technics* of collectivity. *Sociologica*, 14(2), 5–12. doi: 10.6092/issn.1971-8853/11286.

Feldman, J. and Oxley, N. (2021) Crise sanitaire: stratégies et limites de la vie associative en ligne [Pandemic crisis: strategies and limits for associative life online]. *Juris Associations*, 631, 26–7.

Fenton, N and Barassi, V. (2011) Alternative media and social networking sites: the politics of individuation and political participation. *The Communication Review*, 14, 179–96. doi: 10.1080/10714421.2011.597245.

Flanagan, M., Howe, D. C. and Nissenbaum, H. (2008) Embodying values in technology: theory and practice. In J. van den Hoven and J. Weckert (eds), *Information Technology and Moral Philosophy*. Cambridge: Cambridge University Press, pp. 322–53. doi: 10.1017/CBO9780511498725.017.

The Free Network Foundation (2012) Freedom Tower. 15 June, https://commons.thefnf.org/index.php/FreedomTower. Available at https://web.archive.org/web/20130624023330/https://commons.thefnf.org/index.php/Freedom Tower (last accessed 25 January 2022).

Gerbaudo, P. (2012) *The Tweets and the Streets: Social Media and Contemporary Activism*. London: Pluto Press.

Gerbaudo, P. (2017) Social media teams as digital vanguards: the question of leadership in the management of key Facebook and Twitter accounts of Occupy Wall Street, Indignados and UK Uncut. *Information, Communication & Society*, 20(2), 185–202.

Kavada, A. (2015) Creating the collective: social media, the Occupy Movement and its constitution as a collective actor. *Information, Communication & Society*, 18(8), 872–86. doi: 10.1080/1369118X.2015.1043318.

Kharpal, A. (2021) Signal and Telegram downloads surge after WhatsApp says it will share data with Facebook. cnbc.com, 12 January. Available at https://www.cnbc.com/2021/01/12/signal-telegram-downloads-surge-after-update-to-whatsapp-data-policy.html (last accessed 13 January 2022).

Lefebvre, H. (1996 [1968]) The right to the city. In E. Kofman and E. Lebas (eds and trans), *Writings on Cities*. Oxford: Blackwell, pp. 147–59.

Loomio (2015a) How Ouishare is scaling a shared vision across countries. 27 December. Available at https://www.youtube.com/playlist?list=PLfeqYbxvuD29MfdIvQ7hnzg0LMcK4DEDZ (last accessed 25 January 2022).

Loomio (2015b) How the P2P Foundation does high-level coordination. 27 December. Available at https://youtu.be/KLKU9JbPel4 (last accessed 25 January 2022).

Madrigal, A. (2013) The machine zone: this is where you go when you just can't stop looking at pictures on Facebook. *The Atlantic*, 31 July. Available at https://www.theatlantic.com/technology/archive/2013/07/the-machine-zone-this-is-where-you-go-when-you-just-cant-stop-looking-at-pictures-on-facebook/278185/ (last accessed 13 January 2022).

'Material for journalists and bloggers' (2016) appgree.com. Available at http://www.appgree.com/appgree/en/press/ (last accessed 13 January 2022).

Nesta (2021) Citizen participation and machine learning for a better democracy. Nesta.org.uk. Available at https://www.nesta.org.uk/feature/collective-intelligence-grants/citizen-participation-and-machine-learning-better-democracy/ (last accessed 13 January 2022).

'Organizations using consul' (2021) consulproject.org. Available at https://consulproject.org/en/ (last accessed 13 January 2022).

Phiffer, D. (2013) Occupy.here: a tiny, self-contained darknet. *Rhizome.org*, 1 October. Available at https://rhizome.org/editorial/2013/oct/01/tiny-self-contained-darknet/ (last accessed 13 January 2022).

Polletta, F. (2002) *Freedom Is an Endless Meeting: Democracy in American Social Movements*. Chicago, IL: University of Chicago Press.

rdbartlett (2016) Spreading the collaborative decision-making meme. Loomio blog, 9 February. Available at https://blog.loomio.org/2016/02/09/spreading-the-contagious-idea-of-collaborative-decision-making/ (last accessed 13 January 2022).

Research Center of Citizen Participation/Institute for Democracy and Participation Research of the University of Wuppertal in cooperation with Democracy International (2021) Welcome to the Navigator to Direct Democracy. The Navigator to Direct Democracy. Available at https://www.direct-democracy-navigator.org/ (last accessed 13 January 2022).

Shamir, A. (1979) How to share a secret. *Communications of the ACM*, 22(11), 612–13. doi: 10.1145/359168.359176.

Treré, E. (2019) *Hybrid Media Activism: Ecologies, Imaginaries, Algorithms*. New York: Routledge.

Tufekci, Z. (2017) *Twitter and Teargas: The Power and Fragility of Networked Protest*. New Haven, CT: Yale University Press.

Wilder and Free Network Foundation versus City of New York et al., 1:14-cv-08953-SAS, Document 2, filed November 11, 2014. (1:14-cv-08953), 2021. *Court Listener*, 28 January. Available at https://www.courtlistener.com/docket/4354418/idb/wilder-v-city-of-new-york/ (last accessed 13 January 2022).

Winkler, M. (2020) How COVID-19 is also killing democracy. *Forbes*, 10 April. Available at https://www.forbes.com/sites/hecparis/2020/04/10/how-covid-19-is-also-killing-democracy/ (last accessed 13 January 2022).

Chapter 12

FACIAL RECOGNITION AND THE RIGHT TO APPEAR: INFRASTRUCTURAL CHALLENGES IN ANTI-SURVEILLANCE RESISTANCE

Benedetta Catanzariti

Now that they are preparing the way for the automation of perception, for the innovation of artificial vision, delegating the analysis of objective reality to a machine, it might be appropriate to have another look at the nature of the virtual image. This is the formation of optical imagery with no apparent base, no permanency beyond that of mental or instrumental visual memory. Today it is impossible to talk about the development of the audio-visual without also talking about the development of virtual imagery and its influence on human behaviour, or without pointing to the new industrialisation of vision, to the growth of a veritable market in synthetic perception and all the ethical questions this entails. (Virilio 1994: 59)

The protests sparked by the murder of George Floyd in the summer of 2020 might represent the largest social movement in the history of the United States (Buchanan, Bui and Patel 2020). Data suggests that, between May and June, a little over 25 million people assembled across the country and marched together, speaking out against police brutality and structural racism, asking to divest, defund and abolish the police. Discussions about the demilitarisation of law enforcement have included the divestment of a wider set of surveillance practices: predictive policing, social network analysis and facial recognition. However, as Black Lives Matter (BLM) protests continued, US law enforcement deployed a wide array of surveillance techniques to monitor, target and arrest demonstrators (Kanno-Youngs 2020), undermining their very right to protest. This chapter considers the challenges that the police use of facial recognition poses to public assembly politics. I outline these challenges by discussing notions of visibility and recognition in the context of public assemblies, which relates to the rights of urban citizens to assemble in public space. I bring together Judith Butler's reflections on public assembly politics and science and technology studies (STS) on infrastructures to illuminate how the classification choices underpinning the development of facial recognition, and particularly face datasets, affect the social and material conditions necessary to appear in public and protest – the infrastructural conditions of public assembly politics and public visibility.

FACIAL RECOGNITION IN 2020: NOTES ON ABOLITION

At the beginning of 2020, the *New York Times* published a story about Clearview AI, a small American tech company that had developed a facial recognition app matching faces to a database of three billion images scraped from the Internet. By uploading a face to the system, one could find any publicly available information matching that particular face. Hoan Ton-That, Clearview's founder, had envisioned his app to serve as a ground-breaking tool for law enforcement in the US and Canada. A month later, a BuzzFeed report uncovered that Clearview had provided its technology to more than 2,000 government agencies, law enforcement, and private companies across twenty-seven countries (Mac et al. 2020). Among these, the company had signed contracts with US Immigration and Customs Enforcement (ICE), the Attorney's Office for the Southern District of New York, the FBI, US Customs and Border Protection (CBP), Interpol, local police departments and the US department store Macy's. In the summer of 2020, the Miami police department and the New York police department (NYPD) used Clearview to identify BLM protesters (Lopatto 2020).

In June, 2,435 researchers in technical, legal and social science signed an open letter asking the Springer Editorial Committee to rescind a paper previously accepted for publication. The authors of the paper, among which was a NYPD veteran, claimed to have developed a machine learning system capable of predicting whether someone is a criminal based on a picture of their face. As the open letter notes, this type of claim is characteristic of a larger trend in machine learning research grounded on the assumption that biometric data can serve as an objective marker for criminal behaviour. This assumption is based in turn on physiognomy, the practice of interpreting someone's facial features to infer their moral value, which in the nineteenth century became part of a larger project of social classification that harnessed empirical evidence to justify racism and sexism. Despite being discredited as pseudoscience, this practice continues to re-emerge under the guise of objective statistical models such as machine learning. In recent years, law enforcement and government agencies have adopted machine learning systems claiming that they improve objectivity and transparency – however, these tools perpetuate and reinforce discrimination and racial profiling, hidden behind the rhetoric of scientific and mathematical objectivity (Stop LAPD Spying 2018; Brayne 2020).

In reaction to the increasing awareness in civil society of facial recognition's limitations, errors and biases, and the potential discrimination towards marginalised communities, several US cities have recently banned the use of facial recognition by law enforcement and other municipal authorities. At the beginning of 2020, the European Commission considered a five-year ban on facial recognition in public spaces. Later in the year, Amazon, Microsoft and IBM announced a moratorium on the sale of facial recognition to police departments. These outcomes are the result of years of advocacy by scholars and community activists committed to critical and anti-racist technology (Buolamwini and Gebru 2018; Benjamin 2019; Nkonde 2019; Raji and Buolamwini 2019). However, there are several reasons why these solutions might not be sufficient to mitigate the harms of surveillance technology. First, big tech corporations such as Amazon, Microsoft and IBM are not the biggest players in the facial recognition market. As the Clearview story shows, a constellation of smaller and less well known actors provide policing tools to law enforcement, government agencies, insurance companies and banks with little to no public oversight. Second, while these corporations might have temporarily suspended their sales of facial recognition software, they haven't halted their engagement with law enforcement. For instance, in recent years police departments across the US have partnered with Ring, Amazon's home surveillance camera company, to get access to home owners' security footage without a warrant (Matzakis 2020). Further, Ring's users can upload their footage on Neighbors, a crime-reporting app owned by Amazon that has been known to promote peer-to-peer surveillance and reinforce racism (Haskins 2019). Finally, moratoria often centre the discourse on facial recognition on the concept of accuracy – the use of facial recognition is suspended until it can be proven to be more accurate and 'fair'. Misclassification and misidentification are clearly harmful – most commercial facial recognition systems heavily misclassify darker-skinned individuals, and especially Black women, while the error rate for white men is close to 0 per cent (Buolamwini and Gebru 2018).

However, 'accurate' surveillance tools are equally problematic. Scholars have pointed out how surveillance technologies continue to be employed disproportionately on vulnerable and marginalised communities (Browne 2015; Eubanks 2018). Virginia Eubanks has shown how low-income communities of colour, especially women of colour and immigrants, are subject to intrusive surveillance by US government agencies, who perceived them as inherently dishonest and untrustworthy. As Eubanks notes, 'marginalized people are subject to some of the most technologically sophisticated and comprehensive forms of scrutiny and observation in law enforcement, the welfare system, and the low-wage workplace' (2014: n.p.). In this respect, the Carceral Tech Resistance Network[1] calls for the abolition of the 'police industrial complex': the entanglement of police, academia and private corporations responsible for the creation of police and surveillance tools as solutions to social, political and economic issues.

As millions of people have gathered in the streets across the globe, speaking out against police brutality and structural racism, asking to divest, defund and abolish the police, the question remains, then, how can a person demand an end to police brutality when the very right to gather in a city's public spaces to make those demands may be compromised by ubiquitous surveillance techniques?

NORMS OF RECOGNITION AND THE 'RIGHT TO APPEAR'

In *Notes Toward a Performative Theory of Assembly*, Judith Butler (2015) argues that the material and social conditions of appearance are prerequisites for political participation. While embodied forms of public assembly have a performative dimension that goes beyond that of political speech, not everyone, Butler points out, 'can appear in a bodily form' (2015: 8). Building on her work on gender performativity (1990), Butler argues that social norms shape people's 'conditions of appearance' (2015: 19), excluding from public recognition those who don't align with such norms, such as the gender binary. However, as she points out, in the context of public assembly, exclusion from public

appearance extends beyond gender nonconformity to all marginalised and vulnerable groups. The conditions of appearance, she notes,
include 'infrastructural conditions of staging as well as technological
means of capturing and conveying a gathering, a coming together,
in the visual and acoustic fields' (p. 19). Here, Butler's emphasis is on
the role that both mainstream and social media have in framing social
movements' identity. The media do not simply amplify or silence the
voices of those who demand justice; they participate in the very definition of people's identity. Media constitute 'the site of the hegemonic
struggle over who "we" are' (p. 20). Butler draws on Hannah Arendt's
definition of the public sphere as 'the space of appearance' where
political action takes place (pp. 72–3). According to Arendt, this space
can be 'anywhere and anytime', as political action happens 'between
people' and does not require any specific location (p. 73). However,
Butler argues that Arendt's definition of the public sphere is grounded
on the classic notion of the Greek *polis*, where the domain of public
politics was restricted to male citizens – while women, children, for-
eigners, slaves and lower-status subjects were deemed 'prepolitical' or
'extrapolitical' (p. 78).

Moving away from Arendt, Butler points out that 'we cannot
presume the enclosed and well-fed space of the polis, where all the
material needs are somehow being taken care of elsewhere by beings
whose gender, race or status render them ineligible for public recognition' (p. 96). Moreover, this view ignores the importance of the body
for political participation. Political action requires material supports – it
is 'invariably bodily, even . . . in its virtual forms' (p. 73). These bodily
supports – shelter, food, social and medical care, employment – are
what make the action possible and are, quite often, part of the political struggle, or even its very object. If we take into account the material, bodily conditions underpinning Arendt's space of appearance,
we ought to understand how these conditions are created, who can
or cannot enter such space and who controls it. 'Significantly,' Butler
argues, 'it is precisely this operation of power – the foreclosure and
differential allocation of whether and how the body may appear – that
is excluded from Arendt's explicit account of the political' (p. 88). An
example of such power is the French ban on face coverings that, since
2011, prohibits women from wearing the niqab,[2] the Islamic face veil.
Measures such as this are grounded on a supposed principle of univer-
salism, as opposed to ethnic or religious separatism, that, nonetheless,

fails to recognise the right of those who do not conform with secular norms of appearance.

As I illustrate in the next section and beyond, the right to appear in public spaces is a constitutive property of the right to the city. Often outside the purview of democratic citizen oversight, data infrastructures can condition public visibility by excluding, discriminating against and harming those who don't conform with dominant norms of appearance. From this perspective, a critical discussion on the data infrastructures that regulate access to the public sphere contributes to the formulation of a notion of citizenship that hinges on the right to appear, rather than on legal status.

RECOGNITION AND EXPOSURE: VISIBILITY IN PUBLIC ASSEMBLIES

Public appearance, or visibility, entails recognition. Protesters gathered, and still gather, in the streets to make visible the reality of violence and marginalisation against Black and people of colour (POC) communities. This recognition is premised on an ideal notion of 'public privacy' (Slobogin 2002; Goold 2009; Aston 2017): the right to peacefully gather together without fear of prolonged and pervasive state surveillance, identification and interference. According to this notion, visibility within public assemblies is conditioned on assumed characteristics of public anonymity and homogeneity. In reality, visibility can lead to harmful exposure. This 'paradoxical double bind' of visibility (Brighenti 2007) means that we demand recognition by exposing ourselves to potential harm. This 'heightened bodily exposure' can happen, as Butler points out, when protesters and assembled crowds confront police in the streets, or in situations of territorial occupation, such that encountering a checkpoint, or even walking in public, can make a person vulnerable to violence, incarceration, even death.

Such unwanted and precarious bodily exposure is both the prerequisite and the aim of public assembly politics. Bodily exposure can be a form of political resistance. However, if the aim of politics is to establish better and equal life conditions such as shelter, health care, food and work, then Butler argues that the question of recognition cannot be treated as separate from the built environment, which shapes political action (2015: 127). How we are able to access and use the space of politics – the space of visibility – is critical for recognition. Writes Brighenti:

'It is not simply true that if I am disempowered or a society's outsider, then I am invisible. Rather, what happens is that I access visibility places in ways that are largely or completely out of my control' (2007: 333). When our faces are captured on camera and assigned an identity – a set of demographic characteristics, emotions and personality traits, in ways that are outside our purview – these inferences can have a detrimental impact not only on our individual rights, but also on collective practices of participatory democracy, as scholars and activists have warned about the chilling effect of facial and emotion recognition technologies on protesters and its adverse impact on freedom of assembly and the right to protest (Chowdhury 2020; ARTICLE 19 2021).

Much discussion has taken place about the asymmetrical relationship of visibility underpinning surveillance technologies, and how this asymmetry is informed by practices of social classification and forms of systemic oppression – racism, sexism, ableism and capitalism (Browne 2015; Dubrofsky and Magnet 2015; Zuboff 2019). Facial recognition is and has been deeply entwined with these practices since its very inception. In the next sections, I offer a historical and material account of the practices that inform the work of classification underpinning facial recognition technologies and, in particular, of face datasets. Building on STS work on infrastructures, Stevens and Keyes have argued that facial recognition technology 'has no unifying essence', but it is rather a 'shifting web of programmers, algorithms, datasets, testing standards, formatting requirements, law enforcement agents and other operators and users' (2021: 2). It is only by looking at specific facets of facial recognition technologies that we can recognise what values and politics they perpetuate.

BUILDING INFRASTRUCTURES: FACIAL RECOGNITION IN HISTORY

Technologies that use computer vision to process digital images of the face differ in use and scope. Facial identification – the task of matching a face to a unique identity – is not the same as facial analysis – the task of classifying facial features by race, gender, age, emotions or personality types. However, while surveillance generally involves a process of individual identification, its ultimate goal is social classification, which is, as Brighenti argues, 'a type of classification that is essentially grounded in the *summa divisio* between safe and dangerous subjects'

(2007: 333). In this respect, facial identification and facial analysis are both functions of a project of social classification that is infused with specific cultural and social assumptions.

Early artificial intelligence (AI) research on facial recognition developed in the context of suspect identification, started and funded by US intelligence agencies (Raji and Fried 2021; Stevens and Keyes 2021). Despite the effort of governments and corporations to frame current applications of facial recognition as benign or even humanitarian, this military history 'has shaped everything from the nature of the data collected for benchmarks to the nature of evaluation metrics, and certainly the definition of tasks' (Raji and Fried 2021: 8). AI systems that can 'see' – detect, recognise and classify a face – are trained on large-scale datasets with thousands of facial images categorised according to some form of taxonomy. From the early 1960s until the late 2000s, when social media made large quantities of face images suddenly available, the US government supported facial recognition research by providing mugshot databases as training data. The MEDS dataset, for instance, contained a collection of mugshots of previously arrested and deceased subjects. Write Stevens and Keyes (2021), these subjects, 'whether convicted or not, under laws that may or may not have been valid in the mid-2000s – had their mugshots taken and reused, in some cases up to 40 years after their arrest, for the purpose of further refining law enforcement tools of surveillance and control' (p. 10). Moreover, in the process of data curation – the organisation and standardisation of inconsistent images and metadata – researchers assigned values of gender and race according to their own judgement. Images of injured and bruised subjects, 'screaming and looking away from the camera', were treated as inconsistencies posing a problem to the tagging process, a decision that goes unremarked upon, 'and evidently poses no issue for the purposes of the dataset's developers and users – blood and bruises are not part of their remit unless it interferes with the algorithmic gaze' (p. 12).

In 2019, in response to growing critiques around the disproportionate impact of facial recognition on Black and POC communities, IBM created Diversity in Faces (DiF), a dataset of one million face images sourced from Flickr 'for advancing the study of facial diversity' (Merler et al. 2019: 1). DiF sets out to achieve statistical fairness in face representation by including annotations of craniofacial features such as craniofacial distances, ratios and areas and facial symmetry. As mentioned earlier, the idea that facial features can serve as an objective marker of race and gender identity echoes nineteenth-century efforts to harness empirical evidence – in this case, anthropometric measurements – to justify the classification and discrimination of social groups according by race, gender and class (Gould 1981). The invention of photography and the rise of social statistics further grounded anthropometry as a method of social regulation. Francis Galton's composite portrait applied statistical methods to group classification: by overprinting hundreds of photographs of individuals he believed to be of the same type – 'the criminal', 'the Jew' – Galton hoped to generate portraits of ideal characters and materialise the visual evidence of hereditarian laws (Sekula 1986). The shift from individual identification to group classification relies on statistical inference and pattern recognition that can also be observed in early facial recognition research (Lee-Morrison 2018) and underpins the logics of today's machine learning and Big Data.

MAINTAINING INFRASTRUCTURES: VISIBLE BODIES, INVISIBLE LABOUR

In machine learning, algorithms 'learn' to recognise or classify faces from labelled data. This approach is called supervised learning, and the training data consists of a set of images that have been manually labelled – categorised according to some form of taxonomy, such as 'male' or 'female'. Bowker and Star have famously argued that the technical choices we make about classifications have significant yet often invisible ethical and political implications (Bowker and Star 2000). Similarly, the classification choices embedded in datasets can reinforce and normalise appearances and behaviours that are aligned with cultural and social norms (Uliasz 2020). Datasets govern the way AI systems see the world, and as these are increasingly embedded into our social life, the project of interpreting and labelling images is political, rather than merely technical (Crawford and Paglen 2019). For instance, work in human–computer interaction (HCI) has shown how limitations in gender representation – the exclusion of transgender and gender non-conforming identities from datasets – can cause harm and reinforce stereotypical assumptions about gender appearance (Hamidi, Scheuerman and Branham 2018; Keyes 2018). Furthermore, even if the inclusion of every possible gender expression was technically feasible, this line of research questions the idea that it is possible (and meaningful) to infer gender from facial features. Klaus Scheuerman and colleagues analysed over ninety facial image datasets to investigate the categories and assumptions at work in the definition of gender and race underpinning computer vision; they found that only a few of these datasets contain underlying information on how gender and race identity is classified and that, when such information is available, gender and race are presented as unquestionable and apolitical and assigned on the basis of visible and physical appearance (Scheuerman et al. 2020). However, as the authors note, identity is sociohistorical, rather than merely physical. Ironically, this dissonance is reflected in the variety of interchangeable concepts ('skin type', 'race', 'ethnicity') and categories ('Black', 'African-American', 'Caucasian', 'White', 'Hispanic', 'Indian', 'Middle Eastern', 'Other') that are employed to define race in most datasets (2020: 16–17).

In addition to the social and cultural assumptions that inform how race and gender are framed, the power structures that shape the AI design pipeline can also affect the labelling process. Often, researchers and practitioners rely on out-sourced annotation workers to label face images. These workers can be either employed by annotation companies with traditional managerial structures, or work for on-demand work platforms, such as Amazon's Mechanical Turk. In both cases, workers are often recruited from poor and vulnerable populations to provide data annotation services at competitive prices (Irani 2013; Gray and Suri 2019; Miceli, Schuessler and Yang 2020). After conducting ethnographic observations within three different annotation companies, Miceli and colleagues (2020) concluded that multiple factors contribute to the interpretation and annotation of data. First, standards imposed by commissioning clients (their expectations and requirements) shape the workers' interpretation of the images they are labelling. Second, the distribution of workload among clients, team leaders, reviewers and annotators, internal or outsourced, creates multiple layers of meaning that can infuse the annotation process. Third, standards and layers reinforce the idea that labels are self-evident and discourage annotators from questioning them, normalising the classification choices. Fourth, these annotation companies and their clients are mostly concerned with speed and cost-efficiency, rather than the ethical and social implications of their work. Embedded in the work of classification are technical assumptions that require the annotators to assign mutually exclusive labels to categories like race and gender.

As the authors point out, 'whether such categorisation captures the realities of data subjects or coincides with the values and beliefs of data workers is not negotiated' (Miceli et al. 2020: 5). Finally, while the authors chose companies with traditional management structures, they note how crowdsourced annotation companies, such as Mechanical Turk, make hierarchies of power more opaque and further obfuscate accountability. Here, the material conditions of 'ghost work' (Gray and Suri 2019) – the vulnerable status of crowdsourced workers – can further infuse the annotation process.

HAPPY OR HOSTILE? WHAT FACES (CAN'T) TELL

In recent years, emotion recognition technologies have found applications in sectors ranging from monitoring emotional states of patients for improved health care delivery, to illuminating consumer behaviour in the retail sector and monitoring drivers' attention to enhance road safety. Recent research in computer science suggests that emotion recognition could be used to monitor emotional states of people in airports, public spaces and borders for security reasons and by law enforcement to monitor crowds and identify violent group behaviour (Holder and Tapamo 2017).

What makes possible the idea that AI systems could recognise human emotions, moods or personality types is a popular notion of contemporary psychology: the theory that there is a set of discrete, fixed emotions universally conveyed through the same patterns of facial expressions. Psychologist Paul Ekman developed this theory in the 1960s; he identified six universal emotions (fear, disgust, anger, sadness, surprise and happiness) through the measurement and quantification of facial micro-expressions. In 1978, together with his colleague Wallace Friesen, Ekman published the Facial Action Coding System (FACS). FACS breaks down the movements of facial muscles into twenty-eight action units (AU), along with additional codes for head and eye movements, responsible for the spectrum of facial expressions. Ekman was influenced by Charles Darwin's 1872 *The Expression of Emotions in Man and Animals*, as well as a Princeton Professor, Silvan Tomkins, who insisted on the existence of discrete, biologically determined, affective expressions. Tomkins's fascination with the face manifested in his legendary ability to interpret human expressions. According to a *New Yorker* piece on facial recognition, Tomkins was known to be 'the best face reader there ever was' and that he could 'walk into a post office, go over to the "Wanted" posters, and just by looking at mug shots, tell you what crimes the various fugitives had committed. Tomkins felt that emotion was the code to life and that with enough attention to particulars the code could be cracked' (Gladwell 2002).

Psychologists, cognitive scientists and anthropologists have all challenged Ekman's theory. Recently, psychologist Lisa Feldman Barrett and colleagues have argued that the available scientific evidence fails to support Ekman's view, concluding that the ways in which people communicate emotions vary significantly across cultures and even across the same individual. More importantly, Ekman's theory assumes that it is possible to infer emotional states from facial movements and that the relationship between these is measurable, universal and consistent. Yet research has shown that the face alone is not sufficient to understand someone's emotional state (Barrett et al. 2019). Visual context changes our perception of affective behaviour in unique ways, and contextual information helps us recognise other people's facial expressions. Other factors influence the reliability of Ekman's theory: most experiments ask participants to use a set of predetermined labels (joy, anger, sadness, etc.) to recognise emotions, acting as a constraint on their choices. Moreover, research on emotion perception often employs images of actors performing emotions or uses computer-generated facial expressions, which does not correspond to some person's real, existing emotional state (Barrett et al. 2019: 29).

Despite the ongoing scientific debate, Ekman's theory is the tenet of contemporary emotion recognition technologies. Most of these systems build on Ekman's Emotion FACS (EMFACS), a system designed to match emotions with the facial expressions coded within the FACS. Ekman and his colleagues built a database for the EMFACS data called Facial Action Coding System Affect Interpretation Dictionary (FACSAID), which contains images of coded facial expressions and their assigned emotional meaning (Gates 2011). This approach performs a reverse inference or, as Kelly Gates has noted, a sort of reverse engineering of the emotion it aims to classify. As Gates pointed out, the accuracy of EMFACS depends on the authority of the experts who interpreted facial behaviours and attached meanings to them. Similarly, emotion recognition systems use machine learning algorithms to track the shape and movement of facial features, such as the corners of the mouth, the corners of the eyebrows or the outline of the nose, and compare them to images of facial expressions stored in a training dataset and labelled as specific emotions. As in Ekman's system, the face is treated as information that can be extracted from its context and separated from the subject's intentions.

BRIDGES AND BARRIERS: LESSONS FROM INFRASTRUCTURE STUDIES

A critical analysis of the classification practices and choices that underpin the creation of datasets is useful to understand the limitations of facial recognition technologies. From this perspective, debates about bias or technical solutions, such as improving the information on the phenotypic composition of training datasets or deleting offensive and problematic labels, fail to address the political role of datasets. As Crawford and Paglen (2019) argue, the whole project of 'collecting images, categorizing them, and labeling them is itself a form of politics, filled with questions about who gets to decide what images mean and what kinds of social and political work those representations perform' (p. 33).

Indeed, the machine does not impose the conditions of appearance; they are instead the result of multiple layers of technical assumptions and choices that reinforce dominant social and cultural norms. However, if the right to appear is the prerequisite for political participation, as Butler notes, how do we reconcile recognition with the technical constraints imposed on the bodies entering the visual field? Butler (2015) points out how the 'highly regulated field of appearance does not admit everyone, requiring zones where many are expected not to appear or are legally proscribed from doing so' (p. 35). The norms embedded in facial recognition datasets structure the visual field so that certain identities are excluded from it. Paraphrasing Butler, these identities are *technically proscribed* from appearing. Importantly, Butler notes how

> the compulsory demand to appear in one way rather than another functions as a precondition of appearing at all. And this means that embodying the norm or norms by which one gains recognizable status is a way of ratifying and reproducing certain norms of recognition over others, and so constraining the field of the recognizable. (Ibid.)

Building on Butler's theory of gender performativity, Tobias Matzner argues that data-driven surveillance practices participate in the production of suspect subjects, by containing 'every bit of data under the performative of suspicion', so that a person loses all resources or recourse to contest the suspicions about them (Matzner 2016: 209). Similarly, facial recognition datasets exert performative power over the production of racialised, gendered and criminal identities. In this context, when those who are excluded by the norm that 'they are expected to embody' (Butler 2015: 37) gather in the streets to protest, they are first and foremost reclaiming the field of appearance: the ability to appear in public unconditioned by dominant norms of visibility.

If we look at facial recognition datasets in terms of infrastructure, we can recognise how those norms and conditions of appearance are produced. Building on Bowker and Star's (2000) definition of infrastructure (p. 35), datasets are similarly embedded into larger sociotechnical systems by being integrated into multiple and varied applications; they blur boundaries between public and private use; and their scope goes beyond a single application or use-case. Moreover, as research on data annotation has shown, a dataset, like infrastructure, is part of the norms of a 'community of practice' (p. 35). Power dynamics and classification standards within annotation companies affect the interpretation and labelling of data. Importantly, infrastructure is most visible when it breaks (p. 35). Similar to a power outage manifesting the reach and scope of the electric grid, we realise the extent of facial recognition when cameras cannot see dark skin or when they prompt a wrongful arrest.

Building on the classic example of Robert Moses, the New York city planner who designed the bridges over the Grand Central Parkway low enough so that public transport – hence, low-income families – could not reach the wealthy suburbs of Long Island (Winner 1980), Susan Star (1999) has famously argued that moral values are inscribed in the information environment through everyday design choices and standards. As Star notes, some of these choices are flexible and could be changed with time and knowledge. Others 'present barriers to users that may only be changed by a full-scale social movement' (p. 389). In the light of these considerations, what are the implications for anti-facial recognition resistance? Looking at facial recognition through the lens of infrastructure can inform activist interventions and critiques of these systems in the form of what Bowker (1994) has called 'infrastructural inversion', which is an effort to attend to the often hidden choices, standards and constraints underpinning the development of facial recognition systems.

Star's investigation of infrastructure offers some useful strategies: infrastructures can be inspected through looking for the invisible labour that maintains them and for finding their 'master narratives' and their 'others' (pp. 384–6). Critical literature on data work has shown the often invisible and precarious labour behind much of AI-fuelled automation (Irani 2015; Gray and Suri 2019). Critiques of surveillance technologies are not fully separable from accounts of the capitalist ecosystem that supports the development of such technologies. Identifying and deconstructing master narratives means recognising how we lose sight of the circumstances that gave rise to a given accepted, scientific fact, and how, despite the equivocations that gave rise to it, it achieves the status of truth (Star 1999: 385). Infrastructural reading is a way to challenge and contest those narratives premised on claims that facial recognition systems can actually make a range of inferences from a person's face. In this respect, exposing the culturally and politically situated classification work underpinning facial recognition might have practical consequences for intervention: what would resistance look like if it rejected claims of gender and race recognition, mood or personality detection? Also, this approach might prove useful for academics investigating the implications of facial recognition systems and contesting the imaginaries at work in the use and development of AI surveillance techniques.

CONCLUSION

By looking at facial recognition technologies through the lens of infrastructure, I have sought to illuminate the ways in which these technologies condition public visibility. Public assemblies sit at the uncomfortable intersection of recognition and anonymity. In truth, far from an ideal notion of public privacy, assemblies take place in a visual field within which gender and race, along with other assumptions about identity, are unproblematically assigned to individuals and in which technical choices reinforce the unequal distribution of power. Questions about who can or cannot enter such spaces and who makes these decisions are of foremost importance. If we look at the classification choices embedded in the AI pipeline, we can observe how cultural and political contexts, organisational settings, power structures, standards and discretionary decisions all shape the performative power of these systems. Famously, Bowker and Star (2000) have shown that resistance can take the form of exposing how standards and classifications themselves do political work in the world (p. 49). And since the right to public assembly and private publicity is a component of the broader right to the city, the data infrastructuress constituting these spaces are also a key part of these struggles. From this perspective, illuminating the visual epistemologies that inform the use and development of facial recognition can open up new possibilities for resistance movements to challenge them.

NOTES

1. https://www.carceral.tech/
2. At the time of this writing, and under the ongoing COVID-19 pandemic, France has enforced face mask rules, while simultaneously implementing measures to ban women under the age of 18 from wearing the hijab in public spaces.

REFERENCES

ARTICLE 19. (2021) *Emotion Recognition Technology Report*. Available from https://www.article19.org/emotion-recognition-technology-report/ (last accessed 13 January 2022).

Aston, V. (2017) State surveillance of protest and the rights to privacy and freedom of assembly: a comparison of judicial and protester perspectives. *European Journal of Law and Technology*, 8(1).

Barrett, L. F., Adolphs, R., Marsella, S., Martinez, A. M. and Pollak, S. D. (2019) Emotional expressions reconsidered: challenges to inferring emotion from human facial movements. *Psychological Science in the Public Interest*, 20(1), 1–68.

Benjamin, R. (2019) *Race after Technology: Abolitionist Tools for the New Jim Code*. Cambridge: Polity Press.

Bowker, G. C. (1994) *Science on the Run: Information Management and Industrial Geophysics at Schlumberger, 1920–1940*. Cambridge, MA: MIT Press.

Bowker, G. C. and Star, S. L. (2000) *Sorting Things Out: Classification and Its Consequences*. Cambridge, MA: MIT Press.

Brayne, S. (2020) *Predict and Surveil: Data, Discretion, and the Future of Policing*. New York: Oxford University Press.

Brighenti, A. (2007) Visibility: a category for the social sciences. *Current Sociology*, 55(3), 323–42.

Browne, S. (2015) *Dark Matters: On the Surveillance of Blackness*. Durham, NC: Duke University Press.

Buchanan, L., Bui, Q. and Patel, J. K. (2020) Black Lives Matter may be the largest movement in U.S. history. *New York Times*. Available at https://www.nytimes.com/interactive/2020/07/03/us/george-floyd-protests-crowd-size.html (last accessed 13 January 2022).

Buolamwini, J. and Gebru, T. (2018) Gender shades: intersectional accuracy disparities in commercial gender classification. In *Conference on Fairness, Accountability and Transparency* (pp. 77–91). PMLR.

Butler, J. (1990) *Gender Trouble, Feminism and the Subversion of Identity*. London: Routledge.

Butler, J. (2015) *Notes Toward a Performative Theory of Assembly*. Cambridge, MA: Harvard University Press.

Chowdhury, A. (2020) Unmasking facial recognition: an exploration of the racial bias implication. Available at https://webrootsdemocracy.files.wordpress.com/2020/08/unmasking-facial-recognition-webroots-democracy.pdf (last accessed 13 January 2022).

Crawford, K. and Paglen, T. (2019) *Excavating AI*. Available at https://excavating.ai (last accessed 13 January 2022).

Dubrofsky, R. E. and Magnet, S. A. (eds) (2015) *Feminist Surveillance Studies*. Durham, NC: Duke University Press.

Eubanks, V. (2014) Want to predict the future of surveillance? Ask poor communities. *The American Prospect*. Available at https://prospect.org/api/content/36656b9e-c446-5205-9257-0120f64aabdb/ (last accessed 13 January 2022).

Eubanks, V. (2018) *Automating Inequality: How High-Tech Tools Profile, Police, and Punish the Poor*. New York: St. Martin's Press.

Gates, K. A. (2011) *Our Biometric Future: Facial Recognition Technology and the Culture of Surveillance*, vol. 2. New York: New York University Press.

Gladwell, M. (2002) The naked face. *The New Yorker*. Available at https://www.newyorker.com/magazine/2002/08/05/the-naked-face (last accessed 13 January 2022).

Goold, B. (2009) Surveillance and the political value of privacy. *Amsterdam Law Forum*, 1(4).

Gould, S. J. (1981) *Mismeasure of Man*. New York: W. W. Norton.

Gray, M. L. and Suri, S. (2019) *Ghost Work: How to stop Silicon Valley from Building a New Global Underclass*. Eamon Dolan Books.

Hamidi, F., Scheuerman, M. K. and Branham, S. M. (2018) Gender recognition or gender reductionism? The social implications of embedded gender recognition systems. In *Proceedings of the 2018 CHI Conference on Human Factors in Computing Systems* (pp. 1–13). New York: ACM.

Haskins, C. (2019) Amazon's home security company is turning everyone into cops. *Vice*. Available at https://www.vice.com/en/article/qvyvzd/amazons -home-security-company-is-turning-everyone-into-cops (last accessed 13 January 2022).

Holder, R. P. and Tapamo, J. R. (2017) using facial expression recognition for crowd monitoring. In *Pacific-Rim Symposium on Image and Video Technology* (pp. 463–76). Cham: Springer.

Irani, L. (2013) The cultural work of microwork. *New Media & Society*, 17(5), 720–39.

Irani, L. (2015) Justice for 'data janitors'. Public Books. Available at https:// www.publicbooks.org/justice-for-data-janitors/ (last accessed 13 January 2022).

Kanno-Youngs, Z. (2020) U.S. watched George Floyd protests in 15 cities using aerial surveillance. *New York Times*. Available at https://www.nyt imes.com/2020/06/19/us/politics/george-floyd-protests-surveillance.html (last accessed 13 January 2022).

Keyes, O. (2018) The misgendering machines: trans/HCI implications of automatic gender recognition. In *Proceedings of the ACM on Human–Computer Interaction*, vol. 2 (CSCW) (pp. 1–22).

Lee-Morrison, L. (2018) A portrait of facial recognition: tracing a history of a statistical way of seeing. *Philosophy of Photography*, 9(2), 107–30.

Lopatto, E. (2020) Clearview AI CEO says 'over 2,400 police agencies' are using its facial recognition software. *The Verge*. Available at https:// www.theverge.com/2020/8/26/21402978/clearview-ai-ceo-interview-2400- police-agencies-facial-recognition (last accessed 13 January 2022).

Mac, R., Haskins, C., Sacks, B. and McDonald, M. (2020) How a facial recognition tool found its way into hundreds of US police departments, schools, and taxpayer-funded organizations. BuzzFeed News. Available at https:// www.buzzfeednews.com/article/ryanmac/clearview-ai-local-police-facial -recognition (last accessed 13 January 2022).

Matzakis, L. (2020) Amazon doubles down on ring partnerships with law enforcement. *WIRED*. Available at https://www.wired.com/story/ces-20 20-amazon-defends-ring-police-partnerships/ (last accessed 13 January 2022).

Matzner, T. (2016) Beyond data as representation: the performativity of Big Data in surveillance. *Surveillance & Society* 14, 197–210.

Merler, M., Ratha, N., Feris, R. S. and Smith, J. R. (2019) Diversity in faces. *arXiv preprint* arXiv:1901.10436.

Miceli, M., Schuessler, M. and Yang, T. (2020) between subjectivity and imposition: power dynamics in data annotation for computer vision. *arXiv:2007 .14886 [cs]*.

Nkonde, M. (2019) Automated anti-Blackness: facial recognition in Brooklyn, New York. *Harvard Journal of African American Public Policy*, 20, 30–6.

Raji, I. D, and Buolamwini, J. (2019) Actionable auditing: investigating the impact of publicly naming biased performance results of commercial ai products. In *Proceedings of the 2019 AAAI/ACM Conference on AI, Ethics, and Society* (pp. 429–35).

Raji, I. D. and Fried, G. (2021) About face: a survey of facial recognition evaluation. *arXiv:2102.00813 [cs]*.

Scheuerman, M. K., Wade, K., Lustig, C. and Brubaker, J. R. (2020) How we've taught algorithms to see identity: constructing race and gender in image databases for facial analysis. In *Proceedings of the ACM on Human–Computer Interaction*, 4 (CSCW1), pp. 1–35.

Sekula, A. (1986) The body and the archive. *October*, 39, 3–64.

Slobogin, C. (2002) Public privacy: camera surveillance of public places and the right to anonymity. Miss. 72 *Mississippi Law Journal*, 213

Star, S. L. (1999) The ethnography of infrastructure. *American Behavioral Scientist*, 43(3), 377–91.

Stevens, N. and Keyes, O. (2021) Seeing infrastructure: race, facial recognition and the politics of data. *Cultural Studies*, 35(4–5), 833–53.

Stop LAPD Spying Coalition (2018). Before the bullet hits the body. Available at https://stoplapdspying.org/before-the-bullet-hits-the-body-dismantling -predictive-policing-in-los-angeles/ (last accessed 13 January 2022).

Uliasz, R. (2020) Seeing like an algorithm: operative images and emergent subjects. *AI & Society*, 36(6), 1–9.

Virilio, P. (1994) *The Vision Machine*. Bloomington: Indiana University Press.

Winner, L. (1980) Do artifacts have politics? *Daedalus*, 121–36.

Zuboff, S. (2019) *The Age of Surveillance Capitalism: The Fight for a Human Future at the New Frontier of Power*. London: Profile Books.

Chapter 13

DATA BURDENS: EPISTEMOLOGIES OF EVIDENCE IN POLICE REFORM AND ABOLITION MOVEMENTS

Britt Paris, Morgan Currie, Irene Pasquetto and Jennifer Pierre

In the summer of 2020, the murder of George Floyd by Minneapolis police officer Derek Chauvin widened an already old and painful rift around systemic inequality grounded in racism, made more pronounced by the COVID-19 pandemic.[1] Prior to Floyd's murder, racial health disparities put people of colour at 5.3 times the risk for contracting and suffering acute complications from the COVID-19 pandemic than whites (CDC 2020). Even as pandemic conditions slowed commerce and shut down schools, medical facilities and businesses, the rate at which police killed citizens remained at pre-pandemic levels. In the first few months of the pandemic, police also murdered Breonna Taylor in Louisville, Tommie McGlothen in Shreveport, Louisiana, and Daniel Prude in Rochester, New York, to name just a few of the cases that contributed to a summer of civil unrest across the country and the world.

While this rift had long been clear and palpable, the social and institutional breakdown in the face of the pandemic heightened the urgency of addressing structural inequality wrought by centuries of practices mobilised to sustain white supremacy and capitalism. While COVID-19 had physically isolated people for the most part, activists used online platforms to organise demonstrations, virtual teach-ins, legislative petitions and community mutual aid work around the abolition of policing, many focusing at the grassroots, city-level scale of reform. At the same time, surveillance technologies proliferated, not only to quash these acts of protest (Díaz and Levinson-Waldman 2020; Fowler 2020) but to monitor and control parts of life that the pandemic had forced online (Chin 2020; Cohen 2020; Koonin 2020; Rodriguez and Windwehr 2020; US Courts 2020; Vitak and Zimmer 2020). In online spaces, with their attendant data capture, storage and obfuscated data-sharing practices, Black, Latinx, Indigenous, Muslim, immigrant and LGBTQIA communities, as well as women and minors, are, as Tuck and Yang (2014: 1) note, 'often over-coded, that is, simultaneously hyper-surveilled and invisibilized/made invisible by the state, by police, and by technological design and deployment'. Contemporary technologies' simultaneous overcoding and surveillance of minoritised communities extend epistemic injustices and harmful social structures that authors of social epistemology and critical race theory have been writing about for over a century (Wells-Barnett 1892; Du Bois 1903; Lorde 1984; Collins 1990; Delgado and Stefancic 1993; Solórzano and Yosso 2002; Alcoff 2007; Fricker 2007; Mills 2007; Medina 2013). In this tradition, we use the term 'minoritised' to describe groups oppressed and pushed to the margins by existing social hierarchies that are maintained by the privileged (Muñoz 1999; Crooks and Currie 2021). Critical analyses of the deployment of these 'captivating technologies' in minoritised communities contend that they are primarily used to surveil and control citizens and normalise practices of oppression (Benjamin 2019a). Meanwhile, policy makers, journalists, academics, technologists and other powerful shapers of society too often demand statistical evidence of the disproportionate challenges facing communities of colour as a foundation to enact change; without credible data, those who are oppressed have been discredited, blamed for their own misfortunes or simply ignored, to name a few of the ways epistemic burdens exert their influence (Lorde 1984; Fricker 2007; Noble 2013; Pierre et al. 2021).

Our previous work deals with data around policing as part of the production and performance of power, as city-level police agencies play a major role in controlling the collection, classification and dissemination of data around police homicides of civilians, all while having a vested interest in drawing public attention away from police brutality (Currie et al. 2015, 2016). In this previous work, we noted a significant gap between those most vested in the public dissemination of this data and those having the authority over the data. Additionally, we described a variety of differences in the measurement and attributes of data on police violence, such as scale, granularity and semantics, which greatly affect the consistency and breadth with which this data can be appropriately collected and understood. Though we do not mean to discredit the value and necessity of statistical data and tools, we advocate for a more nuanced understanding of the contextual constraints, power dynamics and perspectives at play in data on policing. The aim of this chapter draws from our previous work, but is distinct. Rather than studying processes around the production of local police data, with this chapter we offer a meditation on using data about police violence to bring about meaningful social change in the context of the city; to this end, we argue that reform-minded data efforts may be well meaning but do not offer the transformation so desperately needed. And although data about police violence in the US are not exclusive to cities, as the following examples will demonstrate, urban spaces are sites of particular intensity, both in the sense of the production of data about police violence as well as the city-level focus of civil society and advocacy-focused groups who collect and analyse them.

In what follows we reflect on efforts by local police agencies and civil society to bring greater transparency around police brutality, now five years from the date of our original study. In the next section, we give an overview of ten of the most populous American cities and nine civil society groups now doing this work. We explore the motivations of these reform-driven efforts around data production. We then propose that data gaps are not the problem, and creating better data will do little to end the harms of the neoliberal, white supremacist, carceral structure of society. After we work through these data-driven, accountability-focused reform efforts, we discuss how they disregard and undermine other types of evidence that abolition groups wield to defund or abolish policing. We conclude that though data-driven efforts to end harmful policing practices are a laudable step, unless they are followed up with meaningful structural change, they serve as little more than a pressure valve that continues to uphold the status quo of police brutality in the US and its disproportionate effects on communities of colour. We suggest that social problems like those of the carceral structure of society can only be truly addressed by the mobilisation of popular struggle around refusing and dismantling policing and carceral infrastructures, as seen in the abolition movement.

REFORMS IN OFFICIAL OPEN POLICE DATA

Government-led data projects have grown significantly in the last five years in response to ever-present evidence that police surveil, brutalise and seek to control minoritised communities at disproportionate rates.

Civilian deaths at the hands of police throughout 2014–15 sparked a national conversation around racist policing and exposed the alarming incompleteness of data on officer violence across the US – a failure long known to many scholars and activists (Sherman and Langworthy 1979; Loftin et al. 2003). In order to access data on police violence, citizens have traditionally had to file onerous Freedom of Information requests to specific agencies, or obtain county-level details through the FBI's Supplementary Homicide Report (SHR), which keeps agencies' self-reported records on 'Felon Killed by Police Officer' (code 81) (Sherman and Langworthy 1979; Federal Bureau of Investigation 2021). The SHR remains an inadequate account of these statistics, however, because it only publishes police homicides declared 'justified' (Fischer-Baum 2014), and many law enforcement agencies across the country are still not required to report these deaths. Data transparency policies remain specific to local law enforcement agencies and vary widely, and there is no legal nation-wide mandate for police agencies to report on these incidents.

To address the lack of transparency around police brutality, the FBI in 2017 launched a National Use-of-Force database to catalogue actions that resulted in the death or serious bodily injury of a person or the discharge of a firearm at a person (Federal Bureau of Investigation 2019). Like SHR, submission to this data collection effort remains voluntary; as of 2020, only 5,030 out of 18,514 law enforcement agencies throughout the United States have submitted. Also at the national level is the Police Data Initiative, begun by the Obama administration and now managed by the non-profit Police Foundation, but only 130 US law enforcement agencies provide data to this effort (Police Data Initiative 2021).

Since 2015, several US cities have also passed open data policies to make it easier for citizens to access data on police violence directly. These data typically tally 'use of force' (also called 'response to resistance' in some cases), 'officer-involved homicides' or 'officer-involved shootings'. Use of force reports typically offer data on incidents of struggle or violence between civilians and police, including the name of the people killed, their race and gender, whether they were armed or unarmed, incident location, and the agencies and race and gender of the officer responsible. Some departments have also begun publishing data on civilian complaints against police forces, as well as on vehicle and pedestrian stops. The data sometimes comes in downloadable files;

other times it is displayed on dashboards and digital maps for citizens to use to locate time- and place-specific information.

Police violence data reporting, however, still remains highly variable from city to city. Some, including those among the US's most populated cities, such as Houston, Phoenix and San Diego, do not publish any use of force data. Other cities report use of force because they are required to. The Chicago Police Department (CPD)'s dashboards detailing use of force and complaints against the CPD members, for instance, exist thanks to a 2018 consent decree, formed after the Illinois attorney general's office sued the CPD in reaction to documented patterns of excessive use of force by its officers (Chicago Police Department 2020).

In cities that publish use of force data, the data may remain aggregate, as with the New York Police Department's Use of Force dashboard (NYC Open Data 2020), made public on 1 January 2020 (NYPD 2020). The dashboard offers no contextual details for incidents, though since 2016 the NYPD also publishes annual Use of Force Reports as PDFs that give further details on weapons use (NYPD 2020).[2] The Los Angeles Police Department's Use of Force webpage, in contrast, has granular, incident-level details (LAPD n.d.) listing officer involved shootings and critical incidents from 2012 to 2017, with links to a page detailing a narrative of each incident,[3] and, in most cases, links to footage posted on YouTube from available video – often bodycams, but also surveillance cameras or aerial footage – as part of a 2018 video release policy (Los Angeles Police Department 2018).[4]

The Philadelphia Police Department website goes further, devoting a major section of its website to 'Accountability', with downloadable Police Reform reports, civilian complaints against police, and lists of officer-involved shootings going back to 2007,[5] including descriptions of the incident detailing the reason the officer was in the area and their interaction with the subject (Philadelphia Police Department 2021). The department also publishes an interactive map showing the geographic relationships between violent crime, sociodemographics and police activity, including officer-involved shootings and car and pedestrian stops, to show the department's increased training, oversight mechanisms and 'rigorous scrutiny to achieve the highest level of accountability'.

Some agencies explicitly link their use of force webpages to ideals of public trust, transparency and accountability (San Jose Police Department n.d.). The Chicago Police Department's Use of Force

Table 13.1 Shows the US top ten most populated cities and whether they publish use of force and other police transparency data.

City	Publishes Use of Force data?	Publishes other types of accountability data	Source URL	Source of Use of Force policy
New York City	Yes		https://www1.nyc.gov/site/nypd/stats/reports-analysis/use-of-force.page	NYPD Patrol Guide
Philadelphia	Yes	Complaints against Police, vehicle and pedestrian stops	https://www.phillypolice.com/accountability/index.html	Use of Force directives
Los Angeles	Yes	Body cam footage	http://www.lapdonline.org/use_of_force	Policy on Use of Force
Houston	No			
Phoenix	No			
San Diego	No			
Chicago	Yes	Complaints against police	https://home.chicagopolice.org/statistics-data/data-dashboards/use-of-force-dashboard/	Use of Force Policy
San Antonio	Yes		https://www.sanantonio.gov/SAPD/Officer-Involved-Shooting	General Manual Procedure 501 – Response to Resistance
Dallas	Yes	Police response to resistance	https://www.dallaspolice.net/ois/ois	Texas HB 1036
San Jose	Yes		https://www.sjpd.org/records/crime-stats-maps/force-analysis-data	Use of Force analysis reports

dashboard describes how the agency draws on the data to design its use of force practices, then subjects this process to public scrutiny. The Dallas Police Department also links the transparency around its officer-involved shooting data to citizens' trust and improved officer training, in order to review best practices in managing officer-involved shootings (Dallas Police Department n.d.).[6]

Table 13.1 shows the diversity of use of force, transparency and open data practices among the police agencies of the top ten most populated US cities, listed here from most to least populated, based on the design of their websites as of January 2020.

These official efforts reflect the belief that increased data transparency will lead to accountability and reforms in policing, which would then reduce discriminatory policing practices. The next section details how community entities, grassroots organisations, university-affiliated groups and media outlets have amplified this call for accountability through data production and use efforts.

CIVIL SOCIETY EFFORTS TOWARDS TRANSPARENCY AND DATA-DRIVEN POLICING REFORM

Over the last two decades, civic efforts to collect and track data on police interactions and killings have developed alongside federal and city-level initiatives. In many cases, including some highlighted in our past research (Currie et al. 2016), such citizen projects provide more thorough and consistent data collection than governmental local, state and federal efforts. These initiatives' core goals range from identifying and resolving gaps in the data, to data collection and access, to increasingly loftier goals such as policy advocacy. Recently, scholars and activists have critiqued the data centredness of some of these projects and have highlighted the potential mismatch between the policy work associated with many of the data-centred projects and anti-police brutality grassroots movements' long-term goals (Komer 2020; Levin 2020; Murray 2020; Roy 2020). In response, a new wave of grassroots projects seeks to focus on data related to alternative methods for community safety and protection to remain more grounded in the goals and motivations of long-term anti-police brutality community movements. This section will outline work from the last two decades of data projects on police–civilian interactions to trace the growing critique of data-centred solutions to police violence.

Data Access and Transparency-Focused Projects

Grassroots-run projects comprise the bulk of civic police violence data collection work done over the last several years. Some of the most comprehensive collections of data, such as Fatal Encounters and the U.S. Police Shootings Database,[7] are grassroots-run. Many of these efforts began with the end goal of collecting and providing access to data to help inform the public and provide potentially useful data to community members.

Journalist D. Brian Burghart created one of the earliest civic police data projects, Fatal Encounters, in 2000. Beginning as a modest early online database of police killings, the website now holds over 28,000 records, and provides a primary searchable and downloadable database along with visualisation tools, public records tools for collecting and providing further data, and memorial pages. The site is impressively comprehensive, with search features allowing queries by name, state, county, gender, city, race, agency, date and unique ID, and visualisations by state, county, race, trends, cause of death and details surrounding death. The site remains one of the most comprehensive by also broadly defining police fatal encounters, striving to collect data on deaths caused by police regardless of on- or off-duty status, intentional and accidental circumstances, and similarly nuanced details. Groups within the project home in on specific focuses, including police-involved suicides and teen deaths. The group has maintained a consistently broad mission: 'to create an impartial, comprehensive, searchable national database of people killed during interactions with the police' (Fatal Encounters 2021). The site was critical in providing early evidence of the scale and magnitude of police killings and continues to promote the need for collecting the data around deaths occurring for any reason within any context.

The U.S. Police Shootings Database claims to be similarly agnostic in its approach. This project is much more bare bones, consisting of a spreadsheet of crowdsourced police shootings. Sources for the spreadsheet entries are largely taken from popular media, but are occasionally sourced from other non-profit or grassroots efforts. Entries are organised with categories covering the date the entry was searched for, the date of the shooting, the state, county and city, the agency name, the victim name, the victim's age, gender and race, whether shots were fired, whether the shooting was legally considered justified, whether the victim was armed, hit or killed, any weapons involved, and the source of the shooting. The database includes entries from 2011 to 2014. Despite the thorough nature of the entries for the collected years, details of the context and origin of the project are sparse and largely unavailable. Focusing on complaints of police interactions with the public, the Citizens Police Data Project provides access to records gained through Freedom of Information requests that would otherwise be cumbersome to obtain. The project is run out of the Invisible Institute in Chicago, a non-profit dedicated to advancing communities through collaborative efforts.

Alongside purely grassroots, civic efforts, universities and news organisations have also contributed to the collection of police data for increasing transparency and accountability. On the university end, the Police Crime Database run by Bowling Green State University collects data on crimes committed by law enforcement officers. The *Washington Post*'s 'Fatal Force' and the *Guardian*'s 'The Counted' are both notably thorough collections of data on killings across the US, drawing on local news reports, social media and the grassroots efforts just described. The *Salt Lake Tribune* and the *Tampa Bay Times* provide police data on specific cities and counties to serve as more localised information sources.

These projects serve as important forays into public data collection and accountability processes, with detailed methodological descriptions and notes on their limitations and constraints. However, these projects do not use this data to propose any specific policy reform. Indeed, with transparency as the focus, the question of how to bring about change in law enforcement, or indeed how to foster greater civic participation in the development of alternative systems of public safety, is largely unaddressed by these projects.

POLICY AND ADVOCACY-FOCUSED PROJECTS

Mapping Police Violence describes itself as 'America's most comprehensive database of killings by police' (Mapping Police Violence 2021). This project differentiates itself from older citizen-led projects, which focused on filling gaps in the public record, by using the data to design frameworks for policy reform. Mapping Police Violence provides a searchable database, a city comparison tool, a collection of information on national trends, a police scorecard tool, and a 2017 report highlighting insights from the founding team. Through the data, Mapping Police

Violence seeks to contextualise patterns of police violence in agencies across the US, and then promote data-driven accountability efforts.

Campaign Zero represents an entry into the data-driven police reform sector of grassroots police data projects. Originating from President Obama's Task Force on 21st Century Policing, the project includes research and community collaborations to provide a 'package of policy solutions to end police violence in America' (campaignzero. org). Following the murder of George Floyd, the campaign released a set of policy demands grounded in a study the group conducted in 2016. The central argument of the campaign consists in the claim that if eight policy shifts are made at the city level, these can reduce police killings by 72 per cent. These eight solutions are most notably summarised in the 8 Can't Wait campaign:

- banning chokeholds and strangleholds
- requiring de-escalation
- requiring warning before shooting
- requiring exhausting all alternatives before shooting
- duty to intervene
- banning shooting at moving vehicles
- requiring use of forces continuums
- requiring comprehensive reporting.

Founders of Campaign Zero include data scientist Samuel Sinyangwe and organiser DeRay McKesson. The organisation's goals and founding ideals centre heavily on aggregate data and statistical analysis, in contrast to the heavy reliance on journalism sources from previous initiatives. Local efforts that mirror this central focus on police reform include the Cop Accountability Project, or CAPStat, based in New York City, which collects and provides access to civil rights lawsuit data between 2015 and 2018 with the aim of improving police misconduct. The Stanford Open Policing Project also contributes to policy change by collecting law enforcement traffic stop data to help policy makers, journalists, researchers and other stakeholders improve interactions between the police and the public.

These advocacy projects to some extent represent a step towards more rigour around police data collection practices and are part of a larger push for meaningful change for those represented in the data. However, by moving away from journalistic sources and focusing on statistical data divorced from contextual details, these projects become further entrenched in data-centring. These efforts form a feedback loop of data production and use among reform-minded organisations: urging police to produce data, different stakeholders use the data to push for police accountability, which is demonstrated, or not, by more data, and so on – a loop that threatens to enact the sort of post-political data fetishism that data justice and social justice scholars warn about.

These campaigns have come under scrutiny and criticism by some abolitionist activist organisations, who highlight the fundamentally different ends envisioned by police reform initiatives versus abolition-ist groups. Reformist efforts largely grant legitimacy to policing with the implicit argument that the carceral structure can be meaningfully reformed by drawing on comprehensive data collection – that if there were no data gaps, police would be more easily indicted for racist practices and held meaningfully accountable, or else can demonstrate successful reform. However, the evidence to date shows that policy reforms of policing practices do not yield meaningful change – many police agencies with a record of violence, such as Minneapolis's, have already adopted several of the 8 Can't Wait proposals (Bergengruen and Berenson 2020; Brown and McHarris 2020). Also, this approach leaves out solutions generated by community organisations that best reflect their needs and more holistically address root causes of police violence, as we discuss in the next sections.

Abolition-Centred Projects

A final category of projects around police killings and police brutality data include those that resist reforming or rehabilitating policing or supporting the need for carceral systems; they are sceptical of the use of data and statistics for understanding the problem of police brutal-ity in the US. Their critique comprises two main concerns, namely the misuse and misinterpretation of statistics about police violence and possible interventions, and the collection of data for surveillance and unethical research practices. Abolitionist groups are responsible for a rival category of projects involving police data that fundamentally decentre the data and critique statistical methods of other data-driven reform groups.

Within this category is the Youth Justice Coalition (YJC), a youth-run activist organisation based in Los Angeles, dedicated to supporting current and formerly incarcerated people started in 2003 (Youth Justice Coalition n.d.). YJC maintains an internally collected database sourced through community interviews as a community resource and narrative tool (Youth Justice Coalition 2014a, 2014b). The work of this project is encapsulated in a graphic on a website (Youth Justice Coalition 2014a), but the work exceeds the information available online. YJC focuses on community care, an approach that aligns closely with the Database for Police Abolition, a national database that tracks proposals for defunding and diminishing police agencies so that activists can draw on tactics used around the country. The goal stated on the website is 'avoiding contributing to the legitimacy of policing'; rather than endorsing any of the policy or activist proposals the website tracks, they aim to 'encourage public engagement with local politics and to assist organizers with their goals' (Database for Police Abolition n.d.). Though they recognise the power of data as evidentiary sources, these databases are access points to community resources and narratives; they are not used as the basis for policy.

Abolition groups were particularly vocal in criticising the research and statistical applications of #8CantWait campaign in support of police reform that arose in the 2020 summer of unrest (8 Can't Wait n.d.; Illing 2020). In response, abolitionist activists and researchers Cherrell Brown and Philip V. McHarris published a public letter arguing that the #8CantWait campaign was based on 'faulty data science' and demanded that the campaign be recalled (2020). Brown and McHarris found 'irreconcilable issues to the data and study design'. In particular, the authors point out issues of generalisation, biases in the research design, and faulty and partial data collection. For example, the study is based on 18 months of data and 91 police departments to argue the policies will lead to a 72 per cent reduction of killings by police; Brown and McHarris say this interval does not offer enough time to achieve causality. The authors also argue that the study includes a limited and insufficient set of control variables and a 95 per cent confidence interval, which they deem to be inappropriate for a study that has life and death implications. Instead, they suggest, the group should have used a 99 per cent confidence interval, as often used in medical sciences. At such a level of confidence, the authors explain, the 8 Can't Wait research findings would not have been statistically significant. The following sentence makes clear the abolitionists' take on the campaign and its use of statistics:

The use of statistics is largely a matter of interpretation. When people invoke data and statistics it can serve as a veneer of empirical proof that renders something difficult to critique. Police also use statistics and interpret them in a way to justify their actions. (Brown and McHarris 2020: n.p.)

While Brown and McHarris's critique is grounded in accusations of faulty statistics, other groups critique the positivist, statistical approach to policy making from a different epistemological perspective, questioning the necessity of data collection altogether. An alternative campaign, called #8toabolition, for instance, focuses on the gap between reform efforts and abolition, arguing that data-focused reform makes oppressive systems 'just bearable enough' and undermines efforts to reimagine what a society with reduced or no policing might look like (#8toAbolition 2022). 8toabolition critiques private–public schemes that pair universities, start-ups and civil society groups with police departments and carceral agencies to develop surveillance technologies, data-sharing arrangements and predictive analytic tools that are disproportionately deployed on vulnerable communities already plagued by the problems of the carceral state. Instead, 8toabolition focuses on diverting energy and funds to community collaborations, emphasising notions of citizen participation and struggle over the very definition of public safety, as well as studies that support minoritised communities' self-determination.

EPISTEMOLOGIES OF EVIDENCE: POLICE ACCOUNTABILITY AND ABOLITION

We now contrast the epistemological bases of data-driven reform efforts we initially reviewed with those of the police abolition groups just mentioned. In what follows, we uncover the narratives of data as evidence in pushing for justice and social change around racist policing. We then connect these epistemological practices to calls for reform and abolition.

Data have long served as forensic evidence encapsulating true processes of the world, both for bureaucratic and sometimes progressive purposes (Hacking 1987; Desrosières and Naish 2002; Bruno, Didier and Vitale 2014). This view belies a positivist belief that data encapsulates the reality of the world that can be acted upon (van Dijk 2005;

Kitchin 2014; Milan and van der Velden 2016; Crooks and Currie 2021). However, data production is a process of collection, classification and storage (Star and Bowker 1999; Bowker 2007; Gitelman 2013), and those processes are often messy. Our previous work around data on police-perpetrated homicides found that decisions about what processes to encapsulate in data, and what to leave out, reveal interpretations and biases about how to represent police practices, and that police agencies exert an outsized influence on how official data on these instances are collected, recorded, stored and made accessible (Currie et al. 2016). This chapter builds upon that previous work to argue that data collection, even if it were completely transparent, does not adequately address the problem of racist policing, because it overlooks and circumvents the lack of dominant groups' political will to change or end policing. Standing beyond the issue of the authenticity and reliability of these automated assessments is the fact that racist policing cannot be fixed by data or data-driven technology, nor by perfect data on these problems. These problems result from a lack of political will within urban, state and federal governance structures to change the balances of social, economic and political power that enable harmful social arrangements and remove the possibility of self-determination. Political problems require political solutions, and, following Lefebvre's (1968) writing around the right to the city (see Lefebvre 1996), inhabitants should be able to collectively shape the processes of dwelling within a city to envision more liberatory outcomes. While the locus of the carceral state extends everywhere, it is in large part enacted through policy developed in cities and other sites of local sovereignty and control, such as the media and education.

Tech abolitionists argue that statistical representations and techno-logical interventions are predicated on an epistemological tradition that values monitoring and control of populations and is disproportionately deployed on minoritised groups (Benjamin 2019a, 2019b; Muigai 2019; Mukharji et al. 2020). As Eubanks (2018), Broussard (2018), Benjamin (2019a, 2019b), Costanza-Chock (2020) and others have shown through their research, the existence and use of data-driven technologies shape user behaviours in ways that are often coercive, as they seek to control users rather than provide meaningful services or care. Consider global concerns by activists and scholars that data-driven policing initiatives, whether facial recognition cameras or predictive database policing, do not rein in crime but rather reinforce discrimination and hyper-visibility of over-policed areas (Ferguson 2017; Stop LAPD Spying Coalition 2018). Moreover, the majority of these technologies are predicated on faulty inputs; logics of colour-blindness, neutrality and resource scarcity; or datasets that produce incorrect assessments (Noble 2018; Cifor et al. 2019; D'Ignazio and Klein 2020). Oftentimes, data collection and algorithms based on these data are not transparent.

In our first iterations of this work around police brutality data in 2015, we were cognizant of the idea that data-driven police accountability efforts, which called for statistical evidence to prove racist policing despite overwhelming evidence from lived experience and narratives of those most affected, are racist (Lanius 2015; Paris and Pierre 2017). But data is not just a tool of oppression; it can also be a means of undermining and foreclosing meaningful critique. Subsequently, we have drawn from critical race theory and social epistemology to argue that this demand for statistical proof of racism disproportionately places an epistemic burden on people who are oppressed by these practices to do the tedious work that will be considered accurate and reliable by the dominant group – but that doubly takes away from time that could be spent on a number of more productive activities, such as building power for political mobilisation within or among urban communities (Paris and Pierre 2017; Pierre et al. 2021). Critical race scholars and cultural studies scholars both note that counter-narratives, or stories from those most affected by racist policing, can be particularly effective in changing discourse and opinions on racist surveillance and law enforcement brutality through grounding more affective ties to the issue (Paris and Pierre 2017). A good example of this is the grassroots research carried out by Los Angeles-based anti-police surveillance network, Stop LAPD Spying, which writes up in-depth case studies of police violence and holds focus groups to collect narratives of citizens' experiences with the police (Stop LAPD Spying Coalition 2015, 2018).

The next section highlights how these conventions around the epistemological bases of data-driven evidence intervene in calls for reform and refusal of policing and policing technologies.

DISMANTLING TECHNOLOGICAL HARM: REFORM AND REFUSAL

The questions we ask are when technocratic solutions are and are not useful, when they might be harmful and, in the case that they are harmful or not useful, how we might dismantle them, ranging from abolition or refusal to incremental change or reform (Pierce 2012). These discussions require us to attend meaningfully to issues of the politics of evidence: whose knowledge, needs and power are currently privileged and how can we create appropriate spaces to adopt counter-practices and self-determination without generating or compounding harm.

The technocratic fix assumes that if we solve problems through analytics or algorithms, fed by data positioned as neutral by elite and benevolent technical experts, society would function perfectly. Necessary critiques of technological solutionism must consider whether existing systems merit repair or revitalisation, for what reasons, and by what means. Technologies do not stand alone, but rather exist in and as infrastructures that that become hidden and obfuscated as possible objects of critique even as they permeate daily life (Bowker 1994; Star and Ruhleder 1994); thus, when these systems cause harm, or become otherwise exposed, many in government and civil society promote reform or repair as the obvious answer (Jackson 2013). This obvious-ness often overrides or obfuscates the need for more critical interroga-tion of the serious implications of reforming systems, requiring us to ask: who calls for the reform? Who undertakes it? Who benefits from the maintenance of a system, and who remains subjugated by it?

Alternatively, carceral abolition is a practice of refusal. Abolition advocates understanding policing not as a 'broken institution' that can be reformed with more community or technological oversight, police force implicit bias training, or diverse representation in law enforce-ment, but one that is ineffective in protecting the public from harm, as it is and always has been predicated on violently maintaining the oppressive order of racial capitalism. As such, police abolitionists, while they vary in practices and perspectives, generally advocate that carceral systems must be defunded, dismantled and even replaced by completely different systems that promote community wellness, foster civic participation in producing alternative systems and, among other things, take systemic oppression into account (Gilmore 2002; Critical Resistance 2012; Kaba 2020). Refusal is a stance that is, as Tuck and Yang note, often exercised by those who are most oppressed in society and who are seen as objects that require carceral control and capture to ensure racist assumptions of social cohesion. Here, police abolition is a code of ethics, a resolute stance: 'It is the posture of an object that will not be removed nor possessed' (Tuck and Yang 2014: 814). The abolition groups' refusal to engage with reformist data-driven technologies and data collection as a mechanism of rehabilitating and justifying policing is part of refusing policing and carceral institutions in their current forms.

CONCLUSION

Our review shows how police data transparency and data-driven police accountability efforts have grown since 2015. But we have to ask ourselves, what end does this transparency serve? We argue that these data efforts contribute to performances of bureaucracy in which transparency is wielded as a solution, rather than meaningful political restructuring. As we've followed data projects focused on police reform over the last six years, we see little evidence that these data reform efforts have meaningfully improved the state of racist police brutality and murder, or that more data will necessarily drive any improvement to the situation (Brown and McHarris 2020; Peeples 2020). Quantitative data collection is not just used to reform historically oppressive social structures, but, as an outcropping of this function, to avoid action, through the expectation that more and more data is required in order to act. Data can be a barrier to doing things, and other forms of evidence of police oppression are overwhelming even when not datafied.

Lacking social and political action, these data reform efforts may bring some superficial form of police accountability, but they only offer ameliorative redress to harms and are not enough to produce transformative change. Instead, as argued by 8toAbolition, data-driven efforts should root epistemological bases of evidence in traditions that are critical of carceral structures and aim to rehabilitate these harmful structures. We end with a question: what if the energy put into data-driven efforts focused on ameliorative or rehabilitative police reform were instead directed towards abolition of carceral structures? This abolitionist stance could well include the abolition of technocratic goals and, sometimes, data and technologies themselves. We argue that such projects are necessary if we are ever to begin reimagining and building capacity for a better future.

Such efforts can take the form of refusal, both within the tech industry and outside it. The mobilisation of refusal will require actionable critiques, movement building and, importantly, envisioning the future we want to take the place of the things we refuse. This movement is already underway, as with the success of #TechWontBuildIt, an organisation of tech workers who mobilised to stop Amazon's contracts with the US Immigration and Customs Enforcement. Abolition groups across the country, such as Critical Resistance and the Stop LAPD Spying Coalition, have long been engaged in critique of carceral institutions; the latter, along with the LA Community Action Network, has ended the LAPD's gang database and stopped its use of drone surveillance. With the impetus coming from anti-carceral and civil society advocates, municipalities across the US have voted down the use of facial recognition technologies in public places. Many of these civil society, abolitionist groups have a clear vision for the future – one in which law enforcement money is spent on communal health and wellness, and in which the right to the city includes those who build solidarity in this mission.

NOTES

1. While our 2015 study used 'police officer-involved homicide' to describe all deaths at the hands of police, here, in cases such as the killing of George Floyd and Breonna Taylor, we use the term 'murder'. The common term 'officer-involved homicide' is how law enforcement agencies frequently classify police acts that result in death, regardless of the circumstances or intention (Pierre et al. 2021). We use the term 'murder', as police abolition advocates sometimes do, to highlight that these deaths are not blameless accidents or self-defence, but the result of intentional structural decisions that overwhelmingly justify and exonerate police for their deadly practices (Gilmore 2002; Critical Resistance 2012; Pierre et al. 2021). These semantic classifications matter – these terms are associated with particular communities and actors, as well as moral and structural obligations.

2. These reports update the NYPD's Annual Firearms Discharge Report going back to 2007. These documents catalogued all shooting incidents, including the number of subjects killed and wounded, the number of innocent bystanders killed and wounded, animal shootings, accidental discharges, unauthorised uses of department firearms, and police suicides with firearms. The also catalogue firearm and electrical weapon discharges, use of impact weapons and pepper spray, and foot or hand strike.

3. The database also has columns with the location, division, and name of the harmed subject.

4. The videos are part of the City's Board of Police Commissioners Critical

Incident Video Release Policy from 2018, which requires video evidence of critical use of force incidents be released to the public within 45 days of the event.

5. The data includes incident details such as date, location, whether the offender was wounded or killed, whether the offender was arrested, whether the officer was wounded or killed, the District Attorney's action, and the Use of Force Review Board's determination.

6. Dallas also publishes 'Police Response to Resistance' data on the city's open data dashboard: https://www.dallasopendata.com

7. https://fatalencounters.org; https://docs.google.com/spreadsheets/d/1cEG Q3eAFKpFBVq1k2mZIy5mBPxC6nBTJHzuSWtZQSVw/edit

REFERENCES

8 Can't Wait (n.d.) 8 Can't Wait. Available at https://8cantwait.org/ (last accessed 14 January 2022).

#8toAbolition (2022) #8toAbolition. Available at https://www.8toabolition .com/ (last accessed 14 January 2022).

Alcoff, L. M. (2007) Epistemologies of ignorance: three types. In S. Sullivan and S. S. N. Tuana (eds), *Race and Epistemologies of Ignorance*. New York: State University of New York Press.

Benjamin, R. (ed.) (2019a) *Captivating Technology: Race, Carceral Technoscience, and Liberatory Imagination in Everyday Life*. Durham, NC: Duke University Press.

Benjamin, R. (2019b) *Race After Technology: Abolitionist Tools for the New Jim Code*. Medford, MA: Polity Press.

Bergengruen, V. and Berenson, T. (2020) 'It was a tinderbox.' How George Floyd's killing highlighted America's police reform failures. *Time*. Available at https://time.com/5848368/george-floyd-police-reform-failures/ (last accessed 14 January 2022).

Bowker, G. C. (1994) *Science on the Run: Information Management and Industrial Geophysics at Schlumberger, 1920–1940*. Cambridge, MA: MIT Press.

Bowker, G. C. (2007) *Memory Practices in the Sciences*. Cambridge, MA: MIT Press.

Broussard, M. (2018) *Artificial Unintelligence: How Computers Misunderstand the World*. Cambridge, MA: MIT Press.

Brown, C. and McHarris, P. V. (2020) #8cantwait is based on faulty data science. Medium. Available at https://medium.com/@8cantwait.faulty/8c antwait-is-based-on-faulty-data-science-a4e0b85fae40 (last accessed 14 January 2022).

Bruno, I., Didier, E. and Vitale, T. (2014) Statactivism: forms of action between disclosure and affirmation. *The Open Journal of Sociopolitical Studies*, 7(2), 198–220.

CDC (2020) Cases, data, and surveillance. Centers for Disease Control and Prevention. Available at https://www.cdc.gov/coronavirus/2019-ncov/co vid-data/investigations-discovery/hospitalization-death-by-race-ethnicity .html (last accessed 14 January 2022).

Chicago Police Department (2020) Use of Force Dashboard. Available at https://home.chicagopolice.org/statistics-data/data-dashboards/use-of-for ce-dashboard/ (last accessed 14 January 2022).

Chin, M. (2020) Exam anxiety: how remote test-proctoring is creeping students out. *The Verge*. Available at https://www.theverge.com/2020/4/29 /21232777/examity-remote-test-proctoring-online-class-education (last accessed 14 January 2022).

Cifor, M. et al. (2019) Feminist Data Manifest-No. Available at https://www .manifestno.com (last accessed 14 January 2022).

Cohen, J. S. (2020) A teenager didn't do her online schoolwork. So a judge sent her to juvenile detention. *ProPublica*. Available at https://www.propub lica.org/article/a-teenager-didnt-do-her-online-schoolwork-so-a-judge-se nt-her-to-juvenile-detention?token=bJH6MWl70nOzorM0BKPSLmZkG0 4qQP2r (last accessed 14 January 2022).

Collins, P. H. (1990) *Black Feminist Thought: Knowledge, Consciousness, and the Politics of Empowerment*. Boston, MA: Unwin Hyman.

Costanza-Chock, S. (2020) *Design Justice: Community-Led Practices to Build the Worlds We Need*. Cambridge, MA: MIT Press.

Critical Resistance (2012) *A World Without Walls: The Critical Resistance Abolition Organizing Toolkit*. Critical Resistance. Available at http://critic alresistance.org/wp-content/uploads/2012/06/CR-Abolitionist-Toolkit-on line.pdf (last accessed 14 January 2022).

Crooks, R. and Currie, M. E. (2021) Numbers will not save us: agonistic data practices. *The Information Society*, 37(4), 201–13.

Currie, M. et al. (2015) The Police Officer Involved Homicide Database Project. In *Social Media Expo*. *iConference*, Newport Beach, CA.

Currie, M. et al. (2016) The conundrum of police officer-involved homicides: counter-data in Los Angeles County. *Big Data & Society*, 3(2), 2053951716663566. doi: 10.1177/2053951716663566.

Dallas Police Department (n.d.) Officer involved shootings data. Dallas Police Department. Available at https://www.dallaspolice.net/ois/ois (last accessed 14 January 2022).

Database for Police Abolition (n.d.) Database for police abolition. Available at https://www.d4pa.org (last accessed 14 January 2022).

Delgado, R. and Stefancic, J. (1993) Critical race theory: an annotated bibliography. *Virginia Law Review*, 79(2), 461–516. doi: 10.2307/1073418.

Desrosières, A. and Naish, C. (2002) *The Politics of Large Numbers: A History of Statistical Reasoning*. Cambridge, MA: Harvard University Press.

Díaz, R. and Levinson-Waldman, Á. (2020). How to reform police monitoring of social media. *Brookings*, 9 July. Available at https://www.brookings.edu/techstream/how-to-reform-police-monitoring-of-social-media/ (last accessed 11 February 2022).

D'Ignazio, C. and Klein, L. F. (2020) *Data Feminism*. Cambridge, MA: MIT Press.

Du Bois, W. E. B. (1903) *The Souls of Black Folk*. Oxford: Oxford University Press.

Eubanks, V. (2018) *Automating Inequality: How High-Tech Tools Profile, Police, and Punish the Poor*. New York: St. Martin's Press.

Fatal Encounters (2021) *Fatal Encounters, Fatal Encounters*. Available at: https://fatalencounters.org/ (Accessed: 29 January 2021).

Federal Bureau of Investigation (2019) FBI Releases 2019 Participation Data for the National Use-of-Force Data Collection. Available at https://www.fbi.gov/news/pressrel/press-releases/fbi-releases-2019-participation-data-for-the-national-use-of-force-data-collection (last accessed 14 January 2022).

Federal Bureau of Investigation (2021) Uniform Crime Reporting (UCR) Program. Federal Bureau of Investigation. Available at https://www.fbi.gov/services/cjis/ucr (last accessed 14 January 2022).

Ferguson, A. (2017) Policing predictive policing. *Washington University Law Review*, 94(5), 1109–89.

Fischer-Baum, R. (2014) Nobody knows how many americans the police kill each year. *FiveThirtyEightPolitics*, 19 August. Available at http://fivethirtyeight.com/features/how-many-americans-the-police-kill-each-year/ (last accessed 14 January 2022).

Fowler, G. A. (2020). Black Lives Matter could change facial recognition forever – if Big Tech doesn't stand in the way. *Washington Post*, 12 June. Available at https://www.washingtonpost.com/technology/2020/06/12/facial-recognition-ban/ (last accessed 11 February 2022).

Fricker, M. (2007) *Epistemic Injustice: Power and the Ethics of Knowing, Epistemic Injustice*. Oxford: Oxford University Press.

Gilmore, R. W. (2002) Fatal couplings of power and difference: notes on racism and geography. *The Professional Geographer*, 54(1), 15–24. doi: 10.1111/0033-0124.00310.

Gitelman, L. (ed.) (2013) *Raw Data Is an Oxymoron*. Cambridge, MA: MIT Press.

Hacking, I. (1987) Prussian Numbers 1860–1882. In L. Krüger, L. Daston and M. Heidelberger (eds), *The Probabilistic Revolution, vol. 1*. Cambridge, MA: MIT Press, pp. 377–94.

Illing, S. (2020) The 'abolish the police' movement, explained by 7 scholars and activists, Vox. Available at https://www.vox.com/policy-and-politics/20 20/6/12/21283813/george-floyd-blm-abolish-the-police-8cantwait-minnea polis (last accessed 14 January 2022).

Jackson, S. M. (2013) Rethinking repair. In T. Gillespie, P. J. Boczkowski and K. Foote (eds), *Media Technologies:Essays on Communication, Materiality and Society*. Cambridge, MA: MIT Press.

Kaba, M. (2020) Yes, we mean literally abolish the police. *New York Times*, 12 June. Available at https://www.nytimes.com/2020/06/12/opinion/sunday/fl oyd-abolish-defund-police.html (last accessed 14 January 2022).

Kitchin, R. (2014) *The Data Revolution: Big Data, Open Data, Data Infrastructures & Their Consequences*. Thousand Oaks, CA: SAGE.

Komer, J. (2020) What's #8CantWait? Movement aims to reform policing, but activists say it won't work. McClatchy Washington Bureau. Available at https://www.mcclatchydc.com/news/nation-world/national/article2433927 61.html (last accessed 29 January 2021).

Koonin, L. M. (2020) Trends in the use of telehealth during the emergence of the COVID-19 pandemic – United States, January–March 2020. *MMWR. Morbidity and Mortality Weekly Report*, 69. doi: 10.15585/mmwr.mm69 43a3.

Lanius, C. (2015) Fact check: your demand for statistical proof is racist. Cyborgology. Available at https://thesocietypages.org/cyborgology/2015/01 /12/fact-check-your-demand-for-statistical-proof-is-racist/ (last accessed 14 January 2022).

LAPD (n.d.) *LAPD Use of Force*. Available at http://www.lapdonline.org/use _of_force (last accessed 14 January 2022).

Lefebvre, H. (1996 [1968]) The right to the city. In E. Kofman and E. Lebas (eds and trans), *Writings on Cities*. Oxford: Blackwell, pp. 147–59.

Levin, N. (2020) Back in the streets: do not let this movement get co-opted by cosmetic reforms. Medium. Available at https://knock-la.com/reform-la pd-black-lives-matter-8-cant-wait-sucks-b85c4fe59558 (last accessed 14 January 2022).

Loftin, C. et al. (2003) Underreporting of justifiable homicides committed by police officers in the United States, 1976–1998. *American Journal of Public Health*, 93, 1117–21.

Lorde, A. (1984) The master's tools will never dismantle the master's house. In A. Lorde, *Sister Outsider: Essays and Speeches*. Berkeley, CA: Crossing Press, pp. 110–14.

Los Angeles Police Department (2018) *Board of Police Commissioners Critical Incident Video Release Policy, LAPD Order no. 6*. Available at http://www.lap donline.org/home/news_view/63555 (last accessed 14 January 2022).

Mapping Police Violence (2021) *Mapping Police Violence, Mapping Police*

Violence. Available at: https://mappingpoliceviolence.org (Accessed: 29 January 2021).

Medina, J. (2013) *The Epistemology of Resistance: Gender and Racial Oppression, Epistemic Injustice, and the Social Imagination*. New York: Oxford University Press.

Milan, S. and van der Velden, L. (2016) The alternative epistemologies of data activism. SSRN Scholarly Paper ID 2850470. Rochester, NY: Social Science Research Network. Available at https://papers.ssrn.com/abstract=2850470 (last accessed 14 August 2022).

Mills, C. W. (2007) Black rights/white wrongs: the critique of racial liberalism. In C. W. Mills, *White Ignorance*. Oxford: Oxford University Press.

Muigai, W. (2019) 'Something wasn't clean': black midwifery, birth, and postwar medical education in *All My Babies*. *Bulletin of the History of Medicine*, 93(1), 82–113. doi: 10.1353/bhm.2019.0003.

Mukharji, P. B. et al. (2020) A roundtable discussion on collecting demographics data. *Isis*, 111(2), 310–53. doi: 10.1086/709484.

Muñoz, J. E. (1999) *Disidentifications: Queers of Color and the Performance of Politics*. Minneapolis: University of Minnesota Press.

Murray, O. (2020) Why 8 won't work: the failings of the 8 can't wait campaign and the obstacle police reform efforts pose to police abolition. *Harvard Civil Rights – Civil Liberties Law Review*. Available at https://harvardcrcl.org/why-8-wont-work/ (last accessed 14 January 2022).

Noble, S. (2013) Google Search: hyper-visibility as a means of rendering Black women and girls invisible. *InVisible Culture*, 19. Available at http://ivc.lib.rochester.edu/google-search-hyper-visibility-as-a-means-of-rendering-black-women-and-girls-invisible/ (last accessed 14 January 2022).

Noble, S. U. (2018) *Algorithms of Oppression: How Search Engines Reinforce Racism*. New York: New York University Press.

NYC Open Data (2020) NYPD Use of Force Database. Available at https://app.powerbigov.us/view?r=eyJrIjoiOGNhMjVhYTctMjk3Ny00MTZjLTliNDAtY2M2ZTQ5YWI3N2ViIiwidCI6IjJiOWY1N2ViLTc4ZDEtNDZmYi1iZTgzLWEyYWZkZDdjNjA0MyJ9 (last accessed 14 January 2022).

NYPD (2020) *NYPD Use of force*. Available at https://www1.nyc.gov/site/nypd/stats/reports-analysis/use-of-force.page (last accessed 14 January 2022).

Paris, B. S. and Pierre, J. (2017) Naming experience: registering resistance and mobilizing change with qualitative tools. *InterActions: UCLA Journal of Education and Information Studies*, 13(1). Available at https://escholarship.org/uc/item/02d9w4qd (last accessed 14 January 2022).

Peeples, L. (2020) What the data say about police brutality and racial bias — and which reforms might work. *Nature*, 583(7814), 22–4. doi: 10.1038/d41586-020-01846-z.

Philadelphia Police Department (2021) Philadelphia Police Department

Accountability. *Philadelphia Police Department*. Available at https://www.phillypolice.com/accountability/index.html (last accessed 14 January 2022).

Pierce, J. (2012) Undesigning technology: considering the negation of design by design. In *Proceedings of the 2012 ACM Annual Conference on Human Factors in Computing Systems – CHI '12*. Austin, TX: ACM Press, p. 957. doi: 10.1145/2207676.2208540.

Pierre, J. et al. (2021) Getting ourselves together: epistemic burden and data-centered participatory design research. In *CHI '21. The ACM Conference on Human Factors in Computing Systems*, Yokohama, Japan.

Police Data Initiative (2021) Police data initiative. *Police Data Initiative*. Available at https://www.policedatainitiative.org/ (last accessed 14 January 2022).

Rodriguez, K. and Windwehr, S. (2020) Workplace surveillance in times of corona. Electronic Frontier Foundation. Available at https://www.eff.org/deeplinks/2020/09/workplace-surveillance-times-corona (last accessed 14 January 2022).

Roy, A. (2020) Serious about racial justice? Then divest from policing. *Medium*. Available at https://knock-la.com/ucla-racial-justice-divest-policing-lapd-72b274924111 (last accessed 14 January 2022).

San Jose Police Department (n.d.) Force analysis data. San Jose Police Department. Available at https://www.sjpd.org/records/crime-stats-maps/force-analysis-data (last accessed 14 January 2022).

Sherman, L. and Langworthy, R. (1979) Measuring homicide by police officers. *Journal of Criminal Law and Criminology*, 70, 546–60.

Solórzano, D. G. and Yosso, T. J. (2002) Critical race methodology: counter-storytelling as an analytical framework for education research. *Qualitative Inquiry*, 8(1), 23–44. doi: 10.1177/107780040200800103.

Star, S. L. and Bowker, G. C. (1999) *Sorting Things Out: Classification and Its Consequences*. Cambridge, MA: MIT Press.

Star, S. L. and Ruhleder, K. (1994) Steps towards an ecology of infra-structure: complex problems in design and access for large-scale collaborative systems. In *Proceedings of the 1994 ACM Conference on Computer Supported Cooperative Work*. New York: ACM (CSCW '94), pp. 253–64. doi: 10.1145/192844.193021.

Stop LAPD Spying Coalition (2015) Body-worn cameras: an empty reform to expand the surveillance state. Available at https://stoplapdspying.org/body-worn-cameras-an-empty-reform-to-expand-the-surveillance-state/ (last accessed 14 January 2022).

Stop LAPD Spying Coalition (2018) Before the bullet hits the body: dismantling predictive policing in Los Angeles. Available at https://stoplapdspying.org/before-the-bullet-hits-the-body-dismantling-predictive-policing-in-los-angeles/ (last accessed 14 January 2022).

Tuck, E. and Yang, K. W. (2014) Unbecoming claims: pedagogies of refusal in qualitative research. *Qualitative Inquiry*, 20(6), 811–18. doi: 10.1177/1077800414530265.

US Courts (2020) Judiciary authorizes video/audio access during COVID-19 pandemic. United States Courts. Available at http://www.uscourts.gov /news/2020/03/31/judiciary-authorizes-videoaudio-access-during-covid -19-pandemic (last accessed 14 January 2022).

Vitak, J. and Zimmer, M. T. (2020) How Covid-19 is changing workplace sur- veillance: American workers' experiences and privacy expectations when working from home. Covid-19 and the Social Sciences – Social Science Research Council (SSRC). Available at https://covid19research.ssrc.org/gr antee/how-covid-19-is-changing-workplace-surveillance-american-worke rs-experiences-and-privacy-expectations-when-working-from-home/ (last accessed 14 January 2022).

van Dijk, T. A. (2005) Critical discourse analysis. In D. Schiffrin, D. Tannen and H. E. Hamilton (eds), *The Handbook of Discourse Analysis*. Oxford: Blackwell, pp. 349–71. doi: 10.1002/9780470753460.ch19.

Wells-Barnett, I. B. (1892) *Southern Horrors: Lynch Law in All Its Phases*. New York: New York Age. Available at https://www.gutenberg.org/files/14975 /14975-h/14975-h.htm (last accessed 14 January 2022).

Youth Justice Coalition (n.d.) Mission and history. Youth Justice Coalition. Available at https://youthjusticela.org/history/ (last accessed 14 January 2022).

Youth Justice Coalition (2014a) Release of data from YJC on law enforcement use of force resulting in a homicide. Available at https://youthjusticela.org /new-release-of-data-from-yjc-on-law-enforcement-use-of-force-resul ting-in-a-homicide/ (last accessed 14 January 2022).

Youth Justice Coalition (2014b) LA County law enforcement use of force resulting in death of community members from January 2007 – August 2014. Available at https://www.njjn.org/uploads/digital-library/LA-Coun ty-Law-Enforcement-Use-of-force-2007-2014-Final.pdf (last accessed 14 January 2022).

Chapter 14

DATA RESISTANCE THROUGH PUBLIC ART: RECLAIMING NARRATIVES IN/OF THE CITY

Pip Thornton

INTRODUCTION

Technologies controlled almost exclusively by large and powerful digital technology companies mediate our everyday lives, which is problematic on many levels. Much of the revenue generated by these companies comes from the exploitation of user data about our social networks, our physical location, our shopping preferences and how we engage with advertising. Events such as the Cambridge Analytica and Facebook scandal and legislation around GDPR (General Data Protection Regulation) have brought issues of data privacy to the fore, but how the media reports on these can obscure their potential importance to the end users of technology products and platforms. Tech-heavy language, legal jargon and geopolitical framing all make it difficult for individual citizens to understand how companies profit from their data.

There is an urgent need to engage citizens with issues surrounding both the value of data and data privacy. This chapter documents the progress of a project that seeks to address this need, using interactive workshops and public art to help us to think critically about data and the power of digital technology companies. The main aim of the project is to investigate alternative ways of making these issues and their significance visible and understandable to the general public. Beginning with a co-design workshop approach that I developed with Susan Lechelt and Chris Elsden, researchers in Human–Computer Interaction at the University of Edinburgh, the project explores how we might design novel experiences to engage citizens with one of our most ubiquitous and mundane technologies, Google's search engine.

This chapter begins with background and context of the methodological approach shaping these artistic interventions and introduces the work the project was built on: my 2016 {poem}.py project, a critique of the monetisation of language through the Google AdWords system (Thornton 2016, 2018). I go into detail about a scoping workshop conducted with Susan and Chris in 2019, an event that asked a group of participants from various strands of academia and the local creative industries to offer design ideas for making public art interventions similar to {poem}.py, but that could reach a wider audience through exhibiting in public spaces. Finally, I describe three creative pieces that emerged from the workshops, discussing their degrees of effectiveness in engaging wider audiences, and identify potential avenues for future work.

CRITIQUING LINGUISTIC CAPITALISM

The starting point for the project was an artistic intervention developed as part of my PhD thesis, 'Language in the Age of Algorithmic Reproduction: A Critique of Linguistic Capitalism'. The project explored the political, economic and cultural effects of the monetisation of language by Google's search and advertising platforms. The resulting work, called {poem}.py, has been an effective method of visualising and exposing the workings of 'linguistic capitalism' (Kaplan 2014) to a wide range of audiences within academia, at digital and data art exhibitions and in the popular technology press. The piece uses poetry to show how language is valued by Google, as each word that passes through the company's search engine receives an economic value by way of an instant auction that takes place so that advertisers can bid for the top spots in the search results. This in turn has an impact on the information we receive through search engine results, both in terms of paid advertising, and the organic, non-advertising results, which are often optimised using the data from Google's ad platform. The {poem}.py project breaks down famous poems to their constituent words and ascribes the monetary value applied to each word by the Google Ads (formerly AdWords) keyword planner. The monetised poems are processed through a Python code script, then printed out as receipts on an analogue point-of-sale receipt printer. This process reveals the tension between the economic value of the poem's words and their value in the context of the poem.

```
                    Daffodils
              by William Wordsworth

                      SALE

  May 24th 2019                   12:47PM
  BATCH #: CRC32
  AUTH #: 2902651734
  AREA #: ALL

        1     i                    £0.33
        1     wandered             £0.00
        1     lonely               £2.37
        1     as                   £0.44
        1     a                    £0.37
        1     cloud                £5.67


        SUBTOTAL:      £9.18
        TAX:           N/A
        TOTAL:         £9.18

              APPROVED

  Thank you for shopping at Google
           CUSTOMER COPY
              {poem}.py
```

Figure 14.1 {poem}.py, Pip Thornton (2019)

In William Wordsworth's poem 'I wandered lonely as a cloud', for instance, the words 'cloud', 'crowd' and 'host' are relatively expensive (Figure 14.1). However, these economic values are not related to Wordsworth's vision of a Cumbrian landscape, but to cloud computing, crowdfunding and web hosting. The project shows what happens to words when, taken out of their communication or descriptive context, they are allowed no other meaning but the most economically lucrative; this creates an 'intentional fallacy' whereby you are not in control of the context of the words you put into the search bar (Jarrett 2014). What comes out the other side will always be the most economically viable version of the words you put in, which is not necessarily the version you intended.

As scholars and technology critics such as Introna and Nissenbaum (2000) and Noble (2018) have noted, search results are far from a bias-free source of accurate information and can be manipulated in many different ways. {poem}.py shows how economic factors govern the search results we rely on in everyday life. By creating physical arte-facts through the receipt printer, and using people's choice of poems, {poem}.py is an educational tool and a means of resistance – it helps people to understand the idea of words having economic values in dif-ferent contexts and the system of linguistic capitalism (Kaplan 2014), which the {poem}.py project critiques. The project is appealing because people can see directly how the words they choose are automatically monetised by the search engine – they can begin to understand the consequences of this process.

To date, however, {poem}.py's audiences have been limited to aca-demic, artistic and technological circles, despite offering an engaging and understandable way to convey the big challenges of digital society. This chapter describes my search to find more effective ways of bring-ing this important critique to a wider audience by adapting this type of intervention into an interactive public artwork that could be installed in different spaces and venues around the city. For example, a projection of various texts onto buildings or infrastructure around the city could turn the {poem}.py project from a small-scale exhibit into a large-scale installation.

Political interventions in public spaces have a long heritage. As a non-violent, far-reaching means of expression, banners, murals, graf-fiti and placards have spread various narratives in cities throughout the world for centuries and have been part of right to the city campaigns. More recent advances in technologies and materials have facilitated new levels of narrative urban protest and resistance, with light projec-tions, digital displays and the support of social media providing effec-tive methods for political protest that is both physically accessible and able to grab the attention of the public and press. While greatly influ-enced by political artists such as Trevor Paglan, Hito Steyerl, Joana Moll and James Bridle, key to any new iterations of {poem}.py was always going to be the harnessing of language as a tool for creativity and expression, especially in the face of its datafication and monetisation by companies such as Google. In this respect, I looked to works such as

Lemn Sissay's landmark poetry, Naho Matsuda's split-flap poetry and the LED and light displays of Jenny Holzer. I drew further inspiration from the subversion of outdoor advertising spaces, for example 'subvertising' by anonymous activist groups such as Brandalism, who hack bus shelter billboards and other street-level (and increasingly online) ad spaces to subvert the logics of capitalism and coercion, as well as more mainstream projects such as Led By Donkeys, which crowdfunds the purchase of larger advertising spaces in order to publicise embarrassing narratives, such as old tweets or other promises from politicians, or to project protest messages onto public buildings or other iconic structures.

With these influences in mind, I was also conscious that any future manifestation of the {poem}.py work should not only harness the power of politics, digital media and word art, but must also reflect and be in sympathy with its geographical context. As I live and work in Edinburgh, such a piece would also operate in the context of this city, a UNESCO city of literature, where its famous writers and words are embedded in its streets. From Scott, Rankin and Welsh to the political and artistic projections and displays on Castle Rock, in alleys, outside galleries, and in the plastering of the city with festival posters, Edinburgh's dramatic public spaces have long been canvases for words. I wanted to explore if my own work might successfully weave its way into this narrative.

Through funding secured from the Edinburgh Futures Institute (EFI) at the University of Edinburgh, Chris, Susan and I set out to undertake a considered co-design approach to scope a range of potential methods to scale up {poem}.py. The funding also covered the costs of prototypes of a large-scale public instantiation of {poem}.py, and their installations at various locations. The goal of the prototypes would be to explore how public language art can guide the general public in making critically informed choices about how they engage with digital technologies, such as search engines.

CO-DESIGN SCOPING WORKSHOPS

In March 2019, Chris, Susan and I received an EFI Research Award for a project entitled *How can creative intervention and public art help us to think critically about data and the power of digital technology companies?* We wanted to work out the best way to magnify poem.py and its political message to wider audiences, and we decided to use inter-active workshops to hear ideas from arts organisations and designers about possible approaches. We invited a mixture of staff from cultural organisations and potential installation venues, such as Edinburgh City of Literature Trust, the Fruitmarket Gallery and the National Library of Scotland, as well as local projection companies and creative practition-ers we recruited through links with local non-profit Creative Edinburgh and Edinburgh University's Creative Informatics.

I began the workshop by describing the {poem}.py project and running a demonstration of its poetry receipts. We deployed a method I had used previously in collaboration with Jessica Foley at Trinity College Dublin, namely to invite participants to write their own short poems, which we asked them to make as 'cheap' or 'expensive' as possible, according to the suggested bid price given to each word by Google at that time. On this previous occasion we had asked participants to write love poems, which we processed through {poem}.py and printed out. We then gave out prizes for the cheapest and most expensive poems. The exercise has proven extremely useful in getting people to really think about the potential economic value each word might have and how popular it might be to advertisers at a particular time of year, especially since the Dublin workshop took place on Valentine's Day. For the Edinburgh workshop, we decided to ask participants to write their cheap and expensive poems on the theme of protest and political poetry, thinking this would harness some equally interesting insights into the contemporary linguistic economy. As with the love poems, the protest poems from the workshop revealed fascinating insights into the relative values of words. When participants really thought creatively and critically about words that might evade the forces of linguistic capi-talism, the 'cheap' poems they came up with tended to be subjectively far more beautiful and intricate than the mostly brash and ugly 'expen-sive' ones (Figure 14.2).

After the demo, we asked participants to think about how we might take the project further to engage our original research question, and specifically to engage wider audiences in public spaces. We discussed the best ways to display the public artwork, whether by projection or otherwise, and what types of texts to use. Poetry was a starting point, but there were other possibilities that might provoke more politically and locally engaging work, such as the Scottish Government Digital Strategy, or local literature. Based on a fusion of the above-mentioned

From Maghera to Petersfield
by Team Text

SALE

17 Jun 2019 2:05PM
BATCH #: CRC32
AUTH #: 2538659777
AREA #: ALL

1	from	£0.33
1	maghera	£0.55
1	to	£0.38
1	petersfield	£1.27
1	tepid	£1.69
1	protestors	£1.40
1	apologise	£0.30
1	for	£0.19
1	their	£0.35
1	warm	£0.63
1	poems	£2.03
1	of	£0.18
1	resistance	£0.58
	SUBTOTAL:	£9.88
	TAX:	N/A
	TOTAL:	£9.88

APPROVED

Thank you for shopping at Google
CUSTOMER COPY
{poem}.py

Figure 14.2 {poem}.py, Pip Thornton (2019)

themes of political and digital art in public spaces and word art, we identified four ingredients, or moving parts, which might make up an intervention: Text, Audience, Venue and Curation. Participants were split into groups to brainstorm these four themes.

Text

As the name suggests, {poem}.py had been mostly based around monetising poetry through Google in order to make visible the workings of linguistic capitalism. I had found that people reacted more strongly to the critique when they had some kind of emotional attachment to the words, so favourite poems were the obvious choice to use as examples. I had at this stage also dabbled in trying out other texts that might also spark emotion in people but that were more overtly political, such as major works by Karl Marx and George Orwell. I wondered whether political, rather than poetic texts, such as speeches, manifestos or news stories, might be effective in engaging wider audiences to start thinking critically about digital technologies and their impacts.

The input from the workshop was extremely insightful on this point, and was a definite challenge to my assumptions, as participants suggested that emotion may be more powerful than politics. People thought that personal, relatable, emotional texts such as diaries, love songs, letters and culturally embedded quotes and poems would have more resonance with the wider public than perhaps inaccessible political texts or classical poetry. Someone suggested that using a diary format, with all its secrets and confessions, might help to highlight the potential sensitivity of the words we commit to various platforms or applications, whilst also being reflective of the secrets that search engines know about us. While there would be ethical considerations in the use of personal material, the monetisation of texts written and produced by the public themselves could have a strong resonance in terms of encouraging critical thinking, as indeed the cheap versus expensive poetry exercises have previously shown.

Another pertinent discussion was about the potential use of Edinburgh-specific texts and media: for example *Trainspotting* quotes, Ian Rankin novels, Harry Potter or Proclaimers lyrics. Such texts, especially when linked to culturally significant localities, such as Rankin's *Fleshmarket Close* novel projected on the steps of the actual Fleshmarket Close, or *Sunshine on Leith* at the Easter Road stadium, would draw attention and make people care more about the treatment and value of the words. Chief among concerns about this approach are issues of copyright, but also the danger of overkill – it was thought that maybe Edinburgh was already oversaturated with Harry Potter references, for example.

Audience

We asked the Audience group to focus specifically on who an intervention might be aimed at and why, which groups of people might benefit the most from learning about the potential risks of digital technologies and who might be receptive to the public art medium. As mentioned, the primary audiences for {poem}.py so far consisted of academics in various disciplines, art exhibition curators and visitors and the already tech savvy, such as followers of the Open Data Institute or readers of *Wired* magazine. While I felt that those who had previously engaged with the project had learned more about the inner workings of Google search and advertising, I worried that, to a certain extent, I was preaching to the converted over issues of digital privacy and data exploitation.

Significant amongst the discussions this group had was a recognition that, in attempting to spread messages *about* digital technology whilst also considering digital *methods*, we must consider audiences who are excluded so far from this particular debate. According to one participant, children are being actively excluded from critical thinking about technology by school policies. Another extremely pertinent point was that, somewhat counter-intuitively, a valuable and necessary audience for these types of critical messages might be data science and computer science students, developers and tech industry workers, as critical thinking is often not taught at universities in informatics and engineering departments, or even considered as part of the start-up culture of the tech industry.

Venue

As {poem}.py had only been shown in indoor locations, I was keen to think about potential venues in public outdoor spaces that might accelerate the message and impact of the project. The Venue group had a lively discussion debating the merits and drawbacks of a wide range of venues, from symbolically significant buildings and locations such as Holyrood Palace, the Scottish Parliament building, the Castle or Edinburgh's famous steps, to more intimate, everyday spaces such as pavements, cash machines and bus shelters. Ideas included harnessing the ephemerality of place by using texts in spaces that can only be accessed from certain vantage points or in certain conditions – for example, the tops of bus shelters or pavement art only visible when it rains. Participants raised questions around hacking commercialised spaces, such as shopping centres and advertising hoardings. These spaces, which carry large amounts of transient footfall, would indeed suggest a wide audience, but it is important to consider the demographics of this footfall in terms of attention spans of shoppers or commuters, for example, and indeed the health and safety aspects of attempts to divert the attention of people on the move (the escalators in Waverley Station were mentioned specifically in this respect). Perhaps the most obvious method of engaging a transient audience would be to take advantage of the pedestrian traffic during the various festivals.

The group were also keen to harness the potential of Edinburgh's famous multi-layered topography, from its steps, wynds and hills, to locations such as the roof of Waverley Station, which is visible to pedestrians and bus passengers from the bridges and other vantage points. Someone suggested magnifying the message on buildings at Waverley Gate that house Amazon's Development Centre and the Microsoft Scotland Offices, as well as other corporate headquarters that keep a low profile in the city.

With many of the ideas of potential venues on which to display texts, the most salient drawbacks revolve around access and permission. Aside from guerrilla installations, such as time-limited projections from the back of a van, many of the installation venues discussed would require permission from either the Council or owners of commercial, proprietary spaces. Inclusivity and access are all-important here, too, as city centre venues are not frequently visited by everybody. Such venues run the risk of only being visible to the same demographics of people. Just as a surveillance camera at a strategic position in a shopping mall will disproportionately capture sections of society who frequent it, so a public artwork is only accessible or visible to certain groups, whether commuters, students, those with jobs, those with mobility or those with knowledge of tech. These are major hurdles if our aim is to spread the message widely.

Curation

The first point to make about this discussion was the acknowledgement that curation is necessarily highly dependent on the other three themes and on parameters such as space, cost, skills, equipment and permissions. The group came up with many ideas around the gamification of {poem}.py, both in digital, physical and hybrid spaces. The concept of a mobile phone application that scans text such as advertising, logos and street signs in different locations highlighted the important issue of geolocation in Google's advertising model, where words differ in price according to where they are searched for. This approach would enable a fun and incisive insight into the workings of linguistic capitalism by playing on the geographic variances in word price, but might not work in a relatively small and concentrated location such as Edinburgh, as Google's geographic targeting is not granular enough to produce differences within such a restricted area. An inter-city version of this app would be much more productive. Combined with such an app could be the use of WiFi hotspots, QR codes or multi-located screens that guide people through planned walks around parts of the city, or indeed through other digital platforms that monetise language, such as Facebook.

Still on the gaming theme, someone suggested that some kind of betting mechanism or slot machine might be an effective way of engaging people in the critique; however, we would have to consider the ethical implications of using gambling as a method. On the non-digital front, a game that challenges people to guess the fluctuating prices of words, similar to the TV show *Play Your Cards Right*, or like a stock market, would be a fun and interactive way of exploring the subject.

Conclusions from the Workshop

Perhaps the most striking observation to come out the workshops, for me at least, was the questioning of why we had used 'Text' as the primary category in the hierarchy of discussion. {poem}.py was always going to be a language-based project, but, as one participant pointed out, logocentrism has its own long history of critique, and perhaps thinking beyond text as words, and indeed foregrounding the themes of audience and venue, might have been a more constructive approach to planning the workshop. Notwithstanding this issue, my assumption that political texts would provide the best material to engage people with the critical message was also squarely challenged by the workshop discussions. Rather than political texts, many participants thought that more personal, emotional texts would be more effective. This point is something I had found before when asking people for their favourite poems to feed through {poem}.py, but, once I started thinking of larger public spaces to use as a canvas, had overlooked.

Copyright, access and permission to use public and private spaces were all also crucially important issues raised in discussions, and in turn raise their own questions around the feasibility of large-scale public artworks on a limited budget and with limited access. We can have wonderful ideas and plans, but, as I will go on to discuss in the next section, without unlimited funds and influence, the practicalities of staging such work more often than not come down to which spaces are available and also a certain degree of serendipity.

Following on from the co-design workshop, I developed three interventions from {poem}.py – each installed with different texts, methods and in very different venues. The next section gives short descriptions of these works – *Newspeak* (2019), *Arcadia* (2020) and *What Are Words Worth?* (2019) – and discusses how they emerged from (or indeed diverged from) workshop discussions. Finally, I reflect self-critically on the effectiveness of each of the projects in their aim to enable people to think critically about digital technologies.

NEWSPEAK (2019)

Shown as part of the Data Lates exhibition at the 2019 Edinburgh Festival Fringe, I developed Newspeak (2019) specifically to fit the large window spaces of the Inspace Gallery City Screens on Potterow in Edinburgh. These windows hosted a number of artworks which were back-projected onto the windows from inside and were only visible in the dark. *Newspeak* (2019) visualised the words of George Orwell's *Nineteen Eighty-Four* as if they were commodities being shown on a stock market ticker tape, with prices for each word based on their fluctuating economic value as the keywords that buy advertising space on Google's search results pages (Figure 14.3). In terms of venue, therefore, the project developed to fit the space and the technology which was on offer, which was a fantastic way of showing the work, but in turn predetermined its audience, who, unless they were specifically travelling to Potterow to visit, would only have seen it if they happened to be walking past at the right time and at the right time of day. Even in festival time, Potterow is not a particularly busy thoroughfare, so most footfall and publicity came out of a launch event, subsequent press, social media and other non-situated engagements.

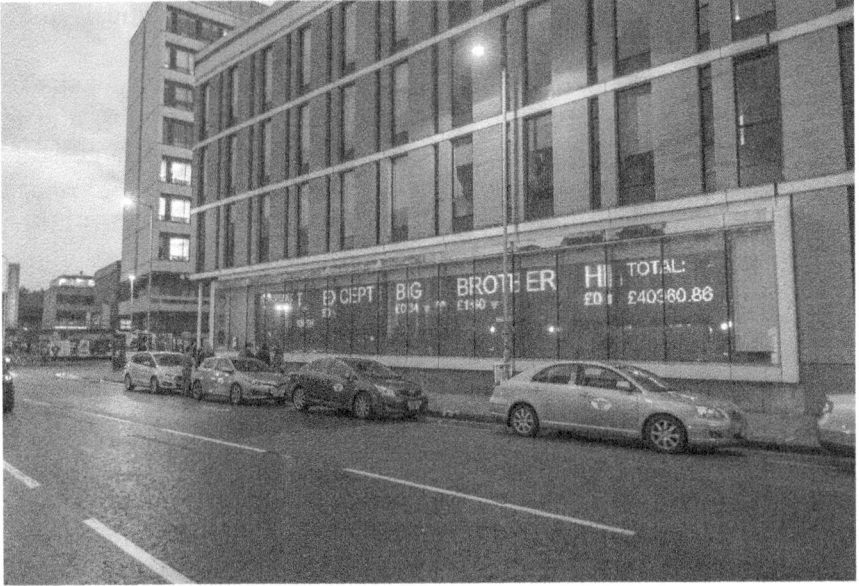

Figure 14.3 *Newspeak*, Pip Thornton (2019). Photo credit: Chris Scott

The choice of text was one I had played with as a {poem}.py receipt prior to the workshop and, although it can be considered a political text, I felt the critique it carries is so embedded in popular culture that it was sufficiently meaningful to a wide audience. Evoking Orwell's vision of Newspeak as a language that 'could only be used for one purpose' (in this case, a commercial one), the project is a political critique of the power held by both Big Brother and Google as mediators of information. The stock market ticker tape visualisation of Orwell's text was a natural progression from the receipt format as a representation of economic exchange, and followed on from the workshop discussions. I was lucky enough to have a curatorial and tech team to make *Newspeak* (2019) happen, as well as the resources to capture the work on film and camera.

And it was ultimately the images of the project being shared on social media and as submissions to competitions that carried the critical message beyond the geographical boundaries of the Edinburgh University campus. *Newspeak* can certainly be classed as a successful intervention if success is measured on acclaim, as it was shortlisted for the Lumen Prize for art and technology in 2020 and was also awarded an honourable mention in the Surveillance Studies Network (SSN) biennial art competition (2020). However, these are prizes situated firmly within the silos of the art and academic worlds respectively, and while *Newspeak* has had considerable impact in those spaces, it was – in this particular situated iteration at least – perhaps lacking in its ability to reach wider audiences.

ARCADIA (2020)

Arcadia is another work for which the venue, and therefore the audience, appeared first, and the text and curation followed. Made for the Fruitmarket Gallery's pop-up space in Waverley Mall, Edinburgh, the work uses LED screens hung in the bookshop's large interior windows to display text that can be seen in the communal mall space below and that mingles with the neon advertising of surrounding commercial stores. Like *Newspeak*, *Arcadia* uses the medium of the scrolling stock market ticker tape, but displays on LED panels rather than by projection. The installation came about after I was approached by a Fruitmarket Gallery curator, Iain Morrison, who had seen {poem}.py and wanted to see if there was a way of displaying it in the bookshop space in the shopping mall. I had recently obtained two long LED panels, and as soon as I saw the layout of the bookshop, I knew they would work very well in the window space (Figure 14.4). Iain and I discussed our mutual love of shopping malls and Walter Benjamin and quickly came to the decision that Walter Benjamin's *Arcades Project* (1999 [1939]) would be the perfect text for this iteration. While it might be considered rather niche, Benjamin's text was carefully chosen for its location both in a bookshop and in a shopping arcade, and also fitted well into the genesis of {poem}.py, as I had already used Benjamin's *Work of Art in the Age of Mechanical Reproduction* essay as a framework for my PhD thesis.

Reimagining the figure of Benjamin's flâneur in the Parisian arcades, the aim of *Arcadia* was to ask viewers to consider their roles as wanderers through the signage of commodified life in today's physical and virtual marketplaces (Wark 2015), where commercial capital accumulates with every search or click as well as each trip to the shopping mall. Benjamin's concern with the very French character of the flâneur – an indolent wanderer with the run of the city – sits alongside the broad mix of visitors to a contemporary shopping mall. This supposedly

Figure 14.4 *Arcadia* (2020). Photo credit: Chris Scott

democratic space, much like the virtual spaces of the Internet, has become a microcosm of modern socioeconomic life. Commercial centres are part of the dwindling public, free spaces available to us and which are understood as always under threat in a capitalist society. Whether for flâneurs, workers or those seeking refuge, from when the mall opens in the morning until late in the evening, *Arcadia* would show glimpses of a text that explores the complex dynamics of this commercial environment.

Arcadia was always going to be a semi-ironic statement installation, rather than one that had any chance of conveying the critical message the project had set out to achieve, but it used the urban fabric as both context and canvas and – alongside *Newspeak* and {poem}.py – has provided rich material for both teaching and secondary public engagement.

WHAT ARE WORDS WORTH? (2019): RECLAIMING THE NARRATIVE FROM WORDSWORTH TO GOOGLE

This iteration of {poem}.py took place as part of the Edinburgh International Festival in 2019. It is chronologically out of order for a reason, as it speaks to some unique aspects of the workshop outputs and also leads very nicely towards concluding comments and reflections generated by this chapter. Once again, this work – an interactive performance piece rather than light-based installation – was to a certain degree led by a predetermined venue, an inside room within the grand surroundings of The Hub, a neo-Gothic former church building near Edinburgh Castle, and home of the International Festival. But what predetermined the work more than the venue was the audience, as I was offered the chance to create an interactive performance-based piece with an audience of international playwrights. This gave me the opportunity to develop some of the gamification ideas I had been having that were developed considerably by some of the workshop discussions. What I had long been wanting to do was to turn {poem}.py into a physical game that controlled where participants can go by the value of the words they utter. I wanted to create a sense of frustration at both the restriction of movement and the constraints and consequences of verbal expression, leading theoretically into new areas of work for me as I began to interrogate spoken rather than just written (or typed) words, with all the privacy implications that Internet of Things devices such as Alexa and Ring doorbells bring to the critique.

The premise of *What Are Words Worth?* (Figure 14.5) was to challenge playwrights to describe well-known plays to their team in the cheapest way possible, as their words were being monetised live through Google, but in a way which also allowed teammates to guess what the play was. Speaking their words into a microphone, their progress through the narrative of the plays was controlled in a series of boxes marked on the floor in luminous tape. Participants could only progress to the next box or scene if their description of the previous scene came in at under a certain amount of money. I was interested in how the playwrights would respond to these restrictions and to see how they might approach writing a play if they could only use the most lucrative or cheapest words currently on the algorithmic market. Would this restrict freedom of expression, or open up radical new ways of seeing, thinking and writing?

While this iteration of {poem}.py was very much a work in progress, we were gifted a small but extremely generous, patient and enthusiastic group of playwrights to work with, and there were some fascinating insights that came out of it, which answered directly the research question of how creative intervention can make people think critically about

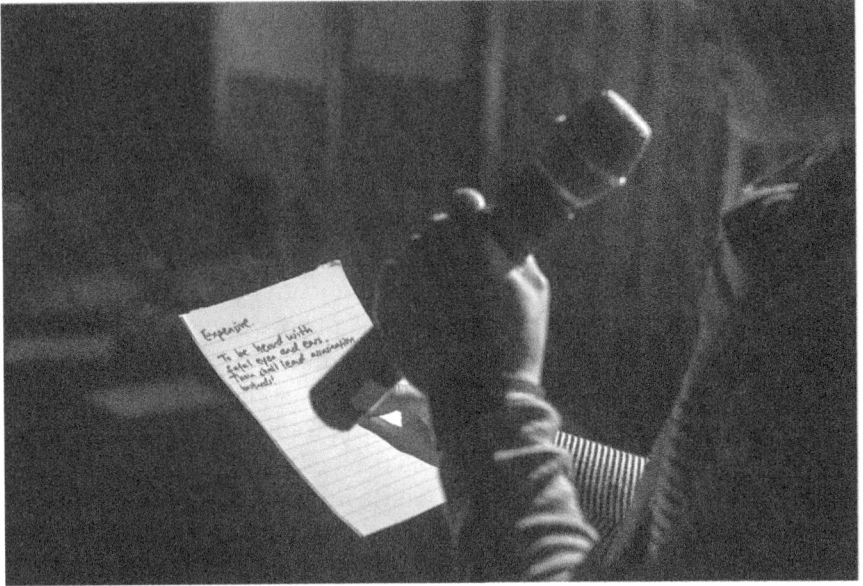

Figure 14.5 *What Are Words Worth?* Pip Thornton (2019). Photo credit:
Chris Scott

the power of digital technology. For example, as participants started
to realise that strong accents, or very slow speech could confuse algorithms while also (crucially) still conveying meaning to their human
teammates, they began to adapt their speech to fool the voice recognition software. Discovering reasons and ways to subvert technologies is
a key tool in critical thinking about digital privacy and the algorithmic
systems that govern our lives; it forms the basis for informed ways of
interacting with digital systems as well as thinking about means of data
resistance. Another interesting lesson learned in terms of choice of
texts was a reminder that the Western canon of literature is not necessarily known by people without English as their first language. One of
the participants in this intervention was from Malaysia and had considerable difficulty trying to convey the storylines of some of the plays
I had chosen, even though I had originally thought 'everyone' would
know them.

CONCLUSIONS

For {poem}.py, and all its current and future iterations, the key point of each work is to challenge the monetisation of language by harnessing the power of language to convey its own critique. Thus poetry, plays, novels and any other texts regain their creative edge in the face of their systemic reduction to bits of data. These projects have been about letting words speak for themselves, rather than be subsumed by forces of linguistic capitalism, and about using language both creatively and critically to translate problems and send messages, not just to make money. Each of the interventions detailed in this chapter succeeded to varying extents in answering the original research question, although – somewhat ironically – it was the physically and geographically bigger works that ultimately proved less effective as stand-alone pieces in helping people to think critically about the power of digital technology companies. Without secondary engagements such as social media, academic outputs and prizes, I would question the actual impact and reach of both *Newspeak* and *Arcadia*, although each had its own aesthetic value as eye-catching and appealing pieces of art. More labour intensive – and perhaps more cost effective – was the workshop exercise of writing cheap and expensive poems, and the *What Are Words Worth?* piece at the International Festival. Despite being held in a closed room with few people, each of these interventions led to meaningful understanding and provided the tools need for critical thinking about these matters.

While I tried to widen the reach of the critique with the large-scale public artworks of *Newspeak* and *Arcadia*, both of these interventions ended up to a certain extent being co-opted back into the spaces in which they were displayed. *Newspeak*, displayed on a building housing an Edinburgh College of Art department, was successful in academic and art circles, as the SSN and Lumen prize nominations showed. Meanwhile *Arcadia*, displayed in a bookshop within a shopping mall, attracted only a small number of people actually familiar with the Benjamin text used and – perhaps most significantly – also attracted the attention of management of Waverley Mall itself, who commissioned a short promotional film about the project. It seems that no matter how critical the work might be, it is very hard to avoid becoming the spectacle.

In some of my previous work I have been extremely critical of digital artwork that fails to interrogate the systems and platforms on which it exists, therefore – in my opinion – losing any critical edge it might have, but it seems that it is not just in digital spaces where this becomes an occupational hazard. Both *Newspeak* and *Arcadia*, displayed on canvases owned respectively by academia and commerce, reflected the marketing needs and reach of their host platforms. Their value in answering the original research question lies in secondary engagements, whereas the personal, intensive and interactive interventions in the workshop and in *What Are Words Worth?*, despite their limited reach, were extremely effective in making their participants think critically about the power of digital technology companies. As I mentioned earlier, the size and scope of any art project or creative intervention will always be governed by the available funds, but what this exercise has shown is that the most effective interventions might actually be the simplest and the cheapest.

So, what does this mean for the future of public art as a means of criticism? It depends heavily on secondary reporting to have the kind of wider impact I was hoping to achieve. Small events work better to achieve the actual goal of the research question. Art prizes and academic outputs have reach and impact primarily in their own circles and networks. I don't want to rely on prizes or the press to give my critique impact, as both have their own potentially problematic structures and business models. For me, then, it's back to workshops in inauspicious venues, with small groups of people, old and young, playing with creating our own poems, plays and other narratives in order to resist and critique the forces of digital and linguistic capitalism.

REFERENCES

Benjamin, W. (1999 [1939]) *The Arcades Project*. Cambridge, MA: Harvard University Press.

Introna, L. D. and Nissenbaum, H. (2000) Shaping the Web: why the politics of search engines matters. *The Information Society*, 16(3), 169–85.

Jarrett, K. (2014) A database of intention? Society of the query reader: Reflections on Web search, 16–29.

Kaplan, F. (2014) Linguistic capitalism and algorithmic mediation. *Representations*, 127(1), 57–63.

Noble, S. U. (2018) *Algorithms of Oppression: How Search Engines Reinforce Racism*. New York: New York University Press.

Thornton, P. (2016) {poem}.py: a critique of linguistic capitalism. Available at

https://pipthornton.com/2016/06/12/poem-py-a-critique-of-linguistic-capi
talism/ (last accessed 14 January 2022).

Thornton, P. (2018) A critique of linguistic capitalism: provocation/interven-
tion. *GeoHumanities*, 4(2), 417–37.

Wark, M. (2015) Benjamedia. *Public Seminar*. Available at https://publicsemin
ar.org/2015/08/benjamedia/ (last accessed 14 January 2022).

POSTSCRIPT: DOING DATA DIALECTICALLY: BETWEEN ALIENATION AND DEMOCRATIC URBAN RENEWAL

Callum McGregor

One way to reflect on this collection is to understand each contribution as part of a broader analysis of the contradictory dynamics of urban datafication. By contradictory dynamics, we mean dynamics in which 'seemingly opposed forces are simultaneously present' (Harvey 2014: 17). This definition of contradiction is useful because it encourages us to think dialectically, rather than dualistically, about urban datafication. In other words, it stresses the undecidability and ambivalence of unfolding processes of datafication: processes which, being neither intrinsically 'progressive' or 'regressive', simultaneously hold potential to enrich and impoverish the fabric of democratic life. Whilst many chapters focus on practices of critique, resistance and refusal, some discuss emerging practices of democratic datafication. Moreover, some chapters offer cogent articulations of what the right to the datafied city could yet be – articulations that are based on careful readings of ambivalent practices and policies. The right to the city, understood as the radical demand framing this collection, is fundamentally about reclaiming urban democracy, and with it, control over our futures. In other words, the right the city is the *'unalienated* right' of 'those who build and sustain urban life . . . to make a city after their hearts desire' (Harvey 2012: xvi, emphasis added). Two points are worth stressing here: first, 'the future' must be understood as a living, material, contradictory potentiality that exists in the present. Second, this conceptual focus on alienation (from our labour, from our urban environments, from ourselves and each other) is necessary for understanding the contradictory potential of datafication.

In the diverse contexts of welfare, education, labour, art and activism, contributors have astutely illustrated the ways in which urban datafication simultaneously forecloses and facilitates the future. Pragmatic yet utopian, this book is an illustration of what it means to 'do' data dialectically by working in and against datafication and mapping emancipatory futures through a sober analysis of the current conjuncture. This approach might frustrate some readers because the book is neither a wholesale denunciation of 'Big Data', nor a parochial insistence that datafication is the vanguard of social change – a master signifier for democratic renewal, as it were. If the book overemphasises practices of critique, resistance and refusal, this is rooted in our editorial instinct that too often the datafied city – along with its attendant 'Californian Ideology' of neoliberal, high-tech disruption (Barbrook and Cameron 1995) – is taken as a fait accompli. From this perspective, what makes datafication and the right to the city such a combustible pairing is obvious: whilst the right to the city demands 'participatory parity' in urban economic and public policy making, there is a patent democratic deficit at the heart of the urban policy fetish for data-driven governance, innovation and growth. Authentic citizen participation means having the opportunity to question and, if necessary, reframe economic and public policy agendas by questioning their assumptions and presuppositions. Take, for example, Zehner's analysis (this volume) of the Edinburgh and South East City Region Deal (CRD) where he argues that 'local communities were not involved in crafting Edinburgh's economic futures. One high-ranking third sector representative describes the emergence of the CRD as "like a spaceship that landed". This observation was confirmed by an Audit Scotland report (2020) which concluded that communities have had very limited direct involvement.'

To be clear, it is not that concerns around data justice are completely absent in data-focused urban policies such as CRDs. The more subtle point is that data justice itself is an ideologically contested concept. Just as social justice has been historically co-opted and recast as 'progressive neoliberalism' (Fraser 2016), data justice will more than likely become a vehicular concept, inflected by various ideological configurations as it is operationalised through policy. Whereas a shallow vision of data justice might represent the problem to be addressed as lack of inclusion and unequal opportunities within the dominant narrative, the right to the city necessitates a deep vision of data justice, which is about the need to redistribute 'projective agency' (Zehner, this volume) – the agency to shape imagined futures – to city dwellers in contexts where the state–corporate nexus hegemonises the urban imaginary and thereby forecloses the realisation of alternative futures. To include citizens as 'makers and shapers' of urban public policy rather than as mere 'users and choosers' (Cornwall and Gaventa 2000) is to recognise that their analyses of the social problems affecting their everyday lives may not be data-centric at all. On the contrary, they may require us to decentre data, to disrupt disruption, as if it were a natural and inevitable phenomenon rather than a socially constructed economic project.

Thus, to understand how datafication might facilitate the realisation of unalienated urban futures we must first understand how alienating practices of datafication foreclose the future by monopolising the urban imaginary. The first way of understanding this is through a political-economic analysis of the ways in which data-centric urban growth strategies intersect insidiously with municipal social services and welfare: data analytics companies and platforms are part of a social policy rationality that combines neoliberal economism with dataism. The familiar rationality of neoliberal economism is that the private sector and its tech start-ups are more agile and efficient at delivering services than the bloated, bureaucratic public sector. Dataism is a particular species of technological solutionism (see Morozov 2013) that recasts complex social phenomena as 'solvable' data analytics models. A number of recent critical social policy studies have highlighted precisely how alienating these increasingly widespread regimes of datafication are, as their algorithms and models perpetuate the misrecognition and objectification of 'problem' groups and communities, even as they are conceivably positioned as vehicles for distributive justice via narratives of efficient and fair resource allocation based on data-driven needs assessments (e.g. Dencik and Kaun 2020; Edwards, Gillies and Gorin, 2021). Even if data analytics experts can genuinely claim to spot empirical patterns, correlations and connections pertaining to social injustices that might otherwise remain unseen or misunderstood, the principle of participatory parity at the heart of the right to the city poses an intrinsic challenge to what Fraser (2008: 414) presciently termed the 'scientistic presumption' of 'justice technocrats':

> Under conditions of injustice, . . . what passes for social 'science' in the mainstream may well reflect the perspectives, and entrench the blind spots, of the privileged. In these conditions, to adopt the scientistic presumption is to risk foreclosing the claims of the disadvantaged. Thus, a theory committed to expanded contestation must reject this presumption. Without denying the relevance

of social knowledge, it must refuse any suggestion that disputes about the 'who' be settled by 'justice technocrats'. (Ibid.)

Note that this position doesn't discount the use of data analytics to empirically identify, and evidence, social injustices experienced by city dwellers. However, it does require that data analytics, when used, must be brought to bear alongside the experiential knowledge and critical deliberation of citizens in order that social problems are not misframed and the citizens who experience them are not misrecognised. In addition to the ways in which datafication forecloses the future through this maldistribution of 'projective agency', there is an additional philosophical argument to be made here that Big Data, 'not differing from statistical reason in any fundamental way', is 'blind to the event' (Han 2017: 76). As Han (ibid.) argues, '[n]ot what is statistically likely, but what is unlikely – the singular, the event – will shape history, in other words, the future of mankind'. Dataism then, is the overarching policy fetish which obfuscates this point by positing a simple correspondence between social reality and data models. In so doing, dataism forecloses alternative futures rather than facilitating them, through its structural inability to reflexively interrogate the ideological parameters of its own models.

Since this coda has so far explained and justified our 'pessimism of the intellect' (critique, resistance, refusal), to paraphrase Gramsci, our 'optimism of the will' must be nourished by positive visions and enactments of the right to the datafied city. If dataism summarily describes the fetishism 'from above' driving urban policy, then we must also caution against a corresponding fetishism 'from below', in which the human desire for the *unalienated* right to the city slides carelessly into a reactionary demand for the *unmediated* right to the city. Srnicek and Williams (2016: 18) have attempted to name this fetish from below 'folk politics', by which they mean 'a collective and historically constituted common sense that has become out of joint with actual mechanisms of power'.

The relationship between alienation and mediation is complex and tightly bound up with the history of socialist political philosophy and its emphasis on positive freedom and social rights. Social rights to a basic level of economic security and welfare, to education, to housing, to health care and so on, provide the necessary material basis for ensuring that citizens have the resources and the capabilities to exercise their political and civil rights. In today's context, data resources must also be considered social rights essential for exercising political and civil rights. In other words, urban data infrastructures, reconceptualised as part of the urban commons, must be reclaimed as a condition of positive freedom, and thus, as a condition of unalienated democratic renewal. Folk politics, for Srnicek and Williams (2016), is characterised by a populist fetishisation of the local and the immediate, a voluntarist conception of political agency and an epistemological populism that is sceptical of mediation and abstraction. The result is reactive episodes of community resistance and direct action lacking a cogent analysis of the wider structural determinants of the social symptoms that they oppose.

In this analysis, purely voluntaristic and populist approaches to the right to the city are alienating, while a sociological imagination facilitated by democratic data use can be empowering for at least three reasons. First, democratic control over data allows citizens and diverse communities to build political solidarity and common cause through co-constructing evidence-based claims that cut across militant particularisms to highlight endemic injustices. Second, horizontal voluntarism propagates its own myths about democratic participation whilst obfuscating the material impediments to participation. It is well documented that community organisations and prefigurative leftist social movements are over-represented by particular social demographics with the required time and economic, social and cultural capital. Finally, populist conspiracy theories act as poor substitutes for people's ontological need to make sense of their social milieus, to develop a sociological imagination. This 'separation between everyday experience and the system we live within results in increased alienation: we feel adrift in a world we do not understand' (Srnicek and Williams 2016: 14).

From this perspective, emerging positive enactments of the right to the datafied city give us reasons to be cautiously hopeful. Take the oft-cited example, by authors in this volume, of Barcelona's 'City Data Commons' and the way that it goes beyond liberal privacy laws (i.e. GDPR) to a commons-based framework of data sovereignty (Bria 2018). However, this developed out of a particular political culture and context. In a majority of cases, struggles for the right to the datafied city will be messy and contradictory, since they exist in and against reality as we find it, not as we would like it to be. This is why, as we struggle to enact urban futures through the right to the datafied city, it is not enough to merely do data democratically, if by that we merely mean the right of ordinary people to participate in the data-centric visions of 'justice technocrats'. Instead, we must critique, resist and refuse, if necessary, by doing data dialectically. This means interrogating its own contradictions in the context of a broader ecosystem of human concern.

REFERENCES

Barbrook, R. and Cameron, A. (1995) The Californian ideology. *Mute*, 1(3). Available at https://www.metamute.org/editorial/articles/californian-ideo logy (last accessed 14 January 2022).

Bria, F. (2018) A new deal for data. In J. McDonnell (ed.), *Economics for the Many*. London: Verso, pp. 164–3.

Cornwall, A. and Gaventa, J. (2000) From users and choosers to makers and shapers: re-positioning participation in social policy. *IDS Bulletin*, 31(4), 50–62.

Dencik, L. and Kuan, A. (2020) Datafication and the welfare state. *Global Perspectives*, pp. 1–18.

Edwards, R., Gillies, V. and Gorin, S. (2021) Problem-solving for problem-solving: data analytics to identify families for service intervention. *Critical Social Policy*. doi: 10.1177/02610183211020294.

Fraser, N. (2008) Abnormal justice *Critical Inquiry*, 34(3), 393–422.

Fraser, N. (2016) Progressive neoliberalism versus reactionary populism: a choice that feminists should refuse. *NORA – Nordic Journal of Feminist and Gender Research*, 24(4), 281–4.

Han, B.-C. (2017) *Psychopolitics: Neoliberalism and New Technologies of Power*. London: Verso.

Harvey, D. (2012) *Rebel Cities*. London: Verso.

Harvey, D. (2014) *Seventeen Contradictions and the End of Capitalism*. London: Profile Books.

Morozov, E. (2013) *To Save Everything Click Here: Technology, Solutionism and the Urge to Fix Problems That Don't Exist*. London: Allen Lane.

Srnicek, N. and Williams, A. (2016) *Inventing the Future: Post-capitalism and a World Without Work*. London: Verso.

INDEX